INTERNATIONAL
HUMAN RIGHT
LEXICON

INTERNATIONAL
HUMAN RIGHTS
LEXICON

SUSAN MARKS
AND
ANDREW CLAPHAM

OXFORD
UNIVERSITY PRESS

OXFORD

UNIVERSITY PRESS

Great Clarendon Street, Oxford OX2 6DP

Oxford University Press is a department of the University of Oxford.
It furthers the University's objective of excellence in research, scholarship,
and education by publishing worldwide in

Oxford New York

Auckland Cape Town Dar es Salaam Hong Kong Karachi
Kuala Lumpur Madrid Melbourne Mexico City Nairobi
New Delhi Shanghai Taipei Toronto

With offices in

Argentina Austria Brazil Chile Czech Republic France Greece
Guatemala Hungary Italy Japan Poland Portugal Singapore
South Korea Switzerland Thailand Turkey Ukraine Vietnam

Oxford is a registered trade mark of Oxford University Press
in the UK and in certain other countries

Published in the United States
by Oxford University Press Inc., New York

British Library Cataloguing in Publication Data

Data available

Library of Congress Cataloging-in-Publication Data

Marks, Susan (Susan R.)
International human rights lexicon / Susan Marks and Andrew Clapham.
p. cm.
Includes index.
ISBN 0–19–876414–6 (hardcover : alk. paper) -- ISBN 0–19–876413–8 (pbk. : alk.
paper) 1. Human rights. I. Clapham, Andrew. II. Title.
K3240.M365 2005
341.4'8--dc22

2005007280

Typeset by Newgen Imaging Systems (P) Ltd., Chennai, India
Printed in Great Britain
on acid-free paper by Biddles Ltd., King's Lynn

ISBN-13: 978-0-19-876413-7
ISBN-10: 0-19-876413-8

3 5 7 9 10 8 6 4

monitoring human rights

Contents

Preface

Like most things, international human rights law can be, and is, studied in many different ways, and with a view to many different questions. One form of enquiry is concerned with the philosophical foundations of human rights law. For example, the question may be examined: do people really have human rights, and if so, what is the scope of these rights, and how is their character as human rights to be explained? Another, quite different sort of enquiry puts that problem aside, and focuses instead on the procedural possibilities that exist for enforcing human rights norms. Here the key issue is often: what action can be taken by people whose human rights have been violated, and how can the avenues of redress available to such people be improved? Yet another style of enquiry delves into particular human rights treaties or normative regimes. A typical investigation might set out by asking: how have the various articles of the International Covenant on Civil and Political Rights been interpreted by the Human Rights Committee and other relevant bodies, and in what ways has that jurisprudence shifted or developed over time?

In this book, while we touch on some of the questions just posed, our main focus is neither philosophical, nor procedural, and nor is it regime-specific. Rather, we survey a range of regimes and debates, with the aim of illustrating something of the diverse articulations of international human rights law with contemporary issues. Thus, instead of proceeding from particular rights, institutions or treaties, we take as our starting point a series of issues (controversies, phenomena, and the groups they most affect)—arranged, as our title announces, alphabetically. In fact, we did not originally plan the alphabetical arrangement. We planned to organise our discussion thematically, around a small number of broadly defined sections. But then we could not decide what should go where. Should 'sexuality' go under 'discrimination', or does it rather belong with 'self-expression'? Is 'disappearance' best considered as an issue of 'the justice system', or does it have more to do with 'exceptional regimes'? The alphabet—that wonderful leveller—solved our problem. In the process, it carried us along, if not actually from swords into ploughshares, then at least from 'arms' to 'work'.

Edward Said once wrote that the point of human rights is to put forward interpretations using the same language as that employed by the dominant power 'to dispute its hierarchy and methods, to elucidate what it has hidden, [and] to pronounce what it has silenced or rendered unpronounceable'. He went on: 'These intellectual procedures require, above all, an acute sense not of how things are separated but of how they are connected, mixed, involved, embroiled, linked'.[1] As well as enabling us to move through the topics we wanted to address without having to fix their relation to one another, the alphabetical arrangement proved congenial to both dimensions highlighted here by Said. On the one hand, it encourages non-linear reading in a way that—we hope—may foster awareness of new and perhaps unexpected linkages. On the other hand, the lexicon format also supports efforts to promote emancipatory change by inviting consideration of international human rights law in relation to the vocabularies that constitute and intersect it. Central to these vocabularies are concepts like democracy, development, fair trial, globalisation, privacy, terrorism, and torture. What is at stake when we talk in these terms? To quote another insightful scholar, Russell Hanson, '[w]hen oppressed people use their oppressors' keywords uncritically, they literally inhabit a world that is defined for them. But when oppressed people use keywords authentically to define their world for themselves, they have liberated themselves in a quite decisive way'.[2]

However it is arranged, a book on the subject of international human rights law must today reckon with a large amount of material, and we are immensely grateful for the generous grant for research and writing we were lucky enough to receive from the John D. and Catherine T. MacArthur Foundation. Thanks to this grant, we were able to enlist help in gathering, sifting and working out what to say about all those treaties, declarations, general comments, and judgments, and eventually in preparing our text for publication. Fiorentina Azizi made an especially

[1] E. Said, *Reflections on Exile* (London: Granta Books, 2001), 430.
[2] R. Hanson, *The Democratic Imagination in America* (Princeton, NJ: Princeton University Press, 1985), 417.

significant contribution. We also have pleasure in acknowledging the assistance of Simon Atrill, Jo Bourke, Théo Boutruche, Drew Gardiner, Hassiba Hadj-Sahraoui, Daniel Joyce, Mecky Kaapanda, Andrew Lang, Claire Mahon, Lisa Oldring and Beatrice Quadranti. Hélène Leggenhager and Monique Nathoo of the Graduate Institute of International Studies handled the accounting and administrative aspects of our grant with exemplary efficiency and good humour. And, in the last stages of the project, we were fortunate that Claire Mahon took on the task of setting up a companion website— www.internationalhumanrightslexicon.org. We invite readers to visit the site; it contains all the primary texts we mention in this book.

As for all the others—students, colleagues, friends and family members—from whom we have learned, and on whom we have leaned, we must leave our expressions of thanks to them for another place. We would like simply to acknowledge the special support we have received from Margaret Clapham, Colin Marks and Mona Rishmawi. We also want to give particular thanks to John Louth and Gwen Booth of Oxford University Press. Two more gracious, affirming and flexible editors could not be imagined. Finally, we wish to mention the unique debt we owe to Antonio Cassese. We both served as his research assistant many years ago at the European University Institute in Florence, and it was that experience which set us both on the course of work reflected here. We are delighted now to record our deep gratitude to Nino for his encouragement and inspiration at that crucial stage.

SUSAN MARKS
ANDREW CLAPHAM

Arms

It is fast becoming a cliché of progressive social commentary that 'small arms are the real weapons of mass destruction'.[1] Approximately half a million people die every year from gunshot wounds, many of them in armed conflict but a large proportion too outside the context of any hostilities.[2] Many more people are seriously injured through the use of firearms, and more still are indirectly affected. Where whole communities are engulfed by gun violence, access may be prevented to schools, land, markets, health clinics, and humanitarian assistance, with disastrous short- and long-term consequences for the inhabitants. Far from being hard to find, these WMDs are in such communities all too visible.

Weapons of mass destruction more traditionally so called have in two cases been outlawed. Under treaties to which most states of the world are parties, bans have been placed on the development, production, stockpiling, transfer and use of biological and chemical weapons.[3] As for nuclear weapons, while the age of deterrence is not yet behind us, lawful use is in practice difficult to imagine.[4] By contrast, and with

---

[1] See, e.g., Kofi Annan, quoted in Amnesty International & Oxfam International, *Shattered Lives* (Control Arms Campaign, 2003), 8, and R. Peters, 'Weapons of Mass Destruction', *International Herald Tribune*, 28 October 2002. By 'small arms' are meant weapons designed for personal use, e.g. revolvers and self-loading pistols, rifles, sub-machine guns, assault rifles, and light machine guns.

[2] See *Small Arms Survey 2004* (Oxford: Oxford University Press, 2004), 174 ff.

[3] See Convention on the Prohibition of the Development, Production and Stockpiling of Bacteriological (Biological) and Toxin Weapons and on their Destruction 1972 and Convention on the Prohibition of the Development, Production, Stockpiling and Use of Chemical Weapons and on their Destruction 1993. See also the antecedent Geneva Protocol for the Prohibition of the Use in War of Asphyxiating, Poisonous or Other Gases, and of Bacteriological Methods of Warfare 1925.

[4] See *Legality of the Threat or Use of Nuclear Weapons*, Advisory Opinion of the International Court of Justice, 8 July 1996, para. 95: 'Thus, methods and means of warfare, which would preclude any distinction between civilian and military targets, or

notable exceptions,[5] conventional weapons have legitimate uses. International law regulates those uses in armed conflict, as part of its regime governing the 'methods and means' of warfare.[6] As just recalled, however, this only covers part of that which requires regulation. What of non-military uses of small arms? What too of the responsibilities of arms suppliers?

In the discussion below, we consider initiatives aimed at enhancing international control of non-military uses of small arms and transfers of weapons generally. Our main focus will be on the ways in which these initiatives draw on, and at the same time help to expand the boundaries of, international human rights law. We begin with firearms use by police and other law enforcement officers. We then look at gun ownership by private people. Finally, we take up the important question of international arms transfers. If small arms are today's weapons of mass destruction, the key questions we will address have to do with the role of international human rights law in that regard. What role has it played in allowing this state of affairs to develop? What role can it now play in supporting efforts to bring about change?

Police violence

In February 2000 demonstrators lined the streets of New York City to protest the acquittal of four officers of the New York Police Department in connection with the fatal shooting of 22-year-old Guinean, Amadou Diallo. Diallo had been stopped as he was walking into his apartment building late one night. Seeing him reach into the inside pocket of his jacket and pull something out, the officers opened fire. In the seconds

which would result in unnecessary suffering to combatants, are prohibited. In view of the unique characteristics of nuclear weapons, to which the Court has referred above, the use of such weapons in fact seems scarcely reconcilable with respect for such requirements.'

[5] See, e.g., Convention on Prohibitions or Restrictions on the Use of Certain Conventional Weapons Which May be Deemed to be Excessively Injurious or to have Indiscriminate Effects, and its Protocols. See also Convention on the Prohibition of the Use, Stockpiling, Production and Transfer of Anti-Personnel Mines and on their Destruction (Ottawa Treaty).

[6] On this, see, e.g., F. Kalshoven & E. Zegveld, *Constraints on the Waging of War*, 3rd ed. (Geneva: ICRC, 2001) and UK Ministry of Defence, *The Manual of the Law of Armed Conflict* (Oxford: Oxford University Press, 2004), chap. 6.

that followed, 41 shots were discharged. Diallo was unarmed, and had no connection to any crime. What he had taken out of his pocket was his wallet, containing papers that would establish his identity.

International efforts to prevent policing of this sort have a basis in norms concerning the right to life. In the contemporary regime of international human rights protection, the starting point for those norms is article 3 of the Universal Declaration of Human Rights: 'Everyone has the right to life, liberty and security of the person'. Building on this, the International Covenant on Civil and Political Rights places on states parties an obligation to respect and ensure the right to life, adding that '[t]his right shall be protected by law' and that '[n]o one shall be arbitrarily deprived of his life'.[7] Similar provisions are included in treaties and other international instruments associated with the various regional human rights systems, among them the African Charter of Human and Peoples' Rights,[8] the American Convention on Human Rights[9] and the European Convention on Human Rights.[10] The European Convention contains an especially detailed provision, which indicates when a deprivation of life will exceptionally be compatible with the Convention, that is to say, when killing will not count as arbitrary. It will not count as arbitrary when it:

results from the use of force which is no more than absolutely necessary:
(a) in defence of any person from unlawful violence;
(b) in order to effect a lawful arrest or to prevent the escape of a person lawfully detained;
(c) in action lawfully taken for the purpose of quelling a riot or insurrection.

We will return to that provision in a moment. For now, let us note two documents in which the concept of arbitrary deprivation of life has been specified in the context of policing. Both texts are considered to set out standards that are implicit in the universal right to life. The first, adopted by the United Nations General Assembly in 1979, is the UN Code of Conduct for Law Enforcement Officials.[11] By 'law enforcement officials' are meant here all those who are authorised to carry out police powers; in some countries and situations, that may include not only police officers, but also military authorities, state security forces, or

---

[7] Art. 6(1).   [8] Art. 4.   [9] Art. 4(1).   [10] Art. 2.
[11] Adopted by UN General Assembly Resolution 34/169 of 17 December 1979.

other officials. The Code of Conduct enunciates a series of points relating to the obligation of such officials to maintain and uphold human rights. Where firearms are concerned, the most important of these points is that '[l]aw enforcement officials may use force only when strictly necessary and to the extent required for the performance of their duty'.[12] According to a commentary incorporated within the Code of Conduct, this means that '[i]n general, firearms should not be used except when a suspected offender offers armed resistance or otherwise jeopardizes the lives of others and less extreme measures are not sufficient to restrain or apprehend the suspected offender'.[13]

The second document is a more detailed elaboration of these points. This is the UN Basic Principles on the Use of Force and Firearms by Law Enforcement Officials, adopted in 1990.[14] With regard to firearms, the general principle is said to be that:

[l]aw enforcement officials shall not use firearms against persons except in self-defence or defence of others against the imminent threat of death or serious injury, to prevent the perpetration of a particularly serious crime involving grave threat to life, to arrest a person presenting such a danger and resisting their authority, or to prevent his or her escape, and only when less extreme means are insufficient to achieve these objectives.[15]

Immediately following this is a stipulation that '[i]n any event, intentional lethal use of firearms may only be made when strictly unavoidable in order to protect life'. Alongside these provisions aimed at law enforcement officials, the Basic Principles also highlight relevant obligations of governments and law enforcement agencies. Selection of law enforcement officials must involve proper screening methods. Training must be provided not only in the use of firearms, but also in non-violent methods. Insofar as violence becomes necessary, police should be equipped with a broad range of types of weapons and ammunition, so as to allow for a differentiated use of force and firearms. Where appropriate, self-defensive equipment and bullet-proof vehicles should also be provided, in order to decrease the need to use weapons of any kind. (This obviously has particular relevance for policing at demonstrations.)[16] Finally, whenever

---

[12] Art. 3.   [13] Commentary to art. 3, para. (c).
[14] Adopted by the Eighth United Nations Congress on the Prevention of Crime and the Treatment of Offenders (1990) U.N. Doc. A/CONF.144/28/Rev.1 at 112.
[15] Principle 9.   [16] Regarding assemblies, see further Principles 12–14.

death or injury is caused, there must be an effective investigation, with appropriate steps to ensure criminal liability in cases where there is evidence of arbitrary or abusive force.[17]

From these two international instruments we can glean, among other things, that the use of firearms can only be justified as a last resort, when, and to the extent, strictly necessary in self-defence or the defence of others against an imminent threat of death or serious injury. In this connection, considerable stress obviously falls on the provision of training, and especially training in the tactical assessment of threats. As one report comments, '[t]oo many police forces around the world are trained *how to fire a gun* but not how to decide *whether it should be fired*, or when'.[18] The responsibilities of governments for preventing firearms abuse by law enforcement officials have also been the subject of some important pronouncements by international human rights courts and supervisory bodies. One case under the European Convention on Human Rights arose out of the fatal shooting by British soldiers of three unarmed people in Gibraltar.[19] The shooting occurred in the context of an operation to avert a bomb attack of which the British Government had received warning. The European Court of Human Rights observed that the obligations entailed by the right to life are not exhausted by the duty of state officials to refrain from arbitrary killing; states parties to the Convention have a positive obligation to protect life, and this calls for the provision of appropriate training, instructions and briefing, along with especially strict operational control where lethal force may be involved. In the circumstances of this case, the European Court determined that the control and organisation of the operation had been flawed in crucial respects. Instructions had been given to the soldiers which had made the use of lethal force 'almost unavoidable'.[20] It followed for the Court that a violation of the Convention had occurred. In terms of the Convention provision quoted above, it had not been established that force had been used which was 'no more than absolutely necessary' in defence of persons from unlawful violence.[21]

[17] See also Principles on the Effective Prevention and Investigation of Extra-Legal, Arbitrary and Summary Executions, recommended by UN Economic and Social Council resolution 1989/65 of 24 May 1989.

[18] *Guns and Policing* (Control Arms Campaign, 2004), 2, available at www. controlarms.org.

[19] *McCann and Others v United Kingdom*, Judgment of the European Court of Human Rights, 5 September 1995.   [20] Ibid., para. 210.

[21] See European Convention on Human Rights, art. 2(2).

Inadequate training, incautious instructions and poor operational control are, then, among the factors that can set the scene for excessive use of firearms by the police. Intensifying these deficiencies is the enduring legacy in some countries of traditions of colonial policing, characterised by only limited safeguards against abuses.[22] The failure to conduct an effective investigation after the event has been the subject of complaints under the European Convention and other treaties on a number of occasions, and plainly, that too can facilitate excesses by weakening expectations of accountability.[23] Lack of expected accountability, of course, also facilitates the deployment of police forces as agents of political repression, and we should not forget the whole range of ways in which firearms may be used by police and other state officials to silence opposition through acts and threats of torture, murder, rape, disappearance, and so on. Nor should we forget the violence that may be used against subordinate populations. Indeed, a further factor very frequently mixed up in cases of arbitrary killing by law enforcement officials is racism, particularly in the form of racial profiling.[24] Together with the violation of the right to life, this implicates the state in a violation of the duty to ensure human rights to all on a non-discriminatory basis.[25] The deadly traces of institutional racism were certainly apparent to those protesting the acquittal of the four officers who killed Amadou Diallo, and a number of initiatives were subsequently introduced in response to the protesters' concerns. At the same time, there was perhaps another consideration shaping that appalling episode—another aspect of the context, on which we have not yet touched, that made this young man vulnerable to the frantic ferocity of the NYPD Street Crime Unit and its semi-automatic pistols. To explore something of this, let us turn now to the issue of private gun ownership.

Gun control

Despite the influential idea that what defines the modern state is a monopoly of the legitimate use of force, the majority of guns are today

---

[22] See *Small Arms Survey 2004* (Oxford: Oxford University Press, 2004), 217.

[23] See, e.g., *Kelly and Others v United Kingdom*, Judgment of the European Court of Human Rights, 4 May 2001.   [24] See further Racism★.

[25] Recognised in general international human rights law, the duty of non-discrimination is also spelled out in relation to the right to personal security and protection from violence in the Convention on the Elimination of All Forms of Racial Discrimination, art. 5(b).

in private hands. According to recent figures, almost 60 per cent are privately owned.[26] The precise relation between firearm accessibility and levels of violence in a society is not fully clear, and is the subject of much debate, especially in the United States. Generally, however, it is plain that firearms facilitate the rapid escalation of disputes and tensions, and increase the likelihood of violent outcomes, whether through intentional shooting or accidents. While mass or serial killings tend to receive the greatest attention, the Geneva-based Small Arms Survey warns against treating firearm violence as simply an affair of lonely psychopaths with unfeasible home armouries. Rather, 'small arms are misused on a daily basis in many communities around the world, making gun violence too banal and too frequent for the international media to cover it'.[27] In this regard, the Survey highlights the particular prevalence of armed crime in areas where there has recently been armed conflict. Part of the importance of post-conflict programmes of disarmament, demobilisation and reintegration thus arises from the need to prevent military weapons from being recycled into criminal activity. The Survey also calls attention to another cyclical pattern. In many communities high levels of gun violence have encouraged people to engage private security firms or acquire small arms themselves. Insofar as security arrangements are privatised in this way, small arms are made to proliferate still further, intensifying the potential for misuse, and hence the insecurity that prompted the attempt to gain protection in the first place. At the same time, high levels of private gun ownership in a society may also encourage firearms abuse by police. This is the further consideration to which we referred above, and it serves as a reminder that in this context, fear of firearm violence is both a response to such violence and an ongoing cause of it.

As is well known, a powerful body of opinion in the United States argues that the existence of armed citizen militias is authorised by the Second Amendment to the United States Constitution, which declares that '[a] well regulated Militia, being necessary to the security of a free State, the right of the people to keep and bear Arms, shall not be infringed'. Others contest this interpretation. Where international law is concerned, gun control is a more recent addition to the rights agenda.

[26] Amnesty International & Oxfam International, *Shattered Lives* (Control Arms Campaign, 2003), 20.
[27] *Small Arms Survey 2004* (Oxford: Oxford University Press, 2004), 173.

The issues that arise are also framed differently. Instead of revolving around the right of individuals to carry arms, discussions in international human rights law revolve around the duty of states to prevent armed crime, as part of their obligation to protect human rights. That is to say, the focus is less on claims about the legitimacy or otherwise of citizen militias than on assertions of the responsibility of governments for taking steps to protect citizens from violence. Of course, the latter affect the former, inasmuch as gun control is likely to be implied. But the main point is that the former cannot determine the latter; whatever position is taken with respect to the question of individual rights of access to firearms, there remain issues to be considered about the firearm-related entailments of international obligations to protect human rights.

We mentioned a moment ago that gun control is a relatively recent addition to the agenda of international human rights law. Let us now elaborate on that. In the background is the traditional preoccupation of international law with defining the international responsibility of states with respect to conduct that is attributable to them. Whose conduct does this cover? Quite obviously, it covers public officials, such as police and other law enforcement officers. It also covers private individuals who act on instructions from a government, or self-appointed vigilantes whose conduct the government acknowledges and effectively 'adopts' as its own.[28] But it does not cover citizens acting in a private capacity. Their activities are clearly not capable of being treated as conduct of the state. With this in mind, the misuse of firearms by private citizens was traditionally viewed in international law as a matter that would presumably engage the responsibility of the individual perpetrator under national criminal law (or international criminal law, if an international crime was involved), but could not engage the responsibility of any state under international human rights law. This is one of the ways in which international human rights law helped to allow small arms to become the real weapons of mass destruction. It failed to hold governments to account for gun control. In effect, it endorsed the daily abuses and all too banal and frequent gun violence recalled above.

---

[28] See International Law Commission, Articles on Responsibility of States for Internationally Wrongful Acts, arts. 5, 8 and 11, adopted by the ILC at its 53rd session, 2001, UN Doc. A/56/10. See further J. Crawford, *The International Law Commission's Articles on State Responsibility: Introduction, Text and Commentaries* (Cambridge: Cambridge University Press, 2002).

From the fact that states cannot be held directly responsible for the conduct of citizens acting in a private capacity, however, it does not follow no state responsibility can exist for regulating that conduct. Governments may still be, and in many circumstances today are, held liable by omission if they fail to exercise due diligence in ensuring that human rights are not abused within the private sphere. This 'due diligence' obligation was articulated by the Inter-American Court of Human Rights in 1988, when it declared Honduras responsible under the American Convention of Human Rights for failing to prevent or adequately respond to the disappearance of Manfredo Velásquez Rodriguez. According to the Inter-American Court,

[a]n illegal act which violates human rights and which is initially not directly imputable to a State (for example, because it is the act of a private person or because the person responsible has not been identified) can lead to international responsibility of the State, not because of the act itself, but because of the lack of due diligence to prevent the violation or to respond to it as required by the Convention.[29]

With regard specifically to the right to life and the right not to have one's life taken arbitrarily, the Inter-American Court said that '[t]hese rights imply an obligation on the part of States Parties to take reasonable steps to prevent situations that could result in [their] violation'.[30] Thus, the right to life may form the basis for a positive obligation to prevent arbitrary killing not only by law enforcement officers, as discussed above, but by non-state actors as well. In a more recent case before the European Court of Human Rights, a Kurdish man had been fatally shot by unknown assailants in Turkey.[31] Though he had reported receiving death threats to the authorities, no action had been taken to protect him. The European Court observed that the obligation undertaken by states parties to the European Convention on Human Rights to secure the right to life includes a duty to take reasonable measures to prevent a real and immediate risk to a person's life. It also includes a duty to undertake an effective investigation after a killing occurs. In neglecting both to provide appropriate protection and to conduct an adequate

[29] *Velásquez Rodriguez v Honduras*, Judgment of the Inter-American Court of Human Rights, 29 July 1988, para. 172.   [30] Ibid., para. 188.

[31] *Akkoç v Turkey*, Judgment of the European Court of Human Rights, 10 October 2000.

investigation, the authorities had failed to comply with the obligations of Turkey under the Convention.

There is gathering momentum behind the idea that international human rights law carries implications for the control of firearms in private hands. In 2002 the UN Commission on Human Rights appointed Barbara Frey as Special Rapporteur, with a mandate to study the prevention of human rights violations committed with small arms and light weapons. In a working paper, Frey notes the existence of 'growing pressure to hold States accountable for patterns of abuses, such as the State's failure to establish reasonable regulation regarding the private ownership of small arms that are likely to be used in homicides, suicides and accidents'.[32] Pursuing this topic in her preliminary report as Special Rapporteur, she highlights the due diligence standard recognised in the case of Manfredo Velásquez Rodriguez and many subsequent interpretive statements. Applying that standard, Frey writes that 'a State may have an affirmative duty under the human rights instruments to ensure that small arms are not used by armed individuals and groups to commit human rights violations'.[33] The most obvious violations that may be committed in this context are, of course, violations of the right to life. But that is not the only human right at stake here. As a threat to public health, with significant impact on mortality and morbidity rates in some countries, firearms misuse by private citizens compromises the right to health. It may also inhibit the exercise of rights of freedom of expression, assembly, association, political participation, and religion. Where violence becomes pervasive in a community, rights to education, food, work, and access to health care facilities may likewise be affected. Finally, and connectedly, guns may impinge on the right to development. As is emphasised in many recent reports, gun violence has indirect effects at almost every level; it undermines the productivity of economic activity, promotes expenditure on protection rather than production, discourages local and foreign investment, reduces the quality and availability of social services, and erodes the norms of trust and reciprocity that make

[32] B. Frey, Working Paper on the question of the trade, carrying and use of small arms and light weapons in the context of human rights and humanitarian norms, 30 May 2002, UN Doc. E/CN.4/Sub.2/2002/39, para. 46.

[33] B. Frey, Preliminary Report on the prevention of human rights violations committed with small arms and light weapons, 25 June 2003, UN Doc. E/CN.4/Sub.2/2003/29, para. 43.

co-ordinated social action possible.[34] Viewed in this light, control of the private possession and use of guns begins to appear inseparable from the protection and fulfilment of human rights. Can the same be said of control of the supply of those guns?

Arms transfers

The five permanent members of the United Nations Security Council are also the world's five leading exporters of small arms and other conventional weapons. Together, China, France, the Russian Federation, the United Kingdom and the United States account for 88 per cent of all conventional arms exports. The United States alone accounts for 45 per cent.[35] In her working paper mentioned above, Barbara Frey observes that efforts to curb firearm violence have spawned a variety of approaches, but that one approach focuses on 'supply-side' issues connected with this market.[36] Without minimising the importance of 'demand-side' initiatives to address the social and political context in which arms misuse occurs, the supply-side approach concentrates on preventing transfers of arms to state and non-state actors who will fore-seeably use them to commit serious violations of human rights or humanitarian law. By 'transfers' is meant here not just commercial sales, but all kinds of exchanges, including those undertaken within the framework of aid programmes or military alliances. Control of arms transfers is hampered by the immensely complex and highly secretive character of the weapons sector, and by the special status which governments commonly accord arms manufacturing companies, whether state-owned or private. On the other hand, the fact that the weapons sector is closely linked with foreign policy and national security has meant that requirements of government authorisation have been imposed on exports and imports of arms in most countries. This lays

[34] See *Small Arms Survey 2003* (Oxford: Oxford University Press, 2003), chap. 4. See also *Guns or Growth?* (Control Arms Campaign, 2004), available at www.controlarms.org.

[35] Amnesty International & Oxfam International, *Shattered Lives* (Control Arms Campaign, 2003), 54.

[36] B. Frey, Working Paper on the question of the trade, carrying and use of small arms and light weapons in the context of human rights and humanitarian norms, 30 May 2002, UN Doc. E/CN.4/Sub.2/2002/39, para. 17.

a basis for international initiatives aimed at tightening at least some links in the chain.

To date, however, the primary concern of international initiatives has been the prevention of illicit transfers of arms, that is to say, transfers not authorised by any government. Thus, for example, a Protocol to the Convention against Transnational Organised Crime was adopted in 2001 (the 'Firearms Protocol'), which obliges states parties to take a variety of measures designed to prevent and punish the illicit manufacturing of, and trafficking in, firearms, their parts and components, and ammunition.[37] This treaty and other comparable international instruments establish the responsibility of governments to co-operate in checking the unauthorised arms trade.[38] But they do little to clarify the responsibilities of governments with respect to the authorisation of arms transfers. As Frey and other analysts stress, that limitation is rendered all the more significant by the ease with which arms acquired in authorised transactions may pass into the illicit arms market. What then of licensing processes? In 1998 the European Union adopted a Code of Conduct on Arms Exports setting out criteria to be taken into account by member states in granting arms export licences. One criterion calls for consideration of respect for human rights in the country of final destination. Specifically, it is declared that member states will:

(a) not issue an export licence if there is a clear risk that the proposed export might be used for internal repression;
(b) exercise special caution and vigilance in issuing licences... to countries where serious violations of human rights have been established by the competent bodies of the UN, the Council of Europe or by the EU.[39]

'Internal repression' is defined for this purpose to include torture and other ill-treatment, extrajudicial execution, disappearance, arbitrary detention, and other major violations of international human rights law. Along similar lines, the Organization for Security and Cooperation in

[37] Protocol against the Illicit Manufacturing of and Trafficking in Firearms, their Parts and Components and Ammunition (2001) (not yet in force).

[38] See, e.g., Inter-American Convention against the Illicit Manufacturing of and Trafficking in Firearms, Ammunition, Explosives and Other Related Materials. See also Programme of Action to Prevent, Combat and Eradicate the Illicit Trade in Small Arms and Light Weapons in All Its Aspects (2001), UN Doc. A/CONF.192/15, chap. IV.

[39] European Union Code of Conduct on Arms Exports, 5 June 1998, EU Doc. 8675/2/98. REV 2, criterion 2.

Europe adopted a document in 2000, expressing the commitment of member states to avoid issuing export licences where there is a clear risk that small arms may be used to violate human rights.[40]

In 2003 a coalition of non-governmental organisations launched a campaign for an international treaty that would build on these and related instruments. While it is believed that all kinds of conventional weapons should be covered, particular emphasis is laid on small arms, given the mass scale of their exchange and impacts. Central to this proposal is the principle that arms transfers should not be authorised by a government which has, or ought reasonably to have, knowledge that the arms to be transferred are likely to be used, or diverted for use, to commit serious violations of human rights or international humanitarian law. Thus, to cite one example given by the coalition, authorisation may be given for the export of guns to a police force that operates in accordance with the UN Basic Principles on the Use of Force and Firearms by Law Enforcement Officials. But authorisation should be denied for the export of guns to a police force which is undisciplined and corrupt, and which uses firearms to commit extra-judicial killings and torture.[41] Or, it could be added, authorisation should be denied for the export of guns to a police force in circumstances where there is a record of persistent diversion for private use to commit violent crime. Plainly, this places on governments an obligation to investigate conditions in countries to which arms transfers are proposed. A rough analogy might be drawn with the investigative obligation entailed by the duty of *non-refoulement* in refugee law.[42] If a government may not return or expel a person to a state in which his or her life or freedom will be at risk on grounds of race, religion, nationality, membership of a social group or political opinion, nor may it sanction the transfer of arms to a country in which the risk arises of serious violations of human rights or humanitarian law.

We noted in the previous section that understandings of state responsibility focused traditionally on public action, to the exclusion of private

[40] OSCE Document on Small Arms and Light Weapons, adopted by the OSCE Forum for Security Co-operation on 24 November 2000, FSC.DOC/1/00. See also the Wassenaar Arrangement's Best Practice Guidelines for Exports of Small Arms and Light Weapons, adopted 11–12 December 2002.

[41] Amnesty International & Oxfam International, *Shattered Lives* (Control Arms Campaign, 2003), 76.

[42] See Convention Relating to the Status of Refugees 1951, art. 33.

conduct. So too, understandings of state responsibility have tended to privilege simple forms of responsibility, as against more complex forms, such as complicity, capacitation, or assistance. This is another way in which international human rights law helped to allow small arms to become the real weapons of mass destruction. It failed to hold governments to account for regulating the transfer of arms, and preventing their foreseeable deployment in extra-judicial killings and other abuses. The developments and proposals highlighted in this section reflect an attempt to correct this. A partial and highly selective antecedent may be the practice of the United Nations Security Council with respect to the imposition of arms-related sanctions on states considered to threaten international peace and security. More pertinently, it is frequently recalled in this context that, despite the general emphasis on simple forms of responsibility, a well-accepted principle of international law makes states responsible for knowing assistance. Thus, a state which assists another state to violate international law becomes liable itself where the assistance is provided with knowledge of the anticipated violation.[43] Barbara Frey writes that the 'effect of this principle is to prohibit States from transferring small arms to another State knowing that the other State will use the arms in violation of international law'.[44] Of course, that only covers state-to-state arms transfers. With regard to transfers more generally, the obligation to regulate transfers may be linked to obligations to co-operate in the protection and fulfilment of human rights, and especially the right to development, as discussed above. In turn, those obligations may also lend support for further supply-side interventions, whether in the mode of 'turning off the tap' or 'draining the pool'.[45] For instance, commercial intermediaries or 'brokers' are recognised to play a pivotal role in the international arms trade, yet brokering activities remain almost entirely unregulated, and indeed unseen. Likewise, efforts to stem the flow of arms

[43] See International Law Commission, Articles on Responsibility of States for Internationally Wrongful Acts, art. 16, adopted by the ILC at its 53rd session, 2001, UN Doc. A/56/10. See further J. Crawford, *The International Law Commission's Articles on State Responsibility: Introduction, Text and Commentaries* (Cambridge: Cambridge University Press, 2002), 148.

[44] B. Frey, Working Paper on the question of the trade, carrying and use of small arms and light weapons in the context of human rights and humanitarian norms, 30 May 2002, UN Doc. E/CN.4/Sub.2/2002/39, para. 73.

[45] See Amnesty International & Oxfam International, *Shattered Lives* (Control Arms Campaign, 2003), 73.

within countries may depend on post-conflict disarmament programmes, improved stockpiling arrangements, and retrieval of illicit arms. Turning off the tap and draining the pool are not traditional modes of engagement for international human rights law, but, through the issue of arms control, they are starting to emerge as essential ones.

Arms and men

We have begun this book with a theme that similarly forms the departure point of an ancient epic poem: 'arms and the man'.[46] With regard to arms, we have recalled the way age-old preoccupations with the rewards and sufferings of battle have come to be accompanied by another, distinctively modern set of concerns about the human and social costs of guns. What, however, of 'the man'? We have not yet spoken about that aspect. Virgil's interest, of course, was in one man in particular—the Trojan Aeneas who would one day found Rome. To capture our broader interests in the relation between human rights and arms control, we need to shift into the plural. Arms and *men*? Surely human rights are concerned with humanity as a whole! Surely bullets kill equally, whatever the victim's sex! Indeed they are, and indeed they do. But from that it does not follow that gender-specific concerns become irrelevant, just as it does not follow that concerns aligned with other social divisions become irrelevant. Quite the contrary, as the succeeding pages will repeatedly illustrate, and as we have already seen in this discussion with regard to racism. To be concerned with the entirety of humanity is necessarily to be concerned with social specificity, and with the way things look when viewed from different points within a social structure.

In considering the gender dimensions of firearms, we can start by noting the prominence of men in firearm-related violence. Men commit the vast majority of firearm-related crimes, and also make up the vast majority of those killed or injured as a result of them. On current global figures, 90 per cent of firearm homicide victims are male.[47] We can also observe the place which guns may occupy in the everyday life of men—the way rifles may be kept as treasured inheritances, worn like

---

[46] Virgil (D. West, trans.), *The Aeneid* (London: Penguin, 1990), 3.
[47] *Small Arms Survey 2004* (Oxford: Oxford University Press, 2004), 178.

pieces of jewellery, or used in parallel economies as tokens of exchange. At the same time, we can point to the association between men and guns within the imaginative or symbolic domain. While the idea of guns as phallic extensions is now a commonplace, the sexualised imagery of guns has always been more complicated than that. As Henri Myrttinen observes in a study of the bearing of forms of masculinity for approaches to disarmament, guns are also used as female sex objects—the bearer's 'bride'—and, more generally, as fetishes of male prowess.[48] Finally, we can register the way all this is bound up with a particular, militarised version of masculinity, which both relies on guns and is enforced by them. As Myrttinen explains, ' "[d]oing" masculinity with the help of a weapon is...the visible manifestation of certain, violent and often militarized enactments of masculinity'.[49] Within those enactments the weapon serves at once as a symbol and as an actual tool for asserting authority and suppressing others—other people, quite obviously, but also other forms of masculinity in which the model of the warrior and armed protector is refused. Myrttinen concludes that post-conflict disarmament, demobilisation and reintegration strategies must be linked to a 'demobilisation' of the distinctive notions of masculinity that foster a fear of disarmament as emasculating and of non-violence as effete.[50]

How do such notions develop? Clearly, the formation of masculinities is embedded in historical and cultural processes that vary considerably across the world, as well as within communities. Likewise, the significance of the display and use of weapons is not constant, but must be investigated in specific social contexts. At the same time, as Charlotte Hooper remarks in another study of masculine identities, '[m]asculinities are not just domestic cultural variables but are to some extent formed by international politics itself'.[51] Wars make men as much as men make wars,[52] and the same can be said of colonial government,

---

[48] H. Myrttinen, 'Disarming Masculinities', *Disarmament Forum* (2003), 37.

[49] Ibid., 44.   [50] See ibid.

[51] C. Hooper, 'Masculinist Practices and Gender Politics: The Operational Masculinities in International Relations' in M. Zalewski and J. Parpart (eds.), *The 'Man' Question in International Relations* (Boulder, Colo.: Westview Press, 1998), 28, 39.

[52] See B. Ehrenreich, 'Forward' in K. Theweleit, *Male Fantasies*, vol. 1 (Cambridge: Cambridge University Press, 1987), xvi ('it is not only men that make wars, it is wars that make men'), quoted in C. Hooper, 'Masculinist Practices and Gender Politics: The Operational Masculinities in International Relations' in M. Zalewski and J. Parpart (eds.), *The 'Man' Question in International Relations* (Boulder, Colo.: Westview Press, 1998), 28, 39.

international conferences, peace-enforcement operations, and a range of other institutions and practices. The image of 'western protector-warriors in the streets of Kabul or Pristina, a "robust", manly but benevolent force, sporting designer shades and displaying their weapons while always ready to assist the poor and helpless women and children they encounter' is especially familiar today.[53] And if masculinities are to some extent formed by international politics, they are also partly shaped by international law, including international human rights law. At the simplest level, permitting access to guns to remain unregulated contributes to the processes that sustain and naturalise militarised traditions of masculine identity—the very militarised traditions that drive down the value of men's right to life and right to health. Of course, unregulated access to guns profoundly affects women too, both in the way violence may be facilitated and subordinate status coercively reinforced, and in the broader outcomes that may be produced. While men are more likely than women to suffer death or injury in consequence of firearm violence, the indirect social and economic effects we described earlier impact upon women at least equally. This then is a final way in which international human rights law helped to allow small arms to become the real weapons of mass destruction. It helped to make guns seem instinctively manly, obscuring alternative and competing forms of masculine identity—and, with them, alternative and competing forms of human life.

[53] H. Myrttinen, 'Disarming Masculinities', *Disarmament Forum* (2003), 37, 39.

Children

The starting point for a consideration of the human rights of children is the insight that children are both the same as adults and different from them. They are the same in that they too have interests and concerns which can benefit from articulation and protection in terms of human rights. But they are also different inasmuch as those interests and concerns are in part distinctive. The idea that children inhabit a distinct developmental space in relation to adults, though certainly not timeless, is quite old. In his classic work on the history of childhood, Philippe Ariès argued that it emerged in Europe in conjunction with social and economic changes between the 15th and 18th centuries.[1] By contrast, the idea that that developmental space comes with human rights is relatively new.

One antecedent to the recognition of children's rights may be the child welfare movement which became established in some countries during the 19th and 20th centuries. In 1924, under the impetus of this movement, the League of Nations adopted the Declaration of the Rights of the Child.[2] Despite its name, this document did not yet recognise rights, but rather enumerated in highly paternalistic language a list of protections which children ought to be given. Another precursor to the recognition of children's rights may be the establishment in some countries of special systems of juvenile justice. Again, however, this initiative remained ambiguous from the perspective of children's rights, as juvenile courts often afforded considerably fewer safeguards against arbitrary detention and miscarriage of justice than ordinary courts. More generally, juvenile justice was hard to separate from the growing

[1] See P. Ariès (R. Baldick, trans.), *Centuries of Childhood* (London: Pimlico, 1996).

[2] Geneva Declaration, adopted by the Assembly of the League of Nations, 26 September 1924. See further G. Van Bueren, *The International Law on the Rights of the Child* (London/Dordrecht: Save the Children/Martinus Nijhoff, 1995).

mid-century preoccupation in government and academic research with 'juvenile delinquency', and with the project of enforcing codes of age- and gender-appropriate behaviour.

The twin concepts of welfare and delinquency that informed these developments continue to be important in structuring approaches to children. On the one hand, we love children, and see them as innocent, unformed and vulnerable. We want to protect, care for, and nurture them. On the other hand, we fear children. We view them as troublesome, unruly, and disturbingly irrational, and want to contain and control their dangerous energies. Alongside these approaches, or perhaps somewhere between or around them, the idea gathered momentum in the late 20th century that children should not just be objects of adult action, whether in the mode of protection or containment. They should also be recognised as subjects of human rights.[3] No doubt many factors contributed to this momentum, but one significant factor appears to have been a new awareness in many countries of serious abuses of state and parental power, which prevailing arrangements patently could not stop.

In 1989 calls to recognise children's rights and create a legal basis for holding governments and others to account with respect to them culminated in the adoption within the framework of the United Nations of the Convention on the Rights of the Child. The Convention entered into force the following year, and quickly became one of the most widely ratified treaties in existence.[4] Since then, a number of further child-specific treaties have been concluded at regional level. Greater attention has also been paid to the implications for children of general human rights treaties. How, then, are the rights of children specified in these various instruments and interpretations? Before turning to this question, we should first pause to consider the legitimacy of the exercise in which the treaties engage. Given their dependence on others to act on their behalf, especially when very young, can children really be recognised as bearers of rights? Should they be? Do children's rights make sense in analytical and strategic terms?

[3] This is to some extent foreshadowed in an initiative within the United Nations to revise the earlier League of Nations Declaration of the Rights of the Child. See UN Declaration of the Rights of the Child, UN GA Res. 1386 (XIV), 20 November 1959.

[4] In the case of some states parties, however, the Convention is subject to far-reaching reservations. For comments on this by the Committee on the Rights of the Child, see their General Comment 5 (General measures of implementation for the Convention on the Rights of the Child: arts. 4, 42 and 44(6)), 3 October 2003, paras. 13–16.

Children as right-bearers

The idea that children should be recognised as bearers of rights has attracted considerable controversy, both from a philosophical standpoint and from a policy perspective. To some scholars, the notion that children have human rights is philosophically incoherent because rights are powers to determine the obligations of others, and children lack the capacity to impose their wills in that way. Yet the assumption that rights are powers to determine the obligations of others is not the only premise from which we can proceed. In a discussion of this argument, Tom Campbell notes that we can also conceptualise rights as legally protected interests.[5] Starting from this premise, there is no difficulty in principle with recognising that children have rights since, however limited their capacities, they clearly have interests. The only question is which of their interests call for legal protection, and whether those rights-generating interests are distinctive compared to the rights-generating interests of adults.

According to Campbell, the 'power' theory is not only uncongenial to the recognition of children's rights. It also inclines us to emphasise those interests of children which have to do with building the requisite volitional and functional capacities needed to assert rights in later life. That is to say, it inclines us to emphasise the interests of children as future adults. As he points out, however, in addition to their interests as future adults, young people have equally compelling interests as children or adolescents and, more generally, as persons. If, as we so often hear, children are our future, they are, after all, also their present, and what counts is not just the time to come, but the actuality of their current lives as well. Campbell observes that the fact that in those current lives children may not be able to act independently in defending their rights cannot mean that they have no rights, for dependency is characteristic of many stages of life, and the need for high levels of assistance and care is a permanent feature for some of us. Human rights cannot be the privilege of those with the greatest capacities for autonomous agency and self-sufficient existence.

---

[5] T. Campbell, 'The Rights of the Minor: as Person, as Child, as Juvenile, as Future Adult' in P. Alston, S. Parker & J. Seymour (eds.), *Children, Rights and the Law* (Oxford: Clarendon Press, 1992), 1.

Alongside the argument that children's rights are philosophically incoherent, the argument is sometimes advanced that, rather than focusing on the rights of children, we should focus on the duties and responsibilities of adults with regard to children. In the assessment of Anne McGillivray, however, the 'argument that anyone is better served by not having rights . . . is deeply suspect in the light of historical experience'.[6] For better or worse, rights are the language of popular equality, access to justice, and political voice. Conversely, exclusion from right-holding is the vocabulary of subordination, exploitation, and paternalism. It signals that someone else knows best. As many have remarked, the notorious practice of referring to colonised and indigenous people as children makes very clear how rightless children supply handy metaphors for oppressive ideologies. Paternalism, we have surely learned, is good for no one—not even real children, whose need for parenting should not be confused with an exemption from the universal interest in anti-paternalist relationships, arrangements and norms.

A final argument sometimes made against the recognition of children's rights is that this introduces a legal dimension into relations that should instead be governed by trust, love, piety, and care. It promotes adversarial relations between children and their parents and other carers, and compromises the affective bond that unites the family and defines the home. A number of points can be made in response to this. One, often highlighted, is that the recognition of children's rights does not introduce a legal dimension into relations that should remain non-legal. That legal dimension is already there. Law is a crucial part of the social environment that determines what it means to be a child, a parent, and a family. It defines when a person is a minor, and who can be a parent. It stipulates what childhood should and should not entail, in terms of work, education, political participation, and social life. It distinguishes between the kinds of trouble that will engage state intervention and the kinds that will not. What is called for is not to keep the law out, but to reorient it so that it more adequately protects and promotes the rights of children.

A second point is related to this. To treat the family as a unity is to overlook the extent to which it is also a structure of power, with young age correlating to subordinate status. Likewise, to naturalise the privacy

---

[6] A. McGillivray, 'Why Children Do Have Equal Rights (Reply to Laura Purdy)' 2 *International Journal of Children's Rights* (1994), 243, 253.

of the home is to ignore the policy and administrative choices that in part determine what can occur there. As we shall see presently, children's rights place obligations on governments to give explicit and systematic attention to the way public decision-making affects the life chances of children. In this regard, turning to a final point, the recognition of children's rights may promote adversarial attitudes. On the other hand, it may equally provide a framework within which the interests of children can be related to, and assessed in the light of, competing considerations and concerns.[7] In the end, Tom Campbell suggests that 'it may be a symptom of the vulnerability and lowly social position of children that their status as right-bearers and the distinctive substance of their rights should be in doubt'. Dismissing both the philosophical objections and the policy qualms, he contends that it is 'arguably a serious defect in any theory of rights that it cannot readily make room for the reality and distinctiveness of children's rights'.[8]

Convention principles

We noted at the beginning that the idea of children inhabiting a distinct developmental space relative to adults goes back quite a long way. In one influential account, its roots can be traced to the early modern period. Despite this, it is, of course, the case that the benefits of that developmental space, and indeed the chance to inhabit it at all, remain in our own time very unevenly distributed. As Madelaine Adelman and Christine Yalda comment, '[s]ocial, economic, and cultural power determine, in part, who is able to live, and who is barred from living, "as a child" '.[9] Against this background, let us now take up the question of how international human rights law specifies the rights of children. In connection with the Convention on the Rights of the Child, the Committee on the Rights of the Child has identified four principles

[7] On this point, see P. Alston, 'The Best Interests Principle: Towards a Reconciliation of Culture and Human Rights', in P. Alston (ed.), *The Best Interests of the Child: Reconciling Culture and Human Rights* (Oxford: Clarendon Press, 1994), 1, 20.

[8] T. Campbell, 'The Rights of the Minor: as Person, as Child, as Juvenile, as Future Adult' in P. Alston, S. Parker & J. Seymour (eds.), *Children, Rights and the Law* (Oxford: Clarendon Press, 1992), 1, 3.

[9] M. Adelman & C. Yalda, 'Seen But Not Heard: The Legal Lives of Young People' 23 *PoLAR: Political and Legal Anthropology Review* (2000), 37, 40.

which should be understood as guiding the interpretation of children's rights.[10] It will be valuable to begin by reviewing these general principles. We can then turn to look at what is provided in the Convention and other treaties on a number of specific issues.

The first of the four Convention principles is the principle of non-discrimination. Under article 2 of the Convention, as under other human rights treaties, states parties assume an obligation to respect and ensure the rights set forth in the Convention 'without discrimination of any kind'. For the Committee, this entails an obligation 'actively to identify individual children and groups of children for whom recognition and realisation of their rights may demand special measures'.[11] In this regard, the Committee highlights the need for data collection to be disaggregated, so as to reveal disparities of gender, social group, region, and other potential axes of discrimination. The Committee also observes that the measures needed to redress discrimination may require changes in legislation, administration and resource allocation, along with educational measures to challenge stereotyping and related practices.

The second Convention principle is that, as stated in article 3(1), the 'best interests of the child' must be a primary consideration in all actions concerning children. The concept of the 'best interests of the child' was initially developed in the context of decision-making about the custody of children in municipal systems of family law. In the context of the Convention, the Committee proposes that one aspect of its significance is to require that all legislative, administrative and judicial bodies give systematic consideration to the question of 'how children's rights and interests are or will be affected by their decisions and actions'.[12] Under article 3(1) it is stated that the need to give due consideration to the best interests of the child applies not only to public or official institutions of this kind, but to 'private social welfare institutions' as well. Thus, another aspect of the significance of the best interests principle is to require that private bodies ensure that their actions relating to children are rooted in attention to the best interests of the children concerned. The Committee notes that processes of privatisation in many countries have resulted in many child-related services being run by businesses, non-governmental

---

[10] See Committee on the Rights of the Child, General Comment 5 (General measures of implementation for the Convention on the Rights of the Child: arts. 4, 42 and 44(6)), 3 October 2003, para. 12.   [11] Ibid.
[12] Ibid.

organisations and other private associations. It emphasises that, in such cases, state parties to the Convention remain liable for ensuring that non-state service providers act consistently with the Convention. According to the Committee, this also creates 'indirect obligations' for those non-state service providers themselves.[13]

The third Convention principle revolves around children's right to life, and the obligation of states parties, set forth in article 6, to 'ensure to the maximum extent possible the survival and development of the child'. For the Committee, the concept of 'development' in this context should be interpreted in the 'broadest sense as a holistic concept, embracing the child's physical, mental, spiritual, moral, psychological and social development'.[14] This principle reinforces the best interests principle, and connects it with the idea that priority should be given to enhancing public provision in such spheres as education, child health care and immunisation, and family support, and to ensuring that what is provided meets the needs of all children. Under article 4 of the Convention, states parties assume an obligation to 'undertake all appropriate legislative, administrative, and other measures for the implementation of the rights recognized'. Where rights to education and health and other social and economic rights are concerned, it is provided that implementation measures must be undertaken 'to the maximum extent of [a state's] available resources and, where needed, within the framework of international co-operation'. The Committee observes that this introduces into the Convention the concept of 'progressive implementation' used in the International Covenant on Economic, Social and Cultural Rights.[15] As in the case of the Covenant, this concept places an onus on states parties to show that they have allocated appropriate proportions of available resources to the implementation of children's rights, and, where necessary have called on international co-operation. It also places an onus on states parties with the capacity to provide international assistance to show that, for their part, they have made appropriate contributions to the global implementation of the Convention.

The final Convention principle identified by the Committee on the Rights of the Child concerns the participation of children in decision-making which affects them. Article 12(1) of the Convention provides

---

[13] Ibid., para. 43. See also paras. 42 and 44. [14] Ibid., para. 12.
[15] Ibid., para. 7.

that states parties 'shall assure to the child who is capable of forming his or her own views the right to express those views freely in all matters affecting the child, the views of the child being given due weight in accordance with the age and maturity of the child'. The idea that children have the right to take part in processes affecting them is an important concomitant to the idea that in those processes the best interests of the child must be a primary consideration. Without it, the best interests principle would scarcely respond to the anti-paternalist impulse we highlighted earlier. Put differently, the principle of participatory decision-making helps to establish the distinctiveness of a rights-based approach in relation to alternative models, whether oriented to welfare, delinquency, or some other concept defined for children by adults. The Committee notes that there is considerable scope for tokenism in moves to involve children in decision-making that affects them. In its words, 'appearing to "listen" to children is relatively unchallenging; giving due weight to their views requires real change'.[16] The Committee considers that article 12(1) also implies the ascertainment of the views of particular children on particular issues—for example, adopted children and children in adoptive families on adoption law and policy. Overall, the Committee stresses the importance of developing channels of communication between children and government which are not mediated through non-governmental organisations or human rights institutions, but are instead direct.

Children's rights: selected issues

We have so far been focusing on the Convention on the Rights of the Child. But this is by no means the only treaty that can be used to defend the rights of children. As Tom Campbell writes, it is 'an elementary if sometimes neglected point that children are people'.[17] Hence, all human rights treaties apply to children, even if it is understood that some elements within them, such as the right to marry, require qualification so as to recognise a minimum age. In addition, there exist a number of

[16] See Committee on the Rights of the Child, General Comment 5 (General measures of implementation for the Convention on the Rights of the Child: arts. 4, 42 and 44(6)), 3 October 2003, para. 12.

[17] T. Campbell, 'The Rights of the Minor: as Person, as Child, as Juvenile, as Future Adult' in P. Alston, S. Parker & J. Seymour (eds.), *Children, Rights and the Law* (Oxford: Clarendon Press, 1992), 1, 17.

other treaties which enumerate specific rights of children, among them the wide-ranging African Charter on the Rights and Welfare of the Child, adopted within the framework of the Organization for African Unity in 1990, and the procedural rights-focused European Convention on the Exercise of Children's Rights, adopted within the framework of the Council of Europe in 1996. Under the auspices of the International Labour Organization, a number of treaties have also been adopted for the protection of children in the sphere of work. Finally, the United Nations and other international organisations have promulgated standards bearing upon the rights on children on a number of issues. Of particular importance are the UN Standard Minimum Rules for the Administration of Juvenile Justice (the 'Beijing Rules'), adopted by the UN General Assembly in 1985.[18] These various treaties and other instruments have significance for a vast array of concerns involving children. Of these, we will focus in the paragraphs that follow on four concerns in particular: child labour, child soldiers, juvenile justice, and violence against children.

Child labour is a very longstanding preoccupation within the International Labour Organization. In ILO Convention 10, adopted in 1921, employment in any public or private agricultural undertaking was prohibited for children under 14. This Convention was later revised by Convention 138, adopted in 1973, which extended the prohibition to all kinds of employment. Article 2(3) of Convention 138 stipulates that the minimum age for employment must be not less than the age for completion of compulsory education, and in any event, not less than 15 years (or, in the case of certain countries and subject to certain conditions, 14 years). In 1999 a further ILO treaty concerning children was adopted, ILO Convention 182. Under this treaty states parties are obliged to prohibit and take immediate steps to eliminate certain forms of labour for all children under the age of 18. Designated the 'worst forms of child labour', these include slavery and slave-like practices such as debt bondage, child prostitution and child pornography, and the use of children in drug trafficking.[19] In the Convention on the Rights of the Child, states parties are left to fix minimum ages for admission to employment, subject to the right of children to be protected from economic exploitation, hazardous work, or work that is likely to interfere with their education or be

[18] UN GA Res. 40/33, 29 November 1985.

[19] See also Optional Protocol to the Convention on the Rights of the Child on the sale of children, child prostitution and child pornography.

harmful to their health or development.[20] For the purpose of this Convention, a child is defined as someone under the age of 18, unless under the law applicable to the child, majority is attained earlier.[21]

As with child labour, protections relating to the recruitment and deployment of children as soldiers indirectly recognise the right of children to conditions of life that are consistent with their developmental and other needs. In the Convention on the Rights of the Child, it is stipulated that states parties 'shall take all feasible measures to ensure that persons who have not attained the age of fifteen years do not take a direct part in hostilities'.[22] States parties are also placed under an obligation not to recruit people under 15 into their armed forces, and when recruiting people between 15 and 18, to 'endeavour to give priority to those who are oldest'.[23] In 2000 an Optional Protocol to the Convention was adopted to extend these restrictions. States parties to the Optional Protocol are obliged to take all feasible measures to ensure that persons under 18 (rather than only 15) do not take a direct part in hostilities.[24] With regard to recruitment, an obligation is imposed not to recruit compulsorily anyone under 18.[25] Voluntary recruitment may occur at a lower age, but states parties are obliged to raise the minimum age of voluntary recruitment from 15 (as provided in the original Convention), and to maintain specified safeguards with respect to recruits under the age of 18.[26] The Optional Protocol also provides that non-state armed groups should not recruit or use in hostilities anyone under the age of 18, and that states parties must take all feasible measures to enforce this.[27] The African Charter on the Rights and Welfare of the Child contains a more robust scheme with respect to state recruitment, providing that no recruits may be under 18, whether compulsory or voluntary.[28] However, it makes no reference to non-state recruitment, even if states parties are again obliged to take all necessary measures to ensure that no one under the age of 18 takes direct part in hostilities. Under the Rome Statute of the International Criminal Court, the conscription or enlisting of children under 15 into an armed force or their use to participate actively in hostilities is included within the category of 'war crimes' over which the International Criminal Court has jurisdiction.[29]

[20] Art. 32.   [21] Art. 1.   [22] Art. 38(2).   [23] Art. 38(3).
[24] Art. 1.   [25] Art. 2.   [26] Art. 3.   [27] Art. 4.   [28] Art. 22(2).
[29] See Art. 8(2)(b)(xxvi) (relating to international armed conflict) and art. 8(2)(e)(vii) (relating to non-international armed conflict).

Norms relating to juvenile justice are concerned with the rights of children in connection with criminal liability, procedure and penalties. The Beijing Rules, mentioned above, contain detailed provisions in this regard, which are broadly reflected in the Convention on the Rights of the Child. Three main issues are addressed. First, the introduction is urged of special laws, procedures and institutions for determining the criminal liability of children.[30] Secondly, the right is recognised of children— as already noted, this refers in the Convention to those under the age of 18—to be treated within the criminal justice system in a manner that takes due account of their age. This entails, among other things, the right to be detained separately from adults, except where this is not in a child's best interests;[31] the right to privacy at all stages of criminal proceedings;[32] and the right to be detained or sentenced to imprisonment only as a last resort, and for the shortest appropriate time.[33] Thirdly, the right is recognised of children to basic guarantees against arbitrary detention and to procedural protections ensuring a fair trial.[34] This last aspect takes on particular importance against the background of special juvenile laws and procedures which have sometimes resulted in reduced procedural protection compared to adult criminal justice.

In one case before the European Court of Human Rights, against the United Kingdom, the applicant had been sentenced to imprisonment upon conviction for murder committed when he was 10.[35] While the Court dismissed his complaint that this was too young an age to be made criminally responsible, it accepted that he had been unable properly to understand, and effectively to participate in, the proceedings against him, with the consequence that his right to a fair trial had been violated. The European Court also considered that the applicant's rights under the Convention had been violated in a number of other ways. Under the applicable English law, offenders under the age of 18 who were convicted of murder were automatically sentenced to be detained 'during Her Majesty's pleasure'. This included an initial period of detention for the purpose of punishment and deterrence, known as the 'tariff', followed by further detention if that was considered necessary for the protection

---

[30] Convention on the Rights of the Child, art. 40(3).   [31] Ibid., art. 37(c).
[32] Ibid., art. 40(2)(b)(vii).   [33] Ibid., art. 37(b).
[34] See ibid., arts. 37 and 40.
[35] *V v United Kingdom*, Judgment of the European Court of Human Rights, 16 December 1999.

of the public. Both the fixing of the tariff and the decision on post-tariff detention were within the discretion of the Home Secretary. In the applicant's case, an initial decision by the Home Secretary on the tariff had been quashed, and no new tariff had been set, leaving the applicant's eventual release date wholly uncertain. The European Court held that these arrangements violated the applicant's right to trial before an independent tribunal, inasmuch as the sentence was fixed by an official of the executive, the Home Secretary. The arrangements were also held to violate the applicant's right, protected in article 5(4) of the European Convention, to have the lawfulness of his detention decided by a court. Since authority to decide on his detention was entirely in the hands of the Home Secretary, and especially given that the latter had not set any tariff, the applicant was effectively denied the right to have his continued detention reviewed by a judicial body.

Turning finally to the issue of violence against children, this too has been the subject of some important judgments by the European Court of Human Rights. A number of early judgments concerned corporal punishment in schools or by order of courts.[36] More recently, however, the European Court has addressed the problem of ill-treatment of children in their homes. Under the Convention on the Rights of the Child, states parties are required to take measures to protect children from violence or neglect by their parents or other carers.[37] In the context of the European Convention, a similar obligation has been held to arise in connection with the right, protected in article 3 of the Convention, not to be subjected to inhuman or degrading treatment. This was made clear in 1998, when the European Court ruled on a complaint against the United Kingdom by a child who had been beaten by his stepfather.[38] Charged with assault, the stepfather had invoked the defence of 'reasonable chastisement', available under English law, and had been acquitted on that basis. The applicant complained that the availability of this defence meant that he was deprived of adequate protection from inhuman or degrading treatment, and the Court accepted this argument.

[36] See, e.g., *Tyrer v United Kingdom*, Judgment of the European Court of Human Rights, 15 March 1978; *Campbell & Cosans v United Kingdom*, Judgment of the European Court of Human Rights, 29 January 1982; and *Costello-Roberts v United Kingdom*, Judgment of the European Court of Human Rights, 23 February 1993.

[37] Art. 19.

[38] *A v United Kingdom*, Judgment of the European Court of Human Rights, 23 September 1998.

The Court confirmed that the prohibition on inhuman and degrading treatment entails not only restraints on state action, but also the duty to take positive measures to ensure that ill-treatment is not administered by private individuals. In a number of later cases, the Court considered the implications of this for the obligations of public authorities to intervene to protect children from serious neglect or abuse. In one case, the Court held that the failure, over a long period of time, to take action to protect children from serious neglect and abuse known to state authorities constituted a violation of the right not to be subjected to inhuman or degrading treatment.[39] In another case the Court reached a similar conclusion, based on a systematic 'lack of investigation, communication and co-operation by the relevant authorities'.[40] In holding the state liable for a violation of the prohibition on ill-treatment, the Court affirmed that a 'failure to take reasonably available measures which could have had a real prospect of altering the outcome or mitigating the harm is sufficient to engage the responsibility of the State'.[41]

Norms concerning child labour, child soldiers, juvenile justice and violence against children illustrate some of the ways in which international human rights law seeks to enhance the possibilities for young people to live in a distinct developmental space, and one that is congenial to their flourishing. But, of course, these norms, even if better implemented, will not in themselves suffice to create the enabling conditions for young people to live 'as children' in this sense. We need to ask: *why* do children take on work, fight in wars, commit crimes, and get abused in homes? As soon as we pose these questions, it becomes clear that children's rights direct attention to some of the most serious social problems we face in the world today. These are problems which affect all societies, whether because they occur in all parts of world or because they are inseparable from historical processes and phenomena that are global in scale. Likewise, they are problems which affect not just children, but also adults. Most point to situations in which adult family members are suffering alongside children. Some also point to situations in which children have been left to head households following the death or debilitation of adult family members in war or through disease. As is

---

[39] *Z & Others v United Kingdom*, Judgment of the European Court of Human Rights, 10 May 2001.

[40] *E & Others v United Kingdom*, Judgment of the European Court of Human Rights, 26 November 2002, para. 100. [41] Ibid., para. 99.

widely recognised, action to implement children's rights must be accompanied by action to improve conditions in the communities and households in which children live. For example, preventing child labour is contingent almost everywhere on raising the income of the family. Likewise, the prevention of violence against children may depend on expanded and better organised family support. To this extent, children's rights are not just about children. The point here is not the well worn adage that 'children are our future'. As noted earlier, they are also their present, and in any event should not be approached instrumentally in this way. Rather, the point is the simple one that children live in a relational present; that is to say, their lives are shaped by the social and economic relations in which they are enmeshed and by the local, national, and global forces that intersect those relations. While children's rights can usefully be invoked to isolate injustices affecting children, their greatest value may lie in connecting these injustices with larger patterns of hardship, exclusion and violence.

Culture

Writing in 1983, Raymond Williams declared 'culture' one of the two or three most complicated words in the English language.[1] Since then, the concept of culture has been through further vicissitudes—'culture wars', identity politics, and resurgent ethnonationalism, to name just a few. To some people working in the social sciences and humanities, the point has been reached where this term has become more trouble than it is worth. To them, culture is best avoided, or even entirely dropped from our vocabularies of social description and analysis. According to other scholars in these fields, however, there remains something distinctive and important that can usefully be captured with this word. According to these scholars, culture should not be dropped, just reinflected.

With these latter arguments in mind, we take up in what follows the question of how human rights relate to culture. We will focus, in particular, on two dimensions of that relationship. One is concerned with the general issue of how human rights stand with respect to culture. Do human rights protect culture, or do they assail it? Is culture an obstacle to human rights, or does it rather belong with efforts to promote them and secure their implementation? The other dimension has to do with the specific phenomenon of cultural rights. Human rights law recognises rights to take part in, and carry forward, cultural practices. What notions of culture underpin these rights? How do those notions compare with the ideas that inform debates about the interrelation of human rights and culture more generally? Are there alternative conceptualisations that could prove more beneficial or more illuminating?

[1] R. Williams, *Keywords* (London: Fontana, rev. ed., 1983), 87.

Culture

In one familiar sense, culture refers to *the arts*. Writing in the 1860s the English poet and critic Matthew Arnold expressed this notion when he characterised culture as the 'best that has been known and thought'. 'Culture', he wrote, 'looks beyond machinery', to 'sweetness and light'.[2] In this sense, then, culture is a way of transcending the mundanity of life in an industrial age. It names the sphere of creativity and refinement and the urgings of the human will to perfection. It also lays the basis for a distinction between 'high culture' and 'low culture', cultivation and popular entertainment. Whereas this usage of the word 'culture' is explicitly evaluative, a second familiar usage intends to be simply descriptive. This is the sense of culture as *the way of life of a particular society or people*. Here culture is pluralised, so that societies and sets of societies correspond to different 'cultures', each having its own values, behaviours and rules. This conception is associated with the beginnings of the academic discipline of anthropology, and it too has important roots in Victorian England. In the 1870s E.B. Tylor defined culture as 'that complex whole which includes knowledge, belief, art, morals, law, custom and any other capabilities acquired by man as a member of society'.[3] For Tylor culture was an evolutionary affair in the manner of Darwinian biology, and non-European societies were species of 'primitive' culture. Along with Matthew Arnold's elitism, however, that perspective later came to seem embarrassing for its arrogance and offensiveness, and culture began to be used instead as a relativising tool, to promote appreciation of the diversity of human societies.

But the basic idea remained in place that the world could be viewed as a collection of distinct cultures, and in its turn this too attracted criticism.[4] Behind the idea of culture as the way of life of a particular society or people—theorists have shown—are three flawed assumptions. The first is an assumption that cultures are determinate things. This misses the fact that cultural life is a structure of change, and that cultures must

---

[2] M. Arnold, *Culture and Anarchy and other writings* (1869) edited by S. Collini (Cambridge: Cambridge University Press, 1993), 53–187, 78.

[3] E. Tylor, *Primitive Culture: Researches into the Development of Mythology, Philosophy, Religion, Art and Custom* (London: John Murray, 1871), vol. I, 1.

[4] See, e.g., J. Clifford, *The Predicament of Culture* (Cambridge, Mass.: Harvard University Press, 1988), on which we draw in this paragraph.

be grasped not as static objects, but as historical processes. Indeed, they must be grasped as extremely complex historical processes, which proceed in non-linear patterns, with cultural forms often emerging and reconfiguring discontinuously, as circumstances allow. Secondly, there is an assumption that cultures are autonomous wholes. Again this is misleading, inasmuch as cultures rarely exist as unified orders, but rather as contradictory assemblages of experiences and ideas. Likewise, they rarely exist as bounded entities, but are instead linked through circuits of borrowing, indigenisation, re-export, imposition, subversion, and so on. Finally, there is an assumption that cultures are pre-political domains of shared values and consensual practices. This also mischaracterises reality, for if cultures are manifestations of shared values and consensual practices, they are at the same time systems of privilege and exclusion. With solidarity and commonality come conflict and contestation. The representation of culture is not a matter of stating facts but of exercising power, and it needs to be assessed in terms of the question of how that power is distributed.

While some scholars have begun to wonder whether the culture concept may be too compromised to remain useful,[5] others have taken the elements of the critique just described as the basis for an alternative formulation. In this latter category is Arjun Appardurai. In his alternative, the focus is shifted from the noun 'culture' (as in the culture of a society or people) to the adjectival uses of culture, so that attention is directed to the 'cultural' dimensions of a social situation or problem.[6] For Appardurai, the nominal use of culture fosters the idea that what is in issue is 'some kind of object, thing or substance'.[7] As soon as we begin to use the word adjectivally, however, we are moved 'into the realm of differences, contrasts and comparisons'. According to him, the 'most valuable feature of the concept of culture is the concept of difference'. In turn, the most valuable features of the concept of difference are that it is a contrastive principle, rather than a substantive property, and that, as a contrastive principle, it works relationally (pointing to similarity and diversity), rather than oppositionally (setting up absolute oppositions).

[5] See, e.g., the essays in N. Dirks (ed.), *In Near Ruins: Cultural Theory at the End of the Century* (Minneapolis and London: University of Minnesota Press, 1998).

[6] A. Appardurai, *Modernity at Large* (Minneapolis: University of Minnesota Press, 1996), esp. 11–15.

[7] For these and the following quotations in this paragraph, see ibid., 12–13.

and trades in processes (pointing to homogenisation and differentiation), rather than things (treating differences as fixed). Of course, as Appardurai observes, there exist in the world many kinds of differences, and only some of them are cultural. Cultural differences, he contends, are those which 'either express, or set the groundwork for, the mobilization of group identities...both within and outside particular social groups'. Thus, his proposal is that culture is best understood, not as a property of particular individuals or groups, but rather as *the dimension of difference*. In his words, culture is a 'heuristic device we can use to talk about difference', and especially about the ways in which in various contexts difference is, or might be, deployed in the mobilisation of group identity.

Culture and human rights

We have surveyed three conceptions of culture: culture as the arts, culture as a particular way of life, and culture as the dimension of difference. Against this background, let us now turn to consider issues and norms relating to culture within the framework of international human rights law. At the centre of contemporary discussions of the relationship between human rights and culture is a debate about the cultural limits of human rights.[8] This debate encompasses a huge variety of arguments, issues and contexts. To focus our consideration of it, we concentrate here on one set of arguments, about 'Asian values' and their effect on human rights. (On the broader question of how the universality of human rights is to be reconciled with global cultural diversity, see Universality★.)

Claims about the significance of Asian values for human rights began to appear in international affairs journals and official statements in the early 1990s,[9] and came to international prominence in meetings associated with the World Conference on Human Rights, held in

[8] See, e.g., M. Mamdani (ed.), *Beyond Rights Talk and Culture Talk* (New York: St Martin's Press, 2000) and R.A. Wilson (ed.), *Human Rights, Culture and Context* (London: Pluto Press, 1997).

[9] See, e.g., K. Mahbubani, 'The West and the Rest' 28 *The National Interest* (Summer, 1992) 3; and B Kausikan, 'Asia's Different Standard' 92 *Foreign Policy* (1993) 24. See further D. Bell, *East Meets West: Human Rights and Democracy in East Asia* (Princeton: Princeton University Press, 2000).

Vienna in 1993.[10] Among the key proponents of the claims have been the Singaporean, Malaysian and Chinese Governments. The arguments advanced are not uniform, but they have a common theme. This is that Asian values are in some fundamental ways at odds with the premises and demands of human rights, especially civil and political rights. While human rights promote individualism and glorify freedom, in Asia the interests of the community come first. Thus, it is said, Asian societies differ from Western societies in placing duties before rights, and social order before individual freedom. Hierarchical relations are more readily accepted than in the West, and there is greater trust in those with authority. Consensus and personal contacts are the preferred methods for resolving social conflict, as distinct from the more adversarial and impersonal approaches promoted by human rights. Given these and other values, and given also their circumstances as developing countries in highly competitive global conditions, it is contended that Asian societies attach more importance to good government than human rights. As Bilahari Kausikan writes, what people in Asia want is 'effective, efficient, and honest administrations able to provide security and basic needs with good opportunities for an improved standard of living'. While acknowledging that good government and human rights are 'overlapping concepts', he observes that 'they are not always the same thing', and good government may, and does, sometimes require administrative detention, press censorship, and other draconian laws. If this is inconsistent with human rights, then that simply confirms that human rights remain, as they started out, an expression of Western traditions and Western worldviews. Where Asia is concerned, writes Kausikan, a 'different standard' must be applied.[11]

This contention sparked considerable controversy at the 1993 World Conference on Human Rights, as well as in the preparatory meetings that preceded the Conference, though it must be said that that controversy included a good deal of shadow-boxing, with both sides putting forward counter-arguments to arguments which had never actually been made. The Declaration issued at the end of the Conference seeks

---

[10] See, e.g., 'Bangkok Declaration', Final Declaration of The Regional Meeting for Asia of the World Conference on Human Rights, Bangkok, 29 March–2 April 1993, UN Doc. A/CONF.157/ASRM/8-A/CONF.157/PC/59, 7 April 1993.

[11] B. Kausikan, 'Asia's Different Standard' 92 *Foreign Policy* (1993) 24, 37–8.

to mediate the various positions with an assertion that, '[w]hile the significance of national and regional particularities and various historical, cultural and religious backgrounds must be borne in mind, it is the duty of States, regardless of their political, economic and cultural systems, to promote and protect all human rights and fundamental freedoms'.[12] But this statement seems at once gloriously self-evident and deeply obscure. In the light of our discussion above, one starting point for a critique of the claims concerning Asian values is to consider how they implicitly conceptualise culture. Clearly, they are informed by the idea that culture refers to *a particular way of life*—in this case, the way of life of the societies of a particular region of the world. As we saw in the previous section, that conception tends to occlude awareness of the extent to which claims to defend prevailing social arrangements are manifestations of power. Indeed, to some critics, the invocation of Asian values is simply a cynical attempt on the part of certain governments and their supporters to justify the repressive measures through which those governments seek to prevent opposition and consolidate their rule. As is frequently observed, the notion that a 'different standard' should be applied to Asia appears to have attracted limited support within popular movements in the region.[13]

To other critics, however, it is wrong to dismiss the Asian values thesis on this basis, for it brings out a number of important points about human rights and their contemporary context. First, it illustrates the consequences of assertions such as those advanced in the United States in the early 1990s that the 'end of history' has arrived, or alternatively that the world is poised to witness a 'clash of civilisations'. If anti-liberal relativism is an unsurprising sequel to post-Cold War liberal triumphalism, the grim vision of inter-civilisational clash for its part invites and endorses the Asian values claims. Secondly, the Asian values thesis also highlights the effects of global economic changes, including trade liberalisation, and reminds us of the way heightened competitive pressures provoke processes of defensive closure. Finally, the idea that a 'different standard' applies in Asia calls attention to the legacy of colonialism,

---

[12] Vienna Declaration and Programme of Action, UN Doc. A/CONF.157/23, 12 July 1993, Part I, para. 5.

[13] See Bangkok NGO Declaration, 24–28 March 1993, UN Doc. A/CONF.157/PC/83, 19 April 1993. Reprinted in *Our Voice: Bangkok NGO Declaration on Human Rights* (Bangkok: Asia Pacific Cultural Forum on Democracy, 1993), 198.

and to the enduringly unequal and exploitative relations that form the background against which human rights are today promoted. As Onuma Yasuaki writes, 'For those who have experienced colonial rule and interventions under such beautiful slogans as "humanity" and "civilization", the term "human rights" looks like nothing more than another beautiful slogan by which great powers rationalize their interventionist policies'.[14] The problem, however, is that, far from challenging imperialism in new form, the Asian values thesis sustains it by renewing the imperialist division between the West and its 'Others' and, with that division, the old Orientalist trope of Asian despotism. To the extent that the thesis reinforces these tenets of colonialism, it helps Western powers to claim for themselves a monopoly of virtue and modernity. At the same time, it permits those powers to go on defining, and hence ordering, life in and with the societies of Asia. As Inoue Tatsuo explains, the evocation of Asian values acts as an 'accomplice of the current version of the Orientalist geopolitics on the Western side', in which the necessity is no longer prescribed of 'conquering the "alien civilization" but [rather] ... of containing it and consolidating the Western sphere of influence'.[15]

In the end, then, what makes the Asian values thesis problematic is that it treats 'Asia' and 'the West' as things, that have determinate essences, form integrated wholes, operate as autonomous entities, and express shared values and consensual practices. In fact, of course, as Kausikan and the others certainly recognise, the most significant commonality of the Asian region is diversity, both across the region and within each country. And if there is more *intra-regional* diversity than the Asian values thesis suggests, there is also less *inter-regional* diversity. The values said to be Asian are by no means absent from Western societies, and vice versa. Asian and Western traditions do not only vary; they overlap, due in part to the colonial encounter itself. Moreover, as many have observed, the fact that administrative detention, press censorship and other draconian laws are felt to be needed is surely a reminder that the values in question are neither uncontested, nor perhaps fully inclusionary. As this brief

[14] Onuma Yasuaki, 'Toward an Intercivilizational Approach to Human Rights' in J. Bauer and D. Bell (eds.), *The East Asian Challenge for Human Rights* (Cambridge: Cambridge University Press, 1999), 103, 105.

[15] Inoue Tatsuo, 'Liberal Democracy and Asian Orientalism' in J. Bauer and D. Bell (eds.), *The East Asian Challenge for Human Rights* (Cambridge: Cambridge University Press, 1999), 27, 43.

review of the Asian values debate confirms, the danger of a conception of culture as a particular way of life is that it may provide ideological support for domination, both within states and among them. This has implications not only for the Asian region, but for contemporary discussions about human rights in the Islamic world as well. It also has implications for debates about the significance of 'traditional practices' for the human rights of women and girls. And, of course, it has notable implications for assessments of the prospects of human rights in Western societies. For, as Inoue again observes, what is bad about the 'polarizing drive of Orientalist dualism [is that it] traps the West as well as Asia in a distorted perception of self-identity'. In the case of the West, this distortion takes the form of 'self-sanctification', and fosters the neglect of 'its own suppressed grim record in terms of democracy and human rights'.[16]

What if, instead of culture as a particular way of life, the animating idea were Appardurai's sense of culture as the dimension of difference? Using culture as a heuristic device to talk about difference might enable us to leave behind the polarising dualisms of Asian values, the 'West and the Rest', and so on, and engage directly with some of the issues to which we have referred in the preceding paragraphs. We might ask: what are the implications of claiming human rights as phenomena that belong to the triumph of the West? What are the implications of casting human rights as stakes in an intercivilisational clash? How does economic liberalisation affect the prospects for human rights protection in developing countries? To what extent is the promotion of human rights shaped by earlier imperial relations? Using culture in the way Appardurai suggests might also help us to develop new ways of using human rights in the negotiation of group identities, and new ways of articulating group identities with human rights regimes. We might ask: how should human rights norms, interpretations and institutions be rethought so as to correct biases and redress exclusions? How can human rights be made more useful to particular groups engaged in emancipatory struggle around the world? How might difference be deployed in the mobilisation of new forms of group identity that escape the inherited categories created for post-colonial societies by imperial powers? Likewise, using

[16] Inoue Tatsuo, 'Liberal Democracy and Asian Orientalism' in J. Bauer and D. Bell (eds.), *The East Asian Challenge for Human Rights* (Cambridge: Cambridge University Press, 1999), 27, 42.

culture in this way might encourage us to scrutinise critically the processes of authenticating or representing culture. Finally, then, we might ask: who has authority to speak for culture? What is the relation between processes of cultural authentication and systems of social hierarchy? How do the cultural dimensions of human rights intersect with the gender and other dimensions?

Cultural rights

Our focus to this point has been on ways in which human rights are said to conflict with culture. But the other side of the relationship between human rights and culture concerns the promotion and protection of culture through human rights. We turn now to consider two aspects of this. The first centres on the right to take part in cultural life, the second on the rights associated with membership of a minority community.

The right to take part in cultural life

The human right 'freely to participate in the cultural life of the community' is asserted in the Universal Declaration of Human Rights.[17] It is guaranteed in article 15 of the International Covenant on Economic, Social and Cultural Rights, under which the states parties recognise 'the right of everyone to take part in cultural life' and undertake to 'respect the freedom indispensable for . . . cultural activity', and it is protected as well under a number of regional human rights systems.[18] It is also reaffirmed, and elaborated, in instruments issued by international organisations, especially the United Nations Educational, Scientific and Cultural Organization. The right to take part in cultural life is understood both as a right of access to cultural activities and as a right to create cultural works. The approach of the Committee on Economic, Social and Cultural Rights in monitoring compliance with article 15 of the

[17] Art. 27. Regarding the right to take part in cultural life, see further H. Nieć (ed.), *Cultural Rights and Wrongs* (Paris: UNESCO Publishing, 1998).

[18] See San Salvador Protocol to the American Convention on Human Rights, art. 14; African Charter on Human and Peoples' Rights, art. 17(2); and American Declaration of the Rights and Duties of Man, art. XIII.

Covenant provides an instructive guide to what is involved.[19] Statements by the Committee suggest that the right of access to cultural activities entails, in the first place, ensuring affordability to the widest possible audience, through the granting of subsidies for 'cultural centres, museums, libraries, theatres, and cinemas'. Secondly, it entails removing barriers to equal participation, through action to redress regional disparities in the availability of cultural facilities, and also to widen the range of works and performances that can be enjoyed by people with disabilities, elderly people, and others with special needs. Finally, it entails preserving the cultural heritage, through measures to safeguard artworks, monuments, archaeological sites, and so on. Alongside these issues of accessibility, cultural participation also engages issues of creative freedom. The right to create cultural works includes the right to disseminate them, and in this respect cultural rights reinforce, and are reinforced by, rights to freedom of expression. Here the concern is with the harassment of authors and artists and the unjustified censorship or destruction of their works.

If we now pause to consider how the term culture is being used in this context, it is obvious from what we have said so far that culture refers here to the arts. Initially, it seems, the right to take part in cultural life was understood as a right to take part in what Matthew Arnold had in mind, the 'best that has been known and thought'. In keeping with the anti-elitist shift we mentioned earlier, however, the distinction between high culture and low culture was later repudiated, and it is now accepted that the right to cultural participation may form the basis of demands for cultural policy that supports not just opera, but soap opera, comic books, and dance music as well. But the concept of cultural life also extends more broadly than this. For, just as the distinction between high culture and low culture has been repudiated, so too the distinction between artistic activity and other symbolic practices has been called into question, and culture has been reconceived to go beyond the sphere of the arts, so as to encompass ways of life. Thus, UNESCO declared, in

[19] We draw here on R. O'Keefe, 'The "Right to Take Part in Cultural Life" under Article 15 of the ICESCR' 47 *International & Comparative Law Quarterly* (1998) 904. See also Committee on Economic, Social and Cultural Rights, General Comment 5 (persons with disabilities), 9 December 1994, paras. 35–8, and General Comment 6 (the economic, social and cultural rights of older persons), 8 December 1995, paras. 39–41.

a Recommendation issued in 1976, that 'the concept of culture has been broadened to include all forms of creativity and expression of groups or individuals, both in their ways of life and in their artistic activities'.[20]

One consequence of this expanded conception of culture is that the right to take part in cultural life can be used as a basis for claims arising out of pressures affecting minority groups within states. To this extent, the right to cultural participation reinforces, and is reinforced by, the rights of members of minority communities, to which we turn in a moment. At the same time, it can be used as a basis for expressing concerns arising out of pressures upon states that emanate from global markets. Noting this aspect, the UNESCO Recommendation asserts the need for 'measures against the harmful effect of "commercial mass culture", which threatens national cultures'.[21] In a similar vein, the Committee on Economic, Social and Cultural Rights calls attention to the danger posed by the 'growing standardization of culture . . . due to the invasion of a cultural model from outside which is accepted purely because of economic factors and due to market forces'.[22] These institutions are right about the need for national measures as a counterweight to market forces. But are they right to diagnose the problem in terms of 'national cultures', 'standardization' and 'invasion of a cultural model from outside'? To speak in these terms is to presuppose that cultures are unitary and autonomous. Yet, as Edward Said has summarised the argument we touched on earlier, '[f]ar from being unitary or monolithic or autonomous things, cultures actually assume more "foreign" elements, alterities, differences, than they consciously exclude'.[23] To speak as UNESCO and the Committee do is equally to presuppose that the reception of cultural forms is a process of passive absorption. Yet, as many today observe, what is actually involved is a far more active and complex kind of engagement, in which processes of homogenisation go hand in hand with processes of heterogenisation. While global cultural diversity may partly depend on state intervention, this seems to suggest that it may also be partly self-sustaining.

[20] Recommendation on Participation by the People at Large in Cultural Life and their Contribution to It, adopted 26 November 1976. UNESCO Doc. 19, C/Resolutions, Annex 1, 29, para. 3(a).

[21] See ibid., 23rd preambular paragraph.

[22] UN Doc. E/1993/22, chap. VII ('General Discussion'), para. 220, quoted in R. O'Keefe, 'The "Right to Take Part in Cultural Life" under Article 15 of the ICESCR' 47 International & Comparative Law Quarterly (1998) 904, 919.

[23] Edward Said, Culture and Imperialism (London: Vintage, 1993), 15.

If the prescription then is sound, the problem with the diagnosis is not just that it involves a mischaracterisation of reality, but that reliance on a conception of culture as way of life may work to support the very market forces that are seen to threaten national culture. This can be illustrated by reference to a ruling of the World Trade Organization Appellate Body in 1997. The case concerned measures that had been adopted in Canada to maintain an environment in which Canadian periodicals could survive competition from the United States. The Appellate Body ruled that most of the measures adopted were incompatible with Canada's obligations under the General Agreement on Tariffs and Trade.[24] In its recommendation the WTO Panel had stressed that the 'ability of any Member to take measures to protect its cultural identity was not at issue in the present case';[25] how, after all, could a few periodicals endanger Canadian national identity? Here we see that a conception of culture as the way of life of a particular society makes it easy to dismiss concerns such as those which motivated the measures adopted in Canada—and which also motivate measures adopted in France, India, Australia and elsewhere with respect to film, among many other sectors. What if, once again, analysis were instead oriented to a conception of culture as the dimension of difference? Using culture in this way might help to keep those concerns in view. By putting aside the idea of culture as a particular way of life, we might be able to shift the focus from the protection of identity to the negotiation of difference, and from the presupposition of things to the investigation of processes. The right to take part in cultural life might then become a way of raising the question of how efforts to negotiate difference are affected by moves to liberalise trade. More generally, it might become a way of directing attention to the problems of mobilising group identity in conditions of intensifying globalisation.

Minority rights

We have been speaking about pressures upon states emanating from global markets. But, as indicated, cultural rights are also concerned with pressures within states affecting minority communities. The idea that

---

[24] WTO Appellate Body, *Canada—Certain Measures Concerning Periodicals*, WT/DS31/AB/R, 30 June 1997.

[25] WTO Panel Report, *Canada—Certain Measures Concerning Periodicals*, WT/DS31/R, 14 March 1997, para. 5.45.

members of minority communities should be protected from assimila-tionist pressures has a long history, and underpins the many 'minorities treaties' that formed part of the post-World War I peace settlement in Europe. Examining one of these treaties in the light of a concern about the situation of Greek-speaking minorities in Albania, the Permanent Court of International Justice observed in 1935 that the aim of the treaties was 'to ensure that nationals belonging to racial, religious or linguistic minorities shall be placed in every respect on a footing of perfect equality with the other nationals of the State' and to ensure for the minority communities the 'means for the preservation of their racial peculiarities, their traditions and their national characteristics'.[26] Indeed, the Permanent Court emphasised, these two objectives are interlocked, for 'there would be no true equality between a majority and a minority if the latter were deprived of its own institutions, and were consequently compelled to renounce that which constitutes the very essence of its being as a minority'.[27]

After the Second World War, the failure of these treaties was widely seen as linked to their imposed and selective character, applying as they did only to minorities within states corresponding to the powers defeated in World War I. Thus, the notion gained acceptance that the best form of minority protection is not the conclusion of treaties with respect to particular communities, but the recognition and protection of universal human rights. At the same time, however, the idea also took root that membership of a minority community entails distinct human rights.[28] This is reflected in the Convention on the Prevention and Punishment of the Crime of Genocide, adopted in 1948, under which certain acts committed with intent to destroy a 'national, ethnical, racial or religious group' were defined as genocide and made international crimes. In a more wide-ranging way, it is reflected as well in the International Covenant on Civil and Political Rights. Article 27 provides: 'In those States in which ethnic, religious or linguistic minorities exist, persons belonging to such minorities shall not be denied the right, in commun-ity with the other members of their group, to enjoy their own culture,

---

[26] *Minority Schools in Albania*, Permanent Court of International Justice, Advisory Opinion of 6 April 1935, Series A/B No. 64, 4, 17. [27] Ibid.

[28] For a variety of perspectives on this idea, see further W. Kymlicka (ed.), *The Rights of Minority Cultures* (Oxford: Oxford University Press, 1995).

profess and practise their own religion, or to use their own language.' Despite this somewhat grudging, or at any rate negative, formulation ('shall not be denied'), the Human Rights Committee has made clear its view that article 27 recognises a right which calls for positive protection, and not only against acts of the state itself, but against acts by others within the state as well.[29] This right is also recognised, and its implications further elaborated in the influential, if not formally binding, UN Declaration on the Rights of Persons Belonging to National or Ethnic, Religious and Linguistic Minorities, adopted in 1992.[30] Following the ethno–nationalist violence in Europe of the early 1990s, two regional treaties for the protection of minority rights were concluded within the framework of the Council of Europe: the Charter for Minority Languages, opened for signature in 1992, and the Framework Convention for the Protection of National Minorities, opened for signature in 1994.[31]

If we take up again the question of how the term culture is used, it appears that culture refers here to the way of life of a particular group, in this case an 'ethnic, religious or linguistic minority' within a state. According to the Human Rights Committee, the protection of minority rights is 'directed towards ensuring the survival and continued development of the cultural, religious and social identity' of minority communities.[32] A number of complaints under article 27 of the Covenant have been brought by members of indigenous communities whose capacity to pursue their traditional livelihoods has been endangered by industrial or other activities.[33] In that context the conception of culture as a particular

---

[29] Human Rights Committee, General Comment 23 (the rights of minorities), 8 April 1994, paras. 6.1–6.2. Regarding the rights of minorities, see further P. Thornberry, *International Law and the Rights of Minorities* (Oxford: Clarendon Press, 1991) and A. Phillips & A. Rosas (eds.), *Universal Minority Rights* (Turku and London: Åbo Akademi University Institute for Human Rights/Minority Rights Group, 1995).

[30] UN GA Res. 47/135, 18 December 1992.

[31] See further G. Pentassuglia, *Minorities in International Law: An introductory study* (Strasbourg: Council of Europe Publishing, 2002).

[32] Human Rights Committee, General Comment 23 (The rights of minorities), 8 April 1994, para. 9.

[33] See, e.g., *Apirana Mahuika v New Zealand*, Communication 547/1993, Views of the Human Rights Committee, adopted 27 October 2000; *Hopu and Bessert v France*, Communication 549/1993, Views of the Human Rights Committee, adopted 29 July 1997; *Länsman and Others v Finland*, Communication 671/1995, Views of the Human Rights Committee, adopted 30 October 1996; *Marshall and Others, as officers of the Grand Council of the Mikmaq Tribal Society v Canada*, Communication 205/1986, Views of the

way of life has formed the basis for a recognition of the significance for indigenous communities of land use and access to resources.[34] Likewise, in connection with the American Convention on Human Rights, it has been stated that 'the close ties of indigenous people with the land must be recognized and understood as the fundamental basis of their cultures'.[35] On this footing, the right has been affirmed to have communal land demarcated and titled so as to ensure control by indigenous owners. Nonetheless, we must again ask whether the conception of culture being used here is adequate to deal with the issues at stake. To speak of culture in this way is to presuppose that cultures have some fixed, determinate 'essence'. Yet, as we have noted, culture is everywhere dynamic, plural and contested. Furthermore, to speak of 'survival' and 'development' is to presuppose that cultures are living organisms that grow and develop, survive or die. Yet, as we have also noted, cultures, and especially subaltern cultures, emerge and re-form discontinuously, as circumstances allow.

Once again, the problem here is not just that reality is mischaracterised, but that asymmetries of power are reinforced. With its organic image of cultural development and its integrated vision of cultural identity, the concept of culture as the way of life of a particular group tends to stabilise actuality and check change. For if at one level minority rights are rights to be different, at another level they can be a way of containing and limiting the possibilities for being different. This has implications for relations between minority and majority communities. Perhaps less obviously, it also has implications for relations within minority communities themselves, as another case involving Canada may serve to illustrate. A complaint was brought to the Human Rights Committee by some English-speaking residents of Quebec concerning a Quebec law under which all public signs had to be in French only.[36] The applicants'

Human Rights Committee, adopted 4 November 1991; *Ominayak and the Lubicon Lake Band v Canada*, Communication 167/1984, Views of the Human Rights Committee, adopted 26 March 1990; and *Kitok v Sweden*, Communication 197/1985, Views of the Human Rights Committee, adopted 27 July 1988.

[34] Human Rights Committee, General Comment 23 (The rights of minorities), 8 April 1994, para. 7. See further P. Thornberry, *Indigenous Peoples and Human Rights* (Manchester: Manchester University Press, 2002).

[35] *The Mayagna (Sumo) Awas Tingni Community v Nicaragua*, Judgment of the Inter-American Court of Human Rights, 31 August 2001, para. 149.

[36] *Ballantyne, Davidson and MacIntyre v Canada*, Communication 385/1989, Views of the Human Rights Committee, adopted 31 March 1993.

customers were English-speaking, and they wished to advertise in English. The Committee ruled that this law violated the applicants' rights to freedom of expression under article 19 of the Covenant. But it did not consider that any issue arose under article 27. '[T]he minorities referred to in article 27 are minorities within...a State, and not minorities within any province', the Committee said. 'English speaking citizens of Canada cannot be considered a linguistic minority.'[37] Just as in the WTO disputes settlement procedure United States periodicals appeared scarcely a threat to Canadian national identity, so here French signs appear scarcely a threat to English-speaking-Canadian identity. The Committee's approach cabins culture, and fixes it territorially. What if, once more, culture were reinflected as the dimension of difference? Using culture 'adjectivally', to direct attention to an aspect of a problem rather than to name a thing, might help to bring into focus the various ways in which social formations differentially affect individuals and groups. In particular, it might help to bring into focus the power imbalances involved, both between groups and within them. Minority rights might then become an invitation to investigate the potentialities, as well as the dangers, associated with the mobilisation of group identity in complex multicultural circumstances.

In a book on the concept of culture, Terry Eagleton writes of the centrality in human life of culture in the sense of '[a]ffection, relationship, memory, kinship, place, community, emotional fulfilment, intellectual enjoyment, a sense of ultimate meaning'. These things, he says, are 'closer to most of us than human rights charters'.[38] Yet, he also observes, '[t]his very intimacy can grow morbid and obsessional' unless it is set within a context that can 'temper these immediacies with more abstract, and in a way more generous affiliations'. Eagleton appears to assume that 'human rights charters', or more generally human rights law, can supply that context. Against the background of our enquiry into the relationship between human rights and culture, we may endorse that assumption. Human rights law can indeed help to temper the excesses of cultural identification. As we have seen, however, it can also serve to entrench those excesses, and to aggravate the morbidity of which Eagleton warns.

---

[37] *Ballantyne, Davidson and MacIntyre v Canada*, Communication 385/1989, Views of the Human Rights Committee, adopted 31 March 1993, para. 11.2.
[38] T. Eagleton, *The Idea of Culture* (Oxford: Blackwell, 2000), 131.

Death Penalty

The campaign to abolish the death penalty is one of the great historic struggles of the international human rights movement. For some, abolition remains among the movement's defining tasks and key ambitions. At one level, it is easy to see why. Deliberately killing a person is pretty much the worst thing you can do to them. The death penalty rationalises deliberate killing, and makes retribution a principle of penal policy. At another level, however, the abolition of the death penalty is not an obvious priority. It is concerned with the forms of punishment, rather than the causes of crime. It calls for recognition of obligations not to kill deliberately, rather than obligations to protect—or, better still, to create conditions that enhance—life. It encourages a focus on state violence, rather than the all too often neglected phenomenon of violence in the private sphere. It orients effort towards national contexts, rather than global systems. Finally, it invites us to dwell on something that affects relatively small numbers of people, rather than on things that affect very large numbers of people. With these points in mind, we might well ask whether, far from constituting a defining task and key ambition, the abolition of the death penalty does not *divert* energies and resources that could more fruitfully be spent on other issues. In what follows we review the principal achievements of abolitionist advocacy within the domain of international human rights law.[1] At the end, we shall return to the question just raised. If the death penalty campaign is a diversion, the possibility still remains, of course, that it is a beneficial diversion.

[1] See further R. Hood, *The Death Penalty: A Worldwide Perspective*, 3rd ed. (Oxford: Oxford University Press, 2002) and W.A. Schabas, *The Abolition of the Death Penalty in International Law*, 3rd ed. (Cambridge: Cambridge University Press, 2002).

The death penalty and human rights

The most conspicuous successes of abolitionist activism within the domain of international human rights law are four treaties, the stated purpose of which is to secure the abolition of the death penalty. One is the Second Optional Protocol to the International Covenant on Civil and Protocol Rights, adopted in 1989. In article 1, the Second Optional Protocol simply states: 'No-one within the jurisdiction of a State Party to the present Protocol shall be executed', and requires states parties to 'take all necessary measures to abolish the death penalty' within their jurisdiction. This is subject to the proviso that the death penalty may be retained for use 'in time of war pursuant to a conviction for a most serious crime of a military nature committed during wartime'.[2] A second treaty is the Sixth Protocol to the European Convention on Human Rights, opened for signature by states parties to the European Convention in 1983. Like the Second Optional Protocol to the Covenant, this obliges states parties to abolish the death penalty, while reserving their right to retain it exceptionally, 'in respect of acts committed in time of war or of imminent threat of war'.[3] In 2002 a further Protocol to the European Convention on Human Rights was adopted—the Thirteenth Protocol—under which that exception is removed. Under this third treaty, then, states parties undertake to abolish the death penalty in all circumstances. The fourth treaty specifically addressed to the abolition of the death penalty is the Protocol to the American Convention on Human Rights to Abolish the Death Penalty, elaborated within the framework of the Inter-American human rights system in 1990 and open to adherence by states parties to the American Convention on Human Rights. This is framed in similar terms to the Second Optional Protocol to the Covenant, in that it bans the death penalty, while allowing for its use 'in wartime in accordance with international law, for extremely serious crimes of a military nature'.[4]

Beyond these treaties, the use of the death penalty is also affected by provisions of general human rights treaties, including those supplemented by the four Protocols just mentioned. Most obviously, it is affected by provisions guaranteeing the right to life. Thus, for instance, the International Covenant on Civil and Political Rights, in article 6, proclaims that '[n]o-one shall be arbitrarily deprived of his life', and goes on to impose a number of

[2] Art. 2.   [3] Art. 2.   [4] Art. 2.

specific restrictions on the use of the death penalty 'in countries which have not abolished' it. We review the various restrictions imposed in this and other treaties below. At the same time, the use of the death penalty is affected by provisions guaranteeing fair trial and requiring the implementation of safeguards against arbitrary detention. It is also affected by provisions guaranteeing non-discrimination and equality before the law. And it is affected by provisions guaranteeing freedom from torture and inhuman or degrading treatment and punishment. As we shall see, these last-mentioned guarantees have served to reinforce existing restrictions concerning fair trial and also introduce further ones. Finally, the use of the death penalty is affected by the provisions of international humanitarian law. Under the Fourth Geneva Convention of 1949 and Protocols I and II of 1977, many of the same restrictions that are imposed in human rights treaties are laid down in the particular context of international and non-international armed conflict. The Fourth Geneva Convention also contains stipulations designed to ensure that occupation of territory does not become an occasion for expanding the scope of the death penalty beyond its extent under the law in force in the occupied territory before the occupation began.[5]

Before turning to the restrictions that apply, it is worth pausing to consider the general character of the state obligations involved. In the case of the four Protocols mentioned above that are aimed at abolition, the obligation is obviously to abolish the death penalty to the extent contemplated, and not to reintroduce it. In the case of the other treaties, there are obligations not to use the death penalty in a way which is inconsistent with the restrictions laid down. An exception might apply where those restrictions have been modified by reservations made at the time of ratification, though the precise effect of reservations in this context is a controversial legal question and remains uncertain. But the obligations of states parties under these treaties also go beyond an obligation not to use the death penalty in a way which is inconsistent with the restrictions laid down. They include as well an obligation not to extradite or deport anyone to another country which is likely to use the death penalty in such a way, at any rate in the case of the person who is extradited or deported. This principle, established in a series of decisions of human rights courts and supervisory bodies, makes states liable for the foreseeable

[5] Art. 68.

consequences of their actions with regard to the imposition of the death penalty in other countries. The states that are made liable, moreover, may themselves be either retentionist or abolitionist. We shall touch on some of these decisions in the succeeding paragraphs. Our focus to this point has been on treaty provisions. However, the restrictions we shall review on the use of the death penalty can also be taken as points of reference for general international law. It follows that they have significance for all states, irrespective of their adherence to particular treaties.[6]

Restrictions and safeguards

Insofar as the death penalty continues to be used, what then are the specific constraints set by international human rights and humanitarian law?

Offence and offender

In the first place, there are restrictions that relate to the offence and the offender. Under article 6 of the Civil and Political Rights Covenant the death penalty may be imposed 'only for the most serious crimes' and 'in accordance with the law in force at the time of the commission of the crime'. The American Convention on Human Rights provides that '[i]n no case shall capital punishment be inflicted for political offenses or related common crimes'.[7] The 'most serious crimes' have been identified, for this purpose, as 'intentional crimes with lethal or other extremely grave consequences'.[8] Thus, for instance, in a case involving armed robbery with no resulting loss of life or serious injury, the Human Rights Committee found that the imposition of the death penalty violated article 6 of the Covenant.[9] In the context of international armed

[6] See UN Economic and Social Council, 'Safeguards guaranteeing protection of the rights of those facing the death penalty', ECOSOC Res. 1984/50, 25 May 1984; 'Implementation of the safeguards guaranteeing protection of the rights of those facing the death penalty', ECOSOC Res. 1989/64, 24 May 1989; and 'Safeguards guaranteeing protection of the rights of those facing the death penalty', ECOSOC Res. 1996/15, 23 July 1996.   [7] Art. 4(4).

[8] ECOSOC Resolution 1984/50, 'Safeguards guaranteeing protection of the rights of those facing the death penalty', para. 1. See also UN Commission on Human Rights, Res. 2003/67, para. 4(d).

[9] *Lubuto v Zambia*, Communication 390/1990, Views of the Human Rights Committee, adopted 31 October 1995, para. 7.2.

conflict, the Fourth Geneva Convention states that the inhabitants of occupied territory may be sentenced to death 'only in cases where the person is guilty of espionage, of serious acts of sabotage against the military installations of the Occupying Power or of intentional offences which have caused the death of one or more persons, provided that such offences were punishable by death under the law of the occupied territory in force before the occupation began'.[10]

With regard to the offender, the Civil and Political Rights Covenant and the American Convention stipulate that the death penalty may not be imposed on people who were under 18 years of age at the time when the crime was committed.[11] This is laid down as well in the UN Convention on the Rights of the Child[12] and other treaties,[13] and has been reaffirmed in many international instruments addressing the death penalty.[14] In a complaint involving a person who was 16 at the time his offence was committed, the Inter-American Commission of Human Rights found that the imposition on him of a death sentence in the United States violated that state's obligations under Inter-American human rights law, as incorporated into the Charter of the Organization of American States.[15] The Inter-American Commission observed, in this context, that the obligation not to impose the death penalty on those who were minors at the time the offence was committed is a universally applicable norm of customary international law, and indeed a fundamental or 'peremptory' norm (*jus cogens*) from which no derogation is permitted.[16] At the same time, the human rights treaties we have

[10] Art. 68.

[11] International Covenant on Civil and Political Rights, art. 6(5); American Convention on Human Rights, art. 4(5). The American Convention also prohibits the imposition of the death penalty on people who were over 70 years of age at the time when the crime was committed.   [12] Art. 37(a).

[13] See, e.g., African Charter on the Rights and Welfare of the Child, art. 5(3) (with art. 2) and Commonwealth of Independent States Convention on Human Rights and Fundamental Freedoms, art. 2(3). See also Fourth Geneva Convention, art. 68 (prohibition on pronunciation of death sentence for protected persons under 18 at the time of the offence).

[14] See, e.g., UN Economic and Social Council, 'Safeguards guaranteeing protection of the rights of those facing the death penalty', ECOSOC Res. 1984/50, 25 May 1984, para. 3; European Union Council Guidelines to EU Policy Towards Third Countries on the Death Penalty, 3 June 1998, para. III (iii); and UN Commission on Human Rights, Res. 2003/67, para. 4(a).

[15] *Domingues v United States*, Case No. 12.285, Report 62/02, 22 October 2002.

[16] Ibid., para. 85.

referred to provide that the death sentence may not be carried out on women who are pregnant. Finally, there is increasing recognition that the death penalty should not be imposed on people suffering from mental illness.[17]

Procedural safeguards

Alongside these restrictions, the use of the death penalty is also conditioned by procedural safeguards. It is an implication—and, in the case of some treaties (such as the Civil and Political Rights Covenant), an explicit aspect—of the right to life that no one may be *arbitrarily* deprived of life. In this respect, the right to life is reinforced by the guarantees of the right to fair trial and prohibitions on arbitrary detention, which apply in all circumstances. With regard specifically to the death penalty, many of the treaties we have mentioned also provide that those sentenced to death must have the right to seek pardon, amnesty or commutation of the sentence. The importance of scrupulous attention to due process in capital trials has been stressed by international courts and human rights bodies. In a General Comment on article 6 of the Covenant, the Human Rights Committee underlines, in particular, the right to fair hearing by an independent and impartial tribunal, the presumption of innocence, the minimum guarantees for the defence, and the right to review by a higher tribunal.[18] In the case of foreign nationals, due process of law in this context has also been understood to require notification of the right of access to consular assistance.[19]

[17] See, e.g., *R. S. v Trinidad & Tobago*, Communication 684/1996, Views of the Human Rights Committee, adopted 2 April 2002. See also UN Economic and Social Council, 'Safeguards guaranteeing protection of the rights of those facing the death penalty', ECOSOC Resolution 1984/50, para. 3; UN Economic and Social Council, 'Implementation of the safeguards guaranteeing protection of the rights of those facing the death penalty', ECOSOC Res. 1989/64, 24 May 1989, para. 1(d); and UN Commission on Human Rights Res. 2003/67, 24 April 2003, para. 4(g).

[18] Human Rights Committee, General Comment 6 (The right to life: art. 6), 30 April 1982, para. 7.

[19] See Advisory Opinion of the Inter-American Court of Human Rights, OC-16/99, 1 October 1999, and *Hilaire, Constantine and Benjamin v Trinidad & Tobago*, Judgment of the Inter-American Court of Human Rights, 21 June 2002. See also *LaGrand Case (Germany v United States of America)*, Judgment of the International Court of Justice, 27 June 2001, and *Case Concerning Avena and Other Mexican Nationals (Mexico v United States of America)*, Order of the International Court of Justice, 5 February 2003.

In a number of complaints by persons sentenced to death, the Human Rights Committee has found that the trial was unfair, and has opined that, in consequence, the death sentence violated the complainant's right to life.[20] At the same time, due process has a bearing in this context on the right not to be subjected to inhuman or degrading treatment. In proceedings against Turkey before the European Court of Human Rights, Kurdish Workers' Party (PKK) leader Abdullah Öcalan made a complaint arising out of his arrest, trial and eventual sentence of death.[21] The Court found that Öcalan's right to liberty and security and to a fair trial had indeed been violated in numerous respects. Among other things, the court trying him was not independent and impartial; undue restrictions were placed on his capacity to prepare his defence; and he was prevented from obtaining legal assistance during police questioning. Approximately three years after Öcalan's death sentence was imposed, but before it had been implemented, Turkey abolished the death penalty, and his sentence was commuted to life imprisonment. Nonetheless, the Court held that the imposition of a death sentence, following an unfair trial, itself violated Öcalan's right not to be subjected to inhuman treatment. Even if the death sentence was no longer going to be carried out, he had had to suffer for several years the consequences of its imposition following an unfair trial.

Death row and execution

A third set of constraints on the use of the death penalty relates to the execution itself, and the length of time spent awaiting it. We mentioned earlier the idea that state obligations concerning the death penalty include not only obligations with respect to the use of the death penalty within a state's own territory, but also obligations with respect to its use in other countries to which persons are extradited or deported. This idea developed in tandem with attention to constraints of the sort we are now considering. In one case, a complaint was brought before the European Court of Human Rights by a person in the United Kingdom

[20] See, e.g., *Campbell v Jamaica*, Communication 248/1997, Views of the Human Rights Committee, adopted 30 March 1992; *Henry and Douglas v Jamaica*, Communication 571/1994, Views of the Human Rights Committee, adopted 25 July 1996; *Yasseen and Thomas v Republic of Guyana*, Communication 676/1996, Views of the Human Rights Committee, adopted 30 March 1998.

[21] *Öcalan v Turkey*, Judgment of the European Court of Human Rights, 12 March 2003.

whose extradition was sought by the United States authorities.[22] He was wanted for trial in the United States on charges of capital murder, and argued that, to extradite him on these charges was to violate rights which the United Kingdom was obligated to protect under the European Convention. The Court accepted that argument, but not on the ground that the United Kingdom would become liable for a violation of his right to life. Rather, the Court noted that, if the applicant was ultimately sentenced to death in the United States, he was likely to spend six to eight years on 'death row', awaiting execution. Given this extensive period, and in the light of his personal circumstances (and in particular, his age and mental state at the time of the offence), extradition would expose him to a 'real risk' of inhuman treatment, in the shape of protracted and rising anguish. Thus, extradition would violate his right not to be subjected to inhuman treatment. In other contexts too a lengthy delay between the date of sentence and the date fixed for execution has been understood to violate the right not to be subjected to inhuman treatment.[23]

A final issue relates to the execution itself, that is to say, the manner in which those condemned are killed. In a General Comment on article 7 of the Civil and Political Rights Covenant (protecting the right not to be subjected to torture or to cruel, inhuman and degrading treatment), the Human Rights Committee observes that, where the death sentence is imposed, it 'must be carried out in such a way as to cause the least possible physical and mental suffering'.[24] A recent resolution of the UN Commission on Human Rights additionally urges governments to ensure that, where capital punishment occurs, it is not 'carried out in public or in any other degrading manner, and to ensure that any application of particularly cruel or inhuman means of execution, such as stoning, [is] stopped immediately'.[25] Like the 'death row phenomenon', this aspect has been the basis for complaints concerning extradition and deportation. In a pair of cases brought against Canada before the Human Rights Committee, two men, Kindler and Ng, were

---

[22] *Soering v United Kingdom*, Judgment of the European Court of Human Rights, 26 June 1989.   [23] See, e.g., *Pratt & Morgan v Jamaica* [1994] 2 Appeals Cases 1.

[24] Human Rights Committee, General Comment 20 (replaces General Comment 7 concerning prohibition of torture and cruel treatment or punishment: art. 7), 10 March 1992, para. 6.

[25] UN Commission on Human Rights, Res. 2003/67, para. 4(i).

extradited to the United States.[26] Kindler had already been convicted and sentenced to death; Ng was to be tried on capital charges. Both complained that their extradition violated Canada's obligations to protect their human rights under the Covenant. While the Committee did not consider that Canada could be deemed to have violated its obligations to protect the right to life, it did find in one case that Canada had violated its obligations to protect the right not to be subjected to cruel and inhuman treatment. In the particular state to which Kindler was sent, the practice at the time was to execute by lethal injection, and the Committee dismissed the complaint. However, in the state to which Ng was sent, the practice was to execute by cyanide gas asphyxiation, and in his case the Committee reached the view that extradition exposed the applicant to a real risk of cruel and inhuman treatment. Since these cases, the Committee has modified its approach with respect to the question of whether extradition to face the death penalty is consistent with the right to life. In a further complaint against Canada, the Committee ruled that, irrespective of the manner of execution, a country such as Canada which has abolished the death penalty violates its obligations with respect to the right to life where it extradites a person to a country in which it may be 'reasonably anticipated' that that person will be sentenced to death, and fails to ensure that any death sentence will not be carried out.[27] Beyond this context, concerns about the manner of execution and its consistency with the right not to be subjected to cruel and inhuman treatment remain.

Abolitionist advocacy

If we now begin to take stock of the developments we have surveyed, it is evident that efforts to secure the abolition of the death penalty have met with considerable success within the domain of international human rights law. As more and more states become parties to treaties that provide for abolition, and as human rights get interpreted in ways

---

[26] *Kindler v Canada*, Communication 470/1991, Views of the Human Rights Committee, adopted 30 July 1993; and *Ng v Canada*, Communication 469/1991, Views of the Human Rights Committee, adopted 5 November 1993.

[27] *Judge v Canada*, Communication 829/1998, Views of the Human Rights Committee, adopted 5 August 2002, para. 10.4.

that imply more and more constraints both for retentionist and (in the context of extradition and deportation) abolitionist states, the death penalty is being progressively abolished. This is reinforced by an assumption—made explicit in some instruments—that the orientation of all change with regard to the death penalty should be towards abolition; that is to say, the range of crimes to which the death penalty applies must not be enlarged, and the death penalty must not be re-established once abolished.[28] Some argue, indeed, that international and national developments have already produced a situation whereby the death penalty can no longer be regarded as consistent with human rights law. In 1995 the South African Constitutional Court ruled that the death penalty could not be reconciled with a constitutional prohibition on cruel, inhuman or degrading treatment or punishment, regardless of the circumstances of its imposition or implementation.[29] Likewise, it is argued, the death penalty can no longer be reconciled with international protection of the right to life. Insofar as provisions in human rights treaties concerning the right to life appear to allow for or contemplate the possibility of lawful execution, on this view these must now be considered to have been modified by subsequent practice. At the least, the fact that the death penalty violates human rights when a trial is unfair, but also when the delay between sentence and execution is too long, limits the scope for lawful execution very considerably. As many have remarked, to achieve fairness is in many cases to generate delay (through legal appeals, applications for commutation, etc.); for the same reason, to achieve expedition is often to generate unfairness.

On the other hand, abolitionist gains are not unambiguous, and restrictions on the use of the death penalty may also be part of the reason why this form of judicial punishment is still retained in some countries. By making the death penalty unlawful in certain circumstances, international human rights law helps to sustain the idea that it is justified and legitimate in other circumstances. Attention is shifted away from the question of *whether* the death penalty should be used, and onto the questions of *when* and *how* it should be used. Central to the resolution of these questions are distinctions such as those we have discussed between adult offenders and juvenile offenders, fair capital trials and

---

[28] See, e.g., American Convention on Human Rights, art. 4(2) and (3).

[29] *State v Makwanyane and Mchunu*, Case No. CCT/3/94, Judgment of the Constitutional Court of the Republic of South Africa, 6 June 1995.

unfair capital trials, lethal injection and cyanide gas asphyxiation. While these distinctions are not without significance, it can be argued that they serve to obscure the fundamental brutality of all forms of deliberate killing, inasmuch as they are an important part of what makes possible the concept of a 'modern' approach to retributive justice. The deployment of DNA testing in US capital trials may be one recent manifestation of that concept. From an abolitionist perspective, supposedly modern approaches simply mask barbarism with a veneer of fairness, compassion and evidentiary sophistication. There is also another, more general way in which restrictions on the use of the death penalty may help, counterproductively, to sustain its use. Speaking about the death penalty, as we have done in this discussion, in rational, calculative terms, tends to sanitise and objectify the conduct involved. Lethal injection and cyanide gas asphyxiation become terms in a technical debate about the correct interpretation of legal norms. Yet the prospects for action to abolish the death penalty in countries that still retain it are surely linked to awareness of the experiential reality of these phenomena for those affected. Viewed from this angle, the process of restricting the death penalty carries with it the risk of dulling the horror, and hence weakening the mobilising effect, that is produced when citizens are left (or made) to register cruelties carried out in their name.

But then, as many contend, abolition of the death penalty is not all that is at stake here. In a recent book about capital punishment in the United States, Austin Sarat writes:

[S]tate killing contributes to some of the most dangerous features of contemporary America. Among them are the substitution of a politics of revenge and resentment for sustained attention to the social problems responsible for so much violence today; the use of crime to pit various social groups against one another and to generate political capital; what has been called an effort to 'govern through crime'; the racializing of danger and, in so doing, the perpetuation of racial fear and antagonism; the erosion of basic legal protections and legal values in favour of short-term political expediency...[30]

If abolition campaigns are also campaigns about the kinds of issues to which Sarat refers, then the significance of abolitionist advocacy goes beyond its capacity to get the death penalty abolished, and resides also

[30] A. Sarat, *When The State Kills: Capital Punishment and the American Condition* (Princeton: Princeton University Press, 2001), 30.

in its capacity to promote change on other levels. In calling attention to the practice of judicially sanctioned killing, abolitionist advocates may at the same time help to call attention to systemic phenomena and pervasive problems, both within the criminal justice system and beyond it. We observed at the beginning that the abolition of the death penalty is not an obvious priority for the human rights movement. Once we take this 'knock-on' potential into account, that observation loses some of its force. To be sure, it does not lose all of its force—but enough perhaps to provide at least a partial answer to the charge that abolitionist advocacy diverts energies and resources which should rather be spent on other issues.

Democracy

That human rights and democracy belong together is today a widely accepted axiom of international affairs. The tacit premise of claims, initiatives and programmes, it is also the explicit message of countless government statements and international declarations. But what precisely is the relation between these two phenomena, the one concerned with basic entitlements and the legal guarantees put in place to protect them, the other focused on political processes and on the allocation and organisation of public power? Is it that, as is sometimes said, democracy provides a congenial environment for the protection of human rights? Is it that the protection of human rights provides a safeguard for democracy? Or are human rights a necessary corrective to democracy? Does democracy require adjusting or supplementing through the protection of human rights?

In what follows we will suggest that the links between human rights and democracy may be closer, as well as more complex, than is implied by any of the possibilities just mentioned. One way of expressing the closeness of the links, which some commentators have proposed, is to characterise democratic governance as itself a human right. After outlining some general features of the interrelation between human rights and democracy, we will discuss that proposal. But first we will need to say something about the concept being brought into contact with human rights here. Of democracy George Orwell once wrote that 'not only is there no agreed definition, but the attempt to make one is resisted from all sides'.[1] In his explanation, '[i]t is almost universally felt that when we call a country democratic we are praising it: consequently the defenders of every kind of régime claim that it is a democracy, and fear

---

[1] G. Orwell, 'Politics and the English Language' (1946) in *Why I Write* (London: Penguin, 2004), 109.

that they might have to stop using that word if it were tied down to any one meaning.'[2] Does this indicate that democracy is simply too slippery a concept to be considered in conjunction with internationally protected human rights, or can we identify something secure around which enquiry might turn?

Democracy

As is well known, the word 'democracy' derives from the name given to the ancient Athenian arrangements of citizen self-government: *demokratia*, meaning 'rule by the people'. In relation to present-day societies, democracy is used variously to refer to electoral politics, multipartyism, interest-group politics, majority rule, political liberalism, participatory decision-making, and a pluralist social and political order, among many other things. Some commentators have concluded from the abundance of contemporary usages that democracy is an 'essentially contested concept', with no stable and undisputed referent. Political theorist David Beetham has shown, however, that each of the usages ultimately appeals to a common core idea.[3] To this extent, democracy has a meaning that is beyond dispute, even if dispute rages over how much democracy is desirable, which domains of life it should relate to, and what its realisation involves. That meaning is concerned with the process that should govern the making of collectively binding rules and policies. In Beetham's words 'a system of collective decision-making can be said to be democratic to the extent that it is subject to control by all members of the relevant association or all those under its authority, considered as equals'.[4] Thus, the core idea of democracy comprises two principles about decision-making competence with respect to public (or other collective) affairs. One, which Beetham labels 'popular control', requires that decision-making be subject to the control of those affected. The other, which he labels 'political equality', requires that that control be distributed among those affected on the basis of equality.

---

[2] G. Orwell, 'Politics and the English Language' (1946) in *Why I Write* (London: Penguin, 2004), 109.

[3] D. Beetham, *Democracy and Human Rights* (Cambridge: Polity Press, 1999), chap. 1.

[4] Ibid., 4–5.

A number of points are worth noticing about this way of conceptualising democracy. First, democracy is defined in terms of principles, rather than institutions and procedures. While, as observed above, institutionally-oriented definitions are quite common, they beg the question of what it is about the relevant institutions or procedures that makes them distinctively democratic. Only by moving to the level of underlying principles can we explain *why* particular institutions and procedures have a claim to be democratic, and what needs to be changed to make them more so. Related to this, Beetham's account also brings into focus a second point. This is that democracy is more a matter of degree than of kind, more a relative issue than an absolute one. If in comparison with highly authoritarian arrangements it might be possible to describe certain arrangements as democratic *tout court*, it will always make sense also to ask how those arrangements might be made *more* democratic. To quote Beetham, the idea of democracy 'always has a critical edge to it'.[5] A third point relates to the nature of that critical edge. One frequently hears it said that democracy may be either direct or representative, participatory or elite, consensual or majoritarian, mass or deliberative, and so on. Once democracy is understood in terms of underlying principles, it becomes clear that these distinctions are misleading. We are not so much faced with a choice between alternative forms of democracy as confronted with the challenge of making effective, or more effective, the principles of popular control and political equality in particular contexts. In devising ways to do this, contemporary societies are invariably led to consider and combine ideas drawn from a range of democratic traditions, in a manner that cuts across the neat distinctions just recalled. A final point is that democracy is not in fact relevant only to 'societies', if by those are meant nationally-demarcated polities. Of course, the sphere of decision-making about public affairs in a state is a major and vitally important arena of democratic life. But it is not, or should not be, the sole arena. Rather, democracy has implications for all the settings in which collective decision-making occurs, whether those settings are national, regional, global or belong to some other level of interaction.[6]

---

[5] Ibid., 4.

[6] On this point, see further D. Held, *Democracy and the Global Order* (Cambridge: Polity Press, 1995). Regarding the implications of democracy at the global level, see also B. Holden (ed.), *Global Democracy: Key Debates* (London: Routledge, 2000).

Democracy and human rights

Let us now return to human rights, and begin taking up the question of their relation with democracy. We will need to deal separately with different rights or sets of rights, for the issues that arise differ somewhat depending on which of them one is considering.

Most commonly recognised as 'democratic' rights are the right to vote and stand for election, along with rights to free expression, assembly, association and movement. Respect for these rights is crucial to popular control over public affairs on a footing of equality, for insofar as they are denied, citizens lack the possibility of sharing in the exercise of legislative authority and of calling those who exercise that authority to account. Denial of these rights also deprives citizens of the possibility of monitoring, criticising and influencing public policy through activities in non-state associations, the media and the other institutions of 'civil society'. In turn, these rights depend on the non-discriminatory guarantee of a range of further rights that provide protection against abuses of state power. Among these further rights are the right to life and to personal liberty and security, the right not to be ill-treated or subjected to forced labour, the right to due process and to protection from retrospective criminal law, the right to privacy, and the right to freedom of thought, conscience and religion. Insofar as such rights go unprotected, secrecy and the suppression of dissent are more apt to characterise political processes than transparency, accountability and contestation. Democracy, then, requires the protection of political and civil rights. But so too the protection of political and civil rights depends on acceptance of the democratic principle that public decision-making is the business of all citizens equally. Only to the extent that that principle governs political life does a secure basis exist for opposing governmental arrangements which deny citizens, or some of them, a say in collective affairs, and demanding arrangements which instead safeguard the right of all to engage in political activity and be free from repressive state action.

What of economic, social and cultural rights? These are sometimes overlooked in discussions of the relation between human rights and democracy, yet the recognition that collective decision-making should be subject to the control of citizens is of limited value to those lacking the capacities or opportunities necessary to exercise that control. If public decision-making is the business of all citizens equally, then all must be not just entitled, but also enabled, to undertake it, and that calls for access to the requisite social, economic and cultural resources. Political equality depends on overcoming material deprivation. Democracy thus requires attention to such social, economic and cultural rights as the right to education and to health, the right to adequate food and housing, the right to work and to safe and healthy conditions of work, and the right to share in the benefits of scientific progress. Can we again reverse this proposition, and maintain that the protection of social, economic and cultural rights likewise demands democracy? Some people argue that these rights are in fact better protected in the context of authoritarian political arrangements. Certainly it is true that conventional democratic institutions have not prevented serious abuses of social, economic and cultural rights. But nor have more authoritarian institutions. Abuses of these rights have occurred in all kinds of polities, and the repudiation of multipartyism and the like has manifestly coexisted with a wide gap between rich and poor. In the end it seems safest to assume that the problem is not too much democracy, but—in all societies, including the 'mature democracies'—too little. That is, at least in part the problem is political exclusion. Of course, by enhancing the extent to which all members of society can participate in the processes of defining distributive priorities, policies and strategies, one does not assure the just distribution of collective resources. But one does surely make it more likely.

A final set of rights of particular interest in this context is minority rights. While these too are sometimes left out of discussions of the relation between human rights and democracy, they form an important part of the equation. For procedures of accountability and participation are once again of limited practical significance where membership in a particular cultural community has the effect of excluding citizens from power and influence. Cultural affiliation is not supposed to count in the allocation of political stakes, yet the reality, of course, is that it frequently does. Cultural minorities are often political minorities. Protection of the right of members of minority communities to maintain and develop their traditions, to profess and practise their religion, and to use and teach their children their own language, is thus crucial if members of minority communities are not to be forced to conform to dominant cultural norms as the price of political inclusion. Democracy, then, requires the protection of minority rights. What, again, of the converse? At first sight it is not at all obvious that the protection of minority rights calls for democracy. On the contrary, conventional democratic procedures appear to be part of the problem, inasmuch as they simply ignore—and, in doing so, reproduce—culturally-based inequalities in the distribution of political chances. To note this, however, is not necessarily to reject the relevance of democracy in this context. It could simply be to question the adequacy of conventional democratic procedures where members of minority communities are concerned, and to assert the need for those procedures to be modified through processes of devolution, institutionalisation of regional autonomy, revised electoral systems, changes to parliamentary procedure, etc. Viewed from this perspective, the protection of minority rights does indeed call for democracy. Without acceptance that control of public decision-making belongs to all citizens equally, modifications of the kind just described become significantly harder to justify, and rights to retain cultural distinctiveness remain vulnerable to the depredations of all-powerful cultural majorities.

We may conclude that human rights are not simply correctives or necessary adjustments to democracy. This might be the case if democracy were defined as majority rule. Rights might then indeed be a mechanism of correction or adjustment, needed to guard against the democratically-sanctioned tyranny not only of cultural majorities, but of contingent political majorities as well. But as soon as we view democracy in terms of underlying principles, as soon as we conceive it in terms of ideas about popular control and political equality that can be used to evaluate the adequacy of prevailing institutions and procedures (including majority rule), it becomes clear that democracy and human rights are more integrally linked. Democracy depends on the protection of human rights. At the same time, the protection of human rights depends on democracy. This is not to say that each automatically brings about the other. As we have noted, the historical record leaves no doubt that moves to establish or deepen democracy can readily coincide with serious abuses of human rights, especially (though not exclusively) social, economic, cultural and minority rights. Likewise, moves to protect human rights can readily coincide with ongoing practices of political exclusion, as where the guarantee of civil and political rights coexists with the marginalisation of minority communities. But nor is it to say that each simply provides a congenial environment for, or helps in safeguarding, the other. Rather, what mutual dependence means in this context is that respect for human rights is a necessary, if not sufficient, condition for efforts to realise the democratic principles of popular control and political equality, and vice versa.

Democratic governance as a human right

In discussing the integral nature of the links that connect human rights and democracy, we have so far been presuming that these nonetheless remain distinct phenomena, their mutual dependence an index precisely of their non-unity. According to some analysts, however, the point has now been reached where democracy must itself be seen as a human right. The leading proponent of this argument for the 'right to democratic governance' is international legal scholar Thomas Franck, who explains it as a response to two related developments of the 1980s and 1990s. The first is the worldwide turn to electoral democracy. The second is the burgeoning practice of election monitoring by international agencies like the United Nations and the Organisation for Security and Cooperation in Europe. In the light of these developments, Franck observes that democracy has passed from being one political system among many to becoming the near-universal basis of government. More than that, democracy has become the sole internationally legitimate basis of government. Whereas previously the organisation of public power was a matter within the sovereign discretion of each state, now the rise of international election observation testifies to a recognition that democratic governance is an essential prerequisite to membership in the community of nations. And if that is the case, then it follows for Franck that there should likewise be a recognition that democratic governance is a universal entitlement, that is to say, a human right. Thus, in his words, 'we have seen the emergence, specifically, of an internationally constituted right to electoral democracy that builds on the human rights canon, but seeks to extend the ambit of protected rights' into the domain of political organisation.[7]

[7] T. Franck, 'Legitimacy and the Democratic Entitlement' in G. Fox & B. Roth (eds.), *Democratic Governance and International Law* (Cambridge: Cambridge University Press, 2000), 25, 26.

The idea of a human right to democratic governance has considerable appeal, especially in the light of evidence which has been put forward by international relations scholars that democracy is linked to peace.[8] But this idea also has difficulties and dangers, and has been questioned on a number of grounds.[9] In the first place, there is doubt as to whether democratic governance really is treated as an essential prerequisite to membership in the community of nations. For some scholars, the argument advanced by Franck and others is an optimistic interpretation of events, which ultimately lacks empirical foundation. To their minds, Franck overstates the significance of international election monitoring, and understates the importance of other factors in decisions about the recognition of new states and governments. Secondly, there is concern about the implications of the argument, and about the way it may be used to carry forward the imperial project of remaking the world to suit the most powerful. One aspect of this relates to the possibility of pro-democratic military intervention. Although the right to democratic governance derives part of its influence from claims concerning the 'democratic peace', to some analysts the recognition of such a right is in fact more likely to promote war. Even if there is no intention to weaken the international legal prohibition of the use of force, they worry that this may in fact be the result. Thirdly, there is also concern about the argument's implications in the light of the conception of democracy that is involved. As is apparent from the previous paragraph, this is a conception that centres on elections and related institutions and procedures. Franck explains that such an admittedly narrow understanding is all that human rights can currently support. However, some scholars fear that recognition of a human right to democratic governance could serve—even if, again, unintentionally—to legitimise the idea that elections are sufficient for democracy. In turn, this could have the consequence of undermining emancipatory struggle by correspondingly delegitimising demands for more far-reaching change. Finally, there is anxiety about another consequence of the preoccupation with elections. This has

---

[8] This is a qualified claim, limited to the assertion of peaceful relations among democratic states. See M. Doyle, 'Kant, Liberal Legacies and Foreign Affairs' 12 *Philosophy and Public Affairs* (1983) 205 and 323.

[9] See various essays in G. Fox & B. Roth (eds.), *Democratic Governance and International Law* (Cambridge: Cambridge University Press, 2000). See also B. Roth, *Governmental Illegitimacy in International Law* (Oxford: Clarendon Press, 1999).

to do with the assumption that what is in issue is the organisation of national politics. In the assessment of some analysts, a right to democratic governance might entail the additional danger of masking the need—especially acute in circumstances of intensifying globalisation—to democratise the many international and other non-national settings in which decision-making about collective life occurs. That is to say, it could lend undue credence to the idea that national democracy alone can suffice.

To question the emergence of democratic governance as a human right is not necessarily to challenge the notion that democracy might plausibly and usefully be brought into closer, or at any rate more transparent, relation with human rights. One way of responding to the misgivings just described is to take the postulated right to democratic governance as a starting point and consider how it might be reformulated. To allay the various concerns, at least two modifications are needed. The first is that democratic governance cannot be characterised as a human right in and of itself. The integral nature of the links which connect democracy and human rights require to be expressed differently. The second modification is that democracy cannot be defined in terms of elections and related procedures. As observed in earlier discussion, the problem with institutional definitions of this sort is that they beg the question of what it is that makes the relevant institutions democratic. Elections may be part of a process that enhances popular control and political equality. But equally they may have little substantive effect on a state's structure of power and influence. Indeed, in some circumstances they may even be regressive from the perspective of popular control and political equality insofar as they may weaken the credibility of those struggling against unjust exclusion. At the same time, there is the point that in any event elections speak only to the democratisation of national politics, whereas decision-making affecting collective life occurs in a wide array of non-national arenas (intergovernmental and non-governmental, public and private, formal and informal) as well. Any attempt to reformulate the right to democratic governance has to draw on a conception of democracy that looks beyond institutions to principles, and beyond national government to the totality of global politics.[10]

If democracy is not to be regarded as a human right in itself, nor—we have shown—is it simply a congenial environment for the protection of

---

[10] See further S. Marks, *The Riddle of All Constitutions* (Oxford: Oxford University Press, 2000), chap. 5.

human rights. Likewise, the protection of human rights is not simply a safeguard for democracy, but nor should it be seen as a guarantee of democratisation in collective affairs. What, then, is the relation between these two phenomena? We have proposed that it is best understood as one of mutual dependence. Whether the focus is on civil and political rights, social, economic and cultural rights or minority rights, the protection of human rights is a necessary (though not sufficient) condition for the realisation of democracy. At the same time, moves to realise democracy are a necessary (though not sufficient) condition for the protection of human rights. George Orwell was certainly right to observe that when we call a country democratic we are praising it. But the thrust of our discussion is that in another sense he was also wrong. To speak of 'calling a country democratic' is to assume that democracy is simply a label which can be applied to particular countries. Once we begin to consider democracy in relation to human rights, however, it becomes clearer than ever that this is inadequate, and that democracy must instead be grasped as an argument, a critical tool, and a set of principles for political life in all its multifarious settings. Above all, it must be grasped as a *question* about what is being done to realise popular control and political equality, and about how arrangements could be improved so as better to reflect those principles.

Detention

People behind bars have long had special significance for the human rights movement, both as catalysts for action and as symbols of injustice. Amnesty International was launched in 1961 with an appeal for the 'forgotten prisoners', those 'prisoners of conscience' languishing in gaols around the world for the crime of expressing an opinion unacceptable to their governments.[1] In the years that followed, famous dissidents imprisoned or placed under house arrest by oppressive regimes were to become icons of the struggle for human rights—Nelson Mandela, Aung San Suu Kyi, Václav Havel, Jacobo Timmerman, and Albie Sachs, to name just a few. Almost more decisively than any other documents, it is the prison diaries and memoirs of people such as these that have engaged and shaped the human rights 'imaginary' or consciousness.

For all that the movement has grown and diversified, detainees still remain a central concern. But the focus of that concern has expanded in a number of important respects. While, of course, continuing to assert the rights of political prisoners and prisoners of conscience, today's activists and progressives are also concerned about the pre-trial rights and prison conditions of ordinary inmates. More than that, and especially in recent years, they have become concerned with security detainees, and with the detention of 'unlawful combatants', 'suspected international terrorists', and asylum-seekers. Thus, attention has turned to the imbrication of detention policies with issues of territory, nation, sovereignty, and citizenship, and with patterns of migration, armed conflict, and post-Cold War geopolitics.

This expansion to encompass security detainees and the rest points to a change on at least three levels. In the first place, there is a change with

---

[1] See P. Benenson, 'The Forgotten Prisoners', *The Observer*, 18 May 1961, available at www.hrweb.org/ai/observer.html.

regard to the *people* in issue. Whereas previously the main focus was on the detention of political opponents and other 'undesirables' within the political community, now it is also on the exclusion or immobilisation of non-nationals. Secondly, there is a change with regard to the *places* in issue. Whereas once the main focus was on detention in fascist, state-socialist and other one-party states, now it is also on the prisons and camps of liberalism's heartlands (and their outposts)—Camp Delta at Guantánamo Bay, Belmarsh prison in the United Kingdom, Australia's detention facility at Woomera. Finally, there is a change with regard to the *policies* in issue. Whereas in the past the main focus was on detention as a means of suppressing dissent and ruling through terror, now it is also on detention as a strategy for containing refugee flows, acting in the domain of national security, and carrying forward the 'war on terror'.

Against the backdrop of these and related changes, we review here the rights of detainees under international human rights law. After outlining the general legal framework, we will look first at the rights of people who are detained without trial or charge in connection with counter-terrorism. Next we will look at the rights of those detained in connection with asylum claims or refugee policy. Finally, we will look at the rights of convicted prisoners. International law sets minimum standards for the treatment of all those in detention, and also recognises the right to judicial review of detention decisions, including in some circumstances decisions about parole. Prolonged administrative detention, inhumane prison conditions, and unfair parole procedures clearly point to important arenas of injustice, but what if the problem of imprisonment is actually much vaster? In the last section of our discussion we will consider the claim that what is at stake here cannot be separated from trends which involve the criminalisation of poverty, as a penal complement to the processes of economic liberalisation.

Arbitrary detention

Protection of the rights of detainees under international human rights law revolves principally around three elements: liberty and security of the person, freedom from arbitrary arrest or detention, and humane and dignified treatment by the detaining authorities. Thus, the Universal Declaration of Human Rights states that everyone has the right to 'liberty and security of person'[2] and that '[n]o-one shall be subjected to arbitrary arrest, detention or exile'.[3] It also affirms the right of everyone not to be 'subjected to torture or to cruel, inhuman or degrading treatment or punishment',[4] and this obviously has particular pertinence for those in custody. The International Covenant on Civil and Political Rights contains similar provisions,[5] as do regional human rights treaties, such as the African Charter of Human and Peoples' Rights, American Convention on Human Rights and European Convention of Human Rights.[6] Some treaties, among them the Covenant, contain a further, explicit affirmation of the right of those in detention to be treated with humanity and respect for their dignity.[7] Some also include a complete ban on imprisonment on the grounds of inability to fulfil a contractual obligation.[8]

Claims by detainees that their rights have been violated have been taken to human rights courts and supervisory bodies on many occasions. We will make reference to a number of the resulting decisions and interpretive documents below. Since 1991 abuses of detainees' rights have also been investigated by the UN Working Group on Arbitrary Detention.[9] Mandated by the UN Commission on Human Rights, the Working Group has competence to examine situations in all states, whether or not they are parties to relevant treaties. In this regard, its principal points of reference are the rights enunciated in the Universal Declaration (quoted above) and a series of more recent non-treaty

---

[2] Art. 3.   [3] Art. 9.   [4] Art. 5.   [5] See arts. 9 and 7.

[6] African Charter on Human and Peoples' Rights, arts. 4, 5 and 6; American Declaration of the Rights and Duties of Man, arts. I, XXV and XXVI; American Convention on Human Rights, arts. 5 and 7; European Convention on Human Rights, arts. 3 and 5; Commonwealth of Independent States Convention on Human Rights and Fundamental Freedoms, arts. 3 and 5; and Revised Arab Charter on Human Rights (2004) (not yet in force), arts. 8, 14, 16(h), 17 and 20.

[7] See, e.g., International Covenant on Civil and Political Rights, art. 10; American Convention on Human Rights, art. 5(2); and Revised Arab Charter on Human Rights (2004) (not yet in force), arts. 16(h), 17 and 20.

[8] See, e.g., International Covenant on Civil and Political Rights, art. 11; American Declaration of the Rights and Duties of Man, art. XXV (obligations of a purely civil character); American Convention on Human Rights, art. 7(7); European Convention on Human Rights, Protocol 4, art. 1; Commonwealth of Independent States Convention on Human Rights and Fundamental Freedoms, art. 8; and Revised Arab Charter on Human Rights (2004) (not yet in force), art. 18.

[9] See Report of the Working Group on Arbitrary Detention, UN Doc. E/CN.4/2004/3, 5 December 2003, para. 1.

instruments drawn up within the framework of the United Nations and regional organisations with the aim of elaborating on the policy implications of those rights. The most important of these instruments is the UN Body of Principles for the Protection of All Persons under Any Form of Detention or Imprisonment, adopted by the UN General Assembly in 1988.[10] The treaties and other instruments we have mentioned so far are concerned with general norms of human rights law. Depending on the context, however, the rights of detainees may additionally need to be considered in the light of other more specific norms, such as those relating to armed conflict or the status of refugees.

In the regime we have just evoked, a pivotal concept is manifestly that of arbitrary detention. Behind this concept stands the obvious point that the right to personal liberty does not entail that every deprivation of liberty is illegitimate. In specifying the boundaries of legitimate detention, international human rights law relies on two principles. One is the principle that no one may be detained otherwise than in accordance with national law. Thus, for example, under the International Covenant on Civil and Political Rights, '[n]o one shall be deprived of his liberty except on such grounds and in accordance with such procedure as are established by law'.[11] This means that the detaining authorities must follow procedures, and act on the basis of grounds, that are clearly and publicly laid down in national law. The other principle is that the implementation of national law must not be arbitrary. With regard to the Covenant, the Human Rights Committee has emphasised that ' "arbitrariness" is not to be equated with "against the law", but must be interpreted more broadly to include elements of inappropriateness, injustice and lack of predictability'.[12] For the Committee, detention can be considered arbitrary 'if it is not necessary in all the circumstances of the case, for example to prevent flight or interference with evidence: the element of proportionality becomes relevant in this context'.[13] In most treaties this aspect is signalled through a general prohibition of arbitrary detention. To quote the Covenant again, '[n]o one shall be subjected to arbitrary arrest

[10] Adopted by UN General Assembly Res. 43/173, 9 December 1988.

[11] Art. 9(1).

[12] *Van Alphen v Netherlands*, Communication 305/88, Views of the Human Rights Committee, adopted 23 July 1990, para 5.8.

[13] *A v Australia*, Communication 560/93, Views of the Human Rights Committee, adopted 3 April 1997, para. 9.2.

or detention'.[14] In one treaty, namely the European Convention on Human Rights, a more differentiated approach is adopted on this issue. Rather than including a general prohibition of arbitrary detention, the European Convention provides an exhaustive list of the specific circumstances in which detention can be reconciled with the right to personal liberty.[15] In each case, however, it is stipulated that those circumstances will not justify deprivation of liberty unless they are themselves 'lawful', and the European Court of Human Rights has explained that the overall purpose, reflected in this stipulation, is to 'protect individuals from arbitrariness'.[16]

Whether deprivation of liberty is consistent with international human rights law depends, then, both on an assessment of its basis in and conformity to national law, and also on broader criteria of appropriateness, reasonableness, and necessity. We can identify five main situations in which these criteria may be met. One is when a person is arrested for the purpose of being brought to trial, and it can be shown that their remand in custody is necessary to prevent flight, interference with evidence, or re-offending, or on some other ground. A second situation is following conviction of an offence, when a person is sentenced to a term of imprisonment. A third situation is when there is medical evidence warranting the involuntary hospitalisation of a person with mental illness. A fourth situation concerns arrest with a view to deportation or extradition. Each of these situations is included in the enumeration of legitimate deprivations of liberty under the European Convention, and is also reflected in interpretations of justifiable (non-arbitrary) detention under other treaties. A final situation differs, in that its basis lies in international humanitarian law. In the particular conditions of international armed conflict, detention will also be justifiable insofar as it is permitted under the Third and Fourth Geneva Conventions or under Protocol I of 1977. In broad terms, this allows for the detention of prisoners of war, along with others considered security threats in occupied territory, and also provides justification for internment within national territory.

The principles we have just outlined are used to determine whether or not there exist grounds for regarding an arrest or detention as legitimate. Linked to the basic right not to be unlawfully or arbitrarily detained,

---

[14] Art. 9(1).   [15] See art. 5(1)(a)–(f).

[16] *Kemmache v France (No. 3)*, Judgment of the European Court of Human Rights, 24 November 1994, para. 42.

however, are a number of procedural rights and safeguards, and it is these that are often the main focus of attention in complaints concerning violations of the right to personal liberty. An initial entitlement relates to the provision of information. In the language of the Covenant, '[a]nyone who is arrested shall be informed, at the time of arrest, of the reasons for his arrest and shall be promptly informed of any charges against him'.[17] Another entitlement concerns judicial supervision of detention on criminal charges. Thus, '[a]nyone arrested or detained on a criminal charge shall be brought promptly before a judge or other officer authorized by law to exercise judicial power and shall be entitled to trial within a reasonable time or to release'.[18] A further entitlement concerns access to justice, whatever the basis or nature of state custody. This is the right to take proceedings before a court for the purpose of challenging the lawfulness of detention, and securing release if the detention is unlawful. Whereas the right to judicial supervision just mentioned presupposes arrest in the context of a criminal investigation, this right applies in all contexts where people are detained, including 'preventive detention',[19] involuntary hospitalisation in connection with mental illness, detention with a view to deportation, and so on. Quoting the Covenant again, '[a]nyone who is deprived of his liberty by arrest or detention shall be entitled to take proceedings before a court, in order that that court may decide without delay on the lawfulness of his detention and order his release if the detention is not lawful'.[20] A final entitlement also applies whatever the custodial context. This is the right to compensation for unlawful detention. 'Anyone who has been the victim of unlawful arrest or detention shall have an enforceable right to compensation.'[21]

Endless war

Commenting on the Bush Administration's 'war on terror', Susan Sontag writes of the emergence of a 'new, pseudo-religious doctrine of war', according to which 'endless war permits the option of endless

[17] International Covenant on Civil and Political Rights, art. 9(2).
[18] Ibid., art. 9(3).
[19] See Human Rights Committee, General Comment 8 (Right to liberty and security of persons: art. 9), 30 June 1982, para. 4.
[20] International Covenant on Civil and Political Rights, art. 9(4).
[21] Ibid., art. 9(5).

incarceration'.[22] In illustrating some of the issues that may arise with respect to detainees' rights, let us begin with this phenomenon of endless or, at any rate, unlimited incarceration as a strategy of 'counter-terrorism'. Supporting the practice is commonly the total or near-total isolation of those concerned from the outside world. Incommunicado detention neutralises safeguards against arbitrary action and inhumane treatment in some very obvious ways. Where detainees are neither brought before a judge, nor allowed access to lawyers and contact with family, the prospects for obtaining judicial scrutiny of the detention and securing an order for release are effectively cancelled. In these circumstances, vulnerability is heightened to ill-treatment, not to mention self-harm and mental illness in the face of a penal process that is without time-frame or discernible path. Among the human rights violated are the right to be brought promptly before a judge following arrest, the right of access to justice for the purpose of challenging the lawfulness of detention, the right to legal representation which is an aspect of the right to fairness in all legal processes, the right to time and facilities for the preparation of a defence and to communicate with a chosen legal representative, and the right to humane treatment.[23] With regard to the last-mentioned right, the violation relates both to the inadequate protection provided against torture and other abuses by state officials, and to the inhumane treatment constituted by isolation of this kind itself.

Under the International Covenant on Civil and Political Rights and a number of other human rights treaties, it is recognised that modified application of the rights protected may sometimes become necessary. This is expressed in terms of an authorisation for governments to take measures derogating from their obligations in the circumstances of a war or other public emergency.[24] Can this authorisation be used to justify counter-terrorist measures that involve the curtailment of safeguards against arbitrary detention and inhumane treatment? We discuss

[22] S. Sontag, 'What have we done?', *The Guardian*, 24 May 2004.

[23] See, e.g., *Lafuente Peñarrieta and others v Bolivia*, Communication 176/1984, Views of the Human Rights Committee, adopted 2 November 1987.

[24] See International Covenant on Civil and Political Rights, art. 4; European Convention on Human Rights, art. 15; Revised European Social Charter, Part V, art. F; American Convention on Human Rights, art. 27; Commonwealth of Independent States Convention on Human Rights and Fundamental Freedoms, art. 35; and Revised Arab Charter of Human Rights (2004) (not yet in force), art. 4.

elsewhere in this book (see Terrorism★) the conditions under which valid derogation may occur. For present purposes what is notable is that certain rights are excluded from the scope of permissible derogation.[25] Among these is the right not to be subjected to torture or inhuman and degrading treatment. The right not to be arbitrarily detained is not specifically listed as a non-derogable right in the treaties that permit derogation. However, the courts and supervisory bodies associated with these treaties have made clear that legal protection against arbitrary detention must remain in place at all times. In the case of the American Convention on Human Rights, this is linked to a provision which prohibits derogation from 'judicial guarantees essential for the protection of' non-derogable rights.[26] The International Covenant on Civil and Political Rights contains no express provision along these lines; nevertheless, with regard to that treaty, the Human Rights Committee has affirmed that '[i]t is inherent in the protection of rights explicitly recognized as non-derogable . . . that they must be secured by procedural guarantees, including, often, judicial guarantees'.[27] In particular, 'the right to take proceedings before a court to enable the court to decide without delay on the lawfulness of detention, must not be diminished by a State party's decision to derogate from the Covenant'.[28] Likewise, the European Court of Human Rights has acknowledged the necessity at all times for 'effective safeguards . . . against arbitrary behaviour and incommunicado detention'.[29]

[25] See International Covenant on Civil and Political Rights, art. 4(2) and Second Optional Protocol, art. 6(2); European Convention on Human Rights, art. 15(2) and Sixth Protocol, art. 3, Seventh Protocol, art. 4(3), and Thirteenth Protocol, art. 2; Revised European Social Charter, Part V, art. F; American Convention on Human Rights, art. 27(2); Commonwealth of Independent States Convention on Human Rights and Fundamental Freedoms, art. 35(2); and Revised Arab Charter of Human Rights (2004) (not yet in force), art. 4(b).

[26] See art. 27(2). Regarding the implications of this for the right to appear before a court to challenge the lawfulness of detention and seek release, see *Habeas Corpus in Emergency Situations*, Advisory Opinion of the Inter-American Court of Human Rights, 30 January 1987. See also *Judicial Guarantees in States of Emergency*, Advisory Opinion of the Inter-American Court of Human Rights, 6 October 1987 and *Castillo Petruzzi and Others v Peru*, Judgment of the Inter-American Court of Human Rights, 30 May 1999, para. 109.

[27] Human Rights Committee, General Comment 29 (States of emergency: art. 4), 24 July 2001, para. 15.   [28] Ibid., para. 16.

[29] *Brannigan & McBride v United Kingdom*, Judgment of the European Court of Human Rights, 26 May 1993, para. 62.

Of course, all of this presupposes the applicability of relevant norms of international human rights law. In connection with Camp Delta at Guantánamo Bay, the United States authorities asserted at the outset that the governing regime was the law of armed conflict. Part of that law is international humanitarian law set forth in the Geneva Conventions, under which protections are also provided for people in detention. However, it was argued that those captured in Afghanistan were 'unlawful combatants', and fell outside the scope of the Geneva Conventions. On an alternative view, international humanitarian law is understood as an all-encompassing regime that leaves no group unprotected. As stated by Jean Pictet in his influential commentary to the Geneva Conventions, '[e]very person in enemy hands must have some status under international law: he is either a prisoner of war and, as such, covered by the Third Convention, a civilian covered by the Fourth Convention, or again, a member of the medical personnel of the armed forces who is covered by the First Convention. *There is no* intermediate status; nobody in enemy hands can be outside the law'.[30] In any event, it is clear that international humanitarian law does not displace international human rights law, but merely complements it where armed conflict is concerned. What then of the further argument that the International Covenant on Civil and Political Rights has no extra-territorial application, and hence could not entail obligations for the United States at Camp Delta, since Guantánamo Bay lies outside national territory? Quite obviously, any attempt to escape responsibility under the Covenant by using an extra-territorial detention facility should be repudiated. Under article 2(1) of the Covenant, a state party undertakes to respect and ensure the rights recognised 'to all individuals within its territory and subject to its jurisdiction'. According to the Human Rights Committee, this is to be read as encompassing everyone within the state's territory and subject to its jurisdiction, regardless of nationality or statelessness, along with everyone subject to the state's jurisdiction or otherwise within its 'power or effective control', regardless of location inside or outside national borders.[31] In a recent opinion, the International Court of Justice reaffirmed that 'the International Covenant on Civil and Political Rights is applicable in

[30] See J.S. Pictet (ed.), *The Geneva Conventions of 1949, Commentary*, vol. IV (Geneva: International Committee of the Red Cross, 1958), 51.

[31] Human Rights Committee, General Comment 31 (The nature of the general legal obligation imposed on states parties to the Covenant), 29 March 2004, para. 10.

respect of acts done by a State in the exercise of its jurisdiction outside its own territory'.[32] Beyond this, norms of customary international law corresponding to the Covenant's stipulations concerning arbitrary detention and humane treatment have universal application.

Refugee policy

Let us turn now to another arena of unlimited incarceration, and one similarly constitutive of the war on terror: the detention of those seeking asylum or recognition as refugees. The practice of detaining asylum-seekers did not start after 11 September 2001, just as the use of detention without trial as a strategy of counter-terrorism did not start then. A general tightening of border controls in the global North has been evident for several decades, and mandatory detention for asylum-seekers arriving without proper documentation (as a considerable proportion unavoidably do) began to be introduced in some countries in the 1980s and '90s. What has changed since September 11 is the context of refugee policy. With the new emphasis on safety, danger and fear, there has emerged a new argument for securing the fortress; in today's public discourse, asylum-seekers are routinely elided with terrorists. To quote one newspaper editorial in which many of the key clichés come together in glorious confusion: 'This sea of humanity is polluted with terrorism and disease and threatens our way of life . . . Blair must say *no more now*, revoke the human rights law *now* and lock up all the illegals *now* until they can be checked'.[33] Indeed, the numbers in detention centres in the United Kingdom have risen sharply in recent years. At the same time, this link with terrorism was made explicit in UK legislation under which non-nationals whom the Home Secretary deemed 'suspected international terrorists' could be held in indefinite detention under immigration law if they could not be deported owing to the risk of ill-treatment at home.[34]

Most commonly, however, detention is not linked to allegations of involvement in criminal activity, let alone large-scale criminal conspiracy,

---

[32] See *Legal Consequences of the Construction of a Wall in the Occupied Palestinian Territory*, Advisory Opinion of the International Court of Justice, 9 July 2004, para. 111.

[33] *The Sun*, Editorial, 27 January 2003, quoted in Z. Bauman, *Wasted Lives* (Cambridge: Polity Press, 2004), 55.

[34] See Anti-Terrorism, Crime and Security Act 2001. On this, see further Terrorism★.

but is rather explained in terms of the need to prevent absconding, or on some other ground related to immigration control. Certainly, no government argues that the mere act of illegal entry for the purpose of seeking recognition as a refugee is a crime, even if the prolonged periods for which asylum-seekers have in some places been held, and the harsh conditions of their custody, may appear to imply that. Equally, no government acknowledges that mandatory detention is designed in part as a deterrent to the initiation or maintenance of refugee applications, even if in some cases that impression has seemed difficult to avoid. To what extent, then, does refugee law provide warrant for the detention of asylum-seekers? To what extent can detention be squared with the right not to be arbitrarily detained under international human rights law? Under the Convention Relating to the Status of Refugees, states parties are prohibited from imposing penalties for illegal entry on refugees who have come directly from a territory where their life or freedom was threatened.[35] The Convention also provides that states parties may not 'apply to the movements of such refugees restrictions other than those which are necessary'.[36] In 1986 the Executive Committee of the United Nations High Commissioner for Refugees issued a statement reaffirming that the detention of asylum-seekers 'should normally be avoided', and declaring that, if necessary, detention should only occur on grounds prescribed by law in four situations: to verify the asylum-seeker's identity; to determine the elements on which the claim to refugee status is based; to deal with cases in which travel documents have been destroyed in order to mislead the authorities of the intended state of refuge; or to protect national security or public order.[37]

This is further elaborated in Guidelines on the Detention of Asylum-Seekers issued by the High Commissioner for Refugees in 1999.[38] The Guidelines begin by observing that 'detention' must be understood as including confinement in any restricted location, whether a prison, closed camp, detention facility or airport 'transit zone', 'where the only opportunity to leave this limited area is to leave the territory'.[39] In one

---

[35] Convention Relating to the Status of Refugees, art. 31(1).

[36] Ibid., art. 31(2).

[37] See UNHCR Executive Committee, Conclusion on Detention of Refugees and Asylum-Seekers, No. 44 (XXXVII-1986).

[38] UNHCR Revised Guidelines on Applicable Criteria and Standards Relating to the Detention of Asylum Seekers, 26 February 1999.　　　　[39] Ibid., guideline 1.

case before the European Court of Human Rights, a group of family members who had been held by the French authorities at Paris-Orly airport for 20 days complained that they had been unlawfully deprived of their liberty, contrary to article 5(1) of the European Convention.[40] The French Government argued that there had been no deprivation of liberty at all, as the transit zone, while 'closed on the French side', was 'open on the outside'; that is to say, the family was free to take another plane out. Following the same approach as the High Commissioner for Refugees, the European Court of Human Rights rejected this logic. Thus, the 'mere fact that it is possible for asylum-seekers to leave voluntarily the country where they wish to take refuge cannot exclude a restriction on liberty', given the possibility that no other country will offer them comparable protection.[41] Returning to the Guidelines, and with regard to the legitimacy of detention, it is stressed that '[a]s a general principle asylum-seekers should not be detained';[42] in different words, '[t]here should be a presumption against detention'. The Guidelines repeat the four exceptional grounds of detention enumerated in 1986, but also highlight the limits of those grounds. For example, 'national security and public order' are said to cover only cases where 'there is evidence to show that the asylum-seeker has criminal antecedents and/or affiliations which are likely to pose a risk to public order or national security should he/she be allowed entry'.[43]

Another issue addressed in the Guidelines concerns procedural safeguards. It is stated that asylum-seekers are entitled, as a minimum: to receive prompt and full communication of the order of detention and their rights in connection with it, in a language and in terms they can understand; to be told of their right to legal assistance; to have the detention decision subjected to automatic review before a judicial or administrative authority independent of the detaining authorities, and to periodic reviews thereafter; to challenge the necessity of the (continued) detention at the review hearing(s) and rebut findings made; and to be in contact with the office of the UN High Commissioner for Refugees and other relevant organisations.[44] In turn, the Guidelines are elaborated in this respect by the UN Working Group on Arbitrary

---

[40] *Amuur v France*, Judgment of the European Court of Human Rights, 25 June 1996.

[41] Ibid., para. 48.

[42] UNHCR Revised Guidelines on Applicable Criteria and Standards Relating to the Detention of Asylum Seekers, 26 February 1999, guideline 2.

[43] Ibid., guideline 3.   [44] Ibid., guideline 5.

Detention, in a statement made in 1999.[45] The Working Group spells out that a maximum period for detention should be set by law; in no case should custody be unlimited or excessive. It also considers that the effective right must always exist to seek prompt judicial review of the lawfulness of the detention and release in the event that it is found unlawful.[46] The detention of asylum-seekers has also been examined by the Human Rights Committee, from the perspective of the right of those concerned to freedom from arbitrary detention. In one case, against Australia, the complainant had been held for more than four years pending the determination of his entitlement to refugee status.[47] He argued that this prolonged detention violated his right not to be arbitrarily detained under article 9(1) of the International Covenant on Civil and Political Rights, and also complained of the impossibility of challenging the lawfulness of his detention in a court, in contravention of article 9(4). The Human Rights Committee upheld these complaints. With regard to article 9(1), the Australian Government had failed to adduce grounds particular to the complaint's case which could justify the lengthy detention. And as for article 9(4), while judicial review of the detention order was available, it was purely formal judicial review, limited to verification of the (self-evident) fact that the complainant fell within the category of those subject to mandatory detention under the relevant legislation. For the Committee, the judicial review that is required must be 'real and not merely formal'.[48] The reviewing court must have the power to order release if the detention is incompatible, not just with national law, but also with the requirements of article 9(1) or other provisions of the Covenant.

Indeterminate sentencing

The forms of detention we have highlighted to this point are instances of administrative or preventive detention. But unlimited incarceration can also occur in the context of imprisonment upon conviction of an offence. It can occur, for example, when a discretionary sentence is

[45] Working Group on Arbitrary Detention, 2000 Report, Annex II, Deliberation No. 5 (1999), UN Doc. E/CN.4/2000/4.   [46] Ibid., principles 7–8.
[47] *A v Australia*, Views of the Human Rights Committee, adopted 3 April 1997.
[48] Ibid., para. 9.5.

imposed on a minor and the duration of the imprisonment is left for the executive authorities to decide. And it may occur in the context of life imprisonment. While sentencing practices and options vary considerably across national jurisdictions, and while the specific implications of a life sentence are also not uniform, a general question arises here about the right not to be arbitrarily detained. Clearly, it is a violation of the right not to be arbitrarily detained to keep people in custody beyond the term of their sentence. Conversely, it is not a violation of the right not to be arbitrarily detained to keep them in custody during the currency of their sentence; unless the trial was unfair, that is a legitimate deprivation of liberty under international human rights law. The question that arises is, where does this leave the right of all detainees to access to justice for the purpose of challenging the lawfulness of their detention, and securing release if the detention is unlawful? Is this entitlement in principle exhausted by the original hearing before the sentencing court, or can it still be invoked during the term of imprisonment, at least where life and discretionary sentences are concerned? This issue has been raised in a series of complaints before the European Court of Human Rights concerning discretionary sentences and life sentences of the kind imposed in the United Kingdom, which comprise a minimum term that must be served having regard to the gravity of the offence (known as the 'tariff'), and a further period of imprisonment that is not fixed in advance, but depends on later assessments of what is necessary to protect the public.

The European Court has affirmed that, in the case of prisoners with discretionary sentences and life sentences of this kind, the right of access to justice is not exhausted by the original hearing.[49] After an initial period has elapsed, people sentenced in this way have the right to seek periodic judicial review of their continued detention, to ensure that there remains justification for detaining them and, if not, to obtain release. In the case of life sentences, the initial period which must elapse first is the minimum term or tariff. The European Court has stressed that, whatever institutional form is adopted with respect to the required periodic judicial review, it must include an oral hearing in the prisoner's

---

[49] Regarding life sentences, see, e.g., *Wynne v United Kingdom (No. 2)*, Judgment of the European Court of Human Rights, 16 October 2003. Regarding discretionary sentences, see, e.g., *Waite v United Kingdom*, Judgment of the European Court of Human Rights, 10 December 2002.

presence, in the context of an adversarial procedure in which the prisoner is legally represented and has the possibility of calling and questioning witnesses. It must also involve a tribunal that is competent to order the prisoner's release. Aside from these implications of the right not to be arbitrarily detained (protected in article 5 of the Convention), the European Court has suggested that the imposition of a sentence of life imprisonment with no possibility of release may violate the right not to be subjected to inhuman treatment (protected in article 3).[50] This idea that 'life should not mean life' is also reflected in the Rome Statute of the International Criminal Court. People sentenced to life imprisonment by the International Criminal Court are entitled to automatic review of their sentence after 25 years, and at periodic intervals thereafter.[51]

Attention to the situation of convicted prisoners provides an occasion to highlight some points about the conditions of detention. Within the framework of intergovernmental discussions concerning criminal justice, the first UN standard-setting document relating to the treatment of prisoners was adopted in 1957.[52] Nine years later, an international guarantee of humane treatment in detention was adopted as part of the International Covenant on Civil and Political Rights. The Covenant specifically affirms the right of '[a]ll persons deprived of their liberty [to] be treated with humanity and with respect for the inherent dignity of the human person'.[53] Further standard-setting documents addressed to prison conditions and related issues appeared throughout the succeeding decades.[54] The UN Body of Principles for the Protection of All Persons under Any Form of Detention or Imprisonment, adopted in 1988, contains an especially

[50] *Wynne v United Kingdom*, Decision on Admissibility of the European Court of Human Rights, 22 May 2003, para. 4.

[51] Rome Statute of the International Criminal Court, art. 110(3) and (5).

[52] Standard Minimum Rules for the Treatment of Prisoners, adopted 30 August 1955 by First United Nations Congress on the Prevention of Crime and the Treatment of Offenders, UN Doc. A/CONF/611, annex I, and approved by ECOSOC resolution 663C (XXIV), 31 July 1957. (See also ECOSOC resolution 2076 (LXII) of 13 May 1977, adding rule 95 concerning persons arrested or detained without charge.)

[53] Art. 10(1). On this and related issues, see Human Rights Committee, General Comment 21 (Humane treatment of persons deprived of liberty: art. 10), 10 April 1992.

[54] Basic Principles for the Treatment of Prisoners, adopted and proclaimed by General Assembly Resolution 45/111 of 14 December 1990; and United Nations Rules for the Protection of Juveniles Deprived of their Liberty, adopted by General Assembly Resolution 45/113 of 14 December 1990.

detailed elaboration of the implications of international human rights law with regard to all those in detention, whether following conviction for an offence or in any other context. For example, the Body of Principles states that the prohibition of cruel, inhuman or degrading treatment or punishment should be interpreted to encompass 'the holding of a detained or imprisoned person in conditions which deprive him, temporarily or permanently, of the use of any of his natural senses, such as sight or hearing', that is to say, the practices of hooding, blindfolding, and the like.[55]

To the extent that international concern with prison conditions has intensified in recent decades, this has been accompanied by a new emphasis on preventing the ill-treatment of detainees, rather than simply condemning, and seeking redress for, abuses which have already occurred. We discuss some of these initiatives, along with other issues relevant to the prevention of ill-treatment in detention, elsewhere in this book (see Torture★). Linked to this interest in preventive approaches is also a new emphasis on the 'positive obligations' of governments with respect to people in state custody—that is to say, the obligations of governments not just to refrain from abusive conduct (their 'negative' obligations), but to take steps as well to protect the right of prisoners to freedom from torture and other ill-treatment, and indeed their right to life. Particular importance is attached in this regard to the obligation of state authorities effectively to investigate allegations of abuse. Thus, for instance, in a series of cases against Bulgaria before the European Court of Human Rights, Roma detainees had died in state custody.[56] Interwoven with issues of racism was the question of the responsibility of the state authorities with respect to the detainees' right to life. There was evidence that the detainees concerned had died at the hands of state agents. In consequence, the responsibility of the state was clearly engaged. But the Court also found the state responsible for a violation of the detainees' right to life, insofar as no effective investigation had been conducted into their deaths. In another case, against Ukraine, the failure to investigate a prisoner's repeated allegations of assault by prison officers was held to violate the prisoner's right not to be

---

[55] UN Body of Principles for the Protection of All Persons under Any Form of Detention or Imprisonment, adopted 9 December 1988, principle 6.

[56] See *Velikova v Bulgaria*, Judgment of the European Court of Human Rights, 18 May 2000; *Anguelova v Bulgaria*, Judgment of the European Court of Human Rights, 13 June 2002; *Nachova and Others v Bulgaria*, Judgment of the European Court of Human Rights, 26 February 2004.

subjected to torture or inhuman or degrading treatment, even though it was not possible for the European Court to determine on the evidence whether the assaults had actually occurred.[57] Yet another case before the European Court, against the United Kingdom, concerned the killing of a prisoner—the applicants' son—by his cell-mate.[58] The cell-mate suffered from acute mental illness, and the Court confimed that the state's obligations in this context may extend to protecting prisoners from other prisoners. In this case, the life of the applicants' son had been placed at risk by the introduction into his cell of a dangerously unstable prisoner, and the Court held that the inadequate nature of the screening process on the cell-mate's arrival in prison, coupled with the failure of relevant agencies (medical profession, police, prosecution and court) to pass information about him to the prison authorities, disclosed a breach of the state's obligations with respect to the right to life.

Invisible hand/iron fist

Our discussion so far has focused on the protection of detainees from unlawful arrest and arbitrary detention, torture and other ill-treatment, inhumane prison conditions, and death in custody. We have considered *how* prisoners are held, and what state authorities must do to secure their rights to life, personal liberty, and humane treatment. But, at least in relation to convicted prisoners, we have not considered *who* is held, *why*, and *with what consequences*. In a series of writings Loïc Wacquant highlights the massive growth of prison populations in recent decades, especially in the United States, but also in other industrialised societies.[59] For Wacquant, this reflects a 'penalisation of poverty', according to which imprisonment is increasingly used to manage the fall-out from social and economic restructuring.[60] The rise of the 'flexible' economy and the widespread dismantling of social protections are rarely seen as linked

[57] *Poltoratskiy v Ukraine*, Judgment of the European Court of Human Rights, 29 April 2003.

[58] *Edwards v United Kingdom*, Judgment of the European Court of Human Rights, 14 March 2002.

[59] See L. Wacquant, *Les Prisons de la misère* (Paris: Editions Raisons d'agir, 1999), and the articles cited below.

[60] See L. Wacquant, 'The Penalisation of Poverty and the Rise of Neo-Liberalism' 9 *European Journal on Criminal Policy and Research* (2001), 401.

with the strengthening of the prison sector, but his argument is that in fact these processes go together. The 'downsizing' of the economic and social state must be understood as forming part of the same set of transformations that is producing an 'upsizing' of the penal state.[61] In his vivid image, 'the "invisible hand" of the casualised labour market finds its institutional complement and counterpart in the "iron fist" of the state which is being redeployed so as to check the disorders generated by the diffusion of social insecurity'.[62]

Wacquant contends that imprisonment serves three functions in this context. It disciplines and subdues recalcitrant or disruptive elements at the lower end of the social order. It 'warehouses' those who have become supernumerary or at any rate the most destitute among them. And it reaffirms the prerogatives and powers of the state within the limited domain now assigned to it. Legitimising these functions is a range of slogans, concepts and practices, most of them originating in the United States but many now also used in some form elsewhere in the industrialised world. In question are phrases like 'zero tolerance', 'three strikes and you're out', 'workfare', and 'prison works', along with measures such as the imposition of curfews and the imprisonment of repeat-offender youths, and developments in the commercialisation of prison operations. If the applicable theory was once rehabilitation, Wacquant observes that penal policy is increasingly oriented to incapacitation—and not only for offenders considered dangerous who need to be prevented from causing harm, but for the de-skilled subproletariat, the poorest of the poor, as well. At the same time, Wacquant highlights the massively disproportionate numbers of African-Americans in United States prisons and the significant imbalance that likewise affects non-white citizens and immigrants in European prisons. What he wryly terms 'carceral affirmative action' points to the role of prisons in the production and reproduction of racial hierarchies.[63] In his account, the prison has taken over from the ghetto in the United States as the key institution for defining, controlling and containing 'untouchable' populations.

[61] See L. Wacquant, 'Deadly Symbiosis: When ghetto and prison meet and mesh' 3 *Punishment and Society* (2001), 95, 97.

[62] L. Wacquant, 'The Penalisation of Poverty and the Rise of Neo-Liberalism' 9 *European Journal on Criminal Policy and Research* (2001), 401, 401–2.

[63] Ibid., 403.

If this analysis is even partly right, it suggests that the expanding purview of the human rights movement, to which we referred in introducing the topic of detainees' rights, may need to expand still further. Alongside concerns about counter-terrorist measures and refugee policies, prison conditions and parole processes, political prisoners and prisoners of conscience, attention may need to be directed to a range of further issues connected with the penalisation of poverty and the consequences of mass incarceration. In the United States, one aspect of this relates to the appalling irony that, after gaining the vote with such struggle, large proportions of African-American men are now losing it under statutes which disenfranchise offenders with felony convictions.[64] More broadly, what needs greater prominence is the character of prison as an engine of social exclusion, generating poverty even as it pulls in the poor. The logic of Wacquant's analysis is, of course, that to reverse the upsizing of the penal state, the downsizing of the economic and social state must also be reversed. Hence, in human rights terms, his conclusion that '[t]he best means of making the prison recede is, again and always, to strengthen and extend social and economic rights'.[65] From this perspective, the rights of detainees are not only a matter of the right to personal liberty, the right not to be subjected to torture and other ill-treatment, and the right to life. They are also, and no less urgently, a matter of the right to social security, the right to education, the right to work, and the right to the non-discriminatory enjoyment of these and other human rights.

[64] See L. Wacquant, 'From Slavery to Mass Incarceration: Rethinking the "race question" in the US' 13 New Left Review (Jan./Feb. 2002), 41, 43.

[65] L. Wacquant, 'The Penalisation of Poverty and the Rise of Neo-Liberalism' 9 European Journal on Criminal Policy and Research (2001), 401, 410.

Development

In recent years human rights have become an important part of debates, policy-making and activism in the field of development. 'Rights-based' approaches to development, premised on the idea that strategies and programmes should be informed by attention to human rights, are now widely endorsed. And just as human rights have entered the arena of development, so too development has become a key issue in discussions, activities and norm-making within the field of human rights. One manifestation of this is the emergence of the 'right to development', embodying the notion that development is the basis of a human right in itself.

At first sight the marriage of development and human rights seems like the most auspicious possible union: two beneficent ideas and practices dedicated to making the world a better place coming together and strengthening each other in the process. On closer inspection, however, a more nuanced assessment is called for, which takes into account the limitations on both sides and in their combination. We discuss various limitations of the human rights approach throughout this book. As to development, it is striking that the effort to establish links with human rights coincides with a time when the contradictory and frequently counter-productive character of the development enterprise could scarcely be plainer. After more than five decades of development activity, improved conditions in some places and at some levels coexist with an increasing gap between the world's richest and poorest, declining per capita incomes in about a third of all countries, and the impoverishment of millions who previously had viable livelihoods. Arturo Escobar speaks to a widely shared experience when he observes that '[u]nderdevelopment became the subject of political technologies that sought to erase it from the face of the Earth, but that ended up multiplying it to infinity'.[1]

Can human rights help to reorient development in ways that might have better prospects of realising the promise of a more equal world? Or do rights-based approaches to development simply prop up a venture that is failing and, as some argue, was misconceived from the outset? And what of the recognition of development as a human right? Can that enhance the capacity of human rights to contribute to the more equal distribution of resources and opportunities? Or does the idea of a right to development serve only to weaken long-established rights and responsibilities? Does it indeed point up shortcomings of human rights law more generally? To some analysts of development, a major part of the problem is that approaches to development have treated the issues involved as technical questions for experts in economics, urban planning, public services, engineering and government, rather than as contestable political questions for those affected. Finally, then, can human rights help to refocus attention on the political stakes of development strategies and programmes? Or do they simply reinforce the depoliticisation of issues, and add yet another layer of technocratic power? In what follows we take up these and related questions.

Development

The project of 'development' is generally traced to the inaugural address of United States President Harry S. Truman in 1949. As one of the components of his agenda for 'peace and freedom', Truman announced a 'program for development', designed to make 'the benefits of our scientific advances and industrial progress available for the improvement and growth of underdeveloped areas'. As he explained, '[g]reater production is the key to prosperity and peace. And the key to greater production is a wider and more vigorous application of modern scientific and technical knowledge'.[2] Science and technology, then,

[1] A. Escobar, *Encountering Development* (Princeton, NJ: Princeton University Press, 1995), 52.
[2] Inaugural Address, 20 January 1949, *Inaugural Addresses of the Presidents of the United States: from George Washington 1789 to George Bush 1989* (Washington, DC: US GPO, 1989), 285, 290.

along with capital investment, were to be the means for bringing to 'underdeveloped' regions the advantages enjoyed by 'developed' societies. In this regard, Truman was quite candid, and indeed emphatic, about the fact that a major aim of his 'program for development' was to establish or consolidate United States influence, and discourage the underdeveloped regions from turning to communism. Truman's programme was later taken up by the United Nations, and, as decolonisation unfolded, a development agenda was embraced by the governments of most newly independent states. Thus was set in train a process which over the course of the succeeding years would lead (rather like human rights) to an extraordinary proliferation of institutions, initiatives and experts, as well as to a new object of academic study and activist engagement.

By the last decades of the 20th century, the tenor of much of this study and activism was sharply critical. In one of the harshest assessments, published in 1992, Wolfgang Sachs denounces development as a dangerous illusion or comforting myth, now best abandoned. 'Delusion and disappointment, failures and crimes have been the steady companions of development,' he writes, 'and they tell a common story: it did not work'.[3] More than that, he contends, the premises on which it is based no longer make sense. In the first place, Truman's idea of progress through limitless growth based on the application of science and technology has been called into question. We have become aware that industrialisation, the technicalisation of agriculture and consumer capitalism carry high environmental costs and risks. Far, then, from holding up the United States and other industrialised countries as models which other nations should seek to emulate, we should be working to transform these 'developed' societies. Secondly, the Cold War context which gave rise to development no longer exists. At the same time, development assistance remains difficult to separate from the efforts of key donors to build strategic and economic relationships, shape international trade, and strengthen particular elites within target countries. The lack of accountability to ordinary citizens, and especially the poorest among them, continues to mean that development activities might benefit some, but do little for many more. Indeed, and this is Sachs's third

---

[3] W. Sachs, 'Introduction' in W. Sachs (ed.), *The Development Dictionary* (London: Zed Books, 1995), 1.

point, experience has shown that in many contexts modernisation has made conditions of life significantly worse. As he writes,

The old ways have been smashed, the new ways are not viable. People are caught in the deadlock of development: the peasant who is dependent on buying seeds, yet finds no cash to do so; the mother who benefits neither from the care of her fellow women in the community nor from the assistance of a hospital; the clerk who had made it in the city, but is now laid off as a result of cost-cutting measures...[4]

Finally, Sachs, in common with many others, highlights the way development portrays people in underdeveloped regions as having only problems and needs, but no agency and few resources. From this perspective, development is problematic because it fosters an image (and, on the part of those concerned, a self-image) of deficiency. Instead of focusing only on what is lacking, and destroying what is there, we should be paying more attention to the possibilities, energies, processes and ideas within communities. More concretely, we should stop treating poor people as consumers of initiatives developed elsewhere, and start attending to the strategies through which they are managing to improve their own circumstances.

These concerns are very widely shared. For most analysts, however, they are reasons not to jettison the development concept, but rather to rethink it and reorient the practices it has spawned. As Maggie Black explains, despite the poor record of development, or indeed because of that record, 'this is not the moment to abandon the vision of a fairer world' which development may serve to project. For '[i]f machinery exists to address "world poverty", optimism insists that it be put to better use'.[5] In fact, of course, approaches to development have been subject to critique and revision from the very beginning. What has changed in recent decades is the need to confront challenges which affect not only the means of development, but also its ends, and not only its prescriptions, but also its premises.

Efforts to reorient development to meet these challenges are reflected in a series of qualifiers which have come to be attached to the word 'development'. Thus, 'human development' seeks to shift the emphasis from economic growth to social conditions, and hence from assessments

[4] W. Sachs, 'Introduction' in W. Sachs (ed.), *The Development Dictionary* (London: Zed Books, 1995), 3.

[5] M. Black, *The No-Nonsense Guide to International Development* (London: Verso, 2002), 27–8.

based exclusively on gross national product per capita to assessments based also on social indicators (life expectancy, infant mortality, literacy, access to services, etc.). 'Sustainable development' directs attention to the need to avoid environmental harms, husband natural resources, and consider precautionary approaches to risk. 'Social development' calls for moves to enhance the extent to which development activities benefit marginalised and vulnerable groups. And 'participatory development' highlights the importance of involving those affected (and in the case of 'women-in-development', women in particular) in the framing, implementation and evaluation of development schemes. Human development has been refined and linked to sustainable, social and participatory development in successive issues of the *Human Development Report*, an annual publication of the United Nations Development Programme since 1990. In 2000 the title of the UNDP's *Human Development Report* was 'Human Rights and Human Development'. This points to a further dimension of recent efforts to reorient development, to which we now turn.

Development and human rights

What is the relationship between development and human rights? On one account, respect for human rights can be an obstacle to development. This account has been elaborated in connection with arguments about the significance for human rights of 'Asian values'.[6] According to one proponent of these arguments, Bilahari Kausikan, 'experience sees order and stability as preconditions for economic growth, and growth as the necessary foundation of any political order that claims to advance human dignity'.[7] It follows for him that developing societies may need to postpone human rights to some extent, to provide a secure, reliable and unified context within which economic development can be pursued. While Kausikan proposes that this applies especially to civil and political rights, such as the right to free speech, the right to free assembly and constraints on preventive detention, many commentators have pointed out that economic and social rights are, if anything, more commonly and comprehensively put to one side, as governments concentrate on boosting economic growth. At any rate, the general point, as expressed

[6] Regarding 'Asian values', see Culture*.
[7] B. Kausikan, 'Asia's Different Standard' 92 *Foreign Policy* (1993), 24, 35.

also by another exponent of the Asian values thesis, Kishore Mahbubani, is that human rights advocates have got things the wrong way around. We need to start putting 'the horse before the cart', he writes, by 'promoting economic development through good government before promoting democracy' and human rights.[8]

In an influential book published in 1999 Amartya Sen argues that this way of approaching the relationship between development and human rights proceeds from a fundamental misconception about the nature of development.[9] To consider whether respect for human rights is or is not conducive to development is to presuppose that development means only economic growth. As we have seen, however, many argue that development must rather be understood in terms of human development and related concepts. More specifically, Sen proposes that development must be understood as a 'process of expanding the real freedoms that people enjoy'.[10] To ask whether respect for human rights is or is not conducive to development is thus to miss the point that human rights are themselves constituent components of development. As he contends, the relevance of substantive freedoms, such as the right to political participation or to basic education,

does not have to be freshly established through their indirect contribution to the growth of GNP or to the promotion of industrialization. As it happens, these freedoms and rights are *also* very effective in contributing to economic progress... But while the causal relation is indeed significant, the vindication of freedoms and rights provided by this causal linkage is over and above the directly constitutive role of these freedoms in development.[11]

On Sen's account, growth of gross national product remains an important means of promoting development, but it cannot be regarded as an end in itself. Rather, as indicated, the end of development is, for him, to expand the real freedoms that people enjoy. This is linked to the idea that poverty is a matter not just of low incomes but rather of what he calls 'capability deprivation', understood as deprivation with respect to the substantive freedoms a person 'enjoys to lead the kind of life he or she has reason to value'.[12] If the goal of development is to redress capability deprivation by expanding freedoms, then it calls for the removal

[8] K. Mahbubani, 'The West and the Rest' 28 *The National Interest* (1992), 3, 11.
[9] A. Sen, *Development as Freedom* (Oxford: Oxford University Press, 1999).
[10] Ibid., 3.   [11] Ibid., 5.   [12] Ibid., 87.

of all the 'major sources of unfreedom: poverty as well as tyranny, poor economic opportunities as well as systematic social deprivation, neglect of public facilities as well as intolerance of overactivity of repressive states'.[13]

Continuing in the line of Sen's conception of development as freedom, the UNDP's *Human Development Report* for 2000 proposes viewing human development and human rights in a more integrated manner. The Report highlights a number of benefits which human rights can bring to approaches to human development. First, human rights connect human development with the idea that others have *duties* to facilitate and enhance development. As observed in the Report, rights imply claims on others that they should ensure, or co-operate in ensuring, access to some social good. In turn, this insistence on justified claims and correlative duties implies such concepts as accountability, culpability and responsibility. Human rights thus broaden the focus of development analysis, to encompass a consideration of the 'actions, strategies and efforts that different duty bearers undertake to contribute to the fulfilment of specified human rights' and hence to the advancement of corresponding facets of human development.[14] They also broaden the focus to encompass a consideration of the responsibilities of different actors when those rights go unfulfilled. Secondly, human rights connect human development with *norms* that require attention to the consequences of development strategies for diverse individuals and groups. Among other things, this entails setting limits on the extent to which governments and others may rely upon utilitarian logics. In the words of the Report, 'individual rights express the limits on the losses that individuals can permissibly be allowed to bear, even in the promotion of noble social goals'.[15] Finally, human rights connect human development with a tradition in which *protection* is key. With human rights comes a reminder that norms and institutions must be put in place to provide security for human development achievements. In this way human rights amplify the 'factual concentration' of development thinking, encouraging scrutiny of the 'extent to which the gains are socially protected against potential threats'.[16]

[13] Ibid., 3. See further chap. 6.
[14] UNDP, *Human Development Report 2000: Human Rights and Human Development* (Oxford: Oxford University Press, 2000), 21.   [15] Ibid., 22.
[16] Ibid., 22–3.

Continuing somewhat further along the line of these elaborations of the concept of human development, the UN High Commissioner for Human Rights has issued a number of statements detailing the features and benefits of 'rights-based' approaches to development.[17] Among the benefits highlighted is again the point that rights-based approaches can enhance the degree to which there exists an authoritative basis for advocacy and for claims on resources. The UNHCHR also stresses the value of the explicit linkage provided with all human rights. As the Committee on Economic, Social and Cultural Rights pointed out in 1990, development cooperation activities by no means 'automatically contribute to the promotion of respect for economic, social and cultural rights'. To avoid harm, rights have to be taken into account at every stage.[18] Rights-based approaches create 'integrated safeguards against unintentional harm by development projects', by requiring that measures of protection be incorporated into development plans, policies and projects. Alongside these advantages, rights-based approaches are said to be distinctive in attaching particular importance to four issues and their interrelation: participation, accountability, non-discrimination and empowerment. Participation calls for the involvement of beneficiaries in ways that go beyond formal consultation and enable them instead to direct development processes. Accountability is concerned with identifying specific duties and duty-bearers and thus moving development cooperation from the domain of charity to that of obligation. Non-discrimination highlights the need to guard against reinforcing pre-existing asymmetries of power and resources, by giving express consideration to the implications of development plans for disadvantaged groups. And empowerment refers to the idea that development activities should be oriented to facilitating and assisting the efforts of communities to improve their own conditions of life.

We have so far been focusing on the introduction of human rights considerations into the equation of development. The other side of the integration of human development and human rights is, of course, the introduction of development issues into the equation of human rights.

---

[17] See, e.g., UN High Commissioner for Human Rights, 'How do rights-based approaches differ and what is the value added?', available at www.unhchr.ch/development/approaches-07.html. See further P. Alston, 'Revitalising United Nations Work on Human Rights and Development' 18 Melbourne University Law Review (1991) 216.

[18] Committee on Economic, Social and Cultural Rights, General Comment 2 (International technical assistance measures: art. 22), 2 February 1990, para. 7.

The right to development

The recognition of development as a human right predates the recent embrace of rights-based approaches to development by quite some time. The right to development emerged in connection with the efforts of newly independent states in the 1960s and 1970s to establish fairer economic and trade relations between the global North and the global South.[19] In its current form the right was first recognised by the UN Commission on Human Rights in 1977.[20] It is protected in the African Charter on Human and Peoples' Rights, opened for signature in 1981. Article 22 of the Charter declares: '(1) All peoples shall have the right to their economic, social and cultural development... (2) States shall have the duty, individually or collectively, to ensure the exercise of the right to development'. The right to development is affirmed and elaborated in the UN Declaration on the Right to Development, adopted by the General Assembly in 1986.[21] It is reaffirmed as 'a universal and inalienable right and an integral part of fundamental human rights' in the Vienna Declaration and Programme of Action, adopted at the World Conference on Human Rights in 1993.[22] In 1998 the UN Commission on Human Rights appointed Arjun Sengupta as independent expert on the right to development. In a series of reports Sengupta has elaborated a conception of the right to development as the 'right to a process', and has examined ways in which the implementation of that right may be enhanced.[23]

If the right to development emerged in connection with efforts to establish fairer economic and trade relations, its subsequent history

[19] See G. Abi-Saab, 'The Legal Formulation of a Right to Development' in R. Dupuy (ed.), *The Right to Development at the International Level* (Alphen aan den Rijn: Sijthoff and Noodhoff, 1981), 163.

[20] UN Commission on Human Rights Res. 4 (XXXIII) of 21 February 1977. See also, earlier, the UN Declaration on Social Progress and Development, UN General Assembly Res. 2542 (XXIV), 11 December 1969 (elaborating on the human rights implications of 'social progress and development', but not recognising a 'right to development' in the manner of later instruments).

[21] UN General Assembly Res. 41/128, 4 December 1986.

[22] Vienna Declaration and Programme of Action, UN Doc. A/CONF.157/23, 12 July 1993, Part I, para. 10.

[23] For discussion of the independent expert's first four reports, see Franciscans International (eds.), *The Right to Development* (Geneva: Franciscans International, 2003) (where the reports themselves are also reproduced).

indicates that for some it (also) has another significance. Thus, the right has been championed by some governments from the global South as a way of justifying repressive policies by reference to the goal of development. (To this extent it may have affinities with the arguments, discussed above, that have been advanced in conjunction with claims about the bearing for human rights of Asian values.) Concurrently, the right to development has been resisted by some governments from the global North, anxious to avoid constraints that might impede trade and investment or cause them to lose control over development assistance. Anne Orford observes that both sets of governments have found it convenient to adopt a narrow interpretation of the right, according to which the right to development is essentially a right of states to prioritise a certain economic model of development over human rights.[24] This supports the effort to justify repression, while at the same time making the right easy to discredit. Yet, as Orford also observes, the UN Declaration on the Right to Development additionally, and perhaps more readily, suggests other, far more progressive interpretations.

Let us begin by considering the subject of the right. According to article 2(1) of the UN Declaration, the 'human person is the central subject of development and should be the active participant and beneficiary of the right to development'. Under article 2(3), 'States have the right and duty to formulate appropriate national development policies that aim at the constant improvement of the well-being of the entire population and of all individuals'. And pursuant to article 22(1) of the African Charter, quoted above, '[a]ll peoples shall have the right to their economic, social and cultural development'. While debates about the subject of the right to development often proceed by privileging one or another of these various formulations, read together they can be understood as establishing a right that has both individual and collective dimensions. The 'human person' is the central subject. 'All peoples' have the right, but on the basis that what is in issue is the well-being of the 'entire population and of all individuals' within it. 'States' are entitled to formulate development policies for enhancing the well-being of the entire population and all individuals, in the sense that others may not prevent or obstruct this goal.

---

[24] A. Orford, 'Globalization and the Right to Development' in P. Alston (ed.), *Peoples' Rights* (Oxford: Oxford University Press, 2001), 127, 133.

What then of the entitlement itself? In the UN Declaration three aspects assume particular prominence. One, echoed also in the rights-based approaches to development we considered earlier, concerns the participation of those affected. Thus, the Declaration asserts that development policies should be formulated 'on the basis of [the] active, free and meaningful participation in development' of all individuals.[25] Highlighted in particular is the need for effective measures to ensure an active role for women,[26] upon whom improvements in social circumstances often disproportionately depend, yet who are all too frequently marginalised, or inadequately involved, in decision-making about development. Once again, these provisions make clear that consultation about policies, projects or programmes already decided upon does not suffice. Participation must include the capacity to take part in setting development priorities and directing development processes. A second aspect relates to the distribution of social goods and opportunities. This is obviously connected with the first aspect, inasmuch as marginalisation in decision-making is conducive to disadvantageous outcomes. The Declaration asserts that development policies should also be formulated with a view to the 'fair distribution of the benefits resulting' from development.[27] At the same time, it refers to the obligation to ensure 'equality of opportunity for all in their access to basic resources, education, health services, food, housing, employment, and the fair distribution of income'.[28] These provisions lay a basis for claims about inequity in the distribution of social goods and opportunities, and about inadequacy in the provision of basic services and in the means of a livelihood. Following on from this, a third aspect of the right to development has to do with the relationship between it and other human rights. In a number of its articles, as well as in its preamble, the Declaration indicates that efforts to promote the right to development must remain consistent with respect for other human rights, and indeed should include efforts to promote respect for the full range of human rights. Thus, for instance, article 6(3) declares that 'States should take steps to eliminate obstacles to development resulting from failure to observe civil and political rights, as well as economic, social and cultural rights'. In contrast to the assumption, mentioned earlier, that the right to development can justify repressive policies by reference to the goal of economic development, this may be

---

[25] Art. 2(3).   [26] Art. 8(1).   [27] Art. 2(3).   [28] Art. 8(1).

Development vs. human rights.

taken to reflect a rights-based approach to development, according to which development is inseparable from the goal of enhancing respect for the full range of human rights.

Finally, upon whom are imposed the obligations associated with this entitlement? Under the African Charter, 'States shall have the duty, individually or collectively, to ensure the exercise of the right to development'.[29] Likewise, under the UN Declaration 'States have the primary responsibility for the creation of national and international conditions favourable to the realization of the right to development'.[30] More specifically, 'States have the duty to take steps, individually and collectively, to formulate development policies…',[31] and 'to co-operate with each other in ensuring development and eliminating obstacles to development'.[32] In this regard, the Declaration emphasises that, '[a]s a complement to the efforts of developing countries, effective international co-operation is essential in providing these countries with appropriate means and facilities to foster their comprehensive development'.[33] At the same time, it is declared that '[a]ll human beings have a responsibility for development, individually and collectively…'.[34] As in the case of the subject of the right to development, debates about responsibility for ensuring the right often proceed by privileging one or another of these various formulations. In this way we are encouraged either to focus on international accountability and absolve from responsibility the government of the state concerned, or to focus on national accountability and absolve from responsibility other governments, international institutions and others. Once again, however, the idea that we must make such a choice can be readily refuted. When read as a whole, the UN Declaration can be understood to express a multidimensional approach to accountability, such that responsibility rests with the government of the state concerned, but also other governments, international institutions and indeed everyone. That responsibility, moreover, is not merely a negative duty not to impede development, but also a positive duty to act in ways that help to eliminate obstacles to development and create favourable conditions for it. Anne Orford notes that in conditions of intensifying globalisation, the role of multinational corporations is particularly significant. In the absence of adequate forms of accountability with regard

[29] Art. 22(2).   [30] Art. 3(1).   [31] Art. 4(1).   [32] Art. 3(3).
[33] Art. 4(2).   [34] Art. 2(2).

to multinational corporations, the duties of international institutions, especially international economic institutions, and of states as members of those institutions, also assume a special salience. Analysing the work of the International Monetary Fund, the World Bank and the World Trade Organization, however, she shows that these duties have yet to be registered fully, or even in some contexts at all. While the right to development has a central place in the agenda of the United Nations, Orford's assessment is that it has had little impact on the work of the institutions mostly closely linked to the international economic system.[35]

To some analysts this is not a cause for disquiet, but for relief. Certainly, the emergence of the right to development has by no means been universally welcomed, and from one perspective, it is an unhelpful, even dangerous, departure, best pulled back. We have mentioned the invocation of the right to development in connection with efforts to justify repression. We have also alluded to the way it has been used to deflect attention from the responsibility of the governments of poor countries for improving conditions within their own countries, or alternatively to deter concentration on the obligations of governments of richer states with respect to development elsewhere. Another concern is that the right to development risks submerging long established human rights protections in a right of which the basic features remain indistinct, or at any rate contested. In Yash Ghai's words, the 'fortunes of the disadvantaged are better served by the claims to specific rights like food, shelter, and literacy than an amorphous portmanteau right...'.[36] This is especially the case given that it seems hard to imagine the right ever being enforced through national courts. Viewed from this angle, the right to development politicises issues which could otherwise be approached on more objective, formal and legal terms.

On the other hand, a further concern is that the right to development precisely depoliticises issues which should rather be recognised as inescapably political struggles over public projects, resource allocations and social arrangements. Here the worry is that the right engages officials, activists and scholars in endless debates about right-holders, duty-bearers,

[35] A. Orford, 'Globalization and the Right to Development' in P. Alston (ed.), *Peoples' Rights* (Oxford: Oxford University Press, 2001), 127, *passim*.

[36] Y. Ghai, *Whose Human Right to Development?*, Commonwealth Secretariat Series of Occasional Papers on the Right to Development (London: Commonwealth Secretariat, 1989), 15.

enforcement mechanisms and other formal and procedural questions, diverting attention from the policy choices being made. In this way, it demobilises those who have reason to contest these choices. It also takes up too much imaginative space, and thus debilitates our capacity for envisioning and formulating alternative frameworks. Let us mention one final concern. This is an anxiety that the right to development may entrench a concept—development—which is itself a key part of the problem. We highlighted earlier some of the challenges to which the concept of development has given rise, as well as some of the reorientations initiated to meet those challenges. The concern is that, even after so many reorientations, little has really changed. An evolutionary model continues to hold sway; deficiency endures as the defining characteristic of 'developing' societies; and economic growth remains the overriding concern, with distributive considerations coming well behind.

While there may be answers to some of these points, not all the misgivings can be fully allayed. From this it does not follow, however, that the right to development should be dismissed. For if the right to development has important limitations, it also has the potential to make valuable contributions. As in the case of rights-based approaches to development, it strengthens in some respects the basis for advocacy and resistance, moving claims from the domain of welfare and voluntary assistance to that of entitlement and obligation. In this regard, it also fosters a presumption of responsibility, and prompts consideration of the detailed implications of the responsibilities of particular actors in particular contexts. As a synthetic right, the right to development helps to bring out the links between different human rights and the need for an integrated or, as it is sometimes termed, 'holistic' approach to respect for human rights. As Arjun Sengupta explains, the right to development is not 'merely the sum total' of existing human rights. That is to say, it is not merely a call for 'the realization of those rights individually, but [for] the realization of them together in a manner that takes into account their effects on each other, both at a particular time and over a period of time'.[37] With its emphasis on participation, the right to development helps to ensure that consideration of these effects in turn takes into account the diverse perspectives of those affected. The right to development also highlights

[37] Third report of the independent expert on the right to development, Arjun Sengupta. UN Doc. E/CN.4/2001/WG.18/2, 2 January 2001, para. 11.

the need for a holistic and structural approach to human rights *abuse*. By directing our attention to economic and social issues, it helps us to see what is making abuse possible. Finally, the right to development encourages us to attend to the interconnectedness of life in the contemporary world, the ways in which social conditions in different places (within countries and across them) are linked in patterns of exploitation and co-operation, interdependence and dependency. It thus heightens perceptions of the global dimensions of the struggle to ensure respect for human rights, enriching understanding not only of the problems confronted, but also of the solidarities that might be mobilised for change.

Disability

Until recent years the implications of disability for human rights went very largely unaddressed. International human rights law proceeded for the most part on the twofold assumption that everyone has more or less the same capacities, and that what those capacities make possible is self-sufficiency in adult life. Yet self-sufficiency is very much a relative and variably distributed state. It is more available to some of us than to others. And it is more available to all of us during some periods of our lives than during others. Indeed, as Martha Nussbaum suggests, the relatively high levels of self-sufficiency experienced by people without functional limitations at certain stages of their lives may well be the *exception* rather than the norm, a brief and highly precarious phase between other times in which needs are greater and independence is more elusive. Whether or not that is right, what is clear is that 'the way we think about the needs of [people] with disabilities is not a special department of life, easily cordoned off from the "average case" '.[1] Rather, it belongs at the very centre of our ideas about the nature of human existence and the principles of associative life. It goes to the very core of our concerns about justice, and about the effective enjoyment of human rights. As Nussbaum also observes, even if the way we think about disability *were* a special department of life, it could not be left at the margins of our concerns about justice and human rights. For everyone has the right to self-respect and to the chance to develop and shape their world, and the particular barriers faced by people with disabilities are something that 'a just society ought to address'.[2]

---

[1] M. Nussbaum, 'Disabled Lives: Who Cares?' *New York Review of Books*, 11 January 2001, 34. [2] Ibid., 36.

Outlined below are some of the ways in which international human rights law is beginning to reflect these points.[3] Reference to disability appears only once in the foundational instruments of human rights, in connection with the right to social security.[4] While some other aspects are taken up in later treaties,[5] the sole treaty addressed to the phemonenon of disability discrimination as a whole is a regional convention concluded under the auspices of the Organization of American States.[6] Steps to draft a universal convention on the rights of people with disabilities are currently underway within the framework of the United Nations.[7] In a number of resolutions the UN General Assembly and other international agencies have used existing instruments and principles of human rights law as a basis for the articulation of standards in this field. The most significant of these resolutions are the UN Declaration on the Rights of Disabled Persons,[8] the World Programme of Action Concerning Disabled Persons,[9] and the UN Standard Rules on the Equalization of Opportunities for Persons with Disabilities.[10] There also exist statements by international human rights treaty bodies on the ramifications of treaty rights and obligations in the specific circumstances of disability. The most detailed of these relates to the International Covenant on Economic, Social and Cultural Rights.[11] Finally,

---

[3] See further T. Degener & Y. Koster-Dreese (eds.), *Human Rights and Disabled Persons* (Dordrecht: Nijhoff, 1995); S. Yee & M.L. Breslin (eds.), *Disability Rights Law and Policy: International and National Perspectives* (New York: Transnational, 2002); S.S. Herr, L. Gostin, & H.H. Koh (eds.), *The Human Rights of Persons with Intellectual Disabilities: Different But Equal* (Oxford: Oxford University Press, 2003); and G. Quinn & T. Degener, *The Current Use and Future Potential of United Nations Human Rights Instruments in the Context of Disability* (HR/PUB/02/1) (Geneva and New York: United Nations, 2002). See also Compilation of International Norms And Standards Relating To Disability, available at www.un.org/esa/socdev/enable/discom00.htm.

[4] See Universal Declaration of Human Rights, art. 25.

[5] See, e.g., Convention Concerning Vocational Rehabilitation and Employment (Disabled Persons) (ILO No. 159).

[6] Inter-American Convention on the Elimination of All Forms of Discrimination against Persons with Disabilities, adopted 6 July 1999.

[7] See Draft Comprehensive and Integral International Convention on the Protection and Promotion of the Rights and Dignity of Persons with Disabilities, UN Doc. A/AC.265/2004/WG.1, 27.

[8] UN GA Res. 3447 (XXX), adopted 9 December 1975.

[9] UN GA Res. 37/52, adopted 3 December 1982.

[10] UN GA Res. 48/96, adopted 20 December 1993.

[11] See Committee on Economic, Social and Cultural Rights, General Comment 5 (Persons with disabilities), 9 December 1994; see also Committee on the Elimination of All Forms of Discrimination against Women, General Recommendation 18 (Disabled women), 4 January 1991.

disability-related concerns have been brought before the European Court
of Human Rights, and have received attention within the European Union
legal order. To what extent, then, have the human rights of people with
disabilities been recognised and protected through these various developments? In considering this question, we must begin by noting something of
what is signified by the term 'disability'.

Disability and handicap

Conceptualisations of disability and of the related notion of handicap
have changed in recent decades. In earlier approaches, understandings of
disability were oriented to a medical or diagnostic model, in which the
focus was on the physical or intellectual limitations of individuals and
on their therapeutic and other needs. The impact of such an understanding is still evident in the 1975 UN Declaration on the Rights of
Disabled Persons.[12] As critics have pointed out, the problem with this
way of conceptualising disability is that it presupposes, or at any rate
signals, that the obstacles encountered by people with disabilities are
entirely a function of their own physical or other limitations. But that is
not at all the case. Those obstacles are also, and often in larger part, a
function of the social environment in which the individuals concerned
live. It follows that a more adequate approach to disability must start
from awareness that the issues raised are not just personal but also systemic, and not purely therapeutic but also political and cultural. In this
regard, it helps to think in terms of people 'with disabilities', rather than
'disabled' or 'handicapped' people, inasmuch as those latter formulations
make it seem as if a disability or handicap wholly defines or determines
a person's existence and circumstances. The focus can then shift from an
exclusive preoccupation with the limitations of individuals to a concern
as well with the shortcomings of societies.

   This approach is reflected in the 1982 World Programme of Action
Concerning Disabled Persons, the 1993 Standard Rules on the
Equalization of Opportunities for Persons with Disabilities and subsequent
instruments. According to the Standard Rules, the term 'disability'
encompasses a wide variety of functional limitations linked to physical,

---

[12] See, e.g., art. 1.

intellectual or sensory impairment, medical conditions or mental illness, whether permanent or transitory. 'Handicap', for its part, is said to refer to the loss or limitation of opportunities to take part in the life of the community on an equal level with others. Handicap is thus a function of the 'encounter between the person with a disability and the environment'. It directs attention to 'the shortcomings in the environment and in many organised activities in society, for example, information, communication and education, which prevent persons with disabilities from participating on equal terms'.[13]

As acknowledged in the Standard Rules, these characterisations are still not fully satisfactory, in that they fail to clarify the interaction between societal conditions and the abilities of individuals. One difficulty in this regard is that conditions affecting abilities vary greatly between and within societies. At the same time, they vary greatly with respect to different kinds and degrees of functional limitation. In both these senses, as the World Programme of Action recalls, people with disabilities are by no means a 'homogeneous group',[14] and it is important that the concept of disability not be used to make them seem so. To note this is to highlight the complexity of any enquiry into the role of social factors in the constitution of abilities, but not to diminish the need for that enquiry. Nor is it to diminish the significance of that enquiry for public policy. As disability activists have shown, so long as disability is approached as a matter of individual deficiencies, all that will seem to be required is treatment and adaptation. Once it is understood to implicate also government, law, business, and culture, however, it becomes clear that only much more far-reaching change will suffice.

Disability and human rights

In the World Programme of Action three strategies are proposed as the basis for policy and action concerning disability. First, prevention; that is say, measures to reduce both the occurrence of impairments and the extent to which impairments become causes of functional limitation. Secondly, rehabilitation, in the shape of resources (technical aids, training, etc.) for

[13] UN GA Res. 48/96, adopted 20 December 1993, para. 18. This draws on the approach adopted by the World Health Organization.
[14] UN GA Res. 37/52, adopted 3 December 1982, para. 8.

enabling people with disabilities to achieve their optimal level of physical and other functionality. And finally, the equalisation of opportunities, an aspect given particular emphasis in the later Standard Rules and defined there as 'the process through which the various systems of society and the environment, such as services, activities, information and documentation, are made available' on an equal basis to all, including people with disabilities.[15] If, as indicated earlier, the only reference to disability in the foundational instruments of international human rights law concerns the right to social security, this tripartite programme suggests a very different assessment of the relation between disability and human rights.

On the one hand, it becomes evident as soon as we begin thinking about a strategy of prevention that functional limitations are often themselves the result of human rights abuse. Violations of rights with respect to the provision of health care, food and water, safe conditions of work, and education are frequently involved. Since the vast majority of people with disabilities live in poor countries, a strategy of prevention is inseparable from the eradication of poverty-related diseases, hunger, and sweatshop working practices, and from the co-operation of aid agencies and international business in that regard. In a substantial proportion of cases, functional limitations are linked as well to injuries, psychological trauma, and brutality experienced during armed conflict or civil strife. To this extent, violations may be involved of rights under international humanitarian law, and of the right not to be subjected to torture. A strategy of prevention is thus also inseparable from moves with respect to the control of weapons, the protection of civilians and others in war, and the implementation of safeguards against ill-treatment in detention.

On the other hand, the strategies of rehabilitation and equalisation of opportunities prompt us to reflect on the ways in which functional limitations may be a basis for the denial of human rights. While rehabilitation takes up a long-standing goal of disability policy, equalisation of opportunities orients efforts towards the inclusion of people with disabilities in all aspects of social life. With the strategy of equalisation of opportunities, the democratic principle of equal citizenship assumes fresh significance in relation to disability. But so too does the legal

[15] UN GA Res. 48/96, adopted 20 December 1993, para. 24.

requirement of non-discrimination in the protection of human rights (to which we shall return presently). Questions are raised about the compatibility of subsisting arrangements not just with the right of people with disabilities to social security, but with the non-discriminatory guarantee of the entirety of their human rights—from their rights with respect to education, work and housing, to their rights with respect to privacy, liberty and political representation.

This perspective belongs with the shift away from a medical or diagnostic model of disability. In that model, people with disabilities appear primarily as users of social services, recipients of care, and/or objects of charity. It seems to be their challenge to overcome the limitations of their condition, and adapt as best they can to the world around them. In the approach proposed in the World Programme of Action and subsequent instruments, by contrast, the necessity is also acknowledged for the world to adapt to disability. Steps to meet the needs of individuals with disabilities are seen as inadequate unless linked to moves to modify the social practices and institutions that turn disability into disadvantage. The relationship between people with disabilities and those without them is grasped as a relationship of subordination on the one side and domination on the other, no more natural, immutable or unavoidable than any other structured asymmetry of power. Informing this approach is a recognition that, more than merely users of social services, recipients of care, and/or objects of charity, people with disabilities are, of course, citizens, social agents, and bearers of human rights.

Disability discrimination

Let us now review in a more specific way those aspects of the human rights of people with disabilities which have received particular attention within the framework of international human rights law. A valuable source in this regard is General Comment 5 of the Committee on Economic, Social and Cultural Rights, in which the Committee presents an analysis of the rights of people with disabilities, and the correlative obligations of states parties, under the International Covenant on Economic, Social and Cultural Rights. Since the Covenant to a degree parallels certain articles of the Universal Declaration of Human Rights, and since most states of the world are in any case parties to the Covenant, General Comment 5 has wide-ranging salience.

An initial issue concerns the lack of explicit reference to disability in the Covenant's non-discrimination guarantee. As the Committee emphasises, this does not mean that disability-based discrimination is not covered, but simply that the need to address it specifically was not recognised at the time the Covenant was drafted. Under article 2(2) of the Covenant, the rights enunciated must be exercisable 'without discrimination of any kind' on certain enumerated grounds or 'other status'. While disability is not one of the enumerated grounds, the Committee notes that it is clearly covered as an 'other status'. Thus, the rights recognised in the Covenant must be protected without discrimination on grounds of disability. There is no doubt that disability-based discrimination is likewise prohibited under other human rights treaties, whether (as in the case of some more recent treaties) they explicitly declare disability a ground of prohibited discrimination[16] or (like the Covenant) they do not.[17] The Committee observes that discrimination against people with disabilities takes a wide variety of forms. While some of these involve *de jure* discrimination, many of the most significant involve *de facto* discrimination, achieved through the imposition of material, social and cultural barriers. With this in mind, the Committee defines disability-based discrimination as 'any distinction, exclusion, restriction or preference, or denial of reasonable accommodation based on disability which has the effect of nullifying or impairing the recognition, enjoyment or exercise' of rights.[18]

The concept of 'reasonable accommodation' evoked in this definition is linked to the strategy of equalisation of opportunities mentioned earlier. It has been used to refer to measures needed to eliminate environmental obstacles to participation in social life by people with disabilities. In this connection, the Committee highlights the obligation placed on states

[16] See Convention on the Rights of the Child, art. 23; African Charter on Human and Peoples' Rights, art. 18(4); San Salvador Protocol to the American Convention on Human Rights, art. 18; and Revised European Social Charter, art. 15. See also EU Charter of Fundamental Rights, art. 21.

[17] See, e.g., Explanatory Memorandum to Protocol 12 to the European Convention on Human Rights, para. 20.

[18] Committee on Economic, Social and Cultural Rights, General Comment 5 (Persons with disabilities), 9 December 1994, para. 15.

parties to the Covenant to promote the progressive realisation of the rights recognised, and observes that this obligation includes a 'positive' dimension. That is to say, governments do not fulfil their commitments simply by abstaining from action which might cause discrimination or otherwise adversely affect persons with disabilities. What is required 'in the case of such a vulnerable and disadvantaged group is to take positive action to reduce structural disadvantages and to give appropriate preferential treatment to people with disabilities in order to achieve the objectives of full participation and equality within society for all persons with disabilities'. And '[t]his almost invariably means that additional resources will need to be made available for this purpose and that a wide range of specially tailored measures will be required'.[19] The Committee notes that 'international cooperation [as contemplated in articles 22 and 23 of the Covenant] is likely to be a particularly important element in enabling some developing countries to fulfil their obligations under the Covenant' with respect to people with disabilities.[20]

What kinds of positive action are required? One of the fields in which the effects of disability discrimination have been particularly severe is employment. The Committee observes that the right, recognised in article 6(1) of the Covenant, to the opportunity to gain one's living by work which one freely chooses or accepts is not realised where the only practical option for workers with disabilities is employment in 'sheltered' facilities offering sub-standard conditions. Likewise, this right may be violated where those with certain kinds of disability are effectively confined to work in certain spheres. As emphasised in the World Programme of Action and the Standard Rules, people with disabilities must have equal opportunities with others for productive and gainful employment. This calls for action to modify the physical environment of workplaces, means of transportation, and communications systems, so as to enhance their accessibility to people with disabilities of various kinds. It also calls for the introduction of specialised training schemes and more flexible working practices. Whether people with disabilities work in 'sheltered' facilities or on the open market, the right to the enjoyment of just and favourable conditions of work (protected in article 7 of the Covenant) is a further key concern. The Committee observes that poor labour standards and exploitative rates of pay are no more

[19] Ibid., para. 9.   [20] Ibid., para. 13.

consistent with this right in the case of workers with disabilities than they are in the case of other workers.[21] Within the European Union legal order, work-related discrimination is the subject of a Directive which requires the introduction of national law to prohibit discrimination in employment and occupation on a variety of grounds, including disability.[22] The Directive refers explicitly to the need for 'effective and practical measures to adapt the workplace to the disability, for example adapting premises and equipment, patterns of working time, the distribution of tasks or the provision of training or integration resources'.[23]

Another field in which the effects of disability discrimination have been acute is education. In considering the right to education, addressed in articles 13 and 14 of the Covenant, the Committee indicates that the Covenant should be approached in the light of the Standard Rules.[24] According to that instrument, the guiding principle is equality of educational opportunities within integrated settings.[25] To implement this principle, teachers must be trained, assistant services provided, and modifications to buildings made, so that children with disabilities can be educated, where possible, in regular schools. Insofar as special education remains the most appropriate option, resources must be deployed to ensure that standards are not lower than in the mainstream education system. Alongside these comments regarding rights in the spheres of work and education, the Committee highlights the significance in the context of disability of other rights protected in the Covenant. Among these are rights with respect to housing and to participation in cultural life, two further fields in which disability discrimination is endemic.

But then, as noted earlier, it is not only the non-discriminatory guarantee of economic, social and cultural rights that should concern us. It is also the non-discriminatory guarantee of civil and political rights.

[21] These and other work-related rights of people with disabilities are also spelled out in some detail in instruments adopted within the framework of the International Labour Organization. Among these is the Convention Concerning Vocational Rehabilitation and Employment (Disabled Persons) (ILO No. 159).

[22] EC Council Directive 2000/78/EC, adopted 27 November 2000, OJ 303/16. 2 December 2000, recital 20. Regarding the deadline for implementing the Directive where disability discrimination is concerned, see art. 18.   [23] Ibid., recital 20.

[24] See also Salamanca Statement on Principles, Policy and Practice in Special Needs Education and Framework of Action, UNESCO, 10 June 1994.

[25] UN GA Res. 48/96, adopted 20 December 1993. See Annex, Rule 6.

Disability activists have pointed out that disability-based discrimination in relation to the latter has received relatively little attention. To this extent, the impact of the medical or diagnostic model of disability, in which rehabilitation eclipses citizenship, may endure. Some aspects of civil rights have, however, been addressed. The main normative framework for this has been the European Convention on Human Rights, though it may be that the jurisprudence of the European Court of Human Rights in this respect also provides a guide to the significance of corresponding norms under other regional and international treaties.

In the first place, the European Court has considered the compatibility of procedures for the confinement of mentally ill persons with the latter's right to personal liberty and security, protected in article 5 of the European Convention. It is, of course, recognised that the compulsory admission to psychiatric hospitals of individuals who are mentally ill is at times necessary.[26] However, since this amounts to an interference with personal liberty, the right to liberty and security requires that certain safeguards be implemented and respected. In particular, the confinement must be 'in accordance with a procedure prescribed by law', as well as 'lawful'. The European Court has affirmed that these stipulations demand, first, that appropriate national law must exist governing compulsory admission, and that that law must be followed. Appropriate law for this purpose is law which is both publicly accessible and sufficiently precise, so that it is reasonably foreseeable in its application, whatever its specific character and status within the national legal order. Secondly, the stipulations demand that decisions to confine a person not be arbitrary. In an important early decision, the European Court said that by this is meant that it must be reliably shown by objective medical evidence that the person concerned is mentally ill (or of 'unsound mind' in the language of the Convention); the illness must be of a kind or degree warranting compulsory admission; and this must remain the case throughout the period of admission.[27]

Other aspects of the rights of people with disabilities which have been considered by the European Court of Human Rights relate to

[26] European Convention on Human Rights, art. 5(1)(e).
[27] *Winterwerp v Netherlands*, Judgment of the European Court of Human Rights, 24 October 1979.

social amenities and prison conditions. One case concerned the lack of provision for wheelchair access to a paying beach.[28] The applicant complained that this violated his right to respect for private life under article 8 of the Convention. While the Court acknowledged that article 8 may entail not just negative duties on the part of the state to refrain from interference with private life, but also positive duties to ensure respect for private life in commercial and other non-state relations, it did not consider that any such obligation had been breached in this case. By contrast, the Convention was found to have been violated in a later case concerning prison conditions.[29] Here the applicant, who had severe disabilities, was sentenced to a term of imprisonment following conviction for a criminal offence. The cell in which she was held was entirely unsuitable, and exposed her to health risks, as well as preventing her from washing or going to the toilet without the greatest difficulty. The European Court upheld her complaint that this violated her right not to be subjected to degrading treatment, protected in article 3 of the Convention. Where a court sentences a person with disabilities to a term of imprisonment without ensuring that the prison to which the person will be committed has facilities that are adequate to meet his or her needs, the Court confirmed this may amount to a violation of the prohibition on inhuman or degrading treatment.[30] In the circumstances of this case, the Court accepted that there had been no intention to humiliate or debase the applicant. Nonetheless, this had been the effect of the sentencing court's action.

In December 2001 the UN General Assembly established a committee to consider the drafting of a new treaty that would address the human rights of people with disabilities in a more comprehensive way than is possible under the European Convention, Economic, Social and Cultural Rights Covenant, or other existing treaties.[31] The committee held its first session in August 2002. Among the issues that have come into focus in its deliberations is the question of the relation between development aid or other forms of international assistance and the promotion and protection of the human rights of people with disabilities. Already

[28] *Botta v Italy*, Judgment of the European Court of Human Rights, 24 February 1998.
[29] *Price v United Kingdom*, Judgment of the European Court of Human Rights, 10 July 2001.   [30] Ibid.
[31] See UN GA Res. 56/168, adopted 19 December 2001.

in 1999, a regional treaty with the similar aim of addressing disability discrimination in a comprehensive manner was adopted within the framework of the Organization of American States. The Inter-American Convention on the Elimination of All Forms of Discrimination against Persons with Disabilities is concerned, as its name proclaims, not just with discrimination in relation to particular rights or particular contexts, but with all forms of discrimination against persons with disabilities. The primary obligation imposed on states parties is to 'adopt the legislative, social, educational, labor-related, or any other measures needed to eliminate discrimination against persons with disabilities and to promote their full integration into society'.[32] For this purpose, discrimination is defined along similar lines to those proposed in General Comment 5 of the Committee on Social, Economic and Cultural Rights. It is said to refer to 'any distinction, exclusion, or restriction based on a disability [and related circumstances], which has the effect or objective of impairing or nullifying the recognition, enjoyment, or exercise by a person with a disability of his or her human rights and fundamental freedoms'.[33] Affirmative action is specifically authorised. Among the measures envisaged in the Convention are measures affecting the operations of both government authorities and private entities in relation to employment, transportation, communications, housing, recreation, education, sports, law enforcement and administration of justice, and political and regulatory activities. Specific mention is also made of the need to ensure that new buildings and other facilities and systems facilitate access by persons with disabilities and of the need to eliminate, to the extent possible, existing barriers to accessibility.[34]

We have so far been reviewing the issue of disability discrimination in a rather abstract and one-dimensional way, as if it were a discrete and clearly defined phenomenon. In reality, of course, things are not so simple. Particular individuals often face discrimination on a plurality of grounds (including also sex, class, ethnicity, religion, immigration status, etc.),

---

[32] Art. III(1).   [33] Art. I(2)(a).

[34] Another feature of the Convention is that it establishes a specialised body for the supervision of state obligations with respect to the rights of people with disabilities. See article VI.

intensifying their vulnerability to the effects of discrimination on grounds of disability. Moreover, the specific forms of disability-based discrimination vary, depending on an individual's position within the social structure. This question of the ways in which disability discrimination interacts with, and is mediated by, other factors has received little sustained attention, though it is highlighted in a number of documents. For example, the particular concerns of women with disabilities are mentioned in General Comment 5 of the Committee on Economic, Social and Cultural Rights, as well as in a General Recommendation adopted in connection with the UN Convention on the Elimination of All Forms of Discrimination against Women.[35]

We opened this discussion by recalling that international human rights law must not assume self-sufficiency. But it can help to enhance it. In the context of disability, enhanced self-sufficiency means greater control by people with disabilities over their lives—the right to receive the services they need, to take part in the decision-making processes that affect them, and to benefit from the goods and opportunities on offer in the societies to which they belong. 'Independent living' is an expression that is sometimes used to capture this, and it is now widely acknowledged that, contrary to earlier assumptions, the obstacles to independent living by people with disabilities are rarely insuperable, and often more material, cultural and political than physiological. These points have far-reaching implications for human rights, which are beginning to be spelled out. In relation to social, economic and cultural rights, the need has been highlighted for positive action on a wide variety of fronts in order to realise the rights of people with disabilities. Some of the ways in which practices and institutions violate the civil and political rights of people with disabilities have likewise been acknowledged. In connection with the Inter-American human rights system, a treaty has been adopted on the elimination of disability-based discrimination. Finally, within the framework of the United Nations, the process has been set in train of elaborating a universal treaty on the rights of people with disabilities. These are significant initiatives. Yet they

---

[35] See Committee on Economic, Social and Cultural Rights, General Comment 5 (Persons with disabilities), 9 December 1994; see also Committee on the Elimination of All Forms of Discrimination against Women, General Recommendation 18 (Disabled women), 4 January 1991.

remain a relatively limited and partial response to the implications of disability for human rights. If international human rights law is to become an effective tool in efforts to ensure independent living on the part of people with disabilities and redress their social inequality, a much more systematic approach is likely to be needed than has emerged to date.

Disappearance

In his book *Homo Sacer* Giorgio Agamben describes a condition which he refers to as 'bare life'.[1] This is a complicated concept, but one aspect of it points to a situation in which the significance or worth of a person ceases to be recognised, and that person becomes exposed to death, in the sense that he or she can be killed without consequences. According to Agamben, this situation arises from a particular kind of interaction between two other forms of life: on the one hand, 'natural life' or 'the simple fact of living' (which he associates with the ancient Greek concept *zoe*); on the other, 'political life' or 'the form of the life of a political community' (which he associates with the ancient Greek concept *bios*). Bare life, in his account, arises when political life (*bios*) envelops natural life (*zoe*), only to abandon it, banishing those concerned to a threshold world between life and death. As an example of this predicament, Agamben discusses the Nazi concentration camps. Entry into a camp, he writes, 'meant the definitive exclusion from the political community'.[2] Because those detained 'were lacking almost all the rights and expectations that we customarily attribute to human existence', they came to be situated 'in a limit zone between life and death, inside and outside, in which they were no longer anything but bare life'. Once in this limit zone, Agamben observes, 'the human body is separated from its normal political status and abandoned, in a state of exception, to the most extreme misfortunes'.

Agamben wants us to see the Nazi concentration camps not as aberrations or anomalies, but rather as vivid illustrations of a distinctively modern form of sovereign power—'biopolitical' power—which he characterises in terms of the capacity to produce bare life. If this is right, it invites us to reconsider the marginality of a range of other phenomena

---

[1] G. Agamben (D. Heller-Roazen, trans.), *Homo Sacer* (Stanford: Stanford University Press, 1998). [2] Ibid., 159.

which have tended likewise to be viewed as aberrations or anomalies. Among these is the phenomenon known today as 'enforced or involuntary disappearance'. For this too involves separation from one's normal political status and abandonment to an exceptional regime entailing exposure to extreme misfortunes. Practices of disappearance vary, and range from regimes in which few victims survive to procedures of unacknowledged detention in which deaths are rare and most victims are released with only limited delay. In all cases, however, a common feature is the victims' intense vulnerability while in custody, and their exposure to the infliction of harm without consequences for the perpetrators. Agamben notes that the standard response to what he terms bare life is to call for the reassertion of rights. Yet if sovereignty is bound up with the production of bare life, then so too is law. It follows, in his assessment, that the reassertion of rights is insufficient unless accompanied by efforts to investigate the ways in which law may have helped to make possible the deprivation of rights in the first place. This is an important observation, to which we will return towards the end of this discussion. But first let us take stock of the phenomenon of enforced or involuntary disappearance, and review its engagement with rights from the perspective of international human rights law.

Enforced disappearance

'Enforced disappearance' is a translation of the Spanish phrase *desaparición forzada*, coined in the 1960s to refer to systematic practices of abduction and secret detention used initially in Guatemala, and later elsewhere in Latin America. As explained by a US diplomat, what was involved was unacknowledged detention, usually including torture and eventual killing 'without any semblance of due process'.[3] Enforced disappearance assumed a central place in Chilean state policy after the *coup* in 1973, and was deployed on an unprecedented scale in Argentina after the *coup* there in 1976. In a major study of the Argentinian disappearances, Iain Guest describes how the officers' quarters at the Navy Mechanics School in the centre of Buenos Aires were turned into an 'elaborate concentration camp'.[4] At the gates of the School stood two naval cadets

[3] Claus Ruser, quoted in I. Guest, *Behind the Disappearances* (Philadelphia: University of Pennsylvania Press, 1990), 32.   [4] Ibid., 38.

with peaked hats and gleaming ornamental swords. Guest writes that they seemed to say to passing civilians: 'Look at us with respect and be grateful, ... because our job is to protect you'.[5] Inside the School, the basement of the officers' quarters was transformed into a series of torture rooms (an 'interrogation centre'), a 'hospital', and a photo laboratory; officials worked and lived on the ground, first and second floors; and detainees were kept in tiny cubicles on the third floor and in the loft. Operations were highly organised and constantly refined. 'It was as deliberate, methodical, and calculated as collecting tax.'[6]

Through the efforts of victims' relatives, the Inter-American Commission on Human Rights began to name and condemn the practice of enforced disappearance in 1974. Victims became known as 'disappeared persons', the verb 'to disappear' taking on a transitive sense in the context of events that were far from adventitious, but rather belonged to a well planned strategy of terror and repression. In 1979 the UN Commission on Human Rights requested the preparation of a report on the 'fate of missing and disappeared persons in Chile'. The eventual report contained information about the disappearance of at least 600 people,[7] and in the following year the UN Commission decided to establish a Working Group on Enforced or Involuntary Disappearances—the first of many later 'special procedures'—with a general mandate to investigate 'questions relevant to enforced or involuntary disappearances of persons'. Since 1980 the Working Group has documented some 50,000 cases of enforced disappearance, and continues to document more. If the early cases were mostly in Latin America, the more recent ones come from countries encompassing all regions of the world. Of course, the statistics of the Working Group cannot be assumed to tell the full story. Nonetheless, they begin to confirm that enforced disappearance is a phenomenon of global proportions.

Human rights protection

The right not to be subjected to enforced disappearance is not *as such* recognised in catalogues of internationally protected human rights.

---

[5] Ibid., 37.   [6] Ibid., 32.
[7] See UN Doc. A/34/583/Add. 1, 21 November 1979.

However, this right is entailed by a range of rights which are recognised, both in treaties and in general international human rights law. Among other potentially relevant rights, these include the right to personal liberty and security, the right to life, the right not to be subjected to torture and other ill-treatment, and the right to an effective remedy. Insofar as some treaties allow for modified application or 'derogation' to deal with the exigencies of a war or other national emergency, the right to life and the right not to be subjected to torture and other ill-treatment are excluded from this possibility of derogation.[8] To ensure that those rights remain fully protected, derogation may in practice likewise be impermissible with respect to procedural guarantees associated with the right to personal liberty and security and the right to an effective remedy.[9] Thus, enforced disappearance cannot be justified as an exceptional measure which is necessary to deal with the exigencies of an emergency situation. This is important, because that is precisely the claim which generally supports a policy of systematic disappearance, even if the official position of the government concerned is not attempted justification, but rather denial. The phenomenon of enforced disappearance almost invariably coexists with the assertion that extraordinary measures are needed in order to protect the population from terrorism and ensure national security in the face of subversion or insurgency. In some cases it coexists as well with the formal introduction of martial law or the declaration of a state of emergency or of siege.

Alongside these provisions of general human rights treaties and norms of general international human rights law, a number of specific instruments have been adopted on the subject of enforced disappearance since the latter became part of the human rights agenda in the 1970s.[10] In 1992 the UN General Assembly adopted the UN Declaration on the

[8] Derogation is permitted under the International Covenant on Civil and Political Rights, art. 4; European Convention on Human Rights, art. 15; Revised European Social Charter, art. F; American Convention on Human Rights, art. 27; Commonwealth of Independent States Convention on Human Rights and Fundamental Freedoms, art. 35; and Revised Arab Charter of Human Rights (not yet in force), art. 4.

[9] See UN Human Rights Committee, General Comment 29 (States of Emergency: art 4), 24 July 2001.

[10] See further R. Brody & F. González, '*Nunca Más*: An Analysis of International Instruments on Disappearances' 19 *Human Rights Quarterly* (1997) 365 and N.S. Rodley, *The Treatment of Prisoners under International Law*, 2nd edn. (Oxford: Oxford University Press, 1999), chap. 8.

Protection of All Persons from Enforced Disappearance. The Declaration reaffirms that enforced disappearance constitutes a composite violation of a number of human rights, including those mentioned above.[11] It also reaffirms that '[n]o circumstances whatsoever, whether a threat of war, a state of war, internal political instability or any other public emergency, may be invoked to justify enforced disappearances'.[12] There follow a series of provisions aimed at the prevention and investigation of enforced disappearance and the prosecution of those responsible. Among other things, the Declaration stipulates that enforced disappearance must be made a criminal offence under national law,[13] and that acts constituting enforced disappearance must be considered a continuing offence as long as the fate and whereabouts of the disappeared person remain concealed.[14] The Declaration further provides that those responsible for enforced disappearance may not benefit from amnesty or similar laws.[15] In 1994 a treaty was adopted to address the phenomenon of enforced disappearance within the framework of the Inter-American human rights system: the Inter-American Convention on the Forced Disappearance of Persons. For any state that becomes a party to it, the Convention gives binding force to many of the elements of the UN Declaration. At the same time, it also extends the UN Declaration in an important respect. States parties are obliged to establish jurisdiction to prosecute those responsible for acts of enforced disappearance, both in cases where the acts occurred within their territory or were undertaken by one of their nationals, and also in cases where neither of those connections exists but the alleged offender is present in their territory.[16] Where someone alleged to be responsible for an act of enforced disappearance is present in the territory of a state party, the obligation then arises either to extradite that person for prosecution elsewhere or, failing extradition, to investigate the case and, where appropriate, initiate criminal proceedings.[17] Thus, the Convention applies to enforced disappearance the 'extradite or prosecute' rule, applied in earlier treaties to torture and other phenomena. Discussions have for some years been underway within the United Nations regarding the possible adoption of an international instrument along similar lines to this Inter-American treaty.[18]

[11] Art. 1(2).   [12] Art. 7.   [13] Art. 4.   [14] Art. 17.   [15] Art. 18.
[16] Art. IV.   [17] Art. VI.
[18] See UN Doc. E/CN.4/2004/59, 23 February 2004.

In one of its preambular paragraphs, the Inter-American Convention on the Forced Disappearance of Persons asserts that 'the systematic practice of the forced disappearance of persons constitutes a crime against humanity'. This aspect is further elaborated in the Rome Statute of the International Criminal Court. Enforced disappearance is among those acts which are said to constitute a crime against humanity for the purpose of the Statute when 'committed as part of a widespread or systematic attack directed against any civilian population, with knowledge of the attack'.[19] We will return in a moment to the question of how enforced disappearance is defined in this context, but for the present it is worth highlighting that this provision has been glossed in terms which demand proof of a high level of knowledge and intention on the part of the perpetrator before culpability can be established.[20] Among other things, the perpetrator must have been aware that the arrest, detention or abduction would remain unacknowledged, or that information would be refused about the whereabouts or fate of the person concerned.[21] At the same time, he or she must have intended to remove that person from the protection of the law 'for a prolonged period of time'.[22] The general stipulation, associated with all crimes against humanity, that the crime must have been 'committed as part of a widespread or systematic attack directed against any civilian population, with knowledge of the attack', already narrows the range of cases covered, and the effect of these additional stipulations regarding the *mens rea* is to narrow that range still further. In consequence, only a relatively limited subset of cases of enforced disappearance are likely to count as crimes against humanity for the purpose of International Criminal Court jurisdiction.

By whom? Against whom?

Let us now review some aspects of the international legal framework for protection against enforced disappearance, as elaborated through the

---

[19] Art. 7(1)(i).

[20] See the 'Elements of Crimes', adopted by the Assembly of States Parties to the Rome Statute of the International Criminal Court, 3–10 September 2002, Official Records, ICC-ASP/1/3, Part II.B.

[21] Ibid., art. 7(1)(i), para. 3.

[22] Ibid., art. 7(1)(i), para. 6. See also the definition of enforced disappearance of persons in the Rome Statute, art. 7(2)(i).

instruments we have just mentioned, and as elucidated in decisions of human rights courts and supervisory bodies dealing with complaints brought by relatives of disappeared people. An initial issue concerns the definition of enforced disappearance. Common to all definitions is that enforced disappearance refers to the deprivation of a person's liberty, coupled with a refusal to acknowledge that deprivation of liberty or provide information about the person's whereabouts or fate. Beyond that, the question arises whether a state official must be involved. In the UN Declaration on the Protection of All Persons from Enforced Disappearance, enforced disappearance is stated to occur where:

persons are arrested, detained or abducted against their will or otherwise deprived of their liberty by officials of different branches or levels of Government, or by organized groups or private individuals acting on behalf of, or with the support, direct or indirect, consent or acquiescence of the Government, followed by a refusal to disclose the fate or whereabouts of the persons concerned or a refusal to acknowledge the deprivation of their liberty, which places such persons outside the protection of the law.[23]

A similar definition is given in the Inter-American Convention on the Forced Disappearance of Persons.[24] Under this definition enforced disappearance depends on state involvement, even if that involvement is confined to acquiescence. For the purpose of individual criminal liability, by contrast, the Rome Statute of the International Criminal Court characterises enforced disappearance as action carried out 'by, or with the authorization, support or acquiescence of, a State or a political organization'.[25] The reference to 'political organization', while somewhat opaque, makes clear that at least some, organised non-state actors will also be covered. In a report to the UN Commission on Human Rights, Manfred Nowak expresses the view that the approach taken in this respect in international criminal law should be carried over into international human rights law.[26] However, this remains controversial, and some consider that international human rights law should continue only to concern itself with enforced disappearance by or with the support or acquiescence of state officials.

A second issue concerns the evidence needed to establish state responsibility for enforced disappearance, and the precise nature of

[23] See third preambular paragraph.   [24] Art. II.   [25] Art. 7(2)(i).
[26] See UN Doc. E/CN.4/2002/71, 8 January 2002, para. 73.

that responsibility. In an important judgment rendered in 1988, the Inter-American Court of Human Rights confirmed that state responsibility arises under the American Convention on Human Rights notwithstanding that the concealment of facts means that there will generally be no direct evidence that a person was abducted and detained by agents of the state.[27] It is sufficient that the authorities have failed to respond adequately to allegations backed up by circumstantial or presumptive evidence. In this case, based on a complaint against Honduras, the Court was actually convinced that the disappearance had been carried out by agents acting under cover of public authority. But it said that, even if that had not been proven, the failure of the Honduran authorities to conduct any serious investigation into the disappearance constituted a failure to ensure the rights protected in the Convention, as required by article 1(1). This failure affected not only the right not to be arbitrarily detained, but also other rights. It affected the right not to be subjected to torture or other ill-treatment, both because prolonged incommunicado detention is itself cruel and inhuman treatment, and because the detention carried with it exposure to a regime in which torture was known to be carried out with impunity. And it also affected the right to life. Though the disappeared person's body had never been found, the circumstances were such that it could be presumed he had been executed without trial and his body concealed to prevent punishment. Enforced disappearance has been considered on a number of subsequent occasions by the Inter-American Court of Human Rights, and has also been the subject of decisions by other similar institutions, including the Human Rights Committee and the European Court of Human Rights. Approaches have varied with regard to the implications of the practice for protection of the right to life and the right not to be subjected to torture or other ill-treatment.[28] But one thing that has been consistently emphasised is the importance in this context of the duty to investigate, and the responsibility that is entailed for a state when it fails to discharge that duty.

A third issue, and the last we highlight here, concerns the question *whose* rights are violated where enforced disappearance occurs. In an

---

[27] *Velásquez Rodriguez v Honduras*, Judgment of the Inter-American Court of Human Rights, 29 July 1988.

[28] For an excellent overview, see the report to the Commission on Human Rights of Manfred Nowak, UN Doc. E/CN.4/2002/71, 8 January 2002. Regarding Nowak's assessment of these variable approaches, see further below.

early decision involving Uruguay, the Human Rights Committee made clear that not only the disappeared person but also his or her relatives may be considered victims of a violation of human rights.[29] In this case the Committee observed that a mother had 'the right to know what has happened to her [disappeared] daughter', and stated that, compounding the violations suffered by the daughter, the mother too was a victim of those same violations.[30] The Inter-American Court of Human Rights extended this principle in a later case concerning the disappearance of an American journalist in Guatemala.[31] For technical reasons having to do with the timing of Guatemala's recognition of the Court's jurisdiction, the Court did not deem itself competent to pronounce on violations of the disappeared person's rights. However, even in the absence of findings concerning his rights, the Court declared that the authorities' failure effectively to investigate the disappearance violated the rights of his relatives. In particular, it violated their right to a fair trial, which the Court took to include the right to have those responsible for the disappearance prosecuted and punished, and the right to receive compensation for the damages and injuries sustained. In a later case involving Peru, the Inter-American Court affirmed that, where amnesty or similar laws are promulgated, these too must be regarded as inconsistent with the rights of both disappeared persons and their relatives, inasmuch as they prevent allegations of enforced disappearance from being heard and acted upon.[32] Attention has likewise been focused on the rights of relatives by the European Court of Human Rights. Ruling on a complaint against Turkey in 1998, the Court found that the mother of a disappeared person—though not the disappeared person himself—was the victim of a violation of the right not to be subjected to torture or inhuman treatment.[33] For the Court, the mother's prolonged 'anguish of knowing that her son had been detained and that there is a complete absence of official information as to his subsequent fate' engaged the responsibility of the state in this

[29] *Quinteros Almeida v Uruguay*, Communication 107/1981, Views of the Human Rights Committee, adopted 21 July 1983.   [30] Ibid., para. 14.

[31] *Blake v Guatemala*, Judgment of the Inter-American Court of Human Rights, 24 January 1988.

[32] *Barrios Altos Case (Chumbipuma Aguirre et al v Peru)*, Judgment of the Inter-American Court of Human Rights, 14 March 2001.

[33] *Kurt v Turkey*, Judgment of the European Court of Human Rights, 25 May 1998.

respect.[34] Against the background of these interpretations, some commentators and human rights organisations have begun to speak of an evolving 'right to the truth' on the part of the families of persons subjected to enforced disappearance.

Disappearance and bare life

At the beginning of this discussion we referred to Giorgio Agamben's analysis of the condition of 'bare life'. In this final section we return to that analysis, to see how it may elucidate, or be elucidated by, a consideration of the human rights regime relating to enforced disappearance. Before doing so, however, it will be valuable briefly to revisit the general question of how enforced disappearance is best grasped or conceptualised as a phenomenon. What kind of account is most adequate for capturing the reality of this practice, and hence its *truth*, as experienced in particular contexts by particular people?

In most cases, disappeared people are killed. Perhaps then disappearance is best conceptualised as a form of extrajudicial execution, like other illegal killings by security forces or paramilitary groups, or like other deaths in custody due to torture or the use of force. Certainly, enforced disappearance overlaps with the phenomenon known in the language of the UN human rights system as 'extrajudicial, summary or arbitrary execution'.[35] Yet it is not reducible to that phenomenon. For one thing, most obviously, not all victims are killed. Enforced disappearance refers to the whole spectrum of situations in which people may be held in unacknowledged detention, including situations in which killings are rare. The point about enforced disappearance is not necessarily

[34] *Kurt v Turkey*, Judgment of the European Court of Human Rights, 25 May 1998. In a subsequent judgment, the Court emphasised that 'the *Kurt* case does not however establish any general principle that a family member of a "disappeared person" is thereby a victim of treatment contrary to article 3'. See *Tas v Turkey*, Judgment of the European Court of Human Rights, 14 November 2000.

[35] See especially the work of the UN Special Rapporteur on Extrajudicial, Summary or Arbitrary Executions. For an overview of this mandate and the issues see the reports of the Special Rapporteurs e.g., Report of Special Rapporteur Asma Jahangir, UN Doc. E/CN.4/2004/7, 22 December 2003. See also ECOSOC Resolution 1989/65, 24 May 1989 (annexing 'Principles on the Effective Prevention and Investigation of Extra-Legal, Arbitrary and Summary Executions').

that victims are killed, but that they are *exposed to the possibility* of being seriously harmed or ultimately killed. Secondly, and more importantly, to focus only on the disappeared person's killing is to risk obscuring the circumstances of secret detention that are an important part of the truth of what happened. It may also be to assume too readily that the person has in fact been killed, and reduce the pressure on the authorities to secure his or her release if still alive. Governments have often sought to deal with relatives' demands through legal mechanisms for entering verdicts of presumed death and similar procedures, but relatives have resisted this, in part because of the way it 'closes the file' on the disappeared person, but also because it fails to clarify what actually went on after he or she was taken away.

Perhaps then enforced disappearance is best conceptualised in a manner that focuses on the detention itself. Perhaps it is best understood as a particularly serious form of arbitrary detention. In his report to the UN Commission on Human Rights mentioned above, Manfred Nowak observes that this is indeed how some human rights bodies have viewed enforced disappearance.[36] Among those bodies is the European Court of Human Rights. In the 1998 case involving Turkey to which we referred earlier, the Court decided that an enforced disappearance violated the rights of the disappeared person to personal liberty and security and the rights of his mother not to be subjected to torture or inhuman treatment, but the Court did not consider that it was necessary to make a separate ruling on the consistency of the disappearance with the disappeared person's right to life, nor was it willing, in the absence of specific evidence of ill-treatment, to rule on allegations that the disappeared person's right not to be subjected to torture or inhuman treatment had been violated.[37] Yet, as Nowak argues, this approach too appears inadequate.[38] To treat enforced disappearance only as an 'aggravated form of arbitrary detention' is to miss the way it neutralises safeguards, with inherent consequences for protection of the right to life and the right not to be ill-treated, among other rights. As noted earlier, the Inter-American Court of Human Rights has recognised that every prolonged incommunicado detention constitutes inhuman treatment. Likewise, the Human Rights Committee declared in a case involving the

[36] See UN Doc. E/CN.4/2002/71, 8 January 2002, para. 76.
[37] *Kurt v Turkey*, Judgment of the European Court of Human Rights, 25 May 1998.
[38] Nowak, UN Doc. E/CN.4/2002/71, 8 January 2002, paras. 75–6.

Dominican Republic that 'the disappearance of persons is inseparably linked to treatment that amounts to a violation of article 7' of the Civil and Political Rights Covenant (protecting the right not to be subjected to torture or other ill-treatment).[39]

Thinking about enforced disappearance in terms of 'bare life' can help us to see that there is something distinctive about this form of repression which neither extrajudicial execution nor aggravated detention can capture. With enforced disappearance, victims are indeed abandoned to a limit zone between life and death, membership of a political community and loss of political status, just as Agamben describes. To use his terminology, the disappeared person's arrest—or kidnapping or abduction—marks the point of 'inclusive exclusion',[40] the point at which natural life (*zoe*) gets swallowed up by political life (*bios*), only to be spat out, cast out, and left exposed to the 'most extreme misfortunes'. Agamben's analysis also serves as a valuable reminder that it is not enough simply to condemn enforced disappearance and set about reasserting the rights of which victims have been deprived. 'Never again' is an important message, but it becomes an insufficient and dangerously complacent one when it is not accompanied by efforts to understand the ways in which political and legal arrangements may have enabled or facilitated the deprivation of rights in the first place. As Agamben writes in relation to the Nazi concentration camps,

The correct question to pose concerning the horrors committed in the camps is . . . not the hypocritical one of how crimes of such atrocity could be committed against human beings. It would be more honest and, above all, more useful to investigate carefully the juridical procedures and deployments of power by which human beings could be so completely deprived of their rights and prerogatives that no act committed against them could appear any longer as a crime, . . . [and that] everything [could] truly [have] become possible.[41]

On the other hand, if bare life entails that in the worst sense 'everything has truly become possible', the history of enforced disappearance confirms that *resistance* (even if limited and too often ultimately fruitless) also becomes possible, and that international human rights law can play a part in that resistance.

---

[39] *Mojica v Dominican Republic*, Communication 449/1991, Views of the Human Rights Committee, adopted 15 July 1994, para. 5.7.

[40] G. Agamben (D. Heller-Roazen, trans.), *Homo Sacer* (Stanford: Stanford University Press, 1998), 8.　　　　　　　　　　　　　　　　　　　　[41] Ibid., 171.

Education

In 1979 the band Pink Floyd recorded a song lamenting the conformism of the British education system and the oppressive, often brutal teaching methods that were used.[1] 'We don't need no education,' they sang. 'We don't need no thought control.' To them, the classroom was a place of 'dark sarcasm'. And as for pupils, they were 'just another brick in the wall'. So too each indignity was 'just another brick in the wall' that confined and divided their inner lives. Whatever has or has not changed since that time in British schools, Pink Floyd's theme captures an enduring aspect of educational practice. In Louis Althusser's expression, national systems of education are 'ideological state apparatuses'.[2] They are concerned with the inculcation of values and the transmission of cultural norms. They help to reinforce the status quo by teaching pupils to 'know their place' in society and in the world. They reward obedience, and provide lessons in accepting authority, respecting consensus, and postponing desires. They are crucial agents of social control.

But if education is an agent of social control, it is also, of course, an agent of empowerment. The empowering function of education is not a very attractive theme for anyone writing popular music, but it is the subject of a long-standing tradition in political thought,[3] and is also an important topic in writing about educational philosophy and development policy.[4] In a study for Oxfam, Kevin Watkins remarks that '[f]ew governments have prioritised democracy and empowerment in

---

[1] 'Another Brick in the Wall, Part 2' (R. Waters).

[2] L. Althusser, 'Ideology and Ideological State Apparatuses (Notes towards an Investigation)' (1969), in S. Žižek (ed.), *Mapping Ideology* (London: Verso, 1994), 100, esp. 118–20.

[3] See, e.g., Tom Paine, *The Rights of Man* in M. Foot & I. Kramnick (eds.), *The Thomas Paine Reader* (London: Penguin, 1987), 201.

[4] See, e.g., P. Freire (P. Freire & M. Bergman Ramos, trans.), *Pedagogy of the Oppressed* (London: Penguin, 1996).

developing their education systems'.[5] Nonetheless, educated people have a better chance than uneducated people of '[influencing] institutions, processes, and policies that affect their lives'.[6] The more limited a person's educational opportunities, the less likely it is that he or she will possess the skills needed to monitor government action and participate effectively in public life. Even where education systems are designed with oppressive intent, as in the case of colonial education systems and the Bantu education system that was created in connection with *apartheid* in South Africa, Watkins recalls that education has the potential to foster unplanned outcomes, in the shape of political mobilisation.[7] Althusser also observed that an ideological state apparatus is rarely a solid monolith. Generally, he wrote, 'the resistance of the exploited classes is able to find means and occasions to express itself' somehow within it.[8]

The benefits of education are especially apparent in poor countries. The point is not just that education provides the skills needed to encourage innovation and boost productivity, but also that it improves people's capacity to share in the benefits of economic growth. Education enhances opportunities to earn higher incomes, whether through trading activity or employment. It is also strongly correlated to better health status. In part this has to do with increased access to information, but in part it is likely also to be a function of the greater confidence and assertiveness in demanding services that comes with educational attainment. Women's education, in particular, is widely considered one of the most powerful determinants of public health and infant mortality. And if education is an important factor affecting poverty today, it is widely believed that the emergence of an increasingly 'knowledge-driven' global economy will mean that it becomes an even more important factor in the future. This has implications for the distribution of wealth between countries, as well as within them. The growing gap between 'education-rich' and 'education-poor' countries is being replicated at household level in a growing gap between skilled and unskilled people.[9]

[5] K. Watkins, *The Oxfam Education Report* (Oxford: Oxfam, 2000), 66. The discussion that follows of the interrelation between education, empowerment and poverty-reduction draws extensively from this study.   [6] Ibid., 17.

[7] Ibid., 67.

[8] L. Althusser, 'Ideology and Ideological State Apparatuses (Notes towards an Investigation)' (1969), in S. Žižek (ed.), *Mapping Ideology* (London: Verso, 1994), 100, 113.

[9] See R. Watkins, *The Oxfam Education Report* (Oxford: Oxfam, 2000), 61.

For all its conservatism or even repressiveness, then, education firmly belongs with our aspirations for democratic empowerment and poverty reduction. The extent to which particular educational arrangements can actually help in realising those aspirations depends, of course, on many things, but central among them are presumably decisions about budgets, priorities, and programmes—both at national level and in the context of international assistance. In what follows we examine the bearing on these decisions of the right to education, recognised in international human rights law.

A multiplier-right

The right to education is proclaimed in the 1948 Universal Declaration of Human Rights,[10] and reaffirmed in a number of specific declarations, such as the 1990 World Declaration on Education for All.[11] Among treaties, it is enunciated in the International Covenant on Economic, Social and Cultural Rights[12] and, with respect to children, in the Convention on the Rights of the Child.[13] It is also protected in regional treaties and other instruments, among them the African Charter of Human and Peoples' Rights,[14] the American Declaration of the Rights and Duties of Man,[15] the San Salvador Protocol to the American Convention on Human Rights,[16] and the First Protocol to the European Convention on Human Rights.[17] The particular issue of equal rights in education is taken up in a range of further treaties and other international instruments, including the Convention against Discrimination in Education, the Convention on the Elimination of All Forms of Racial Discrimination,[18] the Convention on the Elimination of All Forms of Discrimination against Women,[19] the 1981 UN Declaration on the Elimination of All Forms of Intolerance and of Discrimination Based on Religion or Belief,[20] and the 1992 UN Declaration on the Rights of Persons Belonging to National or Ethnic, Religious and Linguistic Minorities.[21] Action by the UN Special

---

[10] Art. 26.

[11] Adopted by the World Conference on Education For All, held at Jomtien (Thailand), March 1990. See UN GA Res. 37/178 of 17 December 1982.

[12] Arts. 13 and 14.   [13] Art. 28.   [14] Art. 17(1).   [15] Art. XII.

[16] Art. 13.   [17] Art. 2.   [18] Art. 5(e)(v).   [19] Art. 10.

[20] Art. 5(2).   [21] Art. 4(3) and (4).

Rapporteur on the Right to Education, Katarina Tomaševski, confirms that the right to education also takes effect outside the framework of these treaties, as a right under generally applicable international human rights law.

Before turning to consider what this right entails, it is worth pausing to note the way the right to education cuts across the familiar distinction between civil and political rights on the one hand and social, economic and cultural rights on the other. It can be invoked and analysed as a right that belongs to any of these categories, or to all at the same time. For this reason it is often taken to illustrate in particularly striking fashion the interconnectedness of the various categories of human rights. A related feature is the character of the right to education as—in Katarina Tomaševski's word—a 'multiplier' in relation to other human rights. In discussions about the implementation of this right, a central question is generally that of cost. Given the cost of providing education for all, how can the right to education be fully implemented? Instead, Tomaševski invites us to turn the question around, and consider the cost of denying education to some.[22] When we approach the issues from that perspective, it quickly becomes clear that the right to education, as well as having intrinsic value, has great instrumental significance in relation to the enjoyment of other human rights. This significance parallels the empowering functions we recalled earlier. Through education, the capacity to exercise rights and freedoms may be maximised; without it, that capacity may be virtually disabled. It is in this sense that Tomaševski proposes that the right to education operates as a multiplier. 'It enhances all other human rights when guaranteed and forecloses the enjoyment of most, if not all, when denied.'[23]

The right to education

Some people never attend school, or drop out before they learn to read and write. Others are able to remain at school, but receive education of only poor quality. Others still lack the chance to go to university, while their peers who are equally or less capable have that chance. Educational

---

[22] K. Tomaševski, *Education Denied* (London: Zed Books, 2003), 1.
[23] Ibid.

disadvantage may take an array of different forms. It may also be linked to an array of social divisions. Gender is especially significant in determining access to education in many countries and across the world as a whole. At the same time, gender-based disparities are accompanied, and mediated, by other exclusions. When does educational disadvantage become a violation of international human rights law? To return to Tomaševski's formulation, when can the right to education be considered guaranteed, and when should it be considered denied?

Scope

Although the main focus of advocacy and analysis tends to be basic education, we should begin by observing that the right to education encompasses the full range of levels of education, from primary to higher education. This is not to say, of course, that the same obligations are entailed with respect to all levels of education; human rights law plainly should not, and could not, treat all levels identically. It is simply to say that *some* obligations apply across the spectrum. Thus, under article 13 of the International Covenant on Economic, Social and Cultural Rights:

(a) Primary education shall be compulsory and available free to all;
(b) Secondary education . . . shall be made generally available and accessible to all by every appropriate means, and in particular by the progressive introduction of free education;
(c) Higher education shall be made equally accessible to all, on the basis of capacity, by every appropriate means, and in particular by the progressive introduction of free education;
(d) Fundamental education shall be encouraged and intensified as far as possible for those persons who have not received or completed the whole period of their primary education.[24]

The differentiated nature of the obligations associated with the right to education is very clear here. Primary education (at the least) must be compulsory and free, but the same does not apply to higher education. Equally, higher education may be restricted by reference to capacity, but primary and secondary education should be provided for everyone,

---

[24] International Covenant on Economic, Social and Cultural Rights, art. 13(2).

without any such restriction. These things said, the Committee on Economic, Social and Cultural Rights and the Special Rapporteur on the Right to Education have proposed that the right to education can nonetheless be understood in terms of certain general criteria, which apply in principle to all levels of education.[25] While the Committee is specifically concerned with the interpretation of the Covenant, the Special Rapporteur considers that these criteria may be used in determining the scope of the right to education under general international law and, where appropriate, under other treaties as well. The relevant criteria are expressed as availability, accessibility, acceptability and adaptability. Let us briefly review what each of these connotes in this context.[26]

By *availability* is meant that functioning educational institutions and programmes must be available in sufficient quantity. What is needed for schools to function will obviously depend on the particular circumstances, but in General Comment 13 dealing with article 13 of the Covenant the Committee highlights the need for 'protection from the elements, sanitation facilities for both sexes, safe drinking water, trained teachers receiving domestically competitive salaries, [and] teaching materials'.[27] The Special Rapporteur draws particular attention to the challenge of ensuring the availability of primary education in countries where a majority of primary school-age children live in dispersed rural communities, some of them nomadic. But, as she also emphasises, the availability of education is not just an issue with respect to primary education. It is also an issue with respect to secondary and higher education, and at the least requires that existing levels of provision within these categories not be eroded. Thus, in a complaint against Zaire decided in 1996 the African Commission on Human and Peoples' Rights found that the right to education had been violated when payments had not been

---

[25] Committee on Economic, Social and Cultural Rights, General Comment 13 (The right to education: art. 13), 8 December 1999, para. 6, and Preliminary Report of the Special Rapporteur on the Right to Education, Katarina Tomaševski, UN Doc. E/CN.4/1999/49, 13 January 1999, along with her subsequent reports, e.g., UN Doc. E/CN.4/2002/60, 7 January 2002.

[26] In addition to the sources cited in the previous footnote, see K. Tomaševski, *Human Rights Obligations: Making Education Available, Accessible, Acceptable and Adaptable* (Right To Education Primers No. 3) (2001), available at www.right-to-education.org.

[27] Para. 6(a).

made to lecturers and teachers, and universities and schools had had to be closed for two years.[28]

Accessibility refers to the idea that educational institutions and programmes must be accessible to everyone. The Committee explains accessibility in terms of three overlapping dimensions.[29] The first is non-discrimination in the provision of education. Access to education must be provided to all, especially the most vulnerable groups, in law and in fact. At the same time, measures must be taken to redress discrimination, including de facto discrimination, at all levels of education.[30] The second dimension concerns the elimination of geographical and physical barriers to education. Educational facilities must be located and designed so as to put them within safe reach of all (save in exceptional circumstances, and subject to the provision of appropriate alternative facilities, such as 'distance learning' programmes). The final dimension concerns the elimination of economic barriers to education. Education must be affordable to all. Under article 13 of the Covenant, primary education is required to be available free of charge, and states parties to the Covenant are required progressively to introduce free education at higher levels as well. This criterion of accessibility prompts many questions about educational arrangements and their social contexts. Among the most urgent is the question of how the obstacles may be overcome which deprive girls in many countries of the chance to attend or complete primary school.

Acceptability is concerned with the acceptability to students, and, in appropriate cases, parents, of what is taught and the way educational institutions are organised. Thus, the Committee stresses the need for teaching methods and school curricula to be 'relevant, culturally appropriate and of good quality'.[31] One important aspect of this concerns the language of instruction. It has long been recognised that minority communities have the right to establish at their own expense schools in which their own language is used, subject to those schools meeting

[28] *World Organisation Against Torture and others v Zaire* (Communication Nos. 25/89, 47/90, 56/91 and 100/93), Law Reports of the African Commission on Human and Peoples' Rights, Series A, Vol. 1, 25, para. 81.

[29] Committee on Economic, Social and Cultural Rights, General Comment 13 (The right to education: art. 13), 8 December 1999, para. 6(b).

[30] On the issue of redressing discrimination, see ibid., para. 37.

[31] Ibid., para. 6(c).

minimum educational standards set by the state.[32] However, the question has repeatedly been raised of whether the state should be required to finance education in minority and indigenous languages. Where education in multiple languages is publicly financed, issues have also arisen about the selection of languages and about whether the exclusion of particular languages constitutes discrimination. Another aspect of the acceptability of education concerns religious instruction. The right of parents to ensure the religious and moral education of their children in accordance with their own convictions is affirmed in article 13(3) of the Covenant, as well as in most of the other treaties and other instruments mentioned above. Again, however, precisely what this entails for state-financed and state-subsidised schools, and indeed for state supervision of privately funded education, is a matter of ongoing contestation. The acceptability of education may also be affected by many other matters, among them school discipline (and especially the use of corporal punishment), dress codes, and textbook content. In this way, the right to education intersects with other human rights, such as the right not to be ill-treated, the right to freedom of religion and belief, and the right to freedom of expression, as well as with minority rights, indigenous rights, and children's rights.

Finally, *adaptability* directs attention to the need for educational systems to remain open to review and reconsideration. Whereas the prevailing assumption has tended to be that students must adapt to established educational systems (or be excluded if they cannot), this criterion of adaptability asserts instead that those systems must themselves adapt to the diverse and changing populations they serve. As the Committee explains, 'education has to be flexible so it can adapt to the needs of changing societies and communities and respond to the needs of students within their diverse social and cultural settings'.[33] This raises issues about the adequacy of educational arrangements from the perspective of particular students, especially those generally pushed to the margins of educational policy, such as children with disabilities, refugee children, working children, children in prison, students who are parents, and

[32] See, e.g., *Minority Schools in Albania*, Advisory Opinion of the Permanent Court of International Justice, 6 April 1934, Ser. A/B-No.64, 4 (interpreting the Albanian Declaration to the Council of the League of Nations on 2 October 1921, art. 5).

[33] Committee on Economic, Social and Cultural Rights, General Comment 13 (The right to education: art. 13), 8 December 1999, para. 6(d).

those requiring fundamental education (that is to say, education for those who missed out on primary education). It also raises more general issues about learning environments and teaching programmes. An educational system cannot be said to be adapted to the needs of a society as a whole if it sustains the idea that some people are inferior. Adaptability accordingly demands ongoing efforts to organise educational institutions and frame educational curricula in a way that combats stereotyping and other forms of prejudice. This obligation is explicitly stated in a number of the treaties and international instruments we mentioned earlier and in other treaties as well. For instance, it is enunciated with specific reference to racism against indigenous peoples in ILO Convention 169 concerning Indigenous and Tribal Peoples in Independent Countries.[34]

Obligations

Resource and other constraints affecting education mean that some of the obligations associated with the right to education must be realised progressively. Others, however, take full, immediate effect. Under the Covenant states parties have an immediate obligation to guarantee that the right to education 'will be exercised without discrimination of any kind'.[35] They also have an immediate obligation to 'take steps' towards the full realisation of the provisions of article 13.[36] The Committee has made clear that this calls for steps that are 'deliberate, concrete and targeted', and imposes on governments a 'specific and continuing obligation to move as expeditiously and effectively as possible' towards the full realisation of the right to education. A 'strong presumption' thus arises that retrogressive measures violate state obligations under the Covenant.[37] More positively, constant progress must be demonstrated in enhancing the extent to which the availability, accessibility, acceptability and adaptability of education are respected, protected and fulfilled.

The Committee highlights in General Comment 13 certain immediate obligations which have the character of 'core obligations', or minimum essential attainments, in the sphere of education.[38] These include the

---

[34] Art. 31.   [35] Art. 2(2).   [36] Art. 2(1).

[37] Committee on Economic, Social and Cultural Rights, General Comment 13 (The right to education: art. 13), 8 December 1999, paras. 43–5.

[38] Ibid., para. 57.

obligation to provide primary education for all, and to adopt and implement a national educational strategy which includes the provision for secondary, higher and fundamental education. The core obligations also include the obligation to ensure the right of access to public educational institutions and programmes on a non-discriminatory basis. Some aspects of what is required in this regard are set out in the Convention against Discrimination in Education, adopted within the framework of UNESCO in 1960. Discrimination may, of course, manifest itself in many different ways. One indicator, highlighted by the Committee, is the existence of sharp disparities in spending policies that result in differing qualities of education being provided, for instance, to people in different geographical locations.[39] On the other hand, the Committee makes clear that the adoption of temporary special measures to bring about *de facto* equality for disadvantaged groups does not constitute discrimination, so long as the 'measures do not lead to the maintenance of unequal or separate standards for different groups, and provided they are not continued after the objectives for which they were taken have been achieved'.[40]

As noted earlier in relation to the criterion of acceptability, the right to education must be implemented in a manner that takes into account certain rights of parents, including the right to educate their children in private schools. Thus, article 13(3) of the Covenant recognises the right of parents to choose private education for their children, while article 13(4) acknowledges that private parties have the right to establish and direct educational institutions. In both cases, however, this is subject to the proviso that private educational institutions must conform to minimum educational standards laid down by the state. As this makes clear, a further important obligation that flows from the right to education is the obligation imposed on governments to establish minimum educational standards, and to maintain a 'transparent and effective system to monitor' these standards.[41] In many countries a system of accreditation is used. The adequacy of such systems depends on a variety of factors, including the existence of safeguards to ensure that governments do not abuse their power to confer or deny accreditation.

The UN Special Rapporteur on the Right to Education has observed that the role of governments in education is often viewed in

---

[39] Committee on Economic, Social and Cultural Rights, General Comment 13 (The right to education: art. 13), 8 December 1999, para. 35.   [40] Ibid., para. 32.
[41] Ibid., para. 54.

terms of extremes, according to which the state is either the 'sole funder and provider of education' or 'only the regulator'.[42] In most countries education is in fact provided through a mixture of state-run and privately run institutions, each of which often receives both public and private funds. On the other hand, as Tomaševski stresses, the state's role is never simply that of a regulator. The obligation to set and enforce educational standards is certainly part of its role. But so too, and more generally, is the obligation to guarantee the right of all to available, accessible, acceptable and adaptable education. Where, as in some countries, educational systems are being restructured around the logic of consumer choice, with schools being required to compete for pupils or risk loss of funding and eventual closure, serious questions arise about the compatibility of these changes with the right to education, especially of vulnerable and disadvantaged students.

Our focus so far has been on the obligations of governments with respect to the provision of education within their own country. As is stated in many relevant treaties and other international instruments, however, and as is highlighted by the Committee, the right to education also entails obligations with regard to international co-operation and assistance. Moreover, these obligations require that the right to education be taken into account not only in programmes of development assistance, but also in the negotiation and ratification of treaties, and in action taken by governments as members of international organisations, including international financial institutions.[43] This link between the right to education and the work of the international financial institutions points beyond the obligations of governments, confirming that the international financial institutions themselves have responsibilities in this sphere. Debtor governments cannot be deemed solely liable where strategies inconsistent with their citizens' right to education are imposed on them in connection with loans. Cutbacks in educational expenditure have been a notorious feature of International Monetary Fund programmes and, while the Fund's approach to economic restructuring has changed in recent years, concerns in this regard remain. Thus, the Committee writes that all relevant international organisations 'should

---

[42] K. Tomaševski, *Human Rights Obligations: Making Education Available, Accessible, Acceptable and Adaptable* (Right To Education Primers No. 3) (2001), 29.

[43] Committee on Economic, Social and Cultural Rights, General Comment 13 (The right to education: art. 13), 8 December 1999, para. 56.

enhance their cooperation for the implementation of the right to education at national level...In particular, the international financial institutions, notably the World Bank and IMF, should pay greater attention to the protection of the right to education in their lending policies, credit agreements, structural adjustment programmes and measures taken in response to the debt crisis'.[44]

Education and the GATS

We referred a moment ago to the idea that the right to education must be taken into account not only in the formulation of national educational policy, and not only in the elaboration of programmes of international development assistance, but also in the negotiation and ratification of treaties. One treaty which has particular significance for the right to education is the General Agreement on Trade in Services (GATS), negotiated within the context of the World Trade Organisation. Whereas international trade law was originally focused on trade in goods, the GATS extends the regime to encompass also trade in services. There is currently a lively debate about the implications of the GATS for the right to education. While this debate is currently focused on higher education,[45] in the background is a range of wider issues that may potentially affect other levels of education as well.

Under the GATS trade in services is defined in a way that covers a variety of forms of transnational educational provision, referred to as 'modes of supply'. The most important of these at present is what is sometimes called 'export education'. This is where students leave their own countries to study at institutions abroad. Another form of educational provision which is covered is the sale of courses that may be accessed in foreign countries via CD-ROMs or through the internet. This appears to be an expanding market, with obvious potential in relation not just to higher education, but to other levels of education as well. Other practices covered include the establishment of private

[44] Committee on Economic, Social and Cultural Rights, General Comment 13 (The right to education: art. 13), 8 December 1999, para. 60.

[45] See further J. Knight, 'Trade in Higher Education Services: the Implications of GATS', Report for the Observatory on Borderless Higher Education, March 2002, available at www.obhe.ac.uk.

colleges run or franchised by foreign firms, and the conclusion of contracts under which teachers or researchers are hired to work at institutions abroad. Like other trade treaties, the GATS is concerned with what are referred to as 'barriers' to trade. These are national measures that are considered to limit or restrict trade, and in the case of education they include such measures as the imposition of visa requirements for students studying abroad or teachers teaching abroad, the establishment of quotas on numbers of foreign students who may enrol at educational institutions, and the refusal to grant licences to foreign institutions to issue recognised degrees.

In broad terms, the GATS is designed to facilitate these kinds of education trade by ensuring the removal of these kinds of barriers. It contains some general obligations with respect to the liberalisation of trade in services, and also provides a framework within which governments can choose to make specific commitments with regard to the opening of sectors of their national markets to foreign suppliers. At present, relatively few governments have made commitments in the sphere of education, and of those a significant proportion relate to higher education only. That said, as one analyst puts it, 'GATS is not a neutral agreement. It aims to promote and enforce the liberalization of trade in services. . . . Therefore, in spite of the right of each country to determine the extent of its commitments, with each new round of negotiations, countries are expected to add sectors or sub-sectors to their national schedules of commitments and to negotiate the further removal of limitations on market access and national treatment'. It follows that 'countries that are not interested in either the import or export of education services will most likely experience greater pressures to allow market access to foreign providers'.[46] With the GATS, then, the direction of change is towards the removal of more and more barriers to export education and the like, and towards the removal of those barriers for more and more 'sub-sectors' or levels of education.

While education is among those spheres to which the GATS applies, an exemption is stipulated for measures affecting education services that are provided 'in the exercise of governmental authority'.[47] Thus, barriers to trade associated with these services can be retained consistently with the GATS. There is considerable uncertainty regarding the scope of

[46] Ibid., 9–10.　　　[47] General Agreement on Trade in Services, art. 1(3).

this exemption, however, and it remains unclear to what extent public education will be protected. Part of the reason for this is that, as recalled earlier, public education in many countries is provided through a mixture of state-run and privately run institutions, each of which often receives both public and private funds. This question of the extent to which, and the ways in which, the GATS may affect the role of governments in meeting national educational needs is at the centre of debates about the implications of the GATS for the right to education. Supporters of the GATS highlight the agreement's potential to enlarge educational opportunities, boost transnational interaction, and foster educational investment in poorer countries. This latter aspect is held to be especially important where higher and adult education is concerned, inasmuch as demand far outstrips supply.

Against this, it is observed that, while the GATS may indeed bring benefits of this sort, those social benefits are purely incidental to its main purpose which is economic. Thus, it is the primary purpose of opening markets and expanding opportunities for world trade which must serve as the starting point for any consideration of the agreement's likely winners and losers. With this in mind, critics of the GATS highlight a number of risks which are relevant to the right to education. These risks cannot properly be grasped or assessed without detailed consideration of the agreement and its wider legal and social context. However, the general danger to which they relate is that, as trade in education services grows, the character of education as a public good may be undermined. Instead of being oriented to the needs of society as a whole and the right of everyone to education along the lines described above, education may become increasingly oriented to the generation of profit. It may increasingly be seen as a commodity, offered for sale to students who are now consumers, within a society which is now a market. This has the potential to affect the nature of the education provided, encouraging certain kinds of programmes at the expense of others. It also has implications for the role of the state. Export and other forms of transnational education might supplement, rather than replace, state provision of education services. But they might equally encourage governments to reduce public spending on the sub-sectors of education involved, and limit themselves to the regulation of private institutions. Indeed, there is anxiety that even regulation may prove difficult, in the face of ongoing pressures to open markets to trade in education services to an ever greater extent.

Finally, the commodification of education has implications for students, especially those most disadvantaged. We began this discussion of human rights and education by referring to the grim vision of post-War British education evoked in Pink Floyd's album 'The Wall'. There the wall was an image of enforced conformism, psychic confinement, and growing alienation. But in the background, out of sight, was always another kind of image, still vivid today. This is the wall as a marker of educational exclusion. Certainly, we take up this topic at a time of wide, and in some respects widening, disparities in educational opportunity among and within countries. The precise relationship between this situation and the liberalisation of trade in services remains uncertain. What is clear, however, is that the denial of education exacts an immense human and social cost, and that this is one expenditure which tends not to feature on the export education industry's balance-sheet. In this context, a crucial aspect of the current significance of the right to education is to direct attention to the question of how moves to liberalise education trade affect existing disparities in educational opportunity—how they may help to narrow those disparities, but also how they may serve to widen them still further.

Fair Trial

When the trial of Saddam Hussein began in Iraq, media coverage in many countries included soundbites from ordinary Iraqis. Should Saddam be tried? In one such story, the first respondent says no, his crimes are too many; '[h]e should be cut into pieces'.[1] A second concedes that the former president made mistakes, but asks, did he 'do everything by himself, or was there someone behind him, like the Americans, or Great Britain, or Germany, or Russia or France?' A third replies: 'I believe they should put Saddam on trial, but it should be a fair trial... A fair trial will have the approval of God and this one doesn't.'

At some level, of course, all three responses have validity. Few could doubt at this point that in due course Saddam Hussein probably would be executed, even if not in the way the first respondent suggests. As the head of the Coalition Provisional Authority's Crimes against Humanity Investigations Unit in Iraq confirmed in an article published a few days later, '[t]here is little likelihood... that Saddam will live out his days in a comfortable Dutch prison'.[2] At the same time, it is also true, as the second respondent wants us to recall, that Saddam did not do everything by himself, and that behind him was a fluctuating array of powerful and at times exceptionally supportive governments, including those now seeking his trial. Yet it is in the third statement that many of us will hear most strongly and clearly the voice of reason, sound judgement, and good sense. Expressed there is the firm moral conviction that individual accountability is necessary, but that trial must be fair.

[1] J. Meek, 'Court drama or circus—a nation is hooked', *The Guardian*, 2 July 2004. The succeeding quotations in this paragraph are also from this article.

[2] T. Parker, 'Saddam's trial creates a new legal model', *International Herald Tribune*, 8 July 2004. The context makes clear that Parker is referring to the likelihood that Saddam will be sentenced to death.

Firm moral conviction still leaves plenty of room for argument over specifics and realities, and it is obvious that as a concept, value and practice, fair trial in fact prompts many questions. We examine a number of these in this discussion. From a human rights-oriented perspective, the primary question tends to be: what constitutes a fair trial under international human rights law? Alongside this issue of the scope of the right to a fair trial, however, a range of further questions arises about the context and significance of fair trial guarantees, and we will also need to give some consideration to these. Why is it that people don't get a fair trial? Do we worry too much about whether they do? Do we not worry enough about some aspects of whether they do? When we speak about the fairness of a trial, are we speaking only about the jurisdiction that is exercised, the law that is applied, and the procedures that are followed, or also about the sentence that is imposed?

We mentioned a moment ago an article by the head of the Coalition Provisional Authority's Crimes against Humanity Investigations Unit in Iraq, Tom Parker. In this article Parker explains that the reason Saddam is unlikely to live out his days in a comfortable Dutch prison is that he will 'face penalties under Iraqi law—not penalties deemed appropriate by the international community'.[3] Yet Parker also says that 'by giving Iraqis the power to tackle this task themselves, we will be creating an experienced cadre of judges, lawyers and investigators steeped in international notions of due process'. More than that, a 'televised judicial process conducted according to internationally accepted standards will become a civics class for the whole country'. What are internationally accepted standards, and what kind of civics class does, or should, a televised judicial process conducted according to them provide?

The right to a fair trial

Internationally accepted standards with regard to the right to a fair trial can be gleaned from the Universal Declaration of Human Rights.[4] They can also be gleaned from the International Covenant on Civil and Political Rights, in which the right to a fair trial is reaffirmed and elaborated,[5] and from corresponding provisions laid down in all the regional

---

[3] T. Parker, 'Saddam's trial creates a new legal model', *International Herald Tribune*, 8 July 2004. The succeeding quotations in this paragraph are also from this article.
[4] Arts. 10 and 11.   [5] Art. 14.

human rights systems.[6] Relevant norms are also included in treaties concerned with racial discrimination,[7] torture and cruel, inhuman or degrading treatment,[8] the rights of children,[9] and other issues. Particular aspects of the right to a fair trial are further specified in non-treaty instruments which have been adopted by the UN General Assembly and other organisations with the aim of codifying basic principles on matters such as the independence of the judiciary[10] and the role of lawyers in the administration of criminal justice.[11] Human rights courts and other supervisory bodies have contributed very significantly to the definition of fair trial standards. There exists today a large body of case-law and related material analysing the internationally protected right to a fair trial and the obligations it entails for governments.[12] On a different but related track, recent years have seen the growth of the practice of international trial observation, and this too has spawned influential interpretations of the criteria for a fair trial under international human rights law. A notable example is Amnesty International's *Fair Trials Manual*.[13]

---

[6] European Convention on Human Rights, art. 6; American Declaration of the Rights and Duties of Man, arts. XVIII and XXVI; American Convention on Human Rights, art. 8; African Charter on Human and Peoples' Rights, arts. 7 and 26; Commonwealth of Independent States Convention on Human Rights and Fundamental Freedoms, art. 6; and Revised Arab Charter on Human Rights (2004) (not yet in force), arts. 13, 16 and 17.

[7] International Convention on the Elimination of All Forms of Racial Discrimination, art. 5(a).

[8] Convention against Torture and Other Cruel, Inhuman or Degrading Treatment or Punishment, art. 15.

[9] Convention on the Rights of the Child, arts. 37 and 40; International Covenant on Civil and Political Rights, art. 14(1) and (4). See further Children★.

[10] Basic Principles on the Independence of the Judiciary, adopted by the Seventh United Nations Congress on the Prevention of Crime and the Treatment of Offenders (1985) and endorsed by General Assembly Res. 40/32 of 29 November 1985 and Res. 40/146 of 13 December 1985.

[11] Basic Principles on the Role of Lawyers (1990), Guidelines on the Role of Prosecutors (1990), both adopted at the Eighth United Nations Congress on the Prevention of Crime and the Treatment of Offenders, Havana (1990), UN Doc. A/CONF.144/28/Rev.1, (1990) 118, 189.

[12] See further D. Weissbrodt & R. Wolfrum (eds.), *The Right to a Fair Trial* (Berlin: Springer, 1997) and D. Weissbrodt, *The Right to a Fair Trial under the Universal Declaration of Human Rights and the International Covenant on Civil and Political Rights* (The Hague: Martinus Nijhoff, 2001).

[13] Amnesty International, *Fair Trials Manual* (London: Amnesty International Publications, 1998).

Fair trial standards apply to a wide range of processes, actors and institutions. In the first place, they apply to all kinds of legal proceedings. While our focus in this discussion will be on criminal trials, in principle civil (or other non-criminal) proceedings are also encompassed.[14] Secondly, fair trial standards apply to all parties affected. In the criminal context, the central issue is obviously the defendant's right to a fair trial, and that is what we will concentrate on here. But victims also have rights relating to criminal investigations and proceedings. Equally, they have rights to redress where a human rights violation has occurred, and in this connection the *failure* to initiate criminal proceedings—for example, following the enactment of a general amnesty for officials involved in human rights abuse during a specified period—may violate the right of victims to a fair trial.[15] Finally, fair trial standards apply in all jurisdictional settings. In particular, they are relevant not only in national courts, but also in proceedings before international criminal courts and tribunals. Provisions designed to ensure the consistency of international criminal proceedings with internationally recognised fair trial standards are included in the foundational instruments of the International Criminal Tribunal for the former Yugoslavia and all subsequently established *ad hoc* international courts and tribunals,[16] as well as in the Rome Statute of the International Criminal Court.[17] Our main concern in this discussion will be with the generality of criminal trials, rather than the specificity of international criminal procedures. Nonetheless, we will do well to keep those latter procedures in view, as they not only reflect, but also inform, international definitions of fairness in the administration of criminal justice.

What, then, are the key constituents of a fair trial under international human rights law? An initial constituent relates to the law under which

[14] The right to have civil rights and obligations determined by a court raises some distinct issues and controversies. These have assumed considerable prominence in connection with the European Convention on Human Rights. On this, see J. Wright, *Tort Law & Human Rights* (Oxford: Hart Publishing, 2001) and B. Markesinis, J.-B. Auby, C. Waltjen, & S. Deakin (eds.), *The Tortious Liability of Statutory Bodies* (Oxford: Hart Publishing, 1999).

[15] See, e.g., *Chumbipuma Aguirre and Others v Peru (Barrios Altos* Case), Judgment of the Inter-American Court of Human Rights, 14 March 2001 (and, pursuant to later request for interpretation, 3 September 2001).

[16] See, e.g., art. 21 of the Statute of the International Criminal Tribunal for the former Yugoslavia and para. 106 of the Secretary-General's Report S/25704, 3 May 1993, art. 20 of the Statute of the International Criminal Tribunal for Rwanda. See further S. Zappalà, *Human Rights in International Criminal Proceedings* (Oxford: Oxford University Press, 2003).   [17] See, e.g., arts. 64(2), 67, 68 and 69.

the defendant is tried. Embracing the principle *nullum crimen sine lege*, international human rights law prohibits conviction by reference to retroactive criminal law. In the International Covenant on Civil and Political Rights, this is expressed in the following terms: 'No one shall be held guilty of any criminal offence on account of any act or omission which did not constitute a criminal offence, under national or international law, at the time when it was committed.'[18] Linked to this is a prohibition on the imposition of a heavier penalty than the one that was applicable at the time when the offence was committed.[19] It follows from these stipulations that there must exist a clear and publicly accessible legal basis for all criminal prosecutions and penalties, such that the criminal justice system can be said to be operating in a way that was foreseeable to the defendant. While complaints about the application of retroactive criminal law have been raised in many contexts, it is perhaps in the context of international criminal trials, where the legal basis relied upon by the prosecutorial authorities lies in international law, that this aspect has proved most contentious. In one recent case, the defendant, who was the Minister of the Interior of Sierra Leone, was indicted before the Sierra Leone Special Court in connection with a number of offences under international law alleged to have been committed in his capacity as national co-ordinator of the Civil Defence Forces during the period November 1997 to April 1998. Among these offences was the recruitment as soldiers of children under the age of 15.[20] The defendant argued that in this respect the indictment violated the prohibition on non-retroactive criminal law. Even if international law required states to ban under-15 recruitment, individual criminal liability was not established until after the events in question. The Special Court dismissed this argument, finding that by 1997 customary international law had crystallised not only around the idea that under-15 recruitment should be banned, but also around the idea that it engaged individual criminal responsibility. For a majority of the judges, it was simply not plausible for the defendant, especially given his leadership role, to contend that he did not know his conduct was a criminal act in violation of international law.

---

[18] International Covenant on Civil and Political Rights, art. 15(1). See also Universal Declaration of Human Rights, art. 11(2).   [19] Ibid.

[20] *Prosecutor v Sam Hinga Norman* (Case SCSL-03-I), Decision on Preliminary Motion Based on Lack of Jurisdiction (Child Recruitment), Appeals Chamber of the Special Court for Sierra Leone, 31 May 2004.

A further constituent of a fair trial relates to the character of the tribunal before which the defendant is tried. International human rights law reflects the fundamental precept of the rule of law that trial should be by an independent and impartial tribunal that is established by law and jurisdictionally competent to hear the case. Stipulations to this effect in the International Covenant on Civil and Political Rights and other treaties are supplemented by the UN Basic Principles on the Independence of the Judiciary, adopted by the UN General Assembly in 1985. The Basic Principles address the implications of the right to trial by an independent and impartial tribunal for the separation of powers, the appointment and removal of judges, the assignment of cases, and other related matters.[21] In connection with the International Covenant on Civil and Political Rights, the Human Rights Committee has raised particular concern about the use of military or 'special' courts to try civilians. The Committee has emphasised that, '[w]hile the Covenant does not prohibit such categories of courts, nevertheless the conditions which it lays down clearly indicate that the trying of civilians by such courts should be very exceptional and take place under conditions which genuinely afford the full guarantees [of a fair trial] stipulated in [the Covenant]'.[22] In one case before the European Court of Human Rights, the applicant was a civilian accused of disseminating separatist propaganda in Turkey.[23] Tried and convicted by a special 'National Security Court' comprising two civilian judges and one military judge, he complained that his right to trial by an independent and impartial tribunal had been violated. The European Court upheld the complaint, finding that the presence of a military judge who remained subject to military discipline and executive reappointment meant that the applicant had legitimate cause to doubt that the necessary institutional guarantees of a fair trial were in place. The Inter-American Court of Human Rights reached a similar conclusion in a case challenging 'special' procedures

[21] Basic Principles on the Independence of the Judiciary, adopted by the Seventh United Nations Congress on the Prevention of Crime and the Treatment of Offenders (1985) and endorsed by General Assembly Res. 40/32 of 29 November 1985 and Res. 40/146 of 13 December 1985.

[22] Human Rights Committee, General Comment 13 (Equality before the courts and the right to a fair and public hearing by an independent court established by law: art. 14), 13 April 1984, para. 4.

[23] *Incal v Turkey*, Judgment of the European Court of Human Rights, 9 June 1998.

according to which defendants were brought into court hooded or blindfolded in order to conceal the identity of the judges.[24] Apart from other violations of the defendants' human rights, the Inter-American Court made clear that the use of 'faceless' judges is inconsistent with the right to trial by an independent and impartial tribunal. But concerns about independence and impartiality are not limited to contexts such as these. In another case before the European Court of Human Rights, a jury trial was marred by allegations of racism on the part of jurors.[25] The European Court upheld the applicant's complaint that his right to trial by an impartial tribunal had been violated, on the grounds that the trial judge had failed to take adequate action to exclude legitimate doubts that the applicant might be condemned because of his ethnicity.

Beyond these legal and institutional issues, the constituents of a fair trial under international human rights law revolve largely around the procedures that are followed and the extent to which they protect the rights of the defendant and respect the principle of 'equality of arms' between the prosecution and the defence. This latter principle entails the right to be tried in your presence, the right to be legally represented by counsel of your own choosing and to have legal assistance provided at no cost in appropriate cases, the right to communicate with your counsel, the right to adequate time and facilities to prepare your defence, and the right to call and cross-examine witnesses. Other basic rights include the right to be presumed innocent until proven guilty, the right to be informed promptly and in detail of the charge, the right not to be compelled to testify against yourself or confess guilt, the right not to be tried or punished more than once in the same jurisdiction for the same crime (the principle *ne bis in idem*), the right to be tried without undue delay, the right to be tried in public unless it can be shown that on specified grounds closed proceedings are strictly necessary, the right to the free assistance of an interpreter, and the right to have your conviction and sentence reviewed by a higher tribunal according to law. With slight variations, these rights are enumerated in the International Covenant on Civil and Political Rights and in treaties and other instruments associated with each of the

---

[24] *Castillo Petruzzi and Others v Peru*, Judgment of the Inter-American Court of Human Rights, 30 May 1999.
[25] *Sander v United Kingdom*, Judgment of the European Court of Human Rights, 9 May 2000.

regional human rights systems.[26] They are also enumerated in the instruments that define the jurisdiction and procedures of the *ad hoc* international criminal courts and tribunals, and in the Rome Statute of the International Criminal Court.[27] The Rome Statute also makes explicit some further rights that follow from the principle of equality of arms, the presumption of innocence and the privilege against self-incrimination. These include the right to communicate with your legal representatives freely and in confidence, the right to remain silent without such silence being a consideration in the determination of guilt or innocence, the right not to make an unsworn oral or written statement in your defence, and the right not to have imposed on you any reversal of the burden of proof or onus of rebuttal.[28] The Rome Statute additionally contains safeguards regarding the use of confession evidence.[29] More generally, the Torture Convention prohibits the invocation as evidence in any proceedings of statements made as a result of torture.[30] While we offered a few illustrations of cases involving non-retroactivity and impartiality, we cannot even begin to illustrate or specify the various aspects we have mentioned in this paragraph. Suffice it to say that each has been elaborated in case-law, and in some instances in 'soft' law (non-treaty instruments of international organisations) and other interpretive material as well.[31]

These, then, are the principal constituents of a fair trial under international human rights law. There is one further issue that needs now to be highlighted. Under provisions included in a number of human rights treaties, states parties are permitted temporarily to curtail—'derogate from'—their obligations with respect to certain of the human rights

---

[26] International Covenant on Civil and Political Rights, arts. 14 and 15; European Convention on Human Rights, arts. 6 and 7, and Seventh Protocol, arts. 2, 3 and 4; American Declaration of the Rights and Duties of Man, art. XXVI; American Convention on Human Rights, art. 8; African Charter on Human and Peoples' Rights, arts. 7 and 26; Commonwealth of Independent States Convention on Human Rights and Fundamental Freedoms, arts. 6 and 7; and Revised Arab Charter on Human Rights (2004) (not yet in force), arts. 13, 16, 17 and 19.

[27] Rome Statute of the International Criminal Court, arts. 20–4, 40, 51, 55, 63–8. See also Rules of Procedure and Evidence adopted by the Assembly of States Parties.

[28] Rome Statute of the International Criminal Court, art. 67(1)(b), (g), (h) and (i).

[29] Ibid., art. 65.

[30] Convention against Torture and Other Cruel, Inhuman or Degrading Treatment or Punishment, art. 15.

[31] See L. Doswald-Beck & R. Kolb, *Judicial Process and Human Rights* (Kehl am Rhein: N.P. Engel, 2004).

recognised, where this is rendered necessary by the exigencies of a war or other national emergency.[32] Is the right to a fair trial susceptible to derogation in this way? In all relevant treaties that permit derogation, it is explicitly provided that there may be no derogation from the first constituent we noted, the right not to be prosecuted for conduct that was not an offence at the time it was committed.[33] What of the other constituents? In connection with the International Covenant on Civil and Political Rights, the Human Rights Committee has stated that the possibility of derogation granted to states under the Covenant may never be invoked as justification for deviating from 'fundamental principles of fair trial, including the presumption of innocence', as these have the status of peremptory norms of international law or *jus cogens*.[34] The Committee has also stated that derogation will in practice be barred insofar as procedural guarantees must remain in place to safeguard rights—such as the right to life and the right not to be ill-treated—that are non-derogable under the Covenant. This is made explicit in the American Convention on Human Rights, which calls for the maintenance at all times of 'judicial guarantees essential for the protection' of non-derogable rights.[35] One consequence mentioned by the Committee is that the possibility of derogation may never be invoked as justification for deviation from any aspect of the right to a fair trial in proceedings leading to the imposition of the death penalty.

The civics class and its limits

It is said that the screening on Chinese television of *Starsky and Hutch* and *Hawaii 5-O* has encouraged the assertion in China of 'Miranda rights'.[36] Presumably the same might apply to 'taking the Fifth',

[32] International Covenant on Civil and Political Rights, art. 4; European Convention on Human Rights, art. 15; Revised European Social Charter, Part V., art. F; American Convention on Human Rights, art. 27; Commonwealth of Independent States Convention on Human Rights and Fundamental Freedoms, art. 35; Revised Arab Charter of Human Rights (2004) (not yet in force), art. 4.

[33] International Covenant on Civil and Political Rights, arts. 4(2) and 15; European Convention on Human Rights, arts. 15(2) and 7; American Convention on Human Rights, arts. 27(2) and 9; Commonwealth of Independent States Convention on Human Rights and Fundamental Freedoms, arts. 35(2) and 7; Revised Arab Charter of Human Rights (2004) (not yet in force), arts. 4(b) and 15.

[34] Human Rights Committee, General Comment 29 (States of emergency: art. 4), 24 July 2001, para. 11.   [35] American Convention on Human Rights, art. 27(2).

[36] See M. Gibney, 'Introduction' in M. Gibney (ed.), *Globalizing Rights* (Oxford: Oxford University Press, 2003), 1.

'I demand to see my lawyer' and 'where's your warrant?'. The global circulation of American crime shows and courtroom dramas has assured that these are familiar phrases in most parts of the world. But television does not only contribute to the globalisation of specific legal forms. It may also raise the profile and promote the development of local fair trial guarantees, whether through fictional programmes or reality TV. We mentioned at the beginning of this discussion the remark by Tom Parker of the Coalition Provisional Authority's Crimes against Humanity Investigations Unit in Iraq that a televised judicial process conducted in accordance with internationally accepted standards can serve as a civics class for the whole country. Whatever the prospects of the particular trial which Parker has in mind, as a general matter he is clearly right. At the same time, however, it is also clear that there is deep and wide moral conviction underpinning the idea that people should not be tried under retroactive criminal law, that courts should be independent and impartial, that innocence should be presumed until guilt is proven, and that trial procedures should be structured so as to enable an effective defence of individuals accused of crime. On those basic principles popular instruction is scarcely necessary. Why then do defendants' rights get breached? Why do unfair trials happen? While the reasons are of course unique in every instance, let us briefly survey something of the range of factors and circumstances that may be involved.

In the first place, denial of a fair trial may obviously be linked to the repression of political opposition. Perhaps the most notorious instances of unfair criminal process are the Moscow 'show trials', held between 1936 and 1938. Designed to discredit party leaders and officials whom Stalin regarded as a threat, these trials relied largely on self-incrimination. All those brought before the Military Collegium of the Soviet Supreme Court ultimately confessed to the crimes of which they were accused, and pleaded guilty as charged. Whether or not the same emphasis is placed on self-incrimination, tyranny of this sort continues to account for some of the most egregious violations of the right to a fair trial. A well-known, more recent example is the trial in Nigeria of Kenule Beeson Saro-Wiwa and fellow Ogoni leaders. Saro-Wiwa and his co-defendants were arrested in 1994 and some months later charged with incitement to murder. After trial before a special tribunal the members of which were appointed directly by General Abacha, they were executed in November 1995. As set out in a decision of the African

Commission on Human and Peoples' Rights in 1998, the proceedings violated in almost every pertinent respect the defendants' rights under international human rights law in general and the African Charter of Human and Peoples' Rights in particular.[37] In addition to pre-trial violations and to denial of the right to be tried before an independent and impartial tribunal, the defendants were also denied the right of defence; their counsel were harassed to the point where legal representation became impossible. Likewise, the presumption of innocence was set aside, and the defendants were denied the right of appeal.

Secondly, denial of a fair trial may be a function of institutional shortcomings. What is necessary is not simply for the state to respect the right to a fair trial, but also for governments to put in place a legal and institutional framework which will protect that right—and protect it on a non-discriminatory basis. Thus, the prospects for fair criminal process are bound up with such infrastructural matters as the availability of legal assistance, the functioning of prosecution services, and the selection and training of judges, and with regulatory issues, to do with the adequacy of police, evidence, and penal laws. Legal and institutional shortcomings relating to the administration of criminal justice are the subject of important justice sector reform programmes in developing and 'transition' states. At the same time, they remain a revealing feature of the old liberal world. We mentioned earlier a case before the European Court of Human Rights in which a jury trial was marred by allegations of racism on the part of jurors.[38] The United Kingdom was adjudged responsible for a violation of the applicant's right to a fair trial, on the ground that the trial judge had failed to take adequate action to exclude legitimate doubts about the tribunal's impartiality. The allegations of racism—racist remarks and jokes—were brought to the attention of the judge by one member of the jury. The judge is reported to have communicated the allegations to the jury and then said to them: 'This case has cost an enormous amount of money and I am not anxious to halt it at the moment, but I shall have no compunction in doing so if the situation demands.'[39] He then asked the jurors to tell him if they felt they

---

[37] *International Pen, Constitutional Rights Project, Interights on behalf of Ken Saro-Wiwa Jr. and Civil Liberties Organisation v Nigeria* (Communications 137/94, 139/94, 154/96 and 161/97) 31 October 1998, 24th Ordinary Session, Banjul.

[38] *Sander v United Kingdom*, Judgment of the European Court of Human Rights, 9 May 2000. [39] Ibid., para. 11.

could not put aside any prejudices they may have. In the event, he let the trial continue on the basis of statements refuting the allegations of racism, including one signed by the juror who had first made them. While the European Court did not specifically highlight the manifest possibility that resource constraints had been allowed to overshadow the non-discriminatory enjoyment of human rights, it did observe that a request for vague assurances about setting aside prejudices was hardly commensurate with the seriousness of the allegations. To guarantee fairness, a more robust response was required.

A third contributing factor with regard to the denial of a fair trial concerns the pressures that may be exerted upon defendants' rights by crime victims, and more broadly, by those who consider themselves potential victims of crime. We touch elsewhere in this book on moves to recognise the rights and interests of victims and witnesses, especially—though by no means exclusively—in the context of international criminal trials, where the vulnerability of victims and witnesses is often intense (see Victims*). Here we confine ourselves to noting the contested and sometimes ambiguous significance of victim-oriented reforms from the perspective of fairness in criminal process. Thus, for instance, the use of anonymous evidence is to some analysts a necessary feature of a system of international criminal justice that has to protect those who come forward to give testimony of mass atrocities. To others, it is an unjustified constraint on the right of defendants to cross-examine witnesses. Beyond this concern about the impact on defendants' rights of measures designed to protect victims and witnesses, there is also concern about the way fear of crime may compromise the fairness of criminal processes, by encouraging 'get-tough' approaches to crime control and drives to raise rates of conviction. Of course, fear of crime is not an independent variable, and one very important agent shaping it is the media. If television may provide civics classes, it may also help to legitimate the curtailment of defendants' rights. Most obviously, it may do this by fostering the impression that the citizenry is more concerned with vengeance than fairness. For example, media coverage may give prominence to those who believe someone indicted for trial should instead be summarily executed. But equally, media coverage may legitimate the curtailment of defendants' rights by fuelling exaggerated or distorted fear of crime, such that authoritarian measures in the administration of justice come to appear appropriate and even essential.

We have reviewed a number of phenomena that can have a bearing on the incidence of unfairness in criminal justice: repression of political opposition, institutional shortcomings and biases, and pressures associated with crime victimisation and fear of crime. In doing so, we have also recalled the intuitive moral appeal of basic fair trial standards. But we have not yet said anything about the dangers or downsides those standards may carry. We have not yet considered the possible negative effects of a preoccupation with procedural regularity. Might there be at stake here a form of 'procedural fetishism', which promotes attention to procedures, forms and events in a manner that distracts us from critical engagement with relationships, outcomes and contexts? In this regard, we can note in the first place the way fair trial is treated as a technical problem, a matter of adjusting legal procedures and reforming legal institutions. The question of why defendants' rights get breached and of how policy choices and other factors condition the prospects for a fair trial tends to be pushed into the background. Secondly, we can observe the way fair trial is approached as a formal issue, with limited regard for the consequences that are produced. So long as a trial is formally correct, international human rights law has relatively little to say about sentencing. Yet, to refer only to one aspect of this, if fair trial marks the boundary between an extra-judicial execution and a lawful use of the death penalty, is the main issue really the trial or the killing? Finally, we can observe the way fair trial concentrates attention on particular events, moving systemic phenomena out of the line of sight. This may affect our capacity to perceive, and hence address, problems in the criminal justice system, such as the fact some social groups are disproportionately represented among defendants. It may also affect our capacity to perceive, and hence address, problems unrelated to the criminal justice system; the conduct of legal proceedings may be permitted to absorb attention, energy and resources that need additionally to be devoted to other things. We highlighted at the beginning of this discussion three views about the trial of Saddam Hussein. The same newspaper report actually included a fourth view which we did not then mention. According to this respondent, the trial was a 'circus put on to distract the public from their problems'. In his words, the 'real concern, the important issues in Iraq, are electricity [and] security'.[40]

---

[40] J. Meek, 'Court drama or circus—a nation is hooked', *The Guardian*, 2 July 2004.

Food

Discussions of global hunger typically begin with statistics.[1] According to the latest information, 842 million people are undernourished, most of them in sub-Saharan Africa and south Asia. That corresponds to the total populations of the United States, Canada, Europe and Japan. Hunger and malnutrition cause 10 million deaths every year. That means 25,000 deaths every day. Six million children under five die every year from hunger- and malnutrition-related causes. That represents roughly all the children under five in France and Italy. In some countries up to 70 per cent of the population is undernourished. Between 1995 and 2001 the number of the world's inhabitants who were undernourished *increased* by 18 million. Hunger and malnutrition are the number one risk to health.

It is easy to see why figures like these assume prominence in discussions of global hunger. Clearly, they need to be known. As always, however, statistics cannot capture everything, and can even obscure aspects of reality that are as important as those they reveal. In this case, there is a danger of obscuring at least two crucial points. The first is the point once made by Bertholt Brecht when he said that 'famines do not simply occur; they are organised by the grain trade'. Focusing on numbers tends to make hunger seem like a spontaneous phemonenon, a tragedy that strikes, and a set of facts that are then given. Yet Brecht's sardonic remark is a reminder that hunger represents a policy option. This holds whether we have in mind food emergencies, as he does, or more chronic forms of undernourishment. The organiser may or may not be, or have been, the grain trade, but some constellation of forces has made it happen that certain people are deprived of adequate food.

---

[1] The statistics we give here are drawn from information published by the Food and Agriculture Organization and the UN's World Food Programme. See FAO, *State of Food Insecurity in the World 2003* and www.wfp.org respectively.

This leads to the second crucial point which risks getting obscured by statistics. Just as hunger is not a spontaneous phenomenon, nor is it an anonymous phenomenon. Behind the numbers are people and the various collectivities they form (bureaucracies, corporations, associations, movements, and so on). As Mike Davis puts it in a book on the massive famines of the late Victorian era, '[a]lthough equations may be more fashionable, it is necessary to pin names and faces to the human agents of such catastrophes, as well as to understand the configurations of social and natural conditions that constrained their decisions'.[2] He adds: '[e]qually, it is imperative to consider the resistances, large and small, by which starving laborers and poor peasants attempted to foil the death sentences passed by grain speculators and colonial proconsuls'.[3]

Today's resistances, similarly large and small, differ from their 19th century counterparts in at least one respect: they take place against the background of legal recognition of the right to adequate food. In what follows we examine the significance of this right, and of the related concepts of food security and food sovereignty, for the death sentence-foiling efforts of poor people in our own time. In particular, we examine to what extent the right to adequate food can be used to bring into focus the people, policies and processes that contribute to creating a situation whereby in the 21st century large—and, in some places, increasing—numbers of the world's inhabitants cannot get enough to eat. But first it will be instructive to return with Davis to the 19th century.

A modern invention

Between 1871 and 1902 a series of famines engulfed what later came to be called the 'Third World'. Though these are rarely remembered today, Davis shows that they have crucial importance, both in world history generally and in the history of global hunger in particular.[4] For one thing, there had been no previous record of famine afflicting so many places simultaneously: drought swept in three waves from Egypt to southern Africa, India, China and Brazil. Estimates of the death toll

---

[2] M. Davis, *Late Victorian Holocausts: El Niño Famines and the Making of the Third World* (London: Verso, 2001), 11.   [3] Ibid.

[4] See M. Davis, *Late Victorian Holocausts: El Niño Famines and the Making of the Third World* (London: Verso, 2001).

range from 30 to 50 million. This, of course, was the time of the scramble for Africa, the time when European nations were celebrating their final assault on the uncolonised world. But here we see that what seemed to metropolitan eyes the 'final blaze of imperial glory was, from an Asian or African viewpoint, only the hideous light of a giant funeral pyre'.[5] Beyond the fact that such vast numbers died, however, Davis wants us to register that they died in circumstances which contradict widely held assumptions about the places concerned and their trajectories in relation to capitalist modernity. As he explains, these were not, as is often supposed, ' "lands of famine" becalmed in stagnant backwaters of world history'. They were societies decimated at precisely the moment of their integration into the world economy. In other words, '[m]illions died, not outside the "modern world system", but in the very process of being forcibly incorporated into its economic and political structures'.[6]

How so? Surely these were *natural* disasters. Indeed, Davis describes how the three waves of famine in the late Victorian period corresponded to an exceptionally severe succession of climatic disturbances known as 'El Niño events'. These are rapid warmings of the eastern tropical Pacific Ocean, and are associated with monsoon failure and synchronous drought across vast swathes of Asia, Africa and northeastern South America. However, as Davis also describes, drought 'always has a manmade dimension and is never simply a natural disaster'.[7] The impact of deficient rainfall on food production depends on how much stored water is available, how quickly it is distributed to affected areas, and, where water is a commodity, whether cultivators can afford to buy it. Besides, absolute food scarcity is almost never the issue, and was not the issue with these El Niño famines. Food surpluses were available; the problem was that those whose crops had failed had no chance to get hold of them. Whereas previously systems had been in place for coping with the effects of rainfall variation through local storage, inter-regional assistance and in some cases centralised strategic planning, now enmeshment with global commodity markets destroyed these traditional arrangements and left agriculturists mortally exposed. Davis reports that the famine commissions set up by the British administrators of India at the end of the 19th century understood this. In the words of one, 'supplies of food were at all times sufficient, and it cannot be too frequently repeated that severe privation was chiefly due to the dearth of

---

[5] Ibid., 7.   [6] Ibid., 9.   [7] Ibid., 18.

employment in agriculture [arising from the drought]'. According to another, 'the famine was one of high prices rather than of scarcity of food'.[8] Nature, then, certainly played a part in these catastrophes, but it was government and economics that determined whether crop failures would actually lead to starvation and, if they did, who in the event would die.

We have dwelled a little on Davis's account of what he refers to as the 'late Victorian holocausts'[9] because it brings out two important points about global hunger. The first is that mass starvation is not a token of 'backwardness', but a modern invention. Although the British authorities claimed to have rescued India from 'timeless hunger', there were 31 serious famines in 120 years of British rule, as against 17 recorded famines in the entire previous two millennia.[10] China apparently had especially effective systems of famine prevention in the 18th century. Between 1720 and 1785 parts of China were affected by a series of droughts and floods that were comparable in intensity (even if not in scope) to the El Niño events of the late 19th century, but price monitoring and relief campaigns instituted by the Qing rulers ensured that no mass starvation occurred.[11] The second important point is that mass starvation is not caused by climatic crises; it is the result of social systems that make people vulnerable to the effects of those crises. In the case of the late Victorian famines, Davis argues that the combination of incorporation into global commodity markets and subjection to colonial economic priorities dramatically intensified the vulnerability of farm labourers to natural perturbations. Between 1875 and 1900, years that included the worst famines India had ever experienced, grain exports to Britain were raised from 3 million tons annually to 10 million tons: the equivalent annual nutrition of 25 million people, and an amount that supplied nearly a fifth of British wheat consumption.[12] Meanwhile, the price of grain declined sharply, and with that its producers' purchasing power.[13] Davis observes that loss of local control over common resources (watersheds, acquifers, etc.) and disinvestment by colonial authorities in environmental capital (irrigation systems, granaries, etc.) also played a part in allowing climatic factors to exert the deadly influence they had.

---

[8] Quoted in M. Davis, *Late Victorian Holocausts: El Niño Famines and the Making of the Third World* (London: Verso, 2001), 19.

[9] For an explanation of Davis's use of the word 'holocaust' in this context, see ibid., 22.

[10] See ibid., 287.   [11] See ibid., 280–5.   [12] See ibid., 299.

[13] See ibid., 290.

This idea that starvation is ultimately a policy option rather than simply a natural disaster is highlighted as well by analysts of hunger in the contemporary world. In an often quoted passage Susan George declares that '[h]unger is not a scourge but a scandal'.[14] As she observes, climatic conditions and population pressures may exacerbate market-induced economic crises, but they do not create those crises. They do not create the human decisions and actions which ensure that 'only the poor—wherever they live—go hungry'.[15] In a similar vein, Amartya Sen rejects the 'fatalism' that surrounds the existence of widespread under-nourishment and sporadic famine.[16] In the late 18th century Thomas Malthus predicted that population growth would outstrip food production, with devastating consequences. However, Sen is emphatic that this fear remains, as it always was, misplaced. 'There is, in fact, no significant crisis in world food production at this [the present] time'; the rate of expansion in food output varies, but the overall trend is 'quite clearly upward'.[17] Despite this, the legacy of the Malthusian perspective lives on, and is reflected in a tendency to focus on 'food production only, neglecting food *entitlement*'.[18] In Sen's assessment, we cannot understand hunger in terms of a mechanical balance between food and population. Rather, we have to look at the capacity of individuals and households to 'establish ownership over an adequate amount of food, which can be done either by growing the food oneself (as peasants do), or by buying it in the market (as the nongrowers of food do)'.[19] He notes that people may be—and generally are—forced into starvation even when there is plenty of food around because they lose their ability to buy food in the market through a loss of income (for example, due to unemployment or collapse of the market in what they produce for a living). Conversely, starvation can be averted even when harvests repeatedly fail by better sharing of available food (for example, through the creation of alternative employment or through the provision of social security). For Sen the focal issue must be the 'role of human agency in causing and sustaining famines'.[20] Based on historical research, he has developed the influential claim that in the modern world democratic institutions are crucial to the prevention of famines, inasmuch as they make governments accountable for failure to take protective action.

[14] S. George, *How the Other Half Dies* (London: Penguin, 1991), 23.   [15] Ibid.
[16] A. Sen, *Development as Freedom* (Oxford: Oxford University Press, 1999), 160.
[17] Ibid., 206.   [18] Ibid., 209.   [19] Ibid., 161.   [20] Ibid., 171.

Accountability is clearly important. Yet, in examining the role of human agency in causing and sustaining famines, we must also recognise—as Davis recalls—that famine is a process through which 'benefits accrue to one section of the community while losses flow to the other'.[21] From this perspective, famine must be understood as a form of redistributive social struggle that has a distinctive (and indeed, in the case of each famine, unique) causation and dynamic, but is nonetheless linked at a systemic level to the more everyday manifestations of impoverishment, among them chronic undernourishment and malnutrition. Quoting Davis again, 'famine is part of a continuum with the silent violence of malnutrition that precedes and conditions it, and with the mortality shadow of debilitation and disease that follows it'.[22] Struggle, of course, implies resistance, and Davis remarks that 'the agricultural populations of Asia, Africa and South America did not go gently into the New Imperial order'.[23] He describes the revolts, rebellions, and other interventions through which those affected by the famines of the late Victorian era attempted to defend their livelihoods, or at any rate their lives. What then of today's resistances? As the global order is again being reconfigured, renewed stress is falling on the insight that the obstacles to universal subsistence are not natural, but political. Against the ideology that blames hunger on nature, people are again insisting that nature cannot be considered apart from the institutions, policies and norms which shape its processes and impacts. A particular focus of contemporary activism is the organisation of the global economy, and especially the terms of international trade. We will review some of the principal concerns in that regard later on. Before doing so, we should turn to the international protection of human rights. For if global hunger and its economic determinants are the subject of this activism, the right to adequate food is frequently its favoured idiom.

The right to food

The right to adequate food is recognised in the Universal Declaration of Human Rights, where it is stated that '[e]veryone has the right to

---

[21]   M. Davis, *Late Victorian Holocausts: El Niño Famines and the Making of the Third World* (London: Verso, 2001), 20 (quoting A. Rangasami, '"Failure of Exchange Entitlements" Theory of Famine: A Response', *Economic and Political Weekly* (12 October 1985), 178).
[22]   Ibid., 21.   [23]   Ibid., 13.

a standard of living adequate for the health and well-being of himself and of his family, including [among other necessities] food'.[24] This right is guaranteed in similar terms in the International Covenant on Economic, Social and Cultural Rights.[25] The Covenant also records the specific commitment of states parties to take measures to ensure that all are free from hunger, including measures aimed at boosting 'production, conservation and distribution' and measures designed to secure an 'equitable distribution of world food supplies in relation to need'.[26] The right to adequate food is likewise affirmed in other human rights treaties. Within the framework of the Inter-American human rights system, it is guaranteed in the San Salvador Protocol to the American Convention on Human Rights.[27] And it features as well in a number of treaties concerned with the human rights of children, notably the Convention on the Rights of the Child[28] and the African Charter on the Rights and Welfare of the Child.[29] In 1999 the Committee on Economic, Social and Cultural Rights issued an influential analysis of the right to adequate food (General Comment 12).[30] The following year the UN Commission on Human Rights established a mandate for a Special Rapporteur on the Right to Food, and successive reports of the Special Rapporteur contain extensive commentary on the scope of this right and the obligations it entails, both in general terms and in relation to particular situations.[31] A recent initiative, undertaken under the auspices of the UN Food and Agriculture Organization, is the elaboration of a set of 'Voluntary Guidelines' setting out key elements of an 'enabling environment' for food security.[32] By food security is understood access

[24] Art. 25. On the right to food, see further P. Alston & K. Tomaševski (eds.), *The Right to Food* (Dordrecht: Martinus Nijhoff, 1984); A. Eide et al. (eds.), *Food as a Human Right* (Tokyo: United Nations University, 1984); and Food and Agriculture Organization, *The Right to Food in Theory and Practice* (Rome: FAO, 1998).

[25] Art. 11(1).   [26] Art. 11(2).   [27] Art. 12.

[28] Art. 24(2), esp. (a) and (c), and Art. 27(1) and (3).

[29] Art. 14(2), esp. (a), (c), and (d).

[30] Committee on Economic, Social and Cultural Rights, General Comment 12 (The right to adequate food: art. 11), 12 May 1999. On the related issue of the right to water, the Committee issued a further General Comment in 2002. See General Comment 15 (The right to water: arts. 11 and 12), 26 November 2002.

[31] See, e.g., Third Report of the Special Rapporteur on the Right to Food, Jean Ziegler, UN E/CN.4/2003/54 (10 January 2003).

[32] FAO Voluntary Guidelines to Support the Progressive Realization of the Right to Adequate Food in the Context of National Food Security, adopted 23 September 2004.

by all people to adequate food on the basis of stability of supply. The Guidelines seek to promote at the national level what is referred to as a 'rights-based approach to food security', which emphasises 'human rights, the obligations of States and the roles of relevant stakeholders'. Such an approach is said to highlight in particular the need to engage 'poor and vulnerable people who are often excluded from the processes which determine policies to promote food security'.[33]

In General Comment 12 the Committee on Economic, Social and Cultural Rights makes clear that the starting point for discussion of the right to adequate food must be the circumstance to which Davis, George, Sen and others call attention, that food deprivation is not finally a problem of insufficient output, but of lack of access to available supplies. In the Committee's words, '[f]undamentally, the roots of the problem of hunger and malnutrition are not lack of food but lack of *access to* available food, *inter alia* because of poverty, by large segments of the world's population'.[34] With this in mind, the Committee specifies the normative content of the right to adequate food in terms of the following elements. First, and most straightforwardly, food must be 'available in a quantity and quality sufficient to satisfy the dietary needs of individuals'.[35] The UN Special Rapporteur on the Right to Food, Jean Ziegler, has pointed out that chronic hunger is predominantly a rural problem, and that the 'rural poor suffer from hunger because they lack access to resources such as land, do not hold secure tenure, are bound by unjust sharecropping contracts, or have properties that are so small that they cannot grow enough food to feed themselves'.[36] In this context, availability depends on enhancing access to land, along with water, credit and other resources. Secondly, the food that is available must be 'free from adverse substances', that is to say, safe.[37] One current controversy about food safety concerns

[33] FAO Voluntary Guidelines to Support the Progressive Realization of the Right to Adequate Food in the Context of National Food Security, adopted 23 September 2004, para. 19.

[34] Committee on Economic, Social and Cultural Rights, General Comment 12 (The right to adequate food: art. 11), 12 May 1999, para. 5. (This point likewise informs the reports of the UN Special Rapporteur on the Right to Food.)

[35] Ibid., para. 8. See further para. 9.

[36] Third Report of the Special Rapporteur on the Right to Food, Jean Ziegler, UN Doc. E/CN.4/2003/54 (10 January 2003), para. 16.

[37] Committee on Economic, Social and Cultural Rights, General Comment 12, para. 8. See further para. 10.

genetically modified organisms (GMOs). We mention some aspects of that controversy below. Thirdly, the food that is available must also be 'acceptable within a given culture'.[38] This points to the need to take into account the symbolic significance of food and food consumption, along with 'informed consumer concerns regarding the nature of accessible food supplies'.[39] Finally, such food must be accessible, both economically and physically, and both now and for the future. By 'economic accessibility' the Committee intends that 'personal or household financial costs associated with the acquisition of food for an adequate diet should be at a level such that the attainment and satisfaction of other basic needs are not threatened or compromised'.[40] By 'physical accessibility' the Committee means that adequate food must be within reach of everyone. This highlights the particular needs of those who are not able to work, those who are in prison, and others who at a given time are neither in a position to grow food nor to earn money to buy it. Accessibility now and for the future implies food security or sustainability, that is to say, the availability and accessibility of food supplies over the long term.

What obligations are entailed by the right to adequate food? Quite obviously, as the UN Special Rapporteur on the Right to Food observes, the 'right to food does not mean handing out free food to everyone'.[41] Rather, it means that states are 'obliged to ensure for everyone under [their] jurisdiction access to the minimum essential food which is sufficient, nutritionally adequate and safe, to ensure their freedom from hunger'.[42] Beyond this, there exist overall obligations to respect, protect, and fulfil the right to food.[43] The obligation to respect entails refraining from measures that prevent access to adequate food (for example, evictions from land or destruction of crops). The obligation to protect entails implementing and enforcing regulations (for example, food safety standards) designed to ensure that enterprises and individuals do not deprive people of their access to adequate food. The obligation to fulfil entails proactive steps to facilitate access to food and strengthen food security. Such steps are the main concern of the FAO's Voluntary Guidelines

---

[38] Ibid., para. 8.   [39] Ibid., para. 11.   [40] Ibid., para. 13.

[41] Third Report of the Special Rapporteur on the Right to Food, Jean Ziegler, UN E/CN.4/2003/54 (10 January 2003), para. 18.

[42] Committee on Economic, Social and Cultural Rights, General Comment 12, para. 14.   [43] See ibid., para. 15.

mentioned above. The obligation to fulfil also entails that the state must be the 'provider of last resort', with appropriate arrangements to deal with emergencies and other situations in which people are unable to feed themselves.[44] Everyone of course acknowledges the relevance of resource constraints. Under the International Covenant on Economic, Social and Cultural Rights states parties are required to take steps to realise the rights recognised 'to the maximum of [their] available resources, with a view to achieving progressively the full realization of the rights recognized'.[45] This is understood to imply that whether there is a violation of the right to adequate food depends on whether a government can discharge the burden of proving that it has made every effort to use the entirety of the resources at its disposal and to obtain international assistance. It is also understood to imply an obligation to 'move as expeditiously as possible' towards ensuring adequate food for all.[46] In this regard, the Committee considers that, while some aspects of the right to adequate food may involve progressive realisation, other aspects must be regarded as taking immediate effect. These include the minimum obligation to ensure freedom from hunger. They also include the guarantee in article 2(2) of the Covenant of non-discrimination in the exercise of the right to food.

As is widely recognised, access to adequate food is not only affected by governmental activities. It is also affected by the activities of private business. Multinational corporations today exercise unprecedented levels of control over the production, processing and distribution of food. In some places privatisation programmes have resulted in the exercise of private control over water supply as well. As noted above, the right to adequate food entails a protective obligation which requires measures to ensure that enterprises and others do not deprive people of their access to adequate food. In its General Comment on the right to food, the Committee reaffirms that '[a]s part of their obligations to protect people's resource base for food, States parties should take appropriate steps to ensure that activities of the private business sector and civil society are in conformity with the right to food'.[47] In a later General Comment, the Committee elaborates on this insofar as privatised water is concerned.

[44] See Third Report of the Special Rapporteur on the Right to Food, Jean Ziegler, UN E/CN.4/2003/54 (10 January 2003), para. 18.

[45] International Covenant on Economic, Social and Cultural Rights, art. 2(1).

[46] Committee on Economic, Social and Cultural Rights, General Comment 12 (The right to adequate food: art. 11), 12 May 1999, para. 14.   [47] Ibid., para. 27.

'Where water services...are operated by third parties, States parties must prevent them from compromising equal, affordable, and physical access to sufficient, safe and acceptable water.' The Committee adds that '[t]o prevent such abuses an effective regulatory system must be established,...which includes independent monitoring, genuine public participation and imposition of penalties for non-compliance'.[48] If governments are ultimately accountable for violations of the Covenant, the Committee observes that businesses also have responsibilities for conducting their activities in a manner conducive to respect for the right to adequate food.[49] The UN Special Rapporteur on the Right to Food notes in this regard that under the Universal Declaration of Human Rights the goal of promoting respect for human rights and securing their universal observance is intended to engage 'every individual and every organ of society', which must include corporations.[50]

A final issue highlighted by the Committee on Economic, Social and Cultural Rights concerns the commitment of states parties to the Covenant to take steps to realise social, economic and cultural rights 'individually and through international assistance and co-operation'.[51] With regard to the right to food, the Committee asserts that states parties should 'refrain at all times from food embargoes or similar measures which endanger conditions for food production and access to food in other countries'.[52] More positively, states parties should 'take steps to respect the enjoyment of the right to food in other countries, to protect that right, to facilitate access to food and to provide the necessary aid when required'.[53] Food aid can be ambiguous in its impact, bringing short-term relief from hunger, but also harming local producers by destroying their markets and ultimately putting them out of business. This can have serious consequences for the longer-term food security of the communities involved. Against this background, the Committee

[48] Committee on Economic, Social and Cultural Rights, General Comment 15 (The right to water: arts. 11 and 12), 26 November 2002, para. 24.

[49] See Committee on Economic, Social and Cultural Rights, General Comment 12 (The right to adequate food: art. 11), 12 May 1999, para. 20.

[50] Third Report to the General Assembly of the Special Rapporteur on the Right to Food, Jean Ziegler, UN Doc. A/58/330, 28 August 2003, para. 43. See generally paras. 27–51 for discussion of the bearing of transnational corporations on the right to food.

[51] Art. 2(1).

[52] Committee on Economic, Social and Cultural Rights, General Comment 12 (The right to adequate food: art. 11), 12 May 1999, para. 37.   [53] Ibid., para. 36.

also emphasises that, where food aid is provided, it 'should, as far as possible, be provided in ways which do not adversely affect local producers and local markets, and should be organized in ways that facilitate the return to food self-reliance of the beneficiaries'.[54] Furthermore, '[p]roducts included in international food trade or aid programmes must be safe and culturally acceptable to the recipient population'.[55]

In 2002 the UN Special Rapporteur on the Right to Food, along with the governments of a number of recipient states and some non-governmental organisations, expressed reservations about the safety of food aid being provided by the United States which included GMOs. They argued that, in the face of uncertainty over the medium- and long-term health implications of GMOs, the 'precautionary principle' should apply to require that only non-modified food be supplied by way of food aid. The Government of the United States responded that the Special Rapporteur was using his office to 'challenge the food offered by the American people to avert the scourge of famine and to encourage governments to deny food to their hungry citizens'.[56] According to the US Government, the use of GMOs that enhance plant resistance to disease is essential to overcoming hunger and malnutrition. As noted earlier, however, people are not hungry because there is insufficient (non-genetically modified) food around. They are hungry because they are too poor to buy food and also lack the necessary resources to produce their own. Insofar as the US Government's position alludes to the fear that without GMOs agricultural production will fall behind population growth, this idea has been strongly repudiated by Amartya Sen and other analysts. Sen is particularly forthright about the way an over-concentration on food output-per-head can lead policy-makers to ignore both the structural problems that create vulnerability to famine and hence also the need for preventive action. 'A misconceived theory can kill', he writes, 'and the Malthusian perspective of food-to-population ratio has much blood on its hands.'[57]

---

[54] Committee on Economic, Social and Cultural Rights, General Comment 12 (The right to adequate food: art. 11), 12 May 1999, para. 39.   [55] Ibid.

[56] See Statement on the Report of Mr Jean Ziegler, Special Rapporteur on the Right to Food at the Fifty-seventh Session of the UN General Assembly, in the Third Committee, New York, 11 November 2002.

[57] A. Sen, *Development as Freedom* (Oxford: Oxford University Press, 1999), 209.

Trade law and food

We noted at the beginning of this discussion that hunger is not a
spontaneous phenomenon, just as it is not an anonymous one. According
to Mike Davis, the scene was set for the massive famines of the late
Victorian era by a conjunction of climatic phenomena (the 'El Niño'
events), economic fluctuations, and colonial expansion. Whatever forms
part of today's catastrophic conjunctions, one factor that requires close
scrutiny is the current system of international trade. This system has
helped to raise living standards for large numbers of people, but many
believe it has contributed to undermining the food security of the world's
poorest. At a very general level, the project of liberalising world trade rests
on the theory of 'comparative advantage', according to which each country should concentrate on what it can produce most efficiently.
Encouraging states to capitalise on their advantage compared to other
countries is supposed to boost economic growth and enhance the
possibilities for poverty reduction by increasing export revenues. In the
global South, however, things have not always worked out that way, as market access to industrialised countries has remained restricted. At the same
time, dumping of subsidised commodities from industrialised countries has
undercut local producers. Export orientation has further weakened the
position of local producers, concentrating production in the hands of big
companies and driving smallholders off their land and into urban centres
without employment opportunities. The important point, at any rate, is
that the benefits of international trade appear to have been unevenly
distributed, and that food security is an aspect of that unevenness. As John
Madeley writes in a book about trade and hunger, the questions are always
'who will get the benefit of growth? Will the growth be sustainable, and
will it lead to sustainable development? Above all, does growth lay the basis
for food security?'[58]

At the centre of concern about the impact of the current system of
international trade on the food security of the world's poorest are a
number of the agreements adopted at the conclusion of the Uruguay
Round of trade negotiations that now bind WTO member states. Among
these is the Agreement on Agriculture (AoA). The AoA promotes the
liberalisation of trade in foodstuffs and other agricultural produce. Though

[58] J. Madeley, *Hungry for Trade* (London: Zed Books, 2000), 50–1.

this marked a departure for international trade law, in that goods of this kind previously fell outside the scope of the GATT, it resonated with stipulations that had earlier been imposed on the governments of developing countries by the IMF and World Bank in connection with structural adjustment programmes. The AoA lays down obligations with respect to market access, export subsidies, and domestic support for agriculture. In broad terms, the effect of the obligations is to require the reduction of barriers to importation of agricultural produce, the reduction (with some exceptions) of subsidies to local farmers, and the maintenance of domestic support for agriculture at levels no higher than in 1993. The last of these elements is at the heart of much criticism of the AoA, inasmuch as it has enabled the European Union and the United States to retain significantly higher levels of protectionism than are permissible elsewhere. The agreement allows for some exemptions from liberalisation obligations for food security purposes. However, it is not clear whether these exemptions are adequate to counteract the effect of subsidised imports, constrained export earnings, and cash crop consolidation. More specifically, it is not clear whether the exemptions are adequate to counteract those effects in a way that could preserve or, better still, enhance food security for the poorest people in the global South.

Alongside these issues affecting the liberalisation of trade in agricultural produce, concern about the impact of trade law on global hunger is focused on the Agreement on Trade-Related Intellectual Property Rights (TRIPs). Like the AoA, the TRIPs Agreement expanded the scope of the trade regime, bringing the protection of intellectual property within the framework of international trade law. It also reinforced the AoA's integration of agriculture into the trade regime, for what were to be protected were not just mechanical inventions, literary and artistic works, and other traditional forms of intellectual property, but also plant varieties, which had recently begun to be protected in the United States and some other countries. Under the TRIPs agreement WTO member states are obliged to provide intellectual property protection for new plant varieties. In practice, this has generally meant patents, under which the patent holder is granted exclusive rights to commercial exploitation for a given period. This aspect of the TRIPs agreement has proved controversial because of its actual and potential implications for farming practices and biogenetic diversity. Among other things, there is anxiety about the way patent protection affects access by poor people to food crop seeds. On the one hand, access may be restricted as a result of what is referred to as 'biopiracy', as when a company was granted a patent in the United States for basmati rice. On the other hand, access may also be restricted insofar as GMOs place control over seed in the hands of a small number of multinational corporations. We mentioned earlier the contention of the UN Special Rapporteur on the Right to Food and others that only non-modified food should be supplied as food aid, on the ground that uncertainty about the medium- and long-term health implications of GMOs should engage the 'precautionary principle'. A further concern about GMOs relates to the way they make farmers dependent on big companies. Thus, for instance, seeds have been bred to self-sterilise at the end of each season, forcing farmers to buy new seed every year; seeds have also been bred to germinate only after application of fertilisers supplied by the seed-producing company. Overall, the issue here is the relation between the TRIPs agreement and the commodification of food production. Whereas traditionally farmers have saved and shared seed, today they must increasingly pay for it. But with what money are poor people to do that?

Other Uruguay Round agreements have also given rise to food-related criticism, but we have said enough to illustrate something of the anxiety that exists about the bearing of trade law for hunger and malnutrition. While big corporations and their champions urge the commercialisation of agriculture as the solution to food deprivation, others hear echoes of British statesmen claiming to have rescued India from timeless hunger when their own policies were part of the problem. Some critics have begun to articulate their analyses and prescriptions in terms of the concept of 'food sovereignty'. By this is sometimes meant food self-sufficiency. More commonly, however, food sovereignty refers to control over the production, processing and distribution of food, and is used to contest the policies that are facilitating corporate dominance of the food chain. The right to food can help in promoting food sovereignty in this sense. It can help in underscoring the need for investigation into the systemic sources of food insecurity. It can help in insisting on the questions '[w]hy don't people get enough to eat and who are they?'[59] But it cannot prepare us for, and may even shield from us, the immense redistributive struggle to which these questions point. We get

---

[59] S. George, *How the Other Half Dies* (London: Penguin, 1991), 16.

a glimpse of what is involved when we consider the efforts of those who benefit from the current order to discredit the whole enquiry into causation and distribution, and keep the focus firmly fixed on output, trade and aid. Few have captured this process better, or with greater personal experience of it, than Brazilian priest Helder Câmara. Speaking of his work as bishop of Recife, Câmara famously remarked: 'When I give food to the poor, they call me a saint. When I ask why the poor have no food, they call me a communist.'[60]

---

[60] See B. Lecumberri, 'Brazil's Helder Camara, champion of the poor, dies at 90', Agence France Presse, 29 August 1999, available at www.hartford-hwp.com/archives/42/084.html.

Globalisation

What is globalisation? To some, it denotes above all the ubiquity in today's societies of branded goods and corporate logos. To others, it points to the dizzying pace and staggering turnover of the global financial market. To others still, it evokes the rise of satellite television, world music, and the English language as a lingua franca. To yet others, it is synonymous with the consolidation of international and regional governance, especially through the World Trade Organization. Whatever the focus, most people understand globalisation to refer to important changes in the economic, cultural and political spheres, in connection with economic liberalisation and technological innovation.

Since the late 1990s concern has begun to be expressed in human rights circles about the impact of some of these changes for the enjoyment of human rights. In particular, there is concern about the way developments within the framework of the WTO impinge upon the protection of economic and social rights and the rights of indigenous peoples. There is concern about the effect of global markets on the guarantee of labour rights and civil and political rights. And, exacerbating these worries, there is concern about the opening of a responsibility gap, insofar as the prominent role in conditions of globalisation of international actors other than states (multinational corporations, international organisations, etc.) is not matched by adequate recognition of the responsibility of those actors to respect and ensure human rights.

Beyond the specific context of human rights activism and monitoring, globalisation is, of course, contested through the diverse groups and activities that form the 'anti-globalisation' or 'global citizens' movement. Animating this movement is anxiety about the uneven distribution of the benefits of globalisation. This is sometimes expressed in terms of the emergence of a 'socio-economic global apartheid' in which small enclaves of wealth within and between countries are surrounded by vast areas of poverty. On the other hand, the anti-globalisation movement is also animated by awareness that things need not continue as they have unfolded so far. While globalisation is sometimes depicted as if it were a force of nature, it is in fact a political project, and can be challenged and transformed as such.

Against this background, we explore in what follows something of the relationship between globalisation and human rights. We begin by reviewing in more detail the character of contemporary globalisation and the processes associated with it. We then consider how globalisation engages and affects the protection of human rights. Finally, we turn to the question of the salience of human rights for the struggle to transform globalisation. Whereas some regard human rights as taking on renewed significance and urgency in the context of this struggle, others argue that globalisation effectively sidelines human rights and compels us to pursue change in other arenas and using other vocabularies. Ultimately, then, the issue to be faced is: can human rights contribute to the efforts of those seeking to reshape globalisation in the interests of humanity as a whole, and if so, how?

Globalisation

While the word 'globalisation' is relatively new, and has had general currency only since the 1990s, the phenomenon of transboundary interconnectedness with which it is concerned is clearly very old. As historian A.G. Hopkins explains, political boundaries have always been accompanied by crosscutting frontiers 'mapped by systems of belief, circuits of trade, financial flows, zones of famine and disease, and patterns of migration'.[1] From this it does not follow, however, that the nature and significance of transboundary interconnectedness have remained constant. On the contrary, world history can be told as a story of the mutations of this interconnectedness. At any rate, it is widely recognised that contemporary globalisation has crucial features that make it distinctive in relation to earlier periods. In one of the leading accounts, these features are characterised in terms of the extensity, intensity, velocity and impact of global interactions.[2] By this is meant, first, that contemporary

[1] A.G. Hopkins, 'Introduction: Globalization—An Agenda for Historians' in A.G. Hopkins (ed.), *Globalization in World History* (London: Pimlico, 2002), 1, 9.
[2] D. Held, A. McGrew, D. Goldblattt & J. Perraton, *Global Transformations* (Cambridge: Polity Press, 1999), 15.

globalisation involves a 'stretching' or an *extension* of social, economic and political action across national boundaries, such that events, decisions and activities in one part of the world affect people in distant locations. Secondly, contemporary globalisation involves an *intensification* of transboundary interactions and flows, so that they become less random or sporadic and more systematic and regular. Thirdly, contemporary globalisation involves an *acceleration* of the speed at which people, goods, capital, ideas, information and symbolic forms move around the world, carried by new modes of transportation, diffusion and communication. Finally, the enhanced extensity, intensity and velocity of global interactions together magnify the *impact* of global interconnectedness on the life chances of individuals and communities across the world. Thus, on this account, globalisation is defined as 'a process (or a set of processes) which embodies a transformation in the spatial organisation of social relations and transactions—assessed in terms of their extensity, intensity, velocity and impact—generating transcontinental or interregional flows and networks of activity, interaction, and the exercise of power'.[3]

There is a vibrant debate about the causal dynamics that are driving these developments. While some analysts emphasise the multicausal character of globalisation, others set it within the context of the worldwide consolidation of capitalism. Whatever approach is taken, it is clear that contemporary globalisation is linked with the late 20th century demise of state socialism, and with the embrace in the world's major economic regions of a 'neoliberal' agenda of financial deregulation, trade liberalisation, and privatisation. Globalisation is clearly also linked with the technological revolution that has brought us the internet, mobile phone and satellite broadcast, among other innovations. The processes of globalisation are evident in all domains of life, from the economy to government, culture, and ecology.[4] According to some analysts, they are also reflected in changes affecting identity, tradition, community, nation, interpersonal relations, knowledge, and even the way thought is oriented.[5] These things said, there can be little doubt that the most prominent and widely remarked dimensions of globalisation belong to the economic domain, and in particular to the spheres of trade, finance, and production and distribution.

With regard to trade, globalisation is associated with an unprecedented enlargement in the size and scope of world trade. That is to say, compared

---

[3] Ibid., 16.   [4] Ibid., *passim*.
[5] See, e.g., A. Giddens, *Runaway World* (London: Profile Books, 1999).

to earlier periods, levels of world trade are higher, and trading activities encompass more economies and more commodities. Underpinning these changes is the programme of trade liberalisation that began with the 1947 General Agreement on Tariffs and Trade and led in the 1990s to the establishment of the WTO and the framework of post-Uruguay Round agreements through which the forms of trade and kinds of trade barrier covered by international trade law were expanded in some very significant respects. (We return to these agreements later.) With regard to finance, globalisation is associated with an exponential increase in capital flows across borders. The deregulation of financial markets and lifting of exchange controls in many countries have contributed to the emergence of a round-the-clock pattern of financial trading that encompasses a wider range of 'products', and in greater volumes, than ever before. Although trading takes place at a variety of locations, developments in one market have almost instantaneous ramifications everywhere else, as the East Asian crash of 1997–8 highlighted. Finally, with regard to the production and distribution of goods, globalisation is associated with a process of internationalisation, linked to the growth of companies that organise their activities transnationally (whether through the ownership and control of subsidiaries or through 'outsourcing' based on contractual relationships with local firms). While the 'footloose' character of multi-national corporations is sometimes exaggerated, a significant feature of their operations is the capacity to shift production to places where wages are low and labour conditions undemanding. This is a notable feature of the clothing, footwear and sporting goods industries.

In discussions of globalisation an important theme concerns the effect of these changes on state power. For some analysts, globalisation signifies the demise of the nation-state. For others, the idea that globalisation constrains state power is a convenient myth, which allows national governments to 'blame' policy on ineluctable global forces, and in the process to legitimate economic liberalisation and related developments by portraying them as independent of national action. For most analysts, the truth lies somewhere in between these two positions. The nation-state remains significant. Indeed, in some cases and some respects its powers and functions are greater than ever before, and still growing. On the other hand, while globalisation can certainly serve as a convenient myth, the idea that it constrains state power is not *purely* a myth. For with globalisation come a range of pressures on governments to adopt 'market-friendly policies'. Where trade is concerned, these pressures take the form of the rule-based system of trade liberalisation overseen by the WTO. Where finance is concerned, the global financial market affects the autonomy of governments in the fixing of interest and exchange rates, and also generates indirect pressures for reduced budget deficits, cuts in public expenditure, and the privatisation of state activities. And where production and distribution are concerned, the rise of multinational corporations and the internationalisation of production encourage labour market deregulation, curbs on social provision, and lower levels of corporate taxation. The point is not that globalisation determines national policy, but that, in some important ways, it alters the costs and benefits of particular policy options. To this extent, it changes the context in which state power is exercised. At the same time, it reconfigures the system of global governance more generally, insofar as corporate power acquires enhanced significance.

We have so far been speaking of the effects of globalisation in a rather undifferentiated fashion. Yet one of the most striking features of globalisation is its unevenness. Thus, the impact on state power is mediated by hierarchies between North and South, industrialised and newly industrialising, G8 and the rest. While no government—not even that of the United States—is unconstrained by the global order in its policy choices, some governments are patently very much more constrained than others. At the same time, the impact on societies, communities and individuals is similarly differentiated. If globalisation is often elided with homogenisation, integration and interdependence, it seems equally consistent with disharmony, marginalisation and the further entrenchment of relations of exploitation and dependency. Everything depends on the standpoint from which outcomes are viewed, for globalisation entails a new global division of labour and opportunity, which benefits some and disadvantages others. As David Held and Anthony McGrew observe, 'contemporary economic globalization brings with it an increasingly unified world for elites, national, regional and global, but increasing division within nations as the global workforce is segmented, in rich and poor countries alike, into winners and losers'.[6] In this respect, globalisation both accentuates existing inequalities and generates fresh patterns of

---

[6] D. Held & A. McGrew, *Globalization/Anti-Globalization* (Cambridge: Polity Press, 2002), 54.

184 INTERNATIONAL HUMAN RIGHTS LEXICON

inclusion and exclusion. Alongside the other developments we have highlighted, it is noteworthy that by most measures the gap between the world's richest and poorest is currently at record levels, and continuing to widen. As Held and McGrew also remark, the vigour with which trade liberalisation and neoliberal economics have been promoted contrasts sharply with the relatively feeble global action undertaken to reverse this trend.[7] Indeed, redistributive initiatives, mostly in the form of international aid and 'technical assistance', have been virtually negligible compared with the scale of global poverty.

Let us take up one final issue, bearing upon the question of what globalisation is. Specifically, does it refer to an end-state or to a process? While globalisation is sometimes depicted in terms of a particular end-state or condition ('a borderless world', 'the demise of the nation-state', 'the global village', etc.), most analysts maintain that it is more accurately understood as a *process*, and moreover one that is contradictory, uncertain and open-ended in its trajectory. Contrary to more fatalistic assessments, then, globalisation does not prefigure our future or determine our destiny. But if it is an open-ended process, it is important to recognise that globalisation is also a purposeful *project*. Just as it is sometimes depicted in terms of a particular end-state, so too globalisation is sometimes depicted as if it were an impersonal, autonomous and self-propelling force. Thus, instead of being a phenomenon to be explained, it is made to appear itself the explanation and motor of key changes in the world.[8] To present globalisation in this light is to pretend that 'it has come about without distinctive agents working to promote it'.[9] It is to naturalise or reify globalisation, and hence to obscure its character as the product of human agency, historical contingency and contestable political choice. This insight is the crucial premise and perhaps most significant message of the anti-globalisation movement. What the street protesters, activists and campaigners have helped us to see is that globalisation is a political project, which is neither inherently good nor inherently bad, but rather the 'result of human decisions that can be debated and changed'.[10] And if it is a political project, then the issues it

---

[7] D. Held & A. McGrew, *Globalization/Anti-Globalization* (Cambridge: Polity Press, 2002), 63.

[8] J. Rosenberg, *The Follies of Globalisation Theory* (London: Verso, 2000), 3.

[9] D. Harvey, *Spaces of Hope* (Edinburgh: Edinburgh University Press, 2000), 54.

[10] J. A. Scholte, *Globalization: A Critical Introduction* (London: Palgrave, 2000), 9.

raises are political issues—about democracy, justice and equity, and about the organisation of collective life and the prospects for emancipatory change. To quote Held and McGrew again, globalisation 'projects, into a new context, the cardinal questions of political life concerning power and rule, namely: who rules, in whose interests, by what means and for what ends?'[11]

Globalisation and human rights

As a starting point for examining the relationship between globalisation and human rights, we can highlight the *role of human rights as elements within globalisation*. We noted above that globalisation is a complex phenomenon, best understood as a set of processes that generate transboundary flows and networks of activity, interaction or authority. Though we dwelled a little on certain economic processes, we also noted that globalising processes in fact span all domains of life. In accounts of globalisation, human rights are often mentioned in connection with emergent forms of global consciousness, global governance and global accountability. With respect to global consciousness, theorists of globalisation highlight the worldwide diffusion of the idea of human rights, and the significance of universality in this context in fostering an orientation towards the world as a whole. With respect to global governance, attention is directed to the vast and expanding array of norms and institutions that make up the international human rights regime. This regime is understood to belong with other developments that are dispersing political authority and creating a 'multilayered' system of global governance.[12] And with respect to global accountability, the proliferation, activities and networking of non-governmental organisations in the field of human rights are pointed up, as manifestations of an embryonic global civil society.

From the perspective of human rights analysts, however, the interest of globalisation lies less in the role of human rights as elements within globalisation than in the *implications of globalisation for the protection of human*

[11] D. Held & A. McGrew, *Globalization/Anti-Globalization* (Cambridge: Polity Press, 2002), 58.
[12] D. Held, A. McGrew, D. Goldblattt & J. Perraton, *Global Transformations* (Cambridge: Polity Press, 1999), 65 *et seq.*

rights. In recent years this latter issue has come under intense scrutiny, and there is now a large and expanding literature addressing the impact of globalisation on the enjoyment of human rights,[13] including many UN reports.[14] While some of these studies are more sanguine than others about the prospects for globalisation to have beneficial effects on the enjoyment of human rights, most give considerable attention to the ways in which human rights are at the same time subject to strain. The main focus of the studies is on three aspects, linked to the three dimensions of economic globalisation we discussed earlier: global marketisation, trade liberalisation, and corporate power. Let us consider each of these in turn.

The background to concerns about global marketisation is a long-standing anxiety about the effect on human rights of structural adjustment programmes imposed on developing states in connection with loans by international financial institutions. As is well known, the World Bank and International Monetary Fund began in the 1980s to attach conditions to the provision of financial resources, requiring the restructuring of domestic economies so as to lift exchange controls, remove trade barriers, reduce public expenditure, deregulate labour markets, privatise industries and services, and boost production for export. This had serious consequences for human rights. The requirement to reduce public expenditure affects the capacity of governments to protect the rights to food, education, health, and social security. Labour market deregulation often weakens the right to employment and the right to join and form trade unions. And financial and trade liberalisation, privatisation and the reorientation of production for export exacerbate income inequality and foster social unrest, leading all too often to repressive measures that involve violations of the right to liberty and security, the right to freedom of expression and assembly, the right to privacy, the right to humane

[13] See, e.g., R.A. Falk, *Human Rights Horizons: The Pursuit of Justice in a Globalizing World* (London: Routledge, 2000); A. Brysk (ed.), *Globalization and Human Rights* (Los Angeles: University of California Press, 2002); and M.J. Gibney (ed.), *Globalizing Rights* (Oxford: Oxford University Press, 2003).

[14] See, e.g., 'Globalization and its impact on the full enjoyment of all human rights: preliminary report of the Secretary-General', UN Doc. A/55/342, 31 August 2000. See also the work of the special rapporteurs appointed by the UN Sub-Commission on the Promotion and Protection of Human Rights, J. Oloka-Onyango and Deepika Udagama: UN Doc. E/CN.4/Sub.2/2000/13, 15 June 2000; UN Doc. E/CN.4/Sub.2/2001/10, 2 August 2001; and UN Doc. E/CN.4/Sub.2/2003/14, 25 June 2003 (final report).

treatment, and even the right to life. These various impacts, moreover, are often discriminatory inasmuch as they disproportionately affect women, rural populations, public sector employees, and other specific groups. They also cut across the right to development, with its emphasis on the participation of those affected in setting public policy.

Although the World Bank and IMF have more recently moderated their approaches in a number of ways, there remains concern about the human rights implications of lending practices. At the same time, the kinds of issues just highlighted also arise outside the context of World Bank and IMF lending, as effects of global marketisation. Even if governments are not contractually bound to cut public spending, reduce welfare provision, and drive down labour costs, many have done so on the basis that this is necessary in order to maximise the rewards and minimise the risks associated with the internationalisation of production and the volatility of finance. The question of whether the erosion of core protections really does enhance the competitive position and economic prospects of poor countries in conditions of globalisation is a matter of ongoing debate. Nonetheless, to the extent that developments in the economic sphere are associated with a 'race to the bottom', globalisation carries forward the dangers of structural adjustment for labour and other economic and social rights. Insofar as global marketisation is linked with deepening poverty, marginalisation and insecurity for many people, the conditions for violation of civil and political rights likewise persist.

Like structural adjustment, trade liberalisation brings into focus the way law may contribute to creating the context for downward pressure on human rights. In the case of structural adjustment, as we have just noted, that law takes the form of contractual conditions attached to loans. In the case of trade liberalisation, it takes the form of treaty obligations in the sphere of international trade law, now the subject of a growing body of case-law within the framework of the WTO disputes settlement procedures. At issue are primarily (though not exclusively) the various agreements adopted in 1994 at the Uruguay Round of GATT negotiations, when the scope of international trade regulation was significantly enlarged. The agreements include the General Agreement on Trade in Services (GATS), the Agreement on Trade-Related Aspects of Intellectual Property Rights (TRIPs), the Agreement on Trade-Related Investment Measures (TRIMs), the Agreement on Agriculture (AoA) and the Agreement on the Application of Sanitary and Phytosanitary

Measures (SPS Agreement). Among the concerns that have been raised are the possible dangers of the GATS for the right to education and the right to water, TRIPs for the right to health, the right to food and the rights of indigenous peoples to community-based intellectual property, the AoA for the right to food, and the SPS Agreement for the right to health and for issues of food safety associated with the right to food. Again, the uneven patterning of these impacts needs to be stressed. For all that the agreements may promote non-discrimination and market access, their effect is often further to disadvantage those who are already hardest hit by trade liberalisation.

Beyond those issues, trade liberalisation also affects human rights in two interrelated ways, which have to do with asymmetrical practices of protectionism remaining within the system of international trade law. First, whereas developing countries have opened up their economies, significant barriers block their own access to markets in highly industrialised regions in key sectors, such as agriculture and textiles. As is today widely acknowledged, farm subsidies and high tariffs on labour-intensive manufactured goods in the United States and the European Union are closely linked to declining incomes in poor countries. This has implications for the enjoyment of economic and social rights, and also heightens the danger that governments will use repressive measures to silence protest against falling living standards and disintegrating safety nets. Secondly, while the scope of liberalisation has generally broadened with respect to trade in goods and services, labour markets remain closely guarded, especially in the richest countries. The high, and in some places rising, barriers to the movement of people have direct and indirect implications for a variety of human rights, perhaps all of them, but most obviously for the right to work. These barriers also affect the extent to which the rights of migrant workers are protected in the countries where they are employed.

Turning finally to the growth of corporate power, one level at which this has implications for human rights is indicated by our discussion of global marketisation and trade liberalisation. Changes in the organisation of the global economy have greatly increased the role of business in generating outcomes that threaten human rights. Another level at which the growth of corporate power has implications for human rights concerns the allocation of responsibility for protecting human rights. Whereas the focus of international human rights law has traditionally been on the responsibility of states for ensuring the protection of human rights, the enhanced power and visibility of multinational corporations have led to demands for a more wide-ranging approach. To be sure, the rise of corporate power relative to state power is no zero-sum equation,[15] and, as we observed earlier, few analysts hold with the idea that the state is in general decline. On the contrary, the significance of states as redistributors of wealth and protectors of human rights has assumed all the greater importance in conditions of globalisation. At the same time, however, there is growing pressure for responsibility for the protection of human rights to be extended beyond states, to include multinational corporations and, indeed, other actors within the emerging system of global governance as well, such as international economic institutions.

Where multinational corporations are concerned, the effort to promote and define their responsibility in the field of human rights is reflected in a number of documents elaborated within the framework of the United Nations and other intergovernmental organisations. These include the OECD Guidelines for Multinational Enterprises,[16] the ILO Tripartite Declaration of Principles Concerning Multinational Enterprises and Social Policy[17] and most recently, the Norms on the Responsibilities of Transnational Corporations and Other Business Enterprises with regard to Human Rights, elaborated by the UN Sub-Commission on the Promotion and Protection of Human Rights.[18] At the same time, it has become common practice for large corporations to adopt codes of conduct of their own, under which they express a commitment to 'respect the rule of law, and the human rights and dignity of others' in all their operations and activities.[19] Corporations have also taken part in discussions with government officials, activist organisations, trade unions and other stakeholders, leading to the formulation of detailed

[15] D. Held, A. McGrew, D. Goldblattt & J. Perraton, *Global Transformations* (Cambridge: Polity Press, 1999), 281.

[16] See *OECD Guidelines for Multinational Enterprises: Text, Guidelines, Commentary*, DAFFE/IME/WPG (2000) 15.

[17] Adopted by the Governing Body of the International Labour Office at its 204th Session, November 1977, and amended at its 279th Session, November 2000. See ILO Official Bulletin, vol. LXXXIII, 2000, Series A, No. 3.

[18] UN Doc. E/CN.4/Sub.2/2003/12/Rev.2. By Res. 2003/16 the Sub-Commission approved the text, and decided to transmit the Norms to the Commission on Human Rights for consideration and adoption.

[19] See, e.g., UNOCAL Code of Conduct, available at www.unocal.com/ucl_code_of_conduct/index.htm

framework documents, such as the 'Voluntary Principles on Security and Human Rights'.[20] A related development is the 'Global Compact', launched by UN Secretary-General Kofi Annan in 2000; businesses participating in this compact undertake to support a set of 10 principles in the areas of human rights, labour standards, environmental protection, and anti-corruption.[21] Criticism of these various initiatives has focused on the gap between the fulsomeness of the undertakings made or principles enunciated and the lack of effective procedures for monitoring compliance. In this regard, it may be significant that activist groups are beginning to use some of the documents as a basis for scutinising and challenging corporate conduct.[22] Finally, we should note the moves which have been made to engage national courts in the process of making multinational corporations accountable for human rights abuse committed by them or their subsidiaries abroad.[23] In some instances these cases have resulted in substantial settlements, though it is the political mobilisation surrounding the claimants' situation, rather than the settlements themselves, which has generally been considered decisive.

Where international economic organisations are concerned, calls for recognition of the relationship between their activities and human rights initially met with considerable resistance. In recent years the World Bank and IMF have indicated a greater willingness to take account of human rights in framing loans. However, this falls short of acceptance that responsibility exists to ensure compatibility. There is attention to 'good governance' and, more broadly, to the 'social' and 'political' dimensions of development policy, but to date no systematic process has been put in place for considering the impact of lending practices on the enjoyment of human rights.[24] Within the framework of the WTO, the question of formal linkage between trade law and human rights has proved highly

---

[20] This emerged from discussions between the US and UK Governments and a number of oil and mining companies, human rights organisations, trade unions and business associations. See www.state.gov/www/global/human_rights/001220_fsdrl_principles.html.   [21] See www.unglobalcompact.org

[22] See, e.g., the activities of OECD-Watch, established in 2003, reported at www.oecdwatch.org.

[23] For links to relevant cases, see business-humanrights.org.

[24] For detailed discussion of the implications of human rights for these bodies, see S.I. Skogly, *The Human Rights Obligations of the World Bank and International Monetary Fund* (London: Cavendish, 2001) and M. Darrow, *Between Light and Shade: The World Bank, the International Monetary Fund and International Human Rights Law* (Oxford: Hart Publishing, 2003).

controversial. Proposals for introducing a 'social clause', which would provide for the protection of labour standards through the WTO, have been vigorously opposed. Likewise, appeals for the imposition of trade sanctions for human rights violations by WTO member states have been resisted, in part on the ground that sanctions in this context may be open to legal challenge under current WTO rules. Beyond that concern, many governments and activists fear the consequences such developments could have for the already restricted access which poor countries have to rich country markets. But the issue here is not just the responsibility of the IMF, World Bank, WTO and other international organisations with respect to human rights. Also in question are the implications of the human rights obligations owed by the individual state members of these organisations. Thus, for instance, the UN Development Programme's *Human Development Report* of 2000 emphasises the responsibility of government delegations in WTO negotiations for ensuring that trade agreements are consistent with their obligations under international law to respect, protect and fulfil human rights.[25]

From this brief review of concerns about the implications for human rights of global marketisation, trade liberalisation and corporate power, it is apparent that globalisation is understood as throwing up new problems for human rights law. But that is not the only way of thinking about the impact of globalisation on human rights. Viewed from another angle, globalisation can also be seen as pointing up enduring limitations or shortcomings of human rights law. Thus, in a discussion of the relationship between globalisation and human rights, Tony Evans highlights the deficiencies of a 'problem-solving' approach that, as he puts it, '[m]oves from observing human rights problems to creating solutions, ignoring the intermediate steps of analysis and reflection'.[26] What Evans has in mind is the tendency to concentrate on the elaboration of 'technical fixes' which deal with consequences, but not causes. In his words, '[i]nstead of asking why violations of human rights continue to occur on a global scale, which would include an assessment of structural causes of violations, attention is focused on the sites of violations and identifying those responsible for atrocities. Social, economic and political practices are rarely factored into

---

[25] UNDP, *Human Development Report 2000: Human Rights and Human Development* (Oxford: Oxford University Press, 2000), 84–5. Concerning this report, see Development*.

[26] T. Evans, *The Politics of Human Rights* (London: Pluto Press, 2001), 49, 119.

the analysis of human rights violations'.[27] The danger here is not just that the causes of human rights abuse may be left unaddressed. It is also that human rights law may itself contribute to the incidence of abuse. For where violations are treated as the unfortunate consequence of a global order which is not itself in question, that order is legitimated, and the conditions are sustained that make human rights abuse possible.

Our discussion above, and elsewhere in this book, indicates that in fact aspects of the global order which create the context for human rights violations are currently in question within human rights circles. However, it is not clear to what extent this fully corresponds to the kind of 'critical, more reflective view about the nature of hegemony, power, justice, public goods and processes of social change' for which Evans calls.[28] In conditions of globalisation, such a view poses at least five important challenges. First, and at the most general level, it challenges us to recognise that the violation of human rights is often less a matter of individual turpitude or governmental neglect than of the unintended consequences of well-intended policies. Hence, secondly, it challenges us to ensure that attention to particular violations is not allowed to obscure the need for change to those policies and to the wider systems within which they are generated and implemented. Rather, attention to particular violations must be directed to elucidating that need. Thirdly, it challenges us to address in particular the unintended consequences of law, in order to determine how law might be helping to sustain, or might even be exacerbating, the violation of human rights, even as it also provides tools for enhancing respect for those rights. While the effects of trade law in this regard are currently a key focus of discussion, enquiry must extend as well to other dimensions of law, including, as mentioned, human rights law itself. Fourthly, it challenges us to relate concerns about human rights not just to the state but also to the economy. As noted above, moves are currently underway to promote and define the responsibility of multinational corporations and international organisations in the field of human rights. Careful consideration of these moves is needed, to ensure that the various voluntary codes, solemn declarations and multistakeholder initiatives do not serve simply as 'window-dressing', or worse, co-opt the language of human rights in ways that further entrench the economic relationships they purport to

[27] T. Evans, *The Politics of Human Rights* (London: Pluto Press, 2001), 44.
[28] Ibid., 49.

modify. Finally, the kind of 'critical, more reflective' view, to which Evans refers, challenges us to adopt an approach that is oriented not just to problem-solving but to transformative change.

Anti-globalisation and human rights

The end of the 20th century was marked by an extraordinary event. In November–December 1999, over 'five days that shook the world',[29] huge numbers of demonstrators from many countries turned out to disrupt a meeting of the WTO, and the American city of Seattle became a battleground between protesters and riot police. Since that time, almost all the summits of the WTO, along with those of the IMF, World Bank, G8, World Economic Forum and other global and regional organisations, have been accompanied by mass street protests. Linked to these protests have been a range of further initiatives involving the launch of new campaigns (such as the Jubilee 2000 campaign for debt cancellation), new networks (such as the ATTAC network, with an agenda that includes the demand for a 'Tobin' tax on currency speculation), and new institutions (such as the World Social Forum, established as a grassroots alternative to the World Economic Forum). In the process, new solidarities have also been formed, for one of the most striking features of the developments is the tremendous variety of people, preoccupations and perspectives they bring together. Though this is often called the 'anti-globalisation' movement, it is widely recognised that an important part of what has enabled the movement's mobilisation are the very technological innovations and other developments that are associated with globalisation itself, especially the internet. It is also recognised that globalising processes have the potential to raise living standards and promote social inclusion. Thus, the common theme that is emerging is not so much opposition to globalisation *per se*, as opposition to the particular shape and dynamics of 'corporate-led, corporate-driven'[30] globalisation. Put more positively, the common theme that is emerging is a determination to democratise globalisation, and divert it to the struggle against

---

[29] See 238 *New Left Review* (1999), 1.

[30] See S. George, 'Corporate Globalisation' in Emma Bircham & John Charlton (eds.), *Anti-Capitalism: A Guide to the Movement* (London: Bookmarks Publications, 2001), 11, 14.

poverty and injustice. As George Monbiot writes, 'Our task is . . . not to overthrow globalization, but to capture it, and to use it as a vehicle for humanity's first global democratic revolution'.[31]

Human rights are enlisted in the service of the anti-globalisation movement in a number of different ways. One strategy links human rights to the introduction of an ethical dimension into processes which are currently impelled by the logics of capital accumulation. From this perspective, human rights give expression to a global ethics that makes questions of justice relevant to the global economy. Another strategy associates human rights with the effort to democratise processes which are currently directed by bureaucrats, bankers, industrialists, managers, speculators, entrepreneurs, and other powerful and privileged people, most of them white men. Human rights organisations, networks and activities are seen as elements within an emerging global civil society that is expanding the range of participants in global agenda-setting and promoting the accountability of global actors to those they affect. Yet another strategy uses human rights as templates for the articulation of alternatives to 'corporate-led, corporate-driven' globalisation. Thus, for instance, Michael Hardt and Antonio Negri express a vision of an alternative world in terms of a series of new rights—the 'right to global citizenship', the 'right to a social wage', and the 'right to reappropriation'.[32] A final strategy deployed by the anti-globalisation movement is the most obvious from the perspective of a human rights lawyer. Change is pursued by invoking human rights, and holding governments and others to their legal obligations, whether through international procedures, national courts or in some other forum. At the same time, norms are reinterpreted and the boundaries of responsibility reconsidered, in the light of processes that change the context in which inequality and oppression come to be assessed.

In earlier parts of this discussion we saw that human rights stand in two kinds of relation to globalisation. Human rights are elements within globalisation; at the same time, globalisation affects and challenges human rights. Here we see a third connection: human rights are being used as tools to challenge and transform globalisation. Ultimately, of

---

[31] George Monbiot, *The Age of Consent* (London: Flamingo, 2003), 23.
[32] See M. Hardt & A. Negri, *Empire* (Cambridge, Mass.: Harvard University Press, 2000), 396 *et seq*.

course, the transformation of contemporary globalisation is not a matter of human rights, but of politics. It proceeds, to repeat, from awareness that globalisation is neither an end-state nor a self-propelling process, but a political project which can and must be interrogated and reshaped in the interests of humanity as a whole. Our observations on the 'problem-solving' approach that has tended to characterise enquiry into the impact of globalisation for human rights confirm the need to emphasise this point. In that regard, Tony Evans is right to insist that a 'critical, more reflective' approach is needed, if the language and practice of human rights are not to become obstacles to the necessary structural, socio-economic change. But to recognise this is not to say that human rights cannot provide useful tools for those engaged in anti-globalisation struggle.

One way of understanding the utility of the tools which human rights can provide is suggested by a consideration of the increasing contradiction or disjuncture between the realities of our globalising world and the ideas at the centre of human rights. On the one hand, we confront growing concentrations of power and resources, along with deepening poverty and social marginalisation. On the other hand, the universalisation of human rights brings with it the recognition that everyone on the planet has the equal right to core social goods, as well as basic freedoms and participatory rights. As we noted earlier, the worldwide diffusion, international institutionalisation and networked activism of human rights mean that the universalisation of human rights is itself part of the phenomenon of globalisation. From this perspective, human rights may point to the possibility of transforming globalisation by, so to speak, turning it against itself. In David Harvey's words: 'Perhaps the central contradiction of globalization at this point in our history is the way in which it brings to the fore its own nemesis in terms of a fundamental reconception of the universal right for everyone to be treated with dignity and respect as a fully endowed member of our species.'[33]

[33] D. Harvey, *Spaces of Hope* (Edinburgh: Edinburgh University Press, 2000), 94.

Health

Concerns about health overlap with concerns about human rights in some very obvious ways. Torture, for example, is a serious injury to health and a serious breach of human rights. On the other hand, health programmes and human rights can also point in quite different directions. Medical records, for instance, may be kept in a manner that is inconsistent with respect for the right to privacy or the right of access to information. In what follows we take up and explore further this issue of the interrelation of health and human rights. We begin with a general review of some ways in which health and human rights are connected. We then consider how human rights law specifies the integration of health concerns into human rights. That will lead us into a discussion of the right to the 'highest attainable standard of physical and mental health', recognised in the International Covenant on Social, Economic and Cultural Rights[1] and many other instruments.[2] Sometimes referred to as the 'right to health care', this is today more commonly labelled simply the 'right to health'.[3] The point of the latter formulation is to signal that the issues involved include, but also extend beyond, access to health care facilities. As explained below, this is a broad-based, integrative right, aimed at the totality of the conditions for maximal health. So much for the integration of health concerns into human rights. What of the integration of human rights concerns into health policy and action? Does the human rights framework help in this context, or does it rather serve to obscure or even distort the key issues that fall to be addressed by those engaged in the design of health systems, the

[1] Art. 12.
[2] See further B. Toebes, *The Right to Health as a Human Right in International Law* (Antwerp: Intersentia, 1999).
[3] See V.A. Leary, 'The Right to Health in International Human Rights Law' 1 *Health and Human Rights* (1994) 24.

framing of aid programmes and the provision of medical care? Returning to these questions towards the end, we will briefly survey some of the main lines of debate about the value of a 'rights-based' approach to public health.[4]

Health and human rights

Let us begin, then, by taking stock of some of the ways in which health and human rights may be linked. At least four kinds of linkage can be identified. In the first place, the failure to protect human rights can have adverse consequences for health. We have already noted the example of torture as an obvious case of human rights abuse affecting health. Where a state violates its obligations with respect to human rights by providing inadequate protection against other forms of abuse, an equally obvious danger to health may arise. Thus, for instance, domestic violence, unsafe working conditions and the sexual exploitation of children further illustrate the way inattention to human rights can affect health. Secondly, activities in the field of health may themselves violate human rights. We have given the example of medical records being kept in a manner inconsistent with rights to privacy and information. Likewise, mentally ill people may be involuntarily hospitalised on the basis of procedures that do not fully respect their right to personal liberty and security. Compulsory treatment may be administered in circumstances that cannot be reconciled with rights to physical integrity, privacy, freedom of religion, and possibly even life. And health policies may be elaborated which do not meet obligations of non-discrimination.

Clearly, however, the interrelation between health and human rights need not be negative, and is in fact often mutually strengthening. Thirdly, then, activities in the field of health may also serve to promote the enjoyment of human rights. Since sick children cannot attend school, one example of this may be the way programmes for child health lend support for the right to education. Much more generally, though, programmes of immunisation, treatment for infectious diseases, primary

---

[4] On all the issues raised in this paragraph, see further World Health Organization, *25 Questions & Answers on Health and Human Rights* (Geneva: WHO, 2002). See also J. Mann, S. Gruskin, M. Grodin & G. Annas, *Health and Human Rights: A Reader* (New York and London: Routledge, 1999).

health care, and reproductive and maternal health are crucial to the realisation of many of the most basic human rights, inasmuch as those programmes facilitate physical survival, and beyond that the capacity to take part in collective life. Finally, the protection of human rights may itself assist in raising levels of public health. Of central significance in this regard is obviously the right to health, to which we will turn in a moment. For its part, however, that right calls for the protection of a range of other human rights, among them the right to adequate food and nutrition and the right to safe and potable water. In turn, all these rights engage the principle of non-discrimination. Attention to the ways in which health policies involve discrimination is valuable because it can enhance our understanding of the links between social disadvantage and risk to health.

The right to health

The right to the highest attainable standard of health was first enunciated in 1946 in the Constitution of the World Health Organization, and is reiterated in numerous WHO-sponsored declarations, including the 1978 Alma Ata Declaration on Primary Health Care and the 1998 World Health Declaration. It is recognised in the International Covenant on Economic, Social and Cultural Rights[5] and, with respect to children, in the UN Convention on the Rights of the Child,[6] as well as in key regional treaties and other instruments such as the African Charter of Human and Peoples' Rights,[7] the American Declaration of the Rights and Duties of Man,[8] the San Salvador Protocol to the American Convention on Human Rights,[9] and the Revised European Social Charter.[10] The right to health is likewise recognised in more than a hundred national constitutions, whether explicitly or implicitly through the stipulation of state duties with respect to health, and is explicated in some notable judgments of influential national courts, among them the South African Constitutional Court. The Universal Declaration of Human Rights, while not proclaiming the right to health as such, might be seen to have encouraged these developments with its affirmation that

---

[5] Art. 12.   [6] Art. 24.   [7] Art. 16.   [8] Art. XI.   [9] Art. 10.
[10] Art. 11.

'[e]veryone has the right to a standard of living adequate for the health and well-being of himself and his family, including food, clothing, housing and medical care and necessary social services'.[11] In consequence of the various provisions in treaties, other international instruments, and national constitutions just mentioned, the right to health can also be considered a universal right under general international law.

Scope

If we now begin to consider the content of this right, it is immediately obvious that human rights law cannot purport to protect a right not to fall ill or have disease. The right to health cannot be a right to be healthy. Nor can human rights law purport to protect a right that requires poor governments to set up state-of-the-art health care systems for which they lack both money and other resources. What then does this right entail? An important source of guidance is a General Comment on article 12 of the International Covenant on Economic, Social and Cultural Rights, issued in 2000 by the Committee on Economic, Social and Cultural Rights (General Comment 14).[12] The Committee there characterises the right to health as a 'right to the enjoyment of a variety of facilities, goods, services and conditions necessary for the realization of the highest attainable standard of health'. In this sense, it is an 'inclusive right extending not only to timely and appropriate health care but also to the underlying determinants of health, such as access to safe and potable water and adequate sanitation, an adequate supply of safe food, nutrition and housing, healthy occupational and environmental conditions, and access to health-related education and information, including on sexual and reproductive health'.[14]

The right to health, then, is to be understood as encompassing both health care and the underlying determinants of health. With regard to these elements, General Comment 14 proposes that the right can be taken to imply four interrelated criteria: availability, accessibility, acceptability, and quality. By availability is meant that functioning facilities, goods and services relating to health care and the underlying

---

[11] Art. 25.

[12] The right to the highest attainable standard of health: art. 12, 11 August 2000.

[13] Ibid., para. 9.   [14] Ibid., para. 11.

determinants of health must be available in sufficient quantity. By accessibility is intended that these facilities, goods and services must be available to everyone without discrimination; they must be within safe reach of all members of society, including those with disabilities; they must be affordable for all; and information about them must be available to all. Acceptability refers to the need for the relevant facilities, goods and services to be respectful of medical ethics, culturally appropriate and sensitive to gender and age requirements, and designed to respect confidentiality and actually improve health status. Finally, quality points to the need for the relevant facilities, goods and services to be scientifically and medically appropriate, in the sense, for instance, that skilled personnel are used and good standards of hygiene maintained.

The requirement of non-discrimination is explicitly reflected in the various documents already mentioned, and is also stipulated, with regard to racial discrimination and discrimination against women, in the Convention on the Elimination of All Forms of Racial Discrimination[15] and the Convention on the Elimination of All Forms of Discrimination against Women[16] respectively. This aspect assumes particular importance against the background of a strong correlation between poor health status and asymmetries in health and health-determining systems that favour privileged sections of society. These asymmetries are generally (though not invariably) latent, rather than overt. Clearly, if the problem of health-related discrimination is one of effects, rather than intention, then it becomes all the more vital to direct attention to it, and induce consideration of the ways in which programmes and policies fail adequately to take into account the needs and situation of people belonging to particular groups. In this regard, an intriguing suggestion was put forward by one of the leading analysts of the right to health, Jonathan Mann. According to him, 'inadvertent discrimination is so prevalent [in the field of health] that all public health policies and programmes should be considered discriminatory until proven otherwise'.[17]

---

[15] Art. 5(e)(iv).   [16] Arts. 11(1)(f) and 12.
[17] Jonathan Mann, quoted in World Health Organization, 25 Questions and Answers on Health and Human Rights (Geneva: WHO, 2002), 13.

Obligations

Let us turn now to examine more closely the obligations which the right to health entails for governments. These obligations include both aspects that are to be realised progressively, and aspects that have full, immediate effect. For example, the obligation to eliminate health-related discrimination is an obligation with full immediate effect. By contrast, under article 2(1) of the Covenant on Economic, Social and Cultural Rights, the obligation to implement the right to the highest attainable standard of health is an obligation to take steps, to the maximum of a state's available resources, with a view to achieving progressively the right's full realization. However, *this obligation* is itself an obligation with full, immediate effect. In other words, as General Comment 14 emphasises, steps must be taken, and those steps must be 'deliberate, concrete and targeted towards the full realization of the right to health'.[18] This means that constant progress must be demonstrated. Whether a country is rich or poor, the key issue is improvement in relation to the four criteria mentioned above of availability, accessibility, acceptability, and quality. Thus, there is a 'strong presumption' that retrogressive measures breach a state's obligations.[19]

More positively, the adoption is required of legislative, administrative, budgetary, judicial and promotional measures aimed at enhancing the extent to which all members of society have access to health care and to the underlying determinants of health. As in relation to other rights, the Committee on Economic, Social and Cultural Rights has identified certain 'core obligations' associated with the right to health.[20] These include the obligation to ensure access to essential drugs, adequate safe food, basic housing and sanitation, and an adequate supply of safe and potable water, along with non-discriminatory access to health facilities, goods and services. The core obligations also include the obligation to formulate, implement, and revise as necessary, a national public health strategy and plan of action, which is based on epidemiological evidence and which addresses the health concerns of the whole population. In this regard, the Committee stresses the importance of enabling the participation in health-related decision-making at all levels by those affected by it.

[18] Committee on Economic, Social and Cultural Rights, General Comment 14 (The right to the highest attainable standard of health: art. 12), 11 August 2000, para. 30.
[19] Ibid., para. 32.   [20] Ibid., para. 43.

We mentioned a moment ago that, whether a country is rich or poor, the key issue is constant progress. Clearly, however, resource limitations are not irrelevant. Human rights law recognises that the right to health must, and can only be, implemented within a framework of international assistance and co-operation. This is widely reflected in relevant treaties and other instruments, as well as in the practice of relevant organisations and of states. Thus, for example, article 2(1) of the International Covenant on Economic, Social and Cultural Rights cited above, concerning the obligation to take steps, to the maximum of a state's available resources, with a view to achieving progressively the full realization of the right to health, contains the important stipulation that those steps must be taken 'individually and through international assistance and co-operation, especially economic and technical'.[21] One implication of this is that the obligations of states with respect to the right to health cannot be considered without reference to their activities, whether as donors, recipients, or participants of some other kind, in health-related assistance programmes.

Private interests

The HIV and AIDS pandemics of recent decades illustrate the way disparities in the global distribution of resources are linked to disparities in the global distribution of disease, for HIV and AIDS affect people in poorer countries to an exponentially greater extent than people in rich countries. Against this background, an issue that has taken on immense significance in recent years is the impact of international trade law—and particularly the Agreement on Trade-Related Aspects of Intellectual Property Rights (TRIPs)—on the availability of life-saving drugs. On the one side, drug companies have sought protection for their patent rights, and warned of the dangers of failing to reward pharmaceutical research and development in this way. On the other side, the governments of India and Brazil have been among those asserting the right to produce generic (non-branded) drugs under compulsory licensing schemes, or to benefit from parallel imports of such drugs, where patented HIV-AIDS drugs are too expensive. In their contention, intellectual property rights must yield before the need to ensure access to

[21] See further International Council on Human Rights Policy, *Duties sans frontières: human rights and global social justice* (Geneva: ICHRP, 2003).

life-saving drugs. At the Doha negotiations of the World Trade Organization in 2001 a Ministerial Declaration was adopted, in which it was acknowledged that the TRIPs Agreement does not prevent WTO member states from taking measures to protect public health. The Declaration goes on to affirm that the TRIPs Agreement 'can and should be interpreted and implemented in a manner supportive of WTO Members' right to protect public health and, in particular, to promote access to medicines for all'.[22]

Intellectual property rights are one way in which private interests can intersect with the right to health. Another way arises when health-related facilities or services are provided by private companies, or when private companies undertake activities that affect health or the underlying determinants of health. Given the widespread moves in recent decades to expand the involvement of the private sector in the provision of public services, attention has turned to the question of accountability for the right to health. In the first place, it is clear that the obligation of states to protect the right to health includes an obligation to regulate the activities of individuals, groups and corporations so as to safeguard people within the state's jurisdiction from infringements of their right to health by third parties. Thus, for instance, legislation must be enacted and enforced which protects employees from employment practices detrimental to their health and safety. Likewise, measures must be adopted which protect populations from health risks caused by industrial activities of private companies or public–private partnerships.[23] Secondly, the obligation of states to ensure that health and health-related services are available, accessible, acceptable, and of good quality remains, regardless of whether those services are provided by state agencies or by private companies. Among other things, this means, as stressed in General Comment 14,[24] that payment for health care services must always be based on the principle of equity, and that where the services are privately provided, governments are in no way absolved of their responsibility for ensuring the affordability of health care services for all, including socially disadvantaged groups.

[22] Doha Ministerial Declaration on the TRIPs Agreement and Public Health, adopted 14 November 2001, WT/MIN (01)/DEC/2, para. 4.

[23] See, e.g., *The Social and Economic Rights Action Center and the Center for Economic and Social Rights v Nigeria*, African Commission of Human and Peoples' Rights, 20th Session, 13–27 October 2001, Communication 155/96.   [24] See para. 12(b).

Finally, and in addition to these forms of state accountability, private parties may themselves be accountable with respect to the right to health. According to the Committee on Economic, Social and Cultural Rights, '[w]hile only States are parties to the Covenant and thus ultimately accountable for compliance with it, all members of society—individuals, including health professionals . . . , as well as the private business sector—have responsibilities regarding the realization of the right to health. States parties should therefore provide an environment which facilitates the discharge of these responsibilities'.[25] Where the private business sector is concerned, the argument has been made that the responsibilities mentioned here may be seen as generating duties for corporations to respect, protect and fulfil the right to health.[26] At the same time, there is evidence that corporations have in some cases themselves accepted the responsibility to promote access to health care, and that that acceptance is linked to an awareness on their part of the claims of human rights.

Health policy and the 'rights–based' approach Conflict.

Our discussion so far has focused on the content and implications of the right to health. It remains now to take up the question of whether reference to this right is helpful. At a number of points in this book we touch on general arguments about the value of addressing problems in terms of human rights. Here we confine ourselves to the more specific debate which has unfolded about the value of what is referred to as a 'rights-based' approach to public health. By 'rights-based' approach is meant that the design, implementation and evaluation of health-related policies and programmes are informed by human rights. Two main concerns arise.

One is the concern that a rights-based approach might compromise the capacity of public authorities to protect health, by allowing rights, such as those to privacy and freedom of movement, to get in the way of essential measures to prevent the spread of disease, such as the compulsory administration of drugs or the institution of quarantine. Those supportive of a rights-based approach point out in response that, indeed, the approach

[25] Committee on Economic, Social and Cultural Rights, General Comment 14 (The right to the highest attainable standard of health: art. 12), 11 August 2000, para. 42.

[26] See, e.g., N. Jägers, *Corporate Human Rights Obligations: In Search of Accountability* (Antwerp: Intersentia, 2002), 87–8.

requires that the implications of health-related measures for human rights be considered. However, by no means every restriction of a human right represents a violation of that right. Human rights law recognises that there are circumstances in which the protection of public health justifies restricting certain rights, but it lays down strict conditions that must be met in that event: the restriction must be provided for by law, and carried out in accordance with law; it must serve a legitimate aim; it must be strictly necessary to achieve that aim, in the sense that a less restrictive measure would not be adequate; and it must not be discriminatory in the way it is imposed or applied.[27] Where these criteria have been met, human rights institutions have held programmes of compulsory vaccination, forcible feeding or compulsory administration of drugs to be fully consistent with commitments to protect human rights.[28]

The other main concern is that, even if a rights-based approach does not compromise the capacity of public authorities to protect health, nonetheless it does not help them to do so. It does not help them because public health systems depend on the ranking of priorities, against the background of scarce resources. As Martha Minow explains, the central questions faced by health policy-makers are of the order: 'Who gets to use dialysis equipment? Who goes to the front of the line for the kidney transplant?'[29] And if these are the questions, then what is achieved by saying that everyone has the right of access to health care facilities, goods and services? Where there is not enough dialysis equipment to go around, and there are limited possibilities for kidney transplantation, the whole point is that *not everyone* with renal failure can get to use dialysis equipment, or have a kidney transplant any time soon.

[27] See Siracusa Principles on the Limitation and Derogation of Provisions in the International Covenant on Civil and Political Rights, reproduced in Annex, UN Doc. E/CN.4/1985/4, 28 September 1984, see further, Symposium 'Limitation and Derogation Provisions in the International Covenant on Civil and Political Rights' 7 *Human Rights Quarterly* (1985) 1; and for a more recent restatement of the principles concerning restriction on rights see Human Rights Committee, General Comment 27 (Freedom of movement: art. 12), 2 November 1999, para. 18.

[28] See, e.g., the decisions of the European Commission of Human Rights in *Carlo Boffa and Thirteen Others v San Marino*, Applic. 26536/95, Report of 15 January 1998, and of the European Court of Human Rights in *Herczegfalvy v Austria*, Judgment of 24 September 1992, paras. 79–84.

[29] M. Minow, in *Economic and Social Rights and the Right to Health: An Interdisciplinary Discussion Held at Harvard Law School in September 1993* Harvard Law School Human Rights Program (1995) 2.

For Minow and others, human rights are too absolutist and individualistic a framework to be useful in addressing questions like those just mentioned. From this perspective, a rights-based approach obscures the fundamentally distributive character of the issues at stake. It also encourages disregard for the needs of others, and risks impeding the processes through which fair social choices are made. In Minow's words, '[r]ights rhetoric revolves around the individual, the bearer of the right; it doesn't help us in allocating resources or adjudicating between competing right bearers. Its individualism paralyzes us and frustrates dialogue'.[30]

Minow's question 'who gets to use dialysis equipment?' in fact fell to be addressed some years later in a case before the South African Constitutional Court.[31] In view of a shortage of resources, a policy had been adopted in which automatic access to dialysis was limited to patients suffering from acute renal failure. For those suffering from chronic renal failure, access to dialysis was provided only if they were eligible for a kidney transplant. An assessment had been made that more people could be kept alive through the application of this policy than if untreatable patients were permitted to use dialysis machines. The appellant in this case suffered from chronic renal failure, and was not provided with access to dialysis, as his particular condition rendered him incapable of having a successful kidney transplant. Lacking dialysis treatment, he claimed that his right of access to health care services, protected in section 27 of the 1996 South African Constitution, had been violated. In considering this claim, Justice Sachs observed that '[w]hen rights by their very nature are shared and inter-dependent, striking appropriate balances between the equally valid entitlements or expectations of a multitude of claimants' is a matter of 'defining the circumstances in which the rights may most fairly and effectively be enjoyed'.[32] The Court was persuaded in this case that the circumstances in which dialysis treatment could most fairly and effectively be enjoyed were not those of the appellant. Hence, there was no violation.

The right of access to health care services came into issue again before the South African Constitutional Court in a case arising out of governmental policy concerning mother-to-child HIV transmission.[33] In consequence of this policy, a drug which could have reduced the risk

[30] Ibid.
[31] *Soobramoney v Minister of Health, KwaZulu-Natal*, CCT 32/97, 27 November 1997.
[32] Ibid., para. 54.
[33] *Minister of Health v Treatment Action Campaign*, CCT 8/02, 5 July 2002.

of mother-to-child HIV transmission was not being made available in the public health system. Here the Court found that the right had been violated. For the Court, the government's failure to meet its obligations with respect to the right to health care services was reflected in its failure to make the drug available, when medically indicated, within the public health sector, and in its failure to set out a timeframe for a national programme to prevent mother-to-child transmission of HIV. Accordingly, the Court ordered the authorities to remove the restrictions that had been imposed on the availability of the drug in public hospitals. In doing so, it also emphasised that any future modifications of governmental policy with regard to mother-to-child HIV transmission would have to be consistent with the right of access to health care services protected in the Constitution.

This case, along with the earlier dialysis case, surely suggests that something is indeed achieved by saying that everyone has the right of access to health care facilities, goods and services. A rights-based approach does not, and cannot, obviate the need to make health policy—that is to say, to make choices, rank priorities, and distribute goods and services in the field of health. What it can do, however, is to shape health policy by requiring that the choices that are made, and the systems that are put in place, be *justified* by reference to a series of ideas or principles. One of the most important of these is the principle that health-related programmes must not involve unjust discrimination. Another is the idea that governments are under an obligation to take steps, to the maximum of the state's available resources, to enhance the extent to which all members of society have access to health care facilities, as well as to the underlying determinants of health. Yet another is the idea that this has significant implications for international assistance and co-operation. Another still is the notion that there exist certain core obligations with respect to health, among them the obligation to develop and implement public health strategies and plans of action. And another is the principle that these strategies, and indeed all health-related decision-making, should be the outcome of an inclusive process, which allows for the participation of those affected. As one study observes, the right to health enters with the insight that government policy may be 'a legitimate exercise of power and government prerogative'. But from that it does not necessarily follow that it is 'a justifiable one'.[34]

---

[34] C. Kisoon, M. Caesar & T. Jitoo, *Whose Right? AIDS Review 2002* (Pretoria: Centre for the Study of AIDS, 2002), 15.

Housing

In his book *City of Quartz* Mike Davis describes the stark contrasts that characterise Los Angeles: while planners work to make rich neighbourhoods 'softer' and lovelier, 'a few blocks away the city is engaged in a merciless struggle to make public facilities and spaces as unliveable as possible for the homeless and poor'.[1] Elements of what Davis describes as an increasingly 'sadistic street environment' include the construction of 'bum-proof' bus benches, the closure of public toilets, and the installation of sprinkler systems that drench those sleeping in parks at random intervals. Davis's point, of course, is not just that street conditions should be better for homeless people. It is that no one should have to sleep on bus benches or in parks in the first place. Planning sadism is simply a reminder of that, should one be needed.

Homelessness in cities like Los Angeles is one facet of the wider problem of lack of access to adequate housing. This is a problem of immense proportions, especially in the countries of the global South. Davis reports that in the late 1990s the majority of homeless people in Los Angeles were refugees from El Salvador, and indeed an aspect of the global scale of this problem is that it is frequently linked to displacement of people, within and across national borders. More generally, deprivation in the sphere of housing is inseparable from the phenomena that cause people to be driven from their homes and/or to live in dwellings that do not meet their needs. War, civil strife and 'ethnic cleansing' are some of the most obvious causes, or at any rate contexts, of dispossession. At the same time, access to housing is affected by economic and social factors (among them, industrialisation, urbanisation, structural adjustment, and property speculation), legal and political arrangements (such as security of tenure,

[1] M. Davis, *City of Quartz: Excavating the Future in Los Angeles* (London: Pimlico, 1998), 232.

entitlement to hold property, and stakeholder consultation), and cultural and ideological practices (of the type exemplified by gender bias, racism, and xenophobia).

Against this background, we examine in what follows the significance of human rights, as the basis for what is sometimes referred to today as a 'rights-based' approach to housing problems. In particular, we examine the significance of the 'right to adequate housing', recognised in international human rights treaties and other instruments, and in the constitutions of many countries. It will be instructive to begin with a general review of the various ways in which housing engages issues of human rights. We can then concentrate on the right to adequate housing, looking first at the entitlements and obligations it is seen to entail, and then later at some issues that arise when it is violated through processes of forced eviction.[2]

Housing and human rights

Access to adequate housing affects the enjoyment of a wide range of human rights. In the first place, it affects the right to health. The World Health Organization has stated that housing is the single most important environmental factor bearing upon the incidence of disease and the extent of life expectancy. Access to adequate housing also affects the right to work, in that the prospects of earning a living are severely reduced when a person is homeless or has access only to housing that is beyond reach of places where a living can be earned. Where people are forcibly evicted from their homes, this may also have implications for the right to education. Forced evictions frequently result in children's schooling being disrupted or stopped altogether. Likewise, forced evictions affect the right to personal security. Victims are generally harassed and often beaten. Women and girls become particularly vulnerable to violence, including sexual violence, when deprived of any, or any safe, home. Furthermore, access to housing is a crucial element in the right to privacy. Secure tenure ensures the possibility of creating an intimate

[2] See further S. Leckie, 'The Right to Housing' in A. Eide, C. Krause & A. Rosas (eds.), *Economic, Social and Cultural Rights: A Textbook*, 2nd ed. (The Hague: Nijhoff, 2001), 149; and S. Leckie (ed.), *Returning Home: Housing and Property Restitution Rights of Refugees and Displaced Persons* (New York: Transnational Publishers, 2003).

space within which to act and interact unobserved. Finally, inasmuch as people's homes are often symbols of identities and traditions, housing affects rights to free expression and rights that protect the members of minority communities against cultural assimilation.

At the same time, access to adequate housing is itself affected by the extent to which a number of these and other human rights are enjoyed. Inadequate housing arrangements do not generally get improved unless demands are made by those affected, and in turn, effective demands depend on organised and collaborative activity. It follows that, where rights to free expression, assembly and association are not protected, the prospects for securing change in the sphere of housing are substantially weakened. Non-discrimination guarantees are also crucial to access to adequate housing, in that discrimination usually works on multiple, mutually reinforcing levels. Thus, for instance, racism in relation to work and other social goods and opportunities heightens susceptibility to racism in relation to housing (and vice versa). Bearing in mind that domestic violence severely compromises the safety and hence adequacy of housing, protection of the right to personal security and physical integrity is likewise decisive for access to adequate housing, especially for women and children. This obviously requires protection against threats to these rights not just by state officials, but also by private parties, such as family members. Finally, access to adequate housing may have implications for the choice of locality in which people are able to live, and to this extent may also depend on protection of the rights to choose one's residence and move freely within one's country of residence.

But access to adequate housing engages issues of human rights not only in these ways. International human rights law also protects the right to adequate housing as a human right in and of itself. This right is proclaimed, as a component of the 'right to a standard of living adequate for ... health and well-being', in the Universal Declaration of Human Rights.[3] In similar terms, it is guaranteed in the International Covenant on Economic, Social and Cultural Rights; article 11(1) of the Covenant affirms the right of everyone to an adequate standard of living, including (among other things) adequate housing. The right to housing is likewise recognised in other international and regional treaties, among them the Convention on the Elimination of All Forms of Racial

---

[3] Art. 25(1).

Discrimination,[4] and in many national constitutions. In treaties which contain no explicit guarantee of the right to housing, such as the European Convention on Human Rights and the African Charter of Human and Peoples' Rights, a degree of implicit recognition and indirect protection has developed within the framework of guarantees of the right to home, privacy and family life, and the right to property and peaceful enjoyment of possessions.

The idea that everyone has the right to adequate housing forms the basis for numerous declarations of international standards in the field of housing, and there can be little doubt that this is today a universal right, which applies irrespective of a state's adherence to the Economic, Social and Cultural Rights Covenant or other relevant treaties. The question to which we must now turn is what that right entails. This question takes on particular significance against the background of some rather exaggerated accounts of the implications of the right which have been advanced in recent years, on occasion by those supportive of a rights-based approach to housing problems, but most commonly by the representatives of governments opposed to it. While it is indeed wrong to treat the merits of such an approach as self-evident, it is equally problematic to frame the right to adequate housing in a way that effectively stops discussion of the merits and demerits of a rights-based approach before it can begin.

Access to adequate housing

Let us start, then, with what the right to adequate housing does not, and manifestly cannot, entail. As observed by Rajindar Sachar in a report to the UN Sub-Commission on Prevention of Discrimination and Protection of Minorities, it does not entail that governments must build housing for the entire population. Nor does it entail that housing must be provided free of charge to all who request it.[5] Nor yet does it entail that governments must spend on housing money which they do not have. Rather, it is concerned with the measures required to prevent homelessness; to ensure that everyone has housing which is safe, healthy and in other

---

[4] Art. 5(e).
[5] See Final Report on the Right to Adequate Housing, UN Doc. E/CN.4/Sub.2/ 1995/12.

respects adequate; to eliminate discrimination in the sphere of housing; and to prohibit forced or arbitrary evictions and other acts of unjust dispossession. Determining these measures invites reflection on a wide range of changes that might be needed, not only in the laws, policies and spending priorities of governments, but also in the larger systems that shape and constrain those laws, policies and priorities. Thus, the right to adequate housing has been used as the basis for calls for change in the provisions of international economic law, in the activities of development agencies, international financial institutions and multinational corporations, and in the structure and orientation of global economic life in general. Let us now look in more detail at what is involved.

Entitlements

The right to adequate housing is both less and more than the right to a house—less in the sense just indicated that it does not entail that governments must provide housing free of charge to everyone who requests it, but more in the sense that it asserts the right of everyone to housing which is *adequate*. As is often remarked, a roof over one's head does not exhaust the entitlement. The concept of adequacy in this context is explicated by the Committee on Economic, Social and Cultural Rights in a General Comment on article 11(1) of the Covenant (General Comment 4).[6] While acknowledging that the adequacy of housing is determined in part by social, economic, climatic, ecological and other factors, the Committee identifies seven factors that must always be taken into account. The first is legal security of tenure. Whatever the particular form of tenure (public or private rental, lease, freehold title, native title, co-operative ownership, informal settlement, etc.), housing is not adequate if the members of the household lack legal protection against forced eviction, harassment and other threats. The second factor concerns the availability of services, materials and infrastructure. Housing is not adequate where there is no sustainable access to water, electricity, sanitation, means of refuse disposal and site drainage, emergency services, and so on. Thirdly, the Committee highlights the issue of capacity to meet necessary housing-related costs. Access to adequate housing requires access to affordable housing. This necessitates means- and needs-related

[6] Committee on Economic, Social and Cultural Rights, General Comment 4 (The right to adequate housing: art. 11(1), 13 December 1991.

systems of housing subsidy and housing finance, along with protection from unreasonable levels and increases of rent.

Fourth in the Committee's list is the question of habitability. Housing is only adequate if it provides the inhabitants with adequate space, protects them from cold, heat, damp and other threats to health and structural hazards, and assures their physical safety. The fifth issue highlighted is that of accessibility to all. To ensure access to adequate housing on the part of disadvantaged and vulnerable groups, such as the elderly, those with chronic medical problems and disabilities, refugees and displaced people, and those living in disaster-prone areas, particular attention, and indeed (as the Committee states) 'some degree of priority consideration', must be given to their distinctive needs.[7] This issue of accessibility also points up the importance of land reform in countries where access to land is narrowly circumscribed. The sixth factor emphasised by the Committee concerns the location of housing. Adequate housing must be in a location which allows access to employment options, health-care services, schools and other social facilities. It must also be in a location which does not endanger the health of the inhabitants, due to polluted water or hazardous atmospheric conditions. Finally, the Committee draws attention to the need for what it terms 'cultural adequacy'. By this it means that housing policies should enable the expression of cultural identity, and that the adequacy of housing is linked to the possibility for diversity in relation to it.

Obligations

Turning now to consider the obligations of states with respect to the entitlement of everyone to adequate housing, we can find useful reference points in article 2(1) and (2) of the Covenant. Under article 2(1), as noted in many other places in this book, states parties undertake to 'take steps, individually and through international assistance and co-operation... to the maximum of [their] available resources, with a view to achieving progressively the full realization of the rights recognized in the... Covenant by all appropriate means'. Under article 2(2) states parties undertake to 'guarantee that the rights enunciated in the... Covenant will be exercised without discrimination of any kind as to race, colour, sex,

---

[7] Committee on Economic, Social and Cultural Rights, General Comment 4 (The right to adequate housing: art.11(1)), 13 December 1991, para. 8(e).

language, religion, political or other opinion, national or social origin, property, birth or other status'. This latter stipulation is reinforced, with regard to discrimination against women, by article 3, under which states parties undertake to 'ensure the equal right of men and women to the enjoyment of all' the rights set forth in the Covenant. If more far-reaching commitments are made under other treaty regimes, these provisions of the Covenant can be taken to express a universally applicable baseline. What do they entail in the specific context of housing rights? Again, General Comment 4 is instructive.

One dimension of the obligations associated with the right to adequate housing concerns the action that must be taken by governments. To begin with, the Committee stresses the importance of devising a housing strategy that defines objectives, sets priorities, and identifies available resources, and of doing so in a manner which enables the participation, and takes account of the concerns, of those who currently lack adequate housing. This last aspect is likewise emphasised by the South African Constitutional Court in an important decision interpreting a constitutional guarantee of the right to adequate housing.[8] For the Court, it is an implication of this right that no housing programme can be regarded as reasonable if it fails to address the needs of disadvantaged segments of society.[9] As to the steps to be taken to ensure adequate housing for all, the Committee observes that these will generally include a mix of policy initiatives, resource allocations, and legal and administrative measures. Security of tenure, for instance, requires legal and administrative measures, while the right of all to affordable housing calls for resource allocations for housing subsidies and/or the construction of low-cost public housing. In most countries housing is provided through a combination of public and private sector initiatives, and the Committee also emphasises the importance of creating an enabling environment for community-based initiatives. Thus, appropriate laws and financial arrangements must be put in place to facilitate the contribution which households themselves, in concert with community groups, non-governmental organisations and business enterprises, are able to make to the provision of adequate housing.

A further dimension of the obligations that are associated with the right to housing concerns the principle of non-discrimination. Specific

---

[8] *Government of the Republic of South Africa v Grootboom & Others*, CCT 11/00, 4 October 2000.   [9] Ibid., esp. paras. 43–4.

obligations to prohibit and eliminate racial discrimination in the field of housing are included in the Racial Discrimination Convention.[10] With regard to discrimination on the grounds of gender, the Convention on the Elimination on All Forms of Discrimination against Women imposes an obligation to eliminate discrimination against women in rural areas in the sphere of housing.[11] At the same time, as is widely recognised, gender discrimination also affects access to housing in ways that go well beyond the disadvantages suffered by women in rural areas. Thus, the right to housing may entail an obligation to repeal laws and secure the modification of practices that discriminate against women with regard to personal status, property ownership, inheritance, and access to finance and land. A further group commonly affected by discrimination in the sphere of housing is immigrants. Under the Convention on the Protection of the Rights of All Migrant Workers and Members of their Families, states parties undertake to ensure that migrant workers enjoy equal treatment with nationals with respect to access to housing.[12] While resource constraints may mean that some aspects of the right to adequate housing will need to be progressively fulfilled, the Economic, Social and Cultural Rights Committee has made clear that these and other obligations to ensure non-discrimination in the enjoyment of rights must be understood as obligations of 'immediate effect'.[13]

A final dimension of the obligations that are associated with the right to housing concerns the issue of international co-operation. In principle, the same obligations which apply to a government's activities with respect to its own population also apply to its activities in the field of international development assistance. Thus, the right to adequate housing is not consistent with aid programmes that fail to take account of the situation of disadvantaged and vulnerable groups, or that help to sustain discrimination in the field of housing. At the same time, the right to adequate housing is not consistent with the imposition on another government of measures which force that government to breach its international obligations to ensure adequate housing. In the context of

[10] Art. 5(e).   [11] See art. 14(2).   [12] Art. 43(1).
[13] Committee on Economic, Social and Cultural Rights, General Comment 3 (The nature of States parties obligations: art. 2(1)), 14 December 1990, para. 1, and see General Comment 4 (The right to adequate housing: art.11(1)), 13 December 1991, paras. 6, 9 and 17, and General Comment 7 (The right to adequate housing—forced evictions: art. 11(1)), 20 May 1997, paras. 10 and 17.

structural adjustment programmes and aid conditionality, concern has been expressed about the conduct of international financial institutions and donor governments from this perspective. A related concern bears upon developments within the framework of the World Trade Organization. One aspect of these developments to which Miloon Kothari called particular attention in a report to the UN Commission on Human Rights, is the impact of the General Agreement on Trade in Services (GATS) on the availability of access to water.[14] As we have noted, access to potable water and sanitation facilities is an integral element in the adequacy of housing.[15] In recent years water services have been subject to processes of privatisation in many countries. The concern about the GATS relates to the prospect of further privatisation of water services, in the context of liberalisation within the water sector. More specifically, it relates to the consequences this may have with regard to the coverage, pricing and quality of water services, especially for poor and other marginalised sections of society and those living in remote or neglected areas.

Forced eviction

To this point our main focus has been on the entitlements and obligations associated with the right to adequate housing. Let us now shift the focus to consider some issues surrounding its violation. As our discussion so far indicates, violation of the right to adequate housing can occur in a variety of ways. One very common way, however, involves forced eviction. By forced eviction is meant the involuntary removal of individuals, households or communities from their homes and/or the land they occupy, without the protection of appropriate legal and other safeguards. Forced evictions take place in many different contexts. Settlements may be destroyed to make way for dams, or in connection with other infra-structural projects or commercial ventures. Slums may be 'cleared' in

[14] See Report of the Special Rapporteur on adequate housing as a component of the right to an adequate standard of living, UN Doc. E/CN.4/2002/59 (1 March 2002), esp. paras. 49–65.

[15] The right of access to water is also understood as a human right which generates specific obligations. See Committee on Economic, Social and Cultural Rights, General Comment 15 (The right to water: arts. 11 and 12), 20 January 2003.

conjunction with urban 'beautification' programmes and efforts to attract tourism. Tenancies may be terminated to allow for redevelopment of valuable sites in gentrifying areas. Beyond circumstances of these kinds, forced evictions also form part of practices of ethnic cleansing, population transfer and collective punishment, and lead to internal displacement, refugee movements, and mass exoduses of people during armed conflict.

Forced evictions affect people in many different ways, which commonly entail violations of a number of internationally protected human rights, among them rights to personal security, privacy, home and family life, property and peaceful enjoyment of possessions, and even the right to life. Non-discrimination guarantees are also implicated, insofar as women, minority communities, indigenous peoples or other groups are disproportionately targeted, or at any rate affected. In a case against Turkey arising out of the destruction by state security forces of a Kurdish village in south-eastern Turkey, the European Court of Human Rights held that Turkey was responsible for violations of the applicants' rights to home and private life under article 8 of the European Convention, and their right to peaceful enjoyment of possessions under article 1 of the First Protocol to the Convention.[16] Likewise, in a complaint concerning the destruction of Ogoni villages in Nigeria, the African Commission on Human and Peoples' Rights found that Nigeria was responsible for violations of the rights to property and family life under articles 14 and 18(1) respectively of the African Charter of Human and Peoples' Rights.[17] The villages were attacked by state security forces after the villagers began to protest at the despoliation of their environment by oil companies operating in Ogoniland. The Commission declared that the actions of the Nigerian Government constituted 'massive violations of the right to shelter', and that the 'particular violation by the Nigerian Government of the right to adequate housing as implicitly protected in the Charter also encompasses the right to protection against forced evictions'.[18]

As this confirms, forced evictions also, and perhaps most obviously, violate the right to adequate housing. In a second General Comment

---

[16] *Akdivar & Others v Turkey*, Judgment of the European Court of Human Rights, 16 September 1996.

[17] *The Social and Economic Rights Action Center and the Center for Economic and Social Rights v Nigeria*, 155/96, Decision of the African Commission of Human and Peoples' Rights, October 2001.   [18] Ibid., paras. 62–3.

on housing, dealing with the specific problem of forced evictions,[19] the Committee on Economic, Social and Cultural Rights observes that the obligation to ensure legal security of tenure necessitates the adoption of legislative measures that confer on households the greatest possible security of tenure. That obligation also calls for strict controls to be placed on the circumstances in which evictions may lawfully be carried out, whether of individual households following rent default or property damage, or of whole communities in conjunction with land clearances.[20] At the same time, the Committee also stresses the importance of procedural safeguards, including the right of those affected to participate in decision-making concerning their relocation and resettlement, and the right to seek legal redress in the event of forced eviction. In many countries liberalisation pressures have led to a reduction in the role of the state in the housing sector and an expansion in the scope for property speculation and other forms of commercial activity affecting housing. In consequence, forced evictions are often carried out by or at the behest of private parties. Against this background, the Committee emphasises the need for legislative measures and procedural safeguards to apply not just to state agents, but to private parties as well. The Committee also expresses concern about the complicity of overseas development agencies and international financial institutions in large-scale forced evictions which have occurred in projects for the construction of infrastructure funded by them.[21]

Alongside large-scale forced evictions carried out under the banner of development, mass evictions are, of course, integral to systems of *apartheid*. At the same time, as noted, they may be strategies of ethnic cleansing, manifestations of communal violence, and effects of armed conflict. In this context, one key issue in recent years has been the question of property restitution and return by displaced persons to their homes. Scott Leckie reports that in Bosnia and Herzegovina, Tajikistan, Kosovo and South Africa, among many other countries, large numbers

[19] Committee on Economic, Social and Cultural Rights, General Comment 7 (The right to adequate housing—forced evictions (art. 11(1)), 20 May 1997.

[20] Ibid., paras. 17–18.

[21] See, however, the policies prepared by the World Bank and the OECD: World Bank OP 4.12, December 2001, Involuntary Resettlement; OECD Guidelines for Aid Agencies on Involuntary Displacement and Resettlement, OECD Development Assistance Committee, *Guidelines on Aid and Environment No. 3* (Paris: OECD, 1992).

of displaced people and refugees have in fact been able to assert claims and recover their original homes.[22] Their right to do so is increasingly understood as an aspect of the security of tenure that is in turn an implication of the right to adequate housing. This is reinforced by guarantees of the right to peaceful enjoyment of possessions, protected in some treaties. Thus, for instance, in a complaint arising out of the Turkish occupation of Northern Cyprus, the European Court of Human Rights held that denial of the applicant's right to return to her home in Northern Cyprus violated her right to peaceful enjoyment of her possessions under article 1 of the First Protocol to the European Convention.[23] Highlighting this trend, Leckie writes of the 'emergence of a distinct right of displaced persons and refugees to return to repossess their original homes and lands once they determine it is safe to do so'.[24]

We have reviewed the significance of the right to adequate housing in a wide variety of circumstances, from the sadistic street environments of Los Angeles, to the destruction of Ogoni villages in Nigeria, and the expulsion of ethnic Albanians from Kosovo. A final question prompted by our discussion is: are these circumstances indeed *too* various? Does a rights-based approach to housing problems ultimately impede solutions by over-generalising the problems and occluding awareness of their distinctive features and specific contexts? One answer might be that, while human rights can certainly be deployed in ways that 'flatten out' reality, they are also a setting for the multiplication of individual stories about injustice: the person who could not return home in Northern Cyprus, the Kurdish villagers whose houses got torched one terrible day. At the same time, the juxtaposition of those stories, through their subsumption under a category such as the right to adequate housing, can bring into focus instructive linkages. Thus, the right to adequate housing can be used to invite consideration of the ways in which Salvadorean homeless people in Los Angeles may be affected by some

[22] S. Leckie, 'New Directions in Housing and Property Restitution' in S. Leckie (ed.), *Returning Home: Housing and Property Restitution Rights of Refugees and Displaced Persons* (New York: Transnational Publishers, 2003), 3, 24.

[23] *Loizidou v Turkey*, Judgment of the European Court of Human Rights, 18 December 1996.

[24] S. Leckie, 'New Directions in Housing and Property Restitution' in S. Leckie (ed.), *Returning Home: Housing and Property Restitution Rights of Refugees and Displaced Persons* (New York: Transnational Publishers, 2003), 3, 56.

of the same historical processes that form the context within which Ogoni villages are destroyed and Kosovar Albanians expelled. Especially in current conditions of intensifying global interconnectedness, these events surely cannot be understood without reference to the larger forces that shape our world. Yet housing deprivation and the discrimination, violence and often appalling cruelty associated with it do not fall naturally onto the global agenda. The right to adequate housing can be—and is being used as—a way of putting them there.

International Crimes

At the Paris Peace Conference of 1919 a fascinating conversation took place about the fate of the German Kaiser, Wilhelm II. Should he be exiled, or should he be brought to trial? And if he should be brought to trial, under what law and before what tribunal? For some delegates, there was simply no basis for international criminal proceedings of this sort. International law was concerned with the responsibility of states for breaches of international norms, whereas crime was 'essentially a violation of the law within each national unit, a violation by the [individual] subject of his duty to his sovereign'.[1] Other delegates disagreed. For them, the Kaiser had committed a crime against international law, and if international law was to be upheld, he needed to be prosecuted for that crime before an international tribunal established for the purpose. In Clemenceau's words, '[w]e have today a glorious opportunity to bring about the transfer to international law of the principle of responsibility which is at the basis of national law'.[2] Developing this theme, he urged his fellow delegates 'to reflect that, if they follow my advice, they will to their own glory accomplish something without precedent,—I admit it—they will establish international justice, which until now has existed only in books, and of which we will at last make a reality'.[3] In the event, of course, the tribunal which Clemenceau had in mind was not established. But the idea he advanced that certain breaches of international law have the character of crimes for which individuals should bear responsibility gained ground nonetheless. It was later reaffirmed by the Nuremberg Tribunal in a famous passage: 'Crimes against international law are committed by men, not by abstract entities, and only by punishing

---

[1] See P. Mantoux (ed.), *Paris Peace Conference 1919: Proceedings of the Council of Four (March 24–April 18)* (Geneva: Libraire Droz, 1964), 148 (Orlando).   [2] Ibid., 149.
[3] Ibid., 150.

individuals who commit such crimes can the provisions of international law be enforced.'[4]

Punishment implies prosecution, and so the question immediately arises, *where* are individuals to be prosecuted for international crimes? While national courts will often be the most suitable, Clemenceau's belief has proved compelling that there are circumstances in which international jurisdiction is required. This is reflected in the establishment of the Nuremberg and Tokyo Tribunals after the end of the Second World War. And it is reflected as well in a series of international criminal tribunals established during the last decade of the 20th century and subsequently. The earliest of these, set up during the 1990s, are the International Criminal Tribunal for the former Yugoslavia and the International Criminal Tribunal for Rwanda. Like the Nuremberg and Toyko Tribunals, these are *ad hoc* tribunals, designed to provide for the prosecution of crimes associated with particular historical events.[5] The latest of the tribunals—internationalised criminal courts set up for Cambodia, East Timor and Sierra Leone—are similar in this respect.[6] By contrast, the International Criminal Court, launched by the 1998 Rome Statute and established when that Statute entered into force on 1 July 2002, is not limited to any particular context or set of historical events. With the creation of this Court a permanent international criminal jurisdiction has come into existence.[7]

---

[4] *Trial of Major War Criminals (Goering et al)*, International Military Tribunal (Nuremberg) (London: HMSO, 1946) Cmd. 6964, 41.

[5] Statute of the International Tribunal for the Prosecution of Persons Responsible for Serious Violations of International Law Committed in the Territory of the former Yugoslavia Since 1991 (UN Security Council Res. 827, 27 May 1993); International Criminal Tribunal for the Prosecution of Persons Responsible for Genocide and Other Serious Violations of International Humanitarian Law Committed in the Territory of Rwanda and Rwanda Citizens Responsible for Genocide and Other Violations Committed in the Territory of Neighbouring States, between 1 January 1994 and 31 December 1994 (UN Security Council Res. 955, 8 November 1994).

[6] Regarding Cambodia, see Agreement between the UN and the Royal Government of Cambodia Concerning the Prosecution under Cambodian Law of Crimes Committed During the Period of Democratic Kampuchea: UN Doc. A/57/806 and A/Res/57/228B adopted 13 May 2003. Regarding East Timor, see United Nations Transitional Administration for East Timor, Regulation on the Establishment of Panels with Exclusive Jurisdiction over Serious Criminal Offences, UNTAET/REG/2000/15, 6 June 2000. Regarding Sierra Leone, see Statute of the Special Court for Sierra Leone, Annex to UN Doc. S/2000/915, 4 October 2000.

[7] See further W. Schabas, *An Introduction to the International Criminal Court*, 2nd edn. (Cambridge: Cambridge University Press, 2004) and A. Cassese, P. Gaeta & J. Jones (eds.), *The Rome Statute of the International Criminal Court* (Oxford: Oxford University Press, 2002).

Is the establishment of the International Criminal Court a cause for celebration, or is it a cause for disquiet? The Government of the United States announced in 2002 that the United States would not become a party to the Rome Statute, and sought to prevent the Court having jurisdiction over United States personnel serving in United Nations operations.[8] In doing so, the Government referred to uncertainty about the basis of prosecutorial decisions and, more specifically, a fear that United States nationals might become subject to politically motivated trials. However, these are by no means the only concerns that have been voiced about the Court. Some very different and more general worries have also been expressed, raising a range of quite fundamental questions about the Court and the larger system of international criminal justice of which it forms a part. What purpose is served by the establishment of an international criminal jurisdiction of this sort? Can international criminal justice really deter international crime, in the way that national criminal justice is supposed to do? And if the point is not so much deterrence as retribution, what justifies the infliction of exemplary punishment on selected individuals? Does an international criminal trial individualise responsibility for that which should rather be approached as collective and political? Does it simplify, and hence mystify, that which should rather be understood as complex and multicausal? And what of all that falls outside the international criminal justice system? By establishing individual liability for some forms of violence, might the International Criminal Court help to sanctify the idea that other forms of violence, suffering and deprivation are acceptable, or at any rate unavoidable? These are serious questions, and we will return to them later. First, however, we need to review the scope of international criminal jurisdiction, both under the Rome Statute and more broadly. The key issues to be considered are: what constitutes an international crime; who can be made liable under international criminal law; and how international criminal liability may be determined and punishment imposed.[9]

---

[8] This was achieved by means of a Security Council deferral, valid for one year, of cases against nationals of states for acts relating to operations established or authorised by the United Nations where such states are not parties to the Rome Statute. See Rome Statute, art. 16, and UN Security Council Resolution 1422 (2002), adopted 12 July 2002. The deferral was renewed for one further year, until July 2004, at which point no further renewal was granted.

[9] On these issues, see further A. Cassese, *International Criminal Law* (Oxford: Oxford University Press, 2003), K. Kittichaisaree, *International Criminal Law* (Oxford: Oxford University Press, 2001) and M.C. Bassiouni (ed.), *International Criminal Law*, 2nd edn. (Ardsley: Transnational, 1999).

Scope

A United States Military Tribunal sitting at Nuremberg in 1948 defined an 'international crime' as 'such an act universally recognized as criminal, which is considered a grave matter of international concern and for some valid reason cannot be left within the exclusive jurisdiction of the state that would have control over it under ordinary circumstances'.[10] This is typical of many definitions of the category 'international crime', but the difficulty with it, of course, is that it leaves unanswered the question, which acts are considered grave matters of international concern, and whose assessments count in this regard. It is also misleading, in that some acts which are demonstrably grave matters of international concern and which, by particular treaties, are removed from the exclusive jurisdiction of the state that would normally have control, do not give rise to international criminal responsibility. While a variety of labels have been used to describe acts of this sort, we will call them 'treaty crimes'. They are dealt with in some 300 treaties on topics ranging from aircraft hijacking to drug trafficking and the transboundary movement of hazardous waste. The general thrust of these treaties is that states parties are obliged to proscribe certain acts as criminal offences under their national law, and to co-operate with other states parties with regard to investigation and punishment. One aspect of this is a so-called 'extradite or prosecute' obligation. Where an alleged offender is present within the territory of a state party, an obligation arises either to extradite that person to another state requesting custody for the purpose of prosecution or otherwise to initiate criminal proceedings, even if the offence has no specific connection with the state concerned. Treaty crimes thus entail criminal liability within a wide array of national legal systems—indeed, potentially (were the treaties to attract universal adherence) within all of those systems. But from this it does not necessarily follow that such crimes entail international criminal liability. For that to arise there must exist individual liability under international law.

In respect of which crimes, then, does international criminal liability exist? An initial set can be gleaned from article 5 of the Rome Statute.

[10] *US v List et al*, 19 February 1948, Trials of War Criminals Before the Nuernberg Tribunals under Control Council Law No. 10 (Washington, DC: US Government Printing Office, 1950) Vol. IX 1230, 1241.

Under this provision the International Criminal Court is given jurisdiction to try individuals for three categories of crimes, which we may infer are international crimes: genocide, crimes against humanity and war crimes. Complicated definitions are given for each of these three categories. In broad terms, genocide refers to murder and other acts 'committed with intent to destroy, in whole or in part, a national, ethnical, racial or religious group, as such'.[11] Crimes against humanity refer to a range of acts—again including murder, but also torture, enslavement, deportation or forcible transfer, various forms of sexual violence, enforced disappearance and *apartheid*—'when committed as part of a widespread or systematic attack directed against any civilian population, with knowledge of the attack'.[12] And war crimes refer to 'grave breaches', as specified in the Geneva Conventions of 1949, along with other serious violations of international humanitarian norms applicable both in international and non-international armed conflict.[13] Article 5 of the Rome Statute additionally mentions jurisdiction with respect to the crime of aggression, but only as a potential sphere of jurisdiction. Actual competence to try individuals for this crime is made subject to further agreement over the definition of aggression and the conditions under which the International Criminal Court should exercise jurisdiction with respect to it. The first possible date for the Assembly of States Parties to consider a proposed definition of aggression would be 2009.[14]

Genocide, crimes against humanity and war crimes are likewise the concern of the International Criminal Tribunal for the former Yugoslavia and the International Criminal Tribunal for Rwanda, albeit on the basis of somewhat differing definitions of these categories.[15] In a judgment rendered in 2001, however, the International Criminal Tribunal for the former Yugoslavia declared that international criminal liability is not exhausted by those crimes, but also includes violations of the so-called 'peremptory' norms of international law (*jus cogens*). According to the Tribunal, 'in human rights law the violation of rights which have

---

[11] Art. 6. Regarding the issue of what constitutes a part of a group in this context, see *Prosecutor v Krstić* (Case IT-98-33-A), Judgment of International Criminal Tribunal for the former Yugoslavia (Appeals Chamber), 19 April 2004, paras. 5–38.

[12] Art. 7.   [13] Art. 8.

[14] I.e. seven years after the entry into force of the Rome Statute. See art. 123 of the Statute.

[15] Statute of the International Criminal Tribunal for the former Yugoslavia, arts. 2–5; Statute of the International Criminal Tribunal for Rwanda, arts. 2–4.

reached the level of *jus cogens*, such as torture, may constitute international crimes'.[16] The prohibition on torture is interesting in the present context, in that it straddles many of the categories we are discussing. By virtue of the 1984 UN Convention against Torture and other Cruel, Inhuman or Degrading Treatment or Punishment, torture is a treaty crime, subject—for the states parties to the Convention—to an 'extradite or prosecute' obligation. At the same time, torture is also an international crime. When perpetrated as part of a widespread or systematic attack directed against a civilian population, torture is an international crime for the additional reason that it is a crime against humanity. And when perpetrated in the context of armed conflict, it may also be a war crime, and hence an international crime on that account as well.

Liability

We have emphasised that international criminality engages the responsibility of individuals. We need now to be a little more precise about who can be prosecuted for an international crime. In the first place, *individual officials* can be prosecuted. The Nuremberg Tribunal established this proposition when it rejected the notion that state officials should be given immunity for their acts. As it explained, defence counsel had:

submitted that international law is concerned with the actions of sovereign States, and provides no punishment for individuals; and further, that where the act in question is an act of state, those who carry it out are not personally responsible, but are protected by the doctrine of the sovereignty of the State. In the opinion of the Tribunal, both these submissions must be rejected.[17]

The principle that official capacity in no way affects international criminal liability is explicitly affirmed in the various instruments that establish the more recent institutions. Thus, for example, article 27 of the Rome Statute provides that the Statute 'shall apply equally to all persons without any distinction based on official capacity. In particular, official capacity as

---

[16] *Prosecutor v Celebici* (Case IT-96-21-A), 20 February 2001, Judgment of the International Criminal Tribunal for the former Yugoslavia (Appeals Chamber), para. 172, fn. 225.

[17] *Trial of Major War Criminals (Goering et al)*, International Military Tribunal (Nuremberg) (London: HMSO, 1946) Cmd. 6964, 41.

a Head of State or Government, a member of a Government or parliament, an elected representative or a government official shall in no case exempt a person from criminal responsibility under this Statute'. The article further clarifies that sovereign and diplomatic immunities shall not bar the International Criminal Court from exercising jurisdiction. It should be noted that this last point does not carry over to the situation where an official is being tried for international crimes in a national court, rather than before an international tribunal. In a case concerning a warrant issued in Belgium for the arrest of the then foreign minister of the Democratic Republic of the Congo in connection with alleged war crimes and crimes against humanity, the International Court of Justice made clear that immunities remain relevant before national courts, even where a person is accused of international crimes. The International Court decided in that case that the Congolese foreign minister enjoyed personal inviolability, including freedom from arrest, under the law of sovereign immunity. Thus, Belgium had acted unlawfully in issuing its arrest warrant.[18] That said, once a state official has ceased to hold high-ranking office, he or she may not be able to rely on sovereign immunity to escape prosecution for international crimes, including international crimes committed during his or her tenure in that office.[19]

If those who are (or were at the relevant time) state officials can be prosecuted for international crimes, so too can those with no official status. Secondly, then, *private individuals* are liable for international crimes. This was made clear with respect to the crime of genocide in the 1948 Convention on Prevention and Punishment of Genocide. Article IV of the Convention provides that persons committing genocide are liable 'whether they are constitutionally responsible rulers, public officials or private individuals'. With respect to war crimes, this issue assumes particular importance in the context of non-international armed conflict and, more generally, 'new wars', in which traditional categories structuring the law of armed conflict are blurred.[20] Do individuals fighting as part of a non-state armed group bear individual responsibility for war

[18] *Democratic Republic of the Congo v Belgium*, Judgment of the International Court of Justice, 14 February 2002.

[19] *R v Bow Street Metropolitan Stipendiary Magistrate and Others, ex parte Pinochet Ugarte (No.3)* [1999] 2 Weekly Law Reports 827. See also *Democratic Republic of the Congo v Belgium*, Judgment of the International Court of Justice, 14 February 2002, paras. 59–61.

[20] See M. Kaldor, *New and Old Wars* (Cambridge: Polity Press, 1999).

crimes? The International Criminal Tribunal for the former Yugoslavia has held that they do.[21] This is made clear as well in the Rome Statute, inasmuch as the Statute confers on the International Criminal Court jurisdiction with respect to a range of crimes that can be committed by members of non-state armed groups.[22]

A third category of persons to be considered in this context is *legal persons*, for example, corporations. Although existing international criminal tribunals only have jurisdiction over individuals, there is no reason in principle why international criminal responsibility cannot attach to corporations. Civil proceedings have in fact been brought in the courts of the United States regarding international crimes alleged to have been committed by oil companies operating abroad.[23] Complaints, resulting in large settlements, have also been brought against German companies with respect to the use of slave labour during World War II, and against Swiss banks with respect to the expropriation of assets belonging to victims of Nazi persecution. What, finally, of the international criminal liability of entities that are neither individuals nor corporations? The Statute of the Nuremberg Tribunal provided for declarations of the criminality of organisations, in connection with the conviction of individuals. As is well known, the Tribunal declared as criminal organisations (among others) the Leadership Corps of the Nazi Party, the Gestapo and the SS. In doing so, however, the Tribunal recognised that the concept of a criminal organisation is not without dangers, especially insofar as it forms the basis for guilt by association. Today this concept is by no means unknown in the context of national criminal law; indeed, measures to proscribe or criminalise organisations are a familiar feature of counter-terrorist legislation. However, it retains only limited contemporary pertinence in the context of international criminal law.

---

[21] *Prosecutor v Duško Tadić*, Decision on the Defence Motion for Interlocutory Appeal on Jurisdiction, Appeals Chamber 2 October 1995 (Case IT–94–1–AR72), paras. 95–137 and Separate Opinion of Judge Abi-Saab.

[22] Regarding the international liability of members of non-state groups for acts of torture, see Torture★.

[23] (The proceedings have been brought as civil actions.) See A. Ramasastry, 'Corporate Complicity: From Nuremberg to Rangoon—An Examination of Forced Labor Cases and Their Impact on the Liability of Multinational Corporations' 20 *Berkeley Journal of International Law* (2002) 91.

A long-running debate in international law centred on the question of whether *states* could be regarded as criminally liable, and if so, for what crimes. In its authoritative work on the subject of state responsibility, the International Law Commission sidestepped this question, abandoning the effort to define the international crimes of states.[24] According to the Commission, gross or systematic breaches of obligations under peremptory norms of international law (*jus cogens*) do entail different and more serious international legal consequences than other breaches.[25] But, in its assessment, these are not usefully grasped in terms of the concept of international criminality.

Prosecution

We have seen that prosecution for international crimes may occur, where jurisdiction exists, in courts established by international agreements or international organisations, or it may occur in the ordinary national courts. With regard to the International Criminal Court, it is important to note that the Court is not intended to serve as a substitute for national criminal justice. This is emphasised in the Preamble to the Rome Statute, which states that the International Criminal Court is to be 'complementary to national criminal jurisdictions', and refers to the need for both 'measures at the national level' and enhanced 'international cooperation'. By article 17 of the Rome Statute, international crimes cannot be tried in the International Criminal Court where a state which has jurisdiction with respect to them is undertaking, or has undertaken, a criminal investigation or prosecution, unless that state is or was unwilling or unable genuinely to carry out that investigation or prosecution. By article 20(3), no person who has already been tried in a national court (or another international court) may be tried for the same conduct in the International Criminal Court. Again, this is subject to the proviso that trial can occur if the earlier proceedings were in the nature of a sham prosecution, conducted for the purpose of shielding the

---

[24] International Law Commission (ILC), Articles on Responsibility of States for Internationally Wrongful Acts, art. 40, see Report of the ILC on its 53rd Session, UN Doc A/52/10, November 2001, para. 76. See further J. Crawford, *The International Law Commission's Articles on State Responsibility: Introduction, Text and Commentaries* (Cambridge: Cambridge University Press, 2002), 16–20.   [25] Ibid., art. 41.

person from criminal responsibility, or at any rate not conducted independently or impartially in accordance with recognised norms of due process and with a view to bringing the person to justice.

Let us now examine two further factors that may affect the possibility of prosecution. One relates to the time when the alleged offence occurred. This is an obvious issue in the case of international criminal tribunals which have been set up to provide for the prosecution of crimes associated with historically specific events. Thus, for instance, the jurisdiction of the International Criminal Tribunal for the former Yugoslavia is limited to crimes committed since 1991; the International Criminal Tribunal for Rwanda is limited to crimes committed between 1 January 1994 and 31 December 1994; the Special Court for Sierra Leone is limited to crimes committed after 30 November 1996; and the Cambodian trials are limited to crimes committed between 17 April 1975 and 6 January 1979.[26] But in the case of the International Criminal Court too a temporal limitation applies, in that the Court only has jurisdiction with respect to crimes committed after the entry into force of the Statute on 1 July 2002. Where a state becomes a party to the Statute after that date, the Court only has jurisdiction with respect to crimes committed after the entry into force of the Statute for that state.[27] There is also a procedure for non-parties to the Statute to accept the Court's jurisdiction, in which case jurisdiction takes effect according to the terms of the declaration. Beyond these points, a general limitation arises from the principle *nullum crimen sine lege*: no one may be tried for an international crime that was not recognised at the time the acts said to comprise it were committed. In most contexts criminal proceedings are subject also to temporal restrictions arising from so-called 'statutes of limitations': after a certain period following the commission of acts, exposure to criminal prosecution with respect to them ceases. It is generally accepted that international crimes are an exception in this regard. Thus, for example, article 29 of the Rome Statute provides that 'crimes

---

[26] Statute of the International Criminal Tribunal for the former Yugoslavia, art. 8; Statute of the International Criminal Tribunal for Rwanda, art. 1; Statute of the Special Court for Sierra Leone, Annex to UN Doc. S/2000/915, 4 October 2000, art. 1(1); and Agreement between the UN and the Royal Government of Cambodia Concerning the Prosecution under Cambodian Law of Crimes Committed During the Period of Democratic Kampuchea: UN Doc. A/57/806 and A/Res/57/228B, adopted 13 May 2003, art. 1.　　　　　　　　　[27] Articles 11, 12(3), 24(1) and 126.

within the jurisdiction of the [International Criminal] Court shall not be subject to any statute of limitations'.

Another factor that may affect the possibility of prosecution relates to the place where the alleged offence occurred. Again, this is obvious in the case of tribunals like the International Criminal Tribunal for the former Yugoslavia, the International Criminal Tribunal for Rwanda and the Special Court for Sierra Leone. The first-mentioned can only exercise jurisdiction over crimes committed within the territory of the former Yugoslavia; the second over crimes committed within the territory of Rwanda or by Rwandan citizens within the territory of neighbouring states; and the third over crimes committed within the territory of Sierra Leone. In the case of the International Criminal Court territorial and nationality links remain significant. Proceedings can be commenced when the crime was committed within the territory of a state party to the Rome Statute, or on board a ship or aircraft registered in the territory of a state party. And proceedings can be commenced where the crime was committed by a national of a state party. These bases of jurisdiction are then extended in two further ways. There is jurisdiction in the same circumstances, where the relevant state, although not a party to the Rome Statute, has accepted the Court's jurisdiction. And there is jurisdiction where the United Nations Security Council, having determined the existence of a 'threat to the peace, breach of the peace or act of aggression' under chapter VII of the Charter, refers to the prosecutor a situation in which international crimes appear to have been committed.[28]

Significance

We observed at the outset of this discussion that the concept of international criminality has a long history. It by no means began with the International Criminal Court, and nor is that Court today the only forum in which international crimes will be tried. Our current system of international criminal justice comprises a diverse and expanding array of international tribunals and internationationalised national instances, along with ordinary national courts. The establishment of

[28] Rome Statute, arts. 12–13.

international tribunals has indeed fostered an expansion of the jurisdiction of ordinary national courts with respect to international crimes. From one perspective, it is the recognition that national courts can and should be used to prosecute those responsible for very serious offences against international law that is in fact the most significant aspect of the concept of international criminality. From another perspective, the most significant aspect is the establishment of international criminal courts, and perhaps the International Criminal Court. Either way, the concept of international criminality has given rise to some far-reaching questions, which have taken on particular urgency precisely because the developments just mentioned with regard to national and international jurisdiction are so significant.[29] We highlighted a number of these questions at the beginning, and return briefly to them now. Perhaps we should read them as prompts to keep in view institutional alternatives to international criminal processes, such as truth commissions. On the other hand, those alternatives, of course, raise problems of their own.

First, then, there are questions about the fairness of international criminal trials. On what basis will cases be selected for prosecution? To what extent do international procedures ensure due process? How can international prosecutors, judges and other court officials be held accountable for the fairness of international criminal processes? Secondly, there are questions about the purpose served by international criminal trials. How does deterrence operate in this context? If retribution is part of the purpose, is there a danger of too much punishment being meted out on too few people? And what of the charge that international criminal processes are more a matter of asserting authority and monopolising virtue than of curbing violence and reducing security? It is sometimes contended that the main purpose of international criminal trials is to communicate certain fundamental values to which the international community subscribes. Who defines these values? Who speaks for this community? Against the background of sharp divisions between powerful and powerless, who indeed comprises this community? A third set of questions also concerns the effect of international criminal processes. Here the worry is that these processes may concentrate attention on symptoms, rather than causes. Can individual responsibility be

---

[29] See further I. Tallgren, 'The Sensibility and Sense of International Criminal Law' 13 *European Journal of International Law* (2002) 561.

pursued in ways that do not impede efforts to understand and address the political, economic, social, and indeed legal, conditions within which international crime becomes possible? A related worry is that international criminal processes may contribute to establishing a hierarchy of abuse which provides unintended authorisation for conduct *not* defined as an international crime. Can responsibility for international crime be pursued in ways that do not eclipse responsibility for other forms of violence?

Finally, questions arise about the very idea of subjecting gross atrocities to the rational calculus of the law. To what extent are legal concepts and procedures appropriate and adequate for dealing with practices that so obviously exceed them? Observing the trial in the early 1960s of Adolf Eichmann, Hannah Arendt wrote of the 'inadequacy of the prevailing legal system and of current juridical concepts to deal with the facts of administrative massacres organized by the state apparatus'. She went on:

If we look more closely into the matter we will observe without much difficulty that the judges in all these trials really passed judgment solely on the basis of the monstrous deeds. In other words, they judged freely, as it were, and did not really lean on the standards and legal precedents with which they more or less convincingly sought to justify their decisions.[30]

Our focus in this discussion has mostly been on developments in international criminal law since the 1960s, when Arendt wrote this passage. At one level those developments seem like an answer to her argument. There now exists an array of international courts and tribunals and, with them, a substantial body of 'standards and legal precedents' on which judges can lean. At another level, however, Arendt's insight surely retains its force, as a reminder of the limits of legal redescriptions and analyses, especially in this context. To what extent the 'facts of administrative massacres' are, or could be, captured through our 'prevailing legal systems' and 'current juridical concepts' remains uncertain.

[30] H. Arendt, *Eichmann in Jerusalem* (London: Penguin, 1994), 294.

Media

What is the function of the media in shaping political life? Edmund Burke is said to have characterised the parliamentary reporters' gallery as a *'fourth estate'*, additional to, and in some respects more important than, the three estates or social groups whose representatives actually constituted parliament.[1] This concept of the 'fourth estate' has come to be associated with the idea that the press plays a crucial role in enabling citizens to exercise control over political processes. That is, it has come to be associated with the *democratic* significance of the press, and with the ideal of an informed and vigilant 'public sphere' within which to debate decisions, influence agendas, and scrutinise the action of public officials. However, this is not the only way of thinking about the significance of the media in the contemporary world.

Especially since the advent of radio and television, theorists have high-lighted the character of the media as a powerful sector of the economy and purveyor of ideology. In the mid-20th century Theodor Adorno and Max Horkheimer argued that the mass media (including cinema) should be understood as a 'culture industry', comparable to the steel, electricity and petroleum industries, yet unlike those industries in com-bining economic importance with immense ideological capability.[2] As Adorno and Horkheimer put it, the mass media promise enlightenment, yet bring only 'mass deception'. More recently, Edward Herman and Noam Chomsky have developed this idea, contending that the primary function of the media is to help in 'manufacturing consent'.[3] By the

[1] See Thomas Carlyle, *On Heroes, Hero-Worship, and the Heroic in History* (1841), notes and introduction by M.J. Goldberg (Berkeley, Los Angeles and Oxford: University of California Press, 1993).

[2] See, e.g., M. Horkheimer and T. Adorno (J. Cumming, trans.), *Dialectic of Enlightenment* (New York: Continuum, 1993), first published 1944, 120 *et seq.*, esp. 122.

[3] E.S. Herman and N. Chomsky, *Manufacturing Consent* (New York: Pantheon Books, 1988).

manufacture of consent they mean the process of mobilising popular support for policies and action that are congenial to dominant interests. In countries where there is official state censorship, the marginalisation of dissent is generally clear. But Herman and Chomsky want us to see how this process works in countries like the United States, where official censorship is limited, and the press is supposedly free. Within this kind of context, they claim, the ideological—or, as they call it, 'propaganda'—role of the media is a matter of 'internalized preconceptions, and the adaptation of personnel to the constraints of ownership, organization, market, and political power'.[4] Thus, '[c]ensorship is largely self-censorship' by journalists, editors and media executives, in connection with decisions about the selection of issues to be covered, the volume and nature of that coverage, the tone and placement of stories, and so on.

From this perspective, the idea of the media as a fourth estate is too sanguine, or at any rate outmoded as a description of the modern mass media and its political significance. Yet, from another perspective, this critique is itself outmoded and inadequate, insofar as it fails to take into account what Jean Baudrillard has referred to as the 'implosion of meaning in the media'.[5] According to Baudrillard, '[w]e live in a world where there is more and more information, and less and less meaning'.[6] He explains this loss or 'implosion' of meaning in terms of Marshall McLuhan's famous aphorism that the 'medium is the message', which he takes to signal that content has been absorbed into, and neutralised by, form. In contemporary conditions of media saturation, however, Baudrillard proposes that the medium has also become the message in the further, more far-reaching sense that representations have come to eclipse in significance the events to which they relate: media images are more authoritative than face-to-face experience; news stories serve as ratifications of actual occurrences; opinion polls shape voting in elections; and so on. Not only, then, has content been absorbed into, and neutralised by, form; the *empirical referents* of content have been absorbed and neutralised as well. It follows for Baudrillard that our understanding of the media must change. In his words, '*the medium is the message* not only signifies the end of the message, but also the end of the medium.

---

[4] E.S. Herman and N. Chomsky, *Manufacturing Consent* (New York: Pantheon Books, 1988), xii.

[5] J. Baudrillard (S.F. Glaser, trans.), *Simulacra and Simulation* (Ann Arbor: University of Michigan Press, 1994), 79.   [6] Ibid.

There are no more media in the literal sense of the word...—that is, of a mediating power between one reality and another, between one state of the real and another'.[7] Baudrillard's point is that the media cannot be viewed today as simply representing social reality or mediating between different realities, whether in the mode of a fourth estate or a manufacturer of consent. Rather, media representations substitute for social reality; they become all there is. Thus, in his assessment, it is no longer a question of representation or mediation, reflection or transmission; '[i]t is a question of substituting the signs of the real for the real'.[8]

Each of these accounts plainly has some validity. It is certainly the case that the media are not just channels for the communication of information, but complex commercial enterprises with huge advertising and other revenues and considerable political clout. In recent years, moreover, these enterprises have in some cases expanded exponentially, for example, through cross-sectoral mergers which have established or consolidated vast global conglomerates whose interests span publishing, broadcasting, cinema and the internet. It is also the case that constraints on what is published or broadcast extend beyond restrictions imposed by the state, and include also constraints arising from the organisation and conventions of media undertakings themselves. At the same time, it is clear that, as Baudrillard highlights, information has become more and more available, to the point where it sometimes feels like an enveloping reality all of its own. There can be little doubt that what we see, hear or read in the media shapes in profound ways our experience and expectations of the world and our interactions within it.

On the other hand, it is important not to over-generalise. The great behemoths of the culture industry do not account for the entirety of the world's media. Beyond them, there exists an array of regional and local media outlets, along with a vibrant alternative or 'non-mainstream' media sector. At the same time, media saturation is by no means a universal condition. Some people have no access to media, or no access to media that are transmitted in a language they can understand. Others have access only to media they do not value or trust, and among these may be people whose only access is to media that are affected by extensive and highly coercive state censorship. Finally, and perhaps most importantly, media communication is not a simple one-way process of

---

[7] Ibid., 82.   [8] Ibid., 2.

conveying information and ideas to passive recipients. Most media theorists today emphasise that the information and ideas we take from the media are in part a function of what we bring to our engagement with the media; that is to say, they are in part a function of our own particular circumstances, outlooks, preoccupations, and agendas. On this view, meanings are not received, but made—and made through an active process that includes both producers and their diverse audiences. If this is right, then the notion that mass media audiences are victims of mass deception seems excessively deterministic, as well as being rather condescending.

All of this is a reminder that the media are powerful, but, as Herman and Chomsky themselves observe, 'not all-powerful'.[9] Certainly, the role of the media as a fourth estate or mainstay of the public sphere has by no means disappeared, and nor have the potential and aspiration to enhance their significance as such. The issues we take up in the discussion that follows revolve around the bearing of international human rights law in this regard. What kind of contribution does human rights law make to ensuring that the media remain available for public oversight of political processes? In what ways does human rights law support, or impede, the use of the media as a vehicle for invoking accountability, expressing dissent, and promoting social change? And what is the impact on this situation of the advent of the 'information society', to which Baudrillard alludes? Central to the image (and self-image) of the media as a fourth estate is the right to freedom of expression, and we shall begin by outlining the legal framework for that right. We will then look at how human rights courts and supervisory bodies have articulated the implications of freedom of expression in relation to the various constraints that can affect media activity. As just discussed, these constraints include official state censorship of the media. At the same time, they also go beyond that practice to encompass questions of media control and media access, which are relevant to the phenomenon of self-censorship highlighted by Herman and Chomsky. Our discussion will end with a brief consideration of the opportunities and challenges of the 'new media' from a human rights perspective.

[9] E.S. Herman & N. Chomsky, *Manufacturing Consent* (New York: Pantheon Books, 1988), 306.

The right to freedom of expression

The right to freedom of expression is recognised in the Universal Declaration of Human Rights, which states: 'Everyone has the right to freedom of opinion and expression; this right includes freedom to hold opinions without interference and to seek, receive and impart information and ideas through any media and regardless of frontiers.'[10] In the context of the media, this makes clear that freedom of expression is a right of producers (newspapers, journalists, broadcasters), as well as audiences (readers, viewers, listeners); it includes both the right to impart information and ideas and the right to seek and receive information and ideas, both the right to inform and the right to be informed. The right to freedom of expression is protected in similar terms in the International Covenant on Civil and Political Rights,[11] and in all the regional human rights systems (the African Charter of Human and Peoples' Rights,[12] the American Convention on Human Rights,[13] and the European Convention on Human Rights).[14] Freedom of expression is also protected outside the framework of these treaties, under generally applicable norms of international human rights law.

A large number of declarations, recommendations and other non-treaty instruments have been adopted by international and regional organisations to address specific aspects of freedom of expression. These instruments almost invariably touch on the media, and some contain detailed provisions dealing with the implications of freedom of expression for the media or particular sectors thereof.[15] The UN Commission on

---

[10] Art. 19.   [11] Art. 19.   [12] Art. 9.

[13] Art. 13. See also American Declaration on the Rights and Duties of Man (1948), art. IV (protecting freedom to express and disseminate ideas 'by any medium whatsoever').

[14] Art. 10. See also art. 11 of the Charter of Fundamental Rights of the European Union (2000). Art. 11(2) of the Charter specifically provides that the 'freedom and pluralism of the media shall be respected'.

[15] See, e.g., the Declaration of Principles—Building the Information Society: A Global Challenge for the New Millennium, adopted at the World Summit on the Information Society, held in Geneva in December 2003, Doc. WSIS-03/GENEVA/DOC/4-E; the Inter-American Declaration of Principles on Freedom of Expression, adopted by the Inter-American Commission on Human Rights in October 2000; the Declaration of Principles on Freedom of Expression in Africa, adopted by the African Commission on Human and Peoples' Rights in October 2002; and the Declaration on Freedom of Political Debate in the Media, adopted by the Committee of Ministers of the Council of Europe in February 2004.

Human Rights has established a mandate whereby a Special Rapporteur is appointed to act as a focal point for the Organisation's efforts to promote and protect freedom of opinion and expression, and the reports prepared by successive incumbents of this office also address a variety of issues relevant to media activity.[16] A consistent theme of all these declarations, recommendations and reports, as of judgments and other pronouncements of human rights courts and supervisory bodies confronted with issues of freedom of expression, is the cardinal importance of this freedom and of the media in relation to it. Thus, for example, the Declaration of Principles on Freedom of Expression in Africa, adopted in 2002 by the African Commission on Human and Peoples' Rights, opens with a preambular reaffirmation of 'the fundamental importance of freedom of expression as an individual human right, as a cornerstone of democracy and as a means of ensuring respect for all human rights and freedoms'.[17] Also highlighted in the preamble to the Declaration is 'the key role of the media and other means of communication in ensuring full respect for freedom of expression, in promoting the free flow of information and ideas, in assisting people to make informed decisions and in facilitating and strengthening democracy'.

The fact that freedom of expression is recognised as fundamentally important does not mean, of course, that it is recognised as unqualified or overriding. Under the International Covenant on Civil and Political Rights, restrictions may be imposed on freedom of expression,

but these shall only be such as are provided by law and are necessary:

(a) For respect of the rights or reputations of others;
(b) For the protection of national security or of public order (*ordre public*), or of public health or morals.[18]

Similar stipulations apply under other treaties and under general international human rights law. We return to these stipulations below. For the present, it is sufficient to note that their effect is to require governments to justify the restriction of freedom of expression by reference to specified interests or aims. Among these interests or aims is the protection of national security—a value which, though incontestably

---

[16] See also the work of the OAS Special Rapporteur on Freedom of Expression and the OSCE Representative on Freedom of the Media.
[17] See 32nd Session, 17–23 October 2002, Banjul.   [18] Art. 19(3).

significant, is absolutely vague and generally rooted in considerations that are not publicly verifiable. In what circumstances national security should be accepted as a justification for restricting freedom of expression is an important point of contention,[19] and all the more so in the period since 11 September 2001. Under the Civil and Political Rights Covenant and certain other treaties, the right to freedom of expression is also made subject to the possibility for states to derogate from their obligations in time of 'public emergency'.[20] However, derogation is only permitted if it can be considered necessary and proportionate to the exigencies of the situation confronted. Since in most cases restrictions of the kind discussed in the preceding paragraph are likely to suffice, and may indeed provide a wider basis for restricting freedom of expression than a 'public emergency' could justify, the necessity of derogation may be difficult to establish. Hence, in part, the stress that falls on the question in what circumstances national security should be accepted as a justification for restricting freedom of expression.

From a different angle, the right to freedom of expression must additionally be understood against the background of the prohibitions of abusive invocation of rights and incitement to hatred. The prohibition of abusive invocation of rights is expressed in article 5(1) of the Civil and Political Rights Covenant in the following terms:

Nothing in the present Covenant may be interpreted as implying for any State, group or person any right to engage in any activity or perform any act aimed at the destruction of any of the rights and freedoms recognized herein or at their limitation to a greater extent than is provided for in the present Covenant.

Similar stipulations apply under other treaties and under general international law. Their effect is obviously to limit the extent to which freedom of expression will provide justification for action that undermines human rights. At the same time, a number of treaties explicitly require that incitement to hatred be prohibited by law. Among these treaties is the Civil and Political Rights Covenant, which provides in article 20(2): 'Any advocacy of national, racial or religious hatred that

---

[19] A wide-ranging elaboration of relevant principles is presented in the Johannesburg Principles on National Security, Freedom of Expression and Access to Information, adopted at a conference held in 1995. See UN Doc. E/CN.4/1996/39.

[20] See esp. International Covenant on Civil and Political Rights, art. 4; American Convention on Human Rights, art. 27; European Convention on Human Rights, art. 15.

constitutes incitement to discrimination, hostility or violence shall be prohibited by law.'

Where the media are concerned, these prohibitions of abusive invocation of rights and incitement to hatred are linked to a further qualification on the right to freedom of expression, which arises from the fact that in certain circumstances media activity may constitute an international crime, and one for which freedom of expression provides no excuse. This has been evident at least since 1946, when Julius Streicher, editor-in-chief of the anti-semitic newspaper *Der Stürmer*, was convicted by the International Military Tribunal at Nuremberg.[21] According to the Tribunal, 'Streicher's incitement to murder and extermination at the time when Jews in the East were being killed under the most horrible conditions clearly constitutes persecution on political and racial grounds in connection with war crimes, as defined by the Charter, and constitutes a crime against humanity'.[22] The relevance of international criminal law for publishers and broadcasters was recently reasserted in an important judgment of the International Criminal Tribunal for Rwanda, delivered in 2003.[23] Three Rwandan media executives were indicted in connection with their role in the genocide which took place in that country in 1994. Two were in charge of the radio station *Radio télévision libre des mille collines* (RTLM); the third was the owner and editor of the journal *Kangura*. Together, RTLM and *Kangura* had played a key part in inflaming hatred and fomenting violence against Tutsis and Hutu opponents. RTLM had additionally broadcast the names, addresses, and car licence plates of particular individuals belonging to these groups and of their families, and the evidence before the Tribunal showed that many of those people were in fact killed. The Tribunal found the three accused guilty of genocide, along with conspiracy and incitement to commit genocide, and the crimes of persecution and extermination. In doing so, it observed that '[t]he power of the media to create and destroy fundamental human values comes with great responsibility. Those who control such media are accountable for its consequences'.[24] The Tribunal noted that, in a poor country like Rwanda with low levels of literacy, radio takes on particular

[21] *Judgment of the International Military Tribunal for the Trial of Major War Criminals*, Cmd. 6964 (London: HMSO, 1946).   [22] Ibid., 102.

[23] *Nahimana, Barayagwiza and Ngeze* (Case ICTR-99-52T), Judgment of the International Criminal Tribunal for Rwanda, 3 December 2003.

[24] Ibid., para. 945.

significance. Indeed, the evidence indicated that RTLM was the ambient sound of the genocide, playing in *genocidaires'* cars as they stopped their victims at road-blocks. Meanwhile, another media organisation—Reporters Without Borders—recorded further testimony to the influence of RTLM: the victims' cry, 'Stop that radio!'

A final limitation on the right to freedom of expression stems from international humanitarian law, and concerns restrictions that are laid down for the benefit of prisoners of war and others detained in times of armed conflict. Under the Third Geneva Convention, it is stated that 'prisoners of war must at all times be protected, particularly against acts of violence or intimidation and against insults and public curiosity',[25] and that '[p]risoners of war are entitled in all circumstances to respect for their persons and their honour'.[26] With respect to others who find themselves in the hands of the enemy, the Fourth Geneva Convention for the protection of civilians during wartime likewise provides that:

[p]rotected persons are entitled, in all circumstances, to respect for their persons, their honour, their family rights, their religious convictions and practices, and their manners and customs. They shall at all times be humanely treated, and shall be protected especially against all acts of violence or threats thereof and against insults and public curiosity.[27]

The question of how these provisions affect the media attracted considerable attention in the context of the Iraq war of 2003 and its aftermath. Concerns were initially raised when footage was shown of US prisoners of war being questioned, and of Iraqi prisoners of war surrendering. Likewise, concerns were voiced about the publication of pictures of Saddam Hussein being subjected to undignified forms of medical examination. The practice of showing pictures of prisoners of war and other detainees with pixelated faces, obscuring their identities, is generally considered consistent with the obligation to respect honour and ensure protection from public curiosity. A related controversy of the Iraq conflict had to do with the publication of pictures of military coffins. Under international humanitarian law, the remains of those who have died in connection with a military occupation must be respected.[28] Concern

---

[25] Art. 13.   [26] Art. 14.   [27] Art. 27.

[28] See Protocol I to the Geneva Conventions, art. 34. As glossed in Y. Sandoz, C. Swinarski, & B. Zimmermann (eds.), *Commentary on the Additional Protocols of 8 June 1977 to the Geneva Conventions of 12 August 1949* (Geneva/Dordrecht: ICRC/Nijhoff, 1987), this entails that the remains cannot be despoiled or exposed to public curiosity (para. 1307).

for the privacy of the families, and for the protection of service members from unwarranted and undignified attention, was the stated justification for barring the further release of these pictures. According to some observers, however, this was better understood as a 'sanitising' move, aimed at masking the human costs of the war, and sustaining public support for participation in hostilities and, later, occupation. One of the most frequently voiced anxieties about the media is 'Is there too much violence in the media?' When it comes to war-reporting, however, violence is often more conspicuous for its absence. In this context, Peter Steven suggests that a different question may need to be asked: 'Is there enough violence in the media?'[29]

Constraints on freedom of expression

In the last section we considered the scope and limits of freedom of expression in a fairly general way, against the background of relevant norms of international human rights law, and in the light also of international criminal law and international humanitarian law. Let us now introduce a little more specificity into the discussion by looking at some of the ways in which human rights courts and supervisory bodies have articulated the right to freedom of expression in relation to the various constraints that may affect media activity.

Content restrictions

Perhaps the most straightforward kind of constraint on media activity arises when national authorities take action to prevent or punish publication or broadcasting. Beyond simple 'executive' censorship—the seizure of an issue of a newspaper, for instance, without the possibility of legal redress—which is clearly inconsistent with the right to freedom of expression, state-imposed restriction of media content may take at least three forms. First, publication or broadcasting may be restrained by order of national courts. Under the American Convention on Human Rights (article 13(2)), prior restraint of the news media is prohibited, though subsequent liability may be imposed. Under the European Convention

---

[29] P. Steven, *The No-Nonsense Guide to Global Media* (Oxford/London: New Internationalist/Verso, 2003), 121.

on Human Rights, prior restraint is not expressly prohibited. However, in an early case brought by the *Sunday Times* against the United Kingdom, the European Court of Human Rights applied a strict level of scrutiny to a government's attempt to justify prior restraint.[30] In the Court's terminology, the government was left only a narrow 'margin of appreciation' in this regard. As under other comparable treaties, justification is required by reference to enumerated interests or aims. Specifically, article 10(2) of the European Convention provides that any 'formalities, conditions, restrictions or penalties' imposed on free expression must be

prescribed by law, and . . . necessary in a democratic society, in the interests of national security, territorial integrity or public safety, for the prevention of disorder or crime, for the protection of health or morals, for the protection of the reputation or rights of others, for preventing the disclosure of information received in confidence, or for maintaining the authority and impartiality of the judiciary.

This stipulation is understood to entail that restriction of media content must meet three criteria if it is to remain consistent with the right to freedom of expression. It must be 'prescribed by law', in the sense of having a legal basis which is publicly accessible, as well as clear. It must be directed to one of the specified aims listed in article 10(2). And it must be 'necessary in a democratic society'. This last criterion is understood to imply that the restrictive measure must be necessary in that it responds to a 'pressing social need', and that there must exist a reasonable relationship of proportionality between the measure and the legitimate aim pursued. The *Sunday Times* case concerned an injunction directed to the aim of maintaining the authority of the judiciary. Upon strict scrutiny, however, the European Court was not convinced that in the circumstances the restraint had been either necessary or proportionate, and thus the right to freedom of expression was held to have been violated.

A second way in which media content may be restricted is through the imposition on media organisations or workers of criminal or civil liability. In contrast to prior restraint, this does not formally prevent publication or broadcasting, but rather punishes them after the event and deters future publications or broadcasts by exposing those concerned to

---

[30] *Sunday Times v United Kingdom*, Judgment of the European Court of Human Rights, 26 April 1979.

the risk of a penalty or damages. Restrictions of this kind have been challenged before the European Court of Human Rights in a variety of different contexts. For example, they have been challenged in situations where media organisations or workers have been successfully sued in national courts in connection with derogatory statements about politicians. In one case against Austria, a journalist who was editor of the periodical *Forum* had been convicted for insulting the far-right Austrian Freedom Party leader Jörg Haider, by publishing an article that referred to Haider as an 'idiot' (*Trottel*).[31] The journalist complained that the conviction violated his right to freedom of expression, and the European Court upheld that complaint. For the Court, the restriction here on freedom of expression, while directed to an aim covered by article 10(2) of the Convention (namely, 'protection of the reputation or rights of others'), could not be regarded as 'necessary in a democratic society' for that aim. In explaining this conclusion, the Court stressed that the threshold of necessity cannot be the same for politicians and ordinary citizens. Where the former are concerned, protection of reputation has to be 'weighed against the interests of open discussion of political issues'.[32] In a widely cited passage, the Court said:

As to the limits of acceptable criticism, they are wider with regard to a politician acting in his public capacity than in relation to a private individual. A politician inevitably and knowingly lays himself open to close scrutiny of his every word and deed by both journalists and the public at large, and he must display a greater degree of tolerance, especially when he himself makes public statements that are susceptible of criticism.[33]

Within the framework of the Inter-American human rights system, the Inter-American Commission on Human Rights has expressed a similar view, and has indicated in particular that so-called '*desacato*' laws, which penalise criticism of public officials, are in principle inconsistent with the right to freedom of expression.[34]

[31] *Oberschlick v Austria (No.2)*, Judgment of the European Court of Human Rights, 25 June 1997.   [32] Para. 29.
[33] Ibid.
[34] See Inter-American Declaration of Principles on Freedom of Expression (para. 11), approved 19 October 2000. See also Special Report of the Inter-American Commission on Human Rights on the Compatibility Between '*Desacato*' Laws and the American Convention on Human Rights, OAS/Ser.L/V/88, doc.9 rev., 17 February 1995, 197–212; and Annual Report of the OAS Special Rapporteur for Freedom of Expression 2002, Part V.

A third way in which media content may be restricted is less 'direct', and perhaps less deliberate, than the other ways we have mentioned so far. Particular information may be rendered unavailable, insofar as journalists are forced to reveal their sources. This kind of restriction was considered by the European Court of Human Rights in a case against the United Kingdom, decided in 1996.[35] A journalist had received un-attributable information which was damaging to a company. It turned out that the information had been gleaned from a confidential docu-ment that had probably been stolen by the journalist's source. On the application of the company, the national courts issued an injunction restraining the publication of any information derived from the confi-dential document. At the same time, they also issued an order requiring the journalist to disclose the identity of his source, so that the company could take action against the latter. The journalist refused to comply with this order, and was fined for contempt of court. Before the European Court of Human Rights he complained that the disclosure order and fine violated his right to freedom of expression. He conceded that the restriction of his freedom of expression could be related to a legitimate aim—again, the protection of the reputation or rights of others (in this case, the company). However, he argued that the restriction could not be regarded as necessary for that aim, nor was there a reasonable rela-tionship of proportionality between that aim and the measures adopted. The Court accepted this argument. In its assessment, the injunction was sufficient to protect the reputation and rights of the company. As to the disclosure order, the company's interest in eliminating the residual threat of commercial damage was not sufficient to 'outweigh the vital public interest in the protection of the applicant journalist's source'.[36] In this regard, the Court stressed the 'vital public-watchdog role of the press', and noted the 'potentially chilling effect' in relation to that role of an order for disclosure of journalistic sources. In its words:

Protection of journalistic sources is one of the basic conditions for press free-dom ... Without such protection, sources may be deterred from assisting the press in informing the public on matters of public interest. As a result the vital public-watchdog role of the press may be undermined and the ability of the press to provide accurate and reliable information may be adversely affected.[37]

[35] *Goodwin v United Kingdom*, Judgment of the European Court of Human Rights, 22 February 1996. [36] Para. 45.
[37] Para. 39.

This issue has also arisen in connection with international proceedings, in the context of the International Criminal Tribunal for the former Yugoslavia. Considering the question whether a war correspondent could be subpoenaed to give evidence, the Tribunal has said that a subpoena may only be issued where the evidence sought is 'of direct and important value in determining a core issue in the case' and that evidence 'cannot reasonably be obtained elsewhere'.[38]

Media organisations

Restrictions of the kind just discussed are important constraints on media activity. But, of course, national authorities may also constrain media activity in many other ways. For instance, rather than taking action which affects the publication or broadcasting of particular items, they may take, or contribute to, action which affects the capacity of a media organisation to operate at all. The most obvious case of this is where a media organisation is shut down. In 1999 the African Commission on Human and Peoples' Rights decided on a series of applications against Nigeria arising out of the proscription of a number of newspapers and news magazines and the forcible occupation and sealing up of their premises on which they were produced.[39] The Commission ruled that the state's action violated the right to freedom of expression. In its words:

The proscription of specific newspapers by name and the sealing of their premises, without a hearing at which they could defend themselves, or any accusation of wrongdoing, legal or otherwise, amounts to harassment of the press. ... Decrees like these pose a serious threat to the public of the right to receive information not in accordance with what the government would like the public to know. ... For the government to proscribe a particular publication, by name, is ... disproportionate and not necessary.[40]

---

[38] *Prosecutor v Radoslav Brdjanin Momir Talic* (Case No. IT-99-36-AR 73.9), Decision of the Appeals Chamber (Motion to Appeal the Trial Chamber's 'Decision on Motion on Behalf of Jonathan Randal to Set Aside Confidential Subpoena to Give Evidence'), 11 December 2002, para. 50.

[39] *Constitutional Rights Project, Civil Liberties Organisation and Media Rights Agenda v Nigeria* (Communications 140/94, 141/94 and 145/95), Decisions of the African Commission on Human and Peoples' Rights, November 1999.

[40] Decision on Communication 141/94, paras. 37, 38 and 44.

Insofar as there was a need to protect individuals from defamatory statements in the media, the Court considered that Nigerian libel laws provided entirely adequate protection.

What if a media organisation is not actually shut down, but becomes unable to continue operations, due to the harassment of its associates by those opposed to its editorial policy or perspective? In a judgment delivered in 2000, the European Court of Human Rights stated that the guarantee of freedom of expression in article 10 of the European Convention is not exhausted by the 'negative' duty of public officials not to interfere with the right to freedom of expression; in some circumstances, it may also entail a 'positive' obligation on the part of national authorities to provide protection for the exercise of that right.[41] The judgment related to a complaint against Turkey by the editors and owners of a newspaper that had been subjected to a sustained campaign of intimidation, and had eventually ceased publication. In part, the intimidation consisted of action by the national authorities. There had been a search-and-arrest operation and a large number of prosecutions in connection with particular articles. While the Turkish Government sought to justify this action by reference to links said to exist between the newspaper and illegal activity by the Kurdish Workers' Party (PKK), the European Court upheld the applicants' claim that the measures taken were disproportionate to any legitimate aim of preventing disorder or crime, and hence violated the right to freedom of expression. In addition to these measures, however, the intimidation of the newspaper also consisted of action by unidentified people. A series of very serious attacks had occurred against journalists, distributors and others associated with the newspaper, which had included killings, assaults and arson attacks. The newspaper's concern that it was the victim of a concerted campaign of violent harassment had been brought to the attention of the authorities, but this allegation had never been investigated, and almost no attempt had been made to protect the newspaper's staff and associates. The European Court held that the government's omissions in this regard constituted a further violation of the right to freedom of expression. The government had failed to comply with their 'positive obligation to protect [the newspaper] in the exercise of its freedom of expression'.[42]

[41] *Özgür Günden v Turkey*, Judgment of the European Court of Human Rights, 16 March 2000.   [42] Para. 46.

Besides these actions affecting existing media organisations, national authorities may also prevent a media organisation from setting up operations in the first place. For example, they may impose a prohibitive tax on newsprint, which applies to non-state but not state-run newspapers. Alternatively, they may establish a licensing system, linked to the allocation of frequencies, and refuse licences to all but the national broadcasting organisation. This latter kind of situation has been considered by the European Court of Human Rights on a number of occasions. One case involved Jörg Haider, whose proceedings for insult were the basis for a complaint we noted earlier.[43] Haider was one of a number of applicants who claimed that their right to freedom of expression had been violated because they had been unable to obtain licences to set up radio or television stations in Austria. With very limited exceptions, a public monopoly system of broadcasting was in operation, and no private licences were granted. The Austrian government argued that this system was necessary in order to guarantee diversity and independence on the part of those involved in reporting and programming. However, the Court was not convinced by this argument. The 'far-reaching character of [the] restrictions' entailed by a public monopoly meant that those restrictions could 'only be justified where they correspond to a pressing social need'. Yet, in the Court's assessment, 'it cannot be argued that there are no equivalent less restrictive situations; it is sufficient by way of example to cite the practice of certain countries which either issue licences subject to specified conditions of variable content or make provision for forms of private participation in the activities of the national corporation'.[44] The Court concluded that the restrictions were not necessary, and hence could not be reconciled with the right to freedom of expression of Jörg Haider and others. It is perhaps pertinent to mention at this point that in the other case involving Haider, the editor of *Forum* had been commenting on a speech in which Haider had expressed the view that only those who had risked their lives in the Second World War were entitled to freedom of opinion.

Public access

The constraints affecting media activity which we have reviewed so far involve state action against the media (or, in one case, state inaction in the

---

[43] *Informationsverein Lentia and Others v Austria*, Judgment of the European Court of Human Rights, 24 November 1993.   [44] Para. 39.

face of violent harassment of the media by unidentified others). Yet, as Herman and Chomsky remind us, much censorship is not the result of state repression. Rather, it is self-censorship, the result of internalised preconceptions and structural factors to do with ownership, organisation, market, and political power. Where constraints of this sort are concerned, the right to freedom of expression takes on fresh significance. It becomes less a defence against unjustified interference with media freedom than a demand for public access to the media and for diversity of media content. Put differently, it becomes less a matter of what media organisations should be permitted to do than a matter of what should be expected or required of them.

In one case before the European Court of Human Rights the applicant was a Swiss organisation concerned with animal welfare, which had produced a television advertisement pointing up the cruelty of industrial pig farming and exhorting viewers to eat less meat.[45] With a view to having this advertisement shown on Swiss national television, the organisation had approached the Commercial Television Company. The latter was a private entity which had been placed in charge of advertising on the Swiss Radio and Television Company, which in turn was the only television station providing 'home news' throughout Switzerland. The Commercial Television Company refused to accept the applicant's advertisement on the ground that it was 'political', and by Swiss law political advertising was prohibited. The Commercial Television Company also indicated that it considered the advertisement damaging to its own business interests, as meat sellers might decline to advertise, and it suggested changes which would moderate the advertisement's message. The applicant declined to make these changes. Before the European Court the applicant complained that the decision not to accept the advertisement violated its right to freedom of expression. An initial question was whether the Swiss Government could be held responsible for the actions of the Commercial Television Company. The Government argued that the Commercial Television Company was a private company over which it exercised no supervision. Accordingly, any challenge to that company's decisions had to be pursued on the level of private law, especially as the right to freedom of expression did not

[45] *VgT Verein gegen Tierfabriken v Switzerland*, Judgment of the European Court of Human Rights, 28 June 2001.

entail any right to broadcast (or, in its phrase, 'right to an antenna'). The applicant contended that the fact that television advertising had been privatised could not release the state from its obligation to ensure freedom of expression for all. Sidestepping both of these arguments, the Court held that it was sufficient for the purpose of establishing the responsibility of the state that the refusal to accept the advertisement was consistent with Swiss law, which prohibited political advertising. As it explained, '[i]n effect, political speech by the applicant association was prohibited',[46] with the result that the state became responsible insofar as this constituted a failure to secure the right to freedom of expression to everyone within the jurisdiction. And, indeed, the Court held that it did constitute a failure to secure that right, as the Commercial Television Company's decision could not be justified by reference to any 'pressing social need'. Thus, Switzerland was held to have violated the right to freedom of expression.

Within the Inter-American human rights system, the responsibility of state authorities for private action that unjustifiably impedes media access has long been clear, at least where states parties to the American Convention on Human Rights are concerned. Article 13(3) of the American Convention provides that '[t]he right of expression may not be restricted by indirect methods or means, such as the abuse of government or private controls over newsprint, radio broadcasting frequencies, or equipment used in the dissemination of information, or by any other means tending to impede the communication and circulation of ideas and opinions'. In an Advisory Opinion rendered in 1985, the Inter-American Court of Human Rights proposed that, when read together with article 1 of the American Convention (by which states parties undertake to respect and ensure the rights recognised in the Convention), article 13(3) carries a two-fold significance.[47] On the one hand, it means that a violation may occur where the state imposes restrictions of an 'indirect' character which tend to impede the communication and circulation of ideas and opinions. On the other hand, it means that a violation may also occur where 'private controls' over newsprint, broadcasting, and so on, produce this same result. Thus, alongside the obligation

---

[46] Para. 47.

[47] *Compulsory Membership in an Association Prescribed by Law for the Practice of Journalism*, Advisory Opinion of the Inter-American Court of Human Rights, OC-5/85, 13 November 1985.

to ensure that the right to freedom of expression is not directly or indirectly violated through public action, 'the State also has an obligation to ensure that...violation does not result from the "private controls" referred to in paragraph 3 of Article 13'.[48] This latter obligation assumes particular significance against the background of developments which have produced significant concentrations of ownership and control in the media sector, both within countries and regions and across the world as a whole. Private monopolies or oligopolies are in many countries controlled through competition or antitrust laws, designed to prevent commercial collusion and ensure consumer choice. From the perspective of human rights law, however, the issue is not consumer protection, but citizenship, and the question of whether competition or antitrust laws are adequate to protect the right of everyone to freedom of expression is not a matter of whether those laws can ensure choice. Rather, it is a matter of whether they can ensure inclusory public access and diversity of content—phenomena for which choice may be necessary, but, as experience seems to confirm, for which choice is also wholly insufficient.[49]

The 'new media'

In recent years a distinction has come to be drawn between the 'old media' and 'new media'. By 'new media' are meant computer-based information and communication technologies, and especially the internet, with its web pages, email lists, chatrooms, ezines and blogs. The distinction is not clear-cut, since many organisations within the 'old media', such as newspapers, magazines and television stations, have online operations, and computer technology has also changed the production and appearance of traditional forms of media diffusion in important ways. Nonetheless, it is widely believed that there is something distinctive

[48] Para. 48. The specific context of these comments was a request for an Advisory Opinion on the question of whether laws which require journalists to be licensed by the state are consistent with the right to freedom of expression, protected in article 13 of the American Convention. The Court's Opinion was that such laws are not consistent with freedom of expression inasmuch as they are indirect restrictions which cannot be regarded as necessary, and are thus unjustifiable.

[49] See P. Steven, *The No-Nonsense Guide to Global Media* (Oxford/London: New Internationalist/Verso, 2003), chap. 7.

about cyberspace. In the words of the Declaration adopted at the 2003 World Summit on the Information Society:

Information and Communication Technologies (ICTs) have an immense impact on virtually all aspects of our lives. The rapid progress of these technologies opens completely new opportunities to attain higher levels of development. The capacity of these technologies to reduce many traditional obstacles, especially those of time and distance, for the first time in history makes it possible to use the potential of these technologies for the benefit of millions of people in all corners of the world.[50]

The Declaration goes on to present a vision of the 'Information Society', oriented to ideals which are expressed in terms of such concepts as 'connectivity', 'digital solidarity', 'cyber-security', and 'bridging the digital divide'.

The problem of the 'digital divide'—whereby infrastructure and services relating to the new media are distributed with extreme unevenness, within countries, as well as among them—is also at the centre of ongoing efforts to bring developments in information and communication technology within the frame of human rights. In the 1970s and 1980s UNESCO pursued an initiative aimed at redressing what was then likewise recognised as an extreme imbalance between the rich parts of the world and the poorer parts with regard to communication and information flows. The initiative was known as the 'New World Information and Communication Order' and, in connection with it, the concept was mooted of a 'right to communicate'. In the late 1990s this proposal was revived, and the 'right to communicate' is now linked with demands for universal, ubiquitous, equitable and affordable access to information and communication technology, as an aspect not only of the right to freedom of expression, but also of the right to development. Beyond this move to use human rights law to help in expanding participation in the new media, the new media are themselves seen as useful for the protection of human rights in a large variety of ways. The enhanced availability of information is viewed as facilitating the exposure of abuses and assisting the implementation of rights, while the improved modes of

---

[50] Declaration of Principles—Building the Information Society: A Global Challenge for the New Millennium, adopted at the World Summit on the Information Society, held in Geneva in December 2003, Doc. WSIS-03/GENEVA/DOC/4-E, 12 December 2003, para. 8.

communication are valued for their contribution to the organisation of enforcement activities and to the mobilisation of campaigns for change within business and government.

But, of course, there is also another story to be told here, for the new media open up dangers, as well as opportunities. Where human rights are concerned, the focus in this regard has mainly been on the use of the internet in connection with trafficking of women, child pornography, and hate speech, and on the threats posed for privacy and data protection. To some commentators, however, the dangers associated with the internet extend much more broadly and deeply than this, and have to do with the way the internet presents itself, and is presented, as a domain of transparency, accountability and consensus—a worldwide, 24/7 public sphere for the 21st century. Central to this image is the idea that the internet lends publicity to power, opening to scrutiny by citizens things that would otherwise remain hidden. Yet, as Jodi Dean observes, the operations of power are frequently today all too transparent.[51] In her words:

We know full well that corporations are destroying the environment, employing slave labor, holding populations hostage to their threats to move their operations to locales with cheaper labor. All sorts of horrible political processes are perfectly transparent today. The problem is that people don't seem to mind, that they are so enthralled by transparency that they have lost the will to fight (*Look! The chemical corporation really is trying . . . Look! The government explained where the money went . . .*).[52]

In Dean's assessment, the image of a digital public sphere must be understood as ideology. It obscures the function of the internet as a major infrastructural element of the global economy. In the process, it also obscures the significance and further potentials of the internet as a site of alternative outlooks, initiatives and projects. Advertisements flash out at us from our computer screens for surveillance cameras the size of pencil sharpeners. At the same time, during the Iraq war and subsequently, we could read 'Dear Raed', the blog written from Baghdad by 'Salam Pax'. For example, we could read the following entry on the fourteenth day of bombing: 'Actually too tired, scared and burnt out to write anything . . . No good news, wherever you look.'[53] Clearly,

[51] J. Dean, 'Why the Net is Not a Public Sphere' 10 *Constellations* (2003), 95.
[52] Ibid., 110.
[53] S. Pax, *The Baghdad Blog* (London: Atlantic Books/The Guardian, 2003), 143 (2 April 2003).

networked communications are used in connection with multiple and often sharply conflicting agendas. As Dean proposes, the key ideological manoeuvre is to obscure that fact.

We opened this discussion by highlighting three perspectives on the media, oriented respectively to the concept of the fourth estate, the process of manufacturing consent, and the idea that there has been an implosion of meaning in the media. We noted then that each of these perspectives has some validity, and our brief comments about the internet may suggest that this holds for the new media as well. Where international human rights law is concerned, we have seen that there is a strong rhetorical investment in the role of the media as a fourth estate or 'cornerstone of democracy', and that human rights law in fact contributes to the realisation of that ideal in a range of significant ways. However, we have also seen that that contribution remains constrained insofar as human rights law fails adequately to address the issue of democratisation within media organisations. Greater attention may be needed to the implications of media concentrations, and to the action required to ensure public access to the media and diversity of media content. What, finally, of the suggestion that we live in a world where there is more and more information, and less and less meaning? To some observers, the international human rights regime itself has many features which provide support for that view. On the other hand, the implosion of meaning has its limits. As the case of the three Rwandan media executives reminds us only too clearly, the 'signs of the real' are not all. Beyond those signs, reality retains yet the capacity to burst back with a murderous vengeance.

Privacy

If privacy is today regarded as a social good, to be defended and protected, this was not always so. The English word 'privacy' comes from the Latin *privare* (to deprive), and in its earliest sense meant something along the lines of 'privation'. A 'private' person was someone deprived of official position or rank, or a member of a closed religious order similarly (albeit voluntarily) disengaged from public life. In the army, of course, a private is still an ordinary soldier who lacks the rank of an officer, and (in some usages) is not a public recruit. Beginning in the 16th century, however, the word 'private' began to be used in much more positive ways, to denote privilege, rather than deprivation—privileged access (as in private property) or privileged relations (as in private friends). The domain of the private thus became associated with independence, exclusivity and intimacy, and in the 17th and especially 18th and 19th centuries privacy came to denote the value of a quiet life, the seclusion of the home, the comfort of family and friends. Today, privacy is a legally protected right in many national jurisdictions. At the same time, it receives international legal protection as a human right. We discuss here the human right to privacy, beginning with brief reference to the history of privacy as a right, and then outlining the main contexts in which international protection is currently given. For all this, privacy has never become an unalloyed good, at least from the perspective of some. The positive sense of the word certainly remains strong. But, as we shall see in the last part of the discussion that follows, the earlier negative, or at any rate, equivocal, sense of privacy as privation—now reoriented to a broader set of privations, including ones that affect life within the private domain itself—also retains resonance.

Privacy as a right

The origins of the idea that privacy is, or should be, a legally protected right are generally traced to the late 19th-century United States, and especially to an article by Louis Brandeis and Samuel Warren, published in the *Harvard Law Review* in 1890 under the title 'The Right to Privacy'.[1] It may be that one impetus for the article came from unwelcome publicity surrounding the wedding of Warren's daughter, and indeed, as claims by actors Michael Douglas and Catherine Zeta-Jones against the magazine *Hello!* attest, unwelcome publicity surrounding high-society or celebrity weddings remains an enduring theme of privacy claims.[2] At any rate, the concerns that drove the right to privacy in this early period had to do with unauthorised observation and/or the unauthorised publication of images of powerful or famous people.[3] A number of the cases to which Brandeis and Warren referred in their article were applications for injunctions by the children of people who had died, to restrain publication of death-bed etchings or photographs made of their parents.

In these and related cases, the threat to privacy came from individuals, newspapers or other agents within society. In the 20th century, however, the state became a major focus of concern from the perspective of privacy. For it became clear then that the consolidation of capitalism and the rise of the bourgeois class—the very developments reflected in the emergence of the favourable concept of privacy described above—brought with them strong states and large bureaucracies, and privacy began to encompass an interest in protection from over-intrusive state power. This served to democratise privacy to a degree, in that now it was not just powerful and privileged people who were affected, but ordinary people as well. At the same time, as Michel Foucault showed, disciplinary mechanisms at work in bourgeois society

---

[1]   4 *Harvard Law Review* (1890) 193. The idea of a 'right to privacy' had also been referred to in cases before 1890: see J.W. DeCew, *In Pursuit of Privacy: Law, Ethics and the Rise of Technology* (Ithaca: Cornell University Press, 1997), 14.

[2]   *Douglas and others v Hello! Ltd and others* [2003] EWHC 786 (Ch).

[3]   For a modern case, see *Daily Mirror* in *Campbell v MGN Limited* [2004] UKHL 22.

undercut the protection of privacy (along with other rights) in important respects. Surveillance became dispersed across the whole field of social life, structuring institutions and promoting processes of individual self-monitoring.[4]

In the late 20th and 21st centuries a key preoccupation with regard to the right to privacy has been the impact of the so-called 'information age'. New technologies of data processing, miniaturisation and communication (the internet, digital photography, electronic tagging, etc.) have brought methods for producing, storing and disseminating data that are seen to pose new threats to privacy. In this context, attention has also reverted to the issue of threats to privacy from non-state agents, as these new technologies have been incorporated into the practices of businesses, enhancing their capacities for monitoring employees, would-be employees, and customers. At the same time, questions arise about what privacy can or should mean in societies caught up in the cult of celebrity, confessional culture, and 'reality TV'. These phrases name some of the ways in which the public gaze is today invited, and, indeed, eroticised. Showing us a little—a few details, some selected photographs, one programme series—is a kind of tease that arouses our desire to see more. In the case of famous people, this can be a matter of preserving the economic value of their celebrity. Thus, for Michael Douglas and Catherine Zeta-Jones, privacy did not mean not having their wedding pictures published. It meant not having their wedding pictures published in *Hello!*; they sold the exclusive rights to publish the pictures to another magazine, *OK!*

Against this background, let us turn now to examine the protection of privacy in international human rights law. In doing so, we should note that the concerns we have mentioned do not arise everywhere—at any rate, not in the same manner or to the same extent. This is evident insofar as the cult of celebrity and related phenomena are associated with late-modern social life, and especially with late-modern social life in certain places. Likewise, and more fundamentally, the strong states and large bureaucracies that developed in Europe and the United States with the consolidation of capitalism, and also accompanied the emergence of

---

[4] See esp. M. Foucault (A. Sheridan, trans.), *Discipline and Punish* (London: Penguin, 1991), esp. 195 *et seq.* ('Panopticism').

state socialism, are not universal or universally operative phenomena. For many in the global South, and in poor areas of countries within the global North, the problem is less over-intrusive states than under-intrusive states. More rigorous practices for keeping track of populations might be welcome where public authorities lack the capacity adequately to collect taxes, ensure personal safety, and provide public services. This is not, of course, to say that the right to privacy has no significance in such conditions. It is simply to observe that concerns regarding it may be most likely to surface in connection with moves to expand state power.

Privacy as a human right

The right to privacy entered the arena of internationally recognised human rights with the adoption of the Universal Declaration of Human Rights. Article 12 of the Declaration prohibits arbitrary interference with 'privacy, family, home or correspondence' and attacks on 'honour and reputation', and asserts the right of everyone to legal protection against such interference or attacks. The International Covenant on Civil and Political Rights, in article 17, guarantees the right to privacy in similar terms: '(1) No one shall be subjected to arbitrary or unlawful interference with his privacy, family, home or correspondence, nor to unlawful attacks on his honour and reputation. (2) Everyone has the right to the protection of the law against such interference or attacks.'

The right to privacy is also protected in the Convention on the Rights of the Child[5] and in two regional treaties, the American Convention on Human Rights (article 11) and the European Convention on Human Rights (article 8). Article 11 of the American Convention largely repeats article 17 of the Civil and Political Rights Covenant, re-casting it slightly to lay particular emphasis on the right to have 'honor respected' and 'dignity recognized'.[6] Article 8 of the European Convention is expressed somewhat differently:

(1) Everyone has the right to respect for his private and family life, his home and his correspondence.

[5] Art. 16.
[6] See also American Declaration of the Rights and Duties of Man, art. V.

(2) There shall be no interference by a public authority with the exercise of this right except such as is in accordance with the law and is necessary in a democratic society in the interests of national security, public safety or the economic well-being of the country, for the prevention of disorder or crime, for the protection of health or morals, or for the protection of the rights and freedoms of others.

One aspect of the difference between this provision and article 17 of the Civil and Political Rights Covenant is obviously that in the European Convention the scope for *lawful* interference with privacy is specified, and in some detail. We should not, however, attach too much significance to this, for in the other instruments as well there is a clear presupposition that privacy is a relative value, which may justifiably be restricted in some circumstances, for the sake of other values. The point is to ensure that it is not *arbitrarily* or *unlawfully* restricted.

What, then, are the contexts in which the right to privacy has received protection under the European Convention and the other treaties just mentioned? In the succeeding paragraphs we highlight four kinds of situation in which an 'interference' with private life has been deemed to have occurred, such that justification was required. We should emphasise that this is only an illustrative sample of a much larger array of relevant contexts. As is frequently observed, the right to privacy is something of a 'catch-all' category, made up in part of interests that do not readily fit within the scope of another human right, but yet are believed to merit protection within the overall framework of human rights law. In this respect, while all human rights are tools for asserting claims, the right to privacy may be more elastic than most. Of course, one danger of a catch-all is that it can easily shade into a 'stop-gap', which relieves us of the task of thinking through what is actually at stake.[7] Certainly, the right to privacy has been deployed to address problems of a wide variety of kinds—among others, problems of fair criminal justice, freedom of dissent, non-discrimination and social inclusion, personal security, environmental protection, and the enjoyment of private property. The European Court of Human Rights has proposed that a common thread is the aim of ensuring 'the development,

---

[7] Slavoj Žižek makes this argument in relation to a concept against which the right to privacy is in some respects counterposed: totalitarianism. See S. Žižek, *Did Somebody Say Totalitarianism?* (London: Verso, 2001), esp. 3.

without outside interference, of the personality of each individual in his relations with other human beings'.[8] But what does *that* involve?

First of all, then, the right to privacy has been used to challenge forms of surveillance. Restrictions placed on prisoners' correspondence were the subject of one early complaint under the European Convention.[9] Dismissing the government's contention that these must simply be accepted as an inherent aspect of imprisonment, the European Court of Human Rights confirmed that what is in issue is an interference with the right to privacy. Accordingly, the question is always whether the restrictions can be justified by reference to article 8(2). Outside the prison context, telephone-tapping was the subject of another early judgment of the European Court of Human Rights,[10] and the idea that secret surveillance is an interference with the right to privacy which requires justification is now well established. The implications of this have been considered in complaints about the activities of a country's intelligence and criminal investigation services. They have also been considered in complaints about surveillance of employees by employers. Thus, for instance, in a case against the United Kingdom arising out of the monitoring of calls made by a police officer who had brought a sex discrimination claim against the police authorities, the European Court of Human Rights ruled that this violated the applicant's right to privacy.[11] The interference was not 'in accordance with law', as demanded by article 8(2). To meet this aspect of the justification criteria, the Court has repeatedly insisted that there must exist national legislation which stipulates the categories of people liable to secret surveillance and the procedures that must be followed with respect to the information obtained.

A second context for protection of the right to privacy concerns arrangements for the storage of personal data. The Human Rights Committee has specified in a General Comment on article 17 of the Civil and Political Rights Covenant some of the legal protections that are

---

[8] *Botta v Italy*, Judgment of 24 February 1998, para. 32.
[9] *Golder v United Kingdom*, Judgment of the European Court of Human Rights, 21 February 1975.
[10] *Klass v Germany*, Judgment of the European Court of Human Rights, 6 September 1978.
[11] *Halford v United Kingdom*, Judgment of the European Court of Human Rights, 25 June 1997.

implicit in the right to privacy in this context.[12] Whether information is gathered and held by public authorities or private parties, everyone should have the right to ascertain whether information concerning them is stored, and if so, what information is stored, and for what purpose. They should also have the right to ascertain which bodies control access to their files, and the right to correct inaccurate information or have their file eliminated if it is unlawfully maintained. Shortly after Romania became a party to the European Convention, a complaint was brought by a person who was the subject of a secret intelligence file held by the Romanian authorities, which was being used against him in legal proceedings.[13] The file included personal details going back almost 60 years, some of which were falsely attributed to the applicant. The European Court of Human Rights held that the maintenance of these files breached the applicant's right to privacy on several grounds. As there was no legal framework within national law for regulating the recording and archiving of the information (and, for instance, limiting the time period for which information could be held), the interference with the right to privacy could not be said to be 'prescribed by law'. At the same time, the interference could not be regarded as having pursued one of the aims specified in article 8(2) of the Convention. In particular, the Court observed that national security cannot justify the more or less indiscriminate storage of data, including false data, over such a long period. Finally, the interference could not be deemed 'necessary in a democratic society', inasmuch as it was disproportionate to any legitimate aim, and not protected by judicially supervised safeguards to guard against abuse.

Thirdly, the right to privacy has been at the centre of claims concerning the control of sexuality and sexual activity. An important category of claims of this kind relates to laws that criminalise same-sex sexual relations and in other respects discriminate against gay men and lesbians. The right to privacy has been used as the basis for challenges to laws of this sort in many human rights courts and treaty bodies. After considerable struggle on the part of those affected, it is now widely recognised that prohibitions on same-sex sexual relations and other laws

[12] General Comment 16 (The right to respect of privacy, family, home and correspondence, and protection of honour and reputation), 8 April 1988, esp. para. 10.

[13] *Rotaru v Romania*, Judgment of the European Court of Human Rights, 4 May 2000.

concerning sexual activity which involve sexual orientation discrimination are violations of that right. (On this aspect of the right to privacy, see Sexuality★.) Also impugned by reference to the right to privacy have been laws criminalising consenting sex with more than one person and other sexual practices,[14] along with laws affecting personal status that discriminate against transsexuals. With regard to the latter, the European Court of Human Rights held in a complaint against France that the failure of the French authorities to change the civil register to reflect an applicant's gender reassignment violates the right to privacy.[15] In systems where civil status is not determined by reference to a civil register, but rather by reference to the registration of births, the European Court was initially reluctant to uphold claims by post-operative transsexuals to have the register of births annotated and a new birth certificate issued. However, in a case involving the United Kingdom, the Court was persuaded to uphold such a claim. The 'fair balance that is inherent in the Convention now tilts decisively in favour of the applicant', it said. No significant factors of public interest had been adduced to outweigh the interest of the applicant in legal recognition of her new gender identity.[16]

The final context we mention here relates to environmental regulation. As is evident in our discussion so far, the right to privacy entails for governments not just that they must refrain from interfering with private life without justification. It also entails that they must provide protection against unjustified interferences with privacy, including interferences by private actors. That is to say, it entails 'positive' obligations. A number of complaints under the European Convention have revolved around the claim that failure appropriately to regulate activities which adversely affect the environmental conditions of a person's home is a violation of the positive obligations that flow from the right to privacy. Thus, for example, in a case against Spain, the European Court of Human Rights ruled that the government had violated the applicant's rights under article 8 by failing to close down a waste-treatment plant near her home that was emitting fumes, repetitive noise and noxious odours, and creating a serious health

---

[14] See, e.g., *A. D. T. v United Kingdom*, Judgment of the European Court of Human Rights, 31 July 2000 and *Laskey, Jaggard and Brown v United Kingdom*, Judgment of the European Court of Human Rights, 20 January 1997.

[15] *B v France*, Judgment of the European Court of Human Rights, 25 March 1992.

[16] *I v United Kingdom*, Judgment of the European Court of Human Rights (Grand Chamber), 11 July 2002, para. 73.

hazard.[17] Once again, the Court observed that a 'fair balance' had not been struck, in this case between the town's interest in having the plant and the industry it served and the applicant's effective enjoyment of her right to respect for her home and her private and family life.[18] In another, more recent judgment, the Court addressed a complaint against the United Kingdom about a decision to allow night flights to and from Heathrow Airport.[19] The case was popularly glossed as a contest between the 'right to cheap flights' and the 'right to a good night's sleep'.[20] The Court accepted the argument of the applicants, who were local residents, that the right to privacy includes the right to a good night's sleep. Thus, the result-ant increase in noise levels at night constituted an interference with their rights under article 8. In the circumstances, however, this interference was considered justifiable by reference to the aim of ensuring the 'economic well-being of the country', as permitted in article 8(2).

Shielding private injustice

We have seen that the right to privacy in international human rights law is structured around the idea of protecting private life from unjustified 'interference'. This fits with the conception of privacy which, as we noted at the beginning, developed in the 17th century and subsequently—the positive conception, according to which the domain of the private is associated with independence, exclusivity and intimacy, and privacy expresses a claim to safeguard those values. But it becomes more prob-lematic when we consider that privacy also has another side. For, as fem-inist theorists especially have taught, in the real world the domain of the private is also associated with subordination, exploitation and violence, and the protection of privacy is part of what enables and sustains these wrongs. Thus, privacy has been used to shield violence against women from effective law enforcement, to prevent challenge to racial discrim-ination in the hiring of domestic staff, and to legitimate the exclusion of people from clubs and associations on religious grounds. The concept of the private sphere as a zone of independence, exclusivity and intimacy

[17] *López Ostra v Spain*, Judgment of the European Court of Human Rights, 9 December 1994.   [18] Ibid., para. 58.
[19] *Hatton v United Kingdom*, Judgment of the European Court of Human Rights (Grand Chamber), 8 July 2003.   [20] See *The Sunday Times*, 13 July 2002, 17.

has meant that issues of marital rape, child abuse and domestic labour long remained outside the frame of human rights concern.

Addressing privacy in terms of the protection of private life from unjustified interference is thus unsatisfactory on a number of counts. It masks the often unequal and violent character of private life, perpetuating instead a romanticised conception of family and associational life which is far removed from the actuality of many people's experience. In doing so, it also masks the need for protection of rights within the private sphere, and hence absolves state authorities from responsibility for ensuring that protection. Finally, it masks the extent to which the state has already 'interfered' by making the laws and putting in place the political arrangements that shape the character of life within the private sphere. To speak in this context of 'interference' is to naturalise family and other private relations as pre-legal and pre-political phenomena. This is perhaps the most problematic aspect. For if private relations are naturally as they are now, then efforts to transform their asymmetries and redress their injustices are not just illegitimate invasions of privacy, but absurd and necessarily futile attempts to change nature.

These considerations are reflected in important developments in international human rights law generally, and the right to privacy in particular. With regard to the latter, we have seen in this discussion that privacy is today used in the context of claims both about over-intrusive government and about neglectful government. That is, it is used both to keep the state out and to draw it in. The concept of positive obligations has emerged in human rights law as a way of insisting that state authorities take responsibility for protecting rights within the private sphere.[21] To this extent, the assumption has been challenged that justice between individuals or other private parties is a matter purely for private law, and that human rights law is concerned solely with the regulation of relations between individuals and public authorities. Likewise, the idea has been challenged that states are only internationally responsible under human rights law for harms which result directly from the acts of public authorities. Yet the notion of privacy as protection from unjustified interference remains potent, and when applicants have relied on the right to privacy to demand state action, it has often been to defend the

---

[21] See further A. Clapham, *Human Rights in the Private Sphere* (Oxford: Oxford University Press, 1993).

character of homes as personal castles. For those to whom home means something very different, privacy is—as perhaps it always has been—a more uncertain good, which retains significant traces of its original sense, and mixes the promise of seclusion with the enduring realities of privation and subordinate status.

Protest

In discussions of public protest today, two themes stand out. One is about the way globalisation has fuelled and facilitated protest. Key landmarks in the history of this development are the Zapatista uprising in Chiapas in 1994, launched on the day when the North American Free Trade Agreement entered into force, and the massive 'anti-globalisation' demonstrations staged at Seattle in 1999, when the scheduled ministerial meeting of the World Trade Organization was disrupted. These and subsequent events attest to important changes both in the focus of popular protest and in its organisation—changes which do not supersede earlier forms of protest, but which expand and recontextualise them in significant respects. With regard to the focus of oppositional activity, local and national concerns are today supplemented by, and at times linked to, concerns about regional and global economic and political systems. Thus, demonstrations have been held at all the major intergovernmental summits of the G8, WTO, World Bank and IMF, as well as at the meetings of the World Economic Forum and other organisations, and multinational corporations have likewise been the target of sustained protest campaigns. With regard to the organisation of oppositional activity, enhanced interaction among activists, helped by the revolution in communications and information technology, has enabled agendas, strategies and initiatives to be formulated and implemented on a transnational scale. Beyond the demonstrations and campaigns mentioned above, the anti-war movement, launched to oppose the attack on Iraq in 2003, well illustrates this. At the same time, networking has brought with it a process of 'triangulation' that has unsettled traditional antagonisms, and enabled new alliances to be formed between groups. Thus, trade unions have demonstrated alongside environmentalists, church groups alongside anarchists, and farmers alongside sociology students.

The second theme points in the opposite direction to the one we have just mentioned. This is about the way globalisation has set limits to protest. The concerns to which globalising processes have given rise are extremely varied. Indeed, one of the most widely remarked features of the new context is its diversity. Nonetheless, according to Naomi Klein, opposition is ranged against forces that have a 'common thread', which 'might broadly be described as the privatization of every aspect of life, and the transformation of every activity and value into a commodity'. As Klein observes, '[w]e often speak of the privatization of education, of healthcare, of natural resources', but the 'process is much vaster', and includes, among many other things, 'the way powerful ideas are turned into advertising slogans and public streets into shopping malls'.[1] Yet, of course, when powerful ideas are turned into advertising slogans and public streets into shopping malls, that affects the possibilities for protest against those very developments. Likewise, the possibilities for protest are affected by many other changes. Among them, Neera Chandhoke points to the elaboration of strategies for 'managing' dissent. In her words, protest and struggle have emerged not just as phenomena to be repressed, but as 'problems ... to be resolved through managerial techniques'.[2] That is to say, rather than simply silencing dissent, governments often prefer to signal a willingness to tolerate it, while placing severe constraints on its expression. For Chandhoke the rise of dissent management belongs with moves to enhance the legitimacy and efficacy of programmes of economic liberalisation through the embrace of 'good governance', defined in terms that include pluralism in public affairs. From this perspective, dissent has at one level been co-opted to legitimate economic liberalisation. At the same time it has been limited, for ultimately (as we shall see) private property is private property.

For Naomi Klein, what is required—and what is in fact unfolding—is a 'radical reclaiming of the commons',[3] and clearly an important aspect of that challenge is to reclaim the conditions for reclamation itself, by contesting the limitation and co-optation of protest. The issue we take up here is the bearing of international human rights law with respect to that process. Specifically, we ask: to what extent does international human rights

---

[1] N. Klein, 'Reclaiming the Commons' 9 *New Left Review* (2001), 81, 82.

[2] N. Chandhoke, 'The Limits of Global Civil Society' in M. Glasius, M. Kaldor & H. Anheirer (eds.), *Global Civil Society 2002* (Oxford: Oxford University Press, 2002), 35, 45.

[3] N. Klein, 'Reclaiming the Commons' 9 *New Left Review* (2001), 81, 82.

law recognise the right to protest? In addressing that question, we will review a number of cases before human rights courts and tribunals in which complaints about the scope of legitimate protest have been considered. While some of those cases touch on the sorts of concerns which Klein has in mind when she speaks of the 'privatization of every aspect of life', most revolve around more 'traditional' concerns about political repression and democratic deliberation. That said, if Klein, Chandhoke and others like them are right, these traditional concerns today arise within a new context which has not left them unaffected.

The right to protest

The right to protest is not as such affirmed in any human rights treaty or other instrument. However, it is implicit in guarantees of the right to freedom of expression and the right to freedom of assembly and association. These rights are recognised in the Universal Declaration of Human Rights, where it is stated that '[e]veryone has the right to freedom of opinion and expression; this right includes freedom to hold opinions without interference and to seek, receive and impart information and ideas through any media and regardless of frontiers,'[4] and that '[e]veryone has the right to freedom of peaceful assembly and association'.[5] Rights to freedom of expression, assembly and association are protected in the International Covenant on Civil and Political Rights,[6] as well as in all the regional human rights systems.[7] Decisions of the various courts and tribunals associated with these treaties are replete with statements about the 'paramount importance in any democratic society' of these rights as entitlements to protest.[8] The fact that the right to protest is recognised as important does not mean, of course, that it is recognised as absolute or overriding. Under international human rights law, this right is qualified in three principal ways.

[4] Art. 19.   [5] Art. 20.   [6] Arts. 19, 21 and 22.

[7] See, e.g., African Charter of Human and Peoples' Rights, arts. 9, 10 and 11; American Convention on Human Rights, arts. 13, 15 and 16; American Declaration of the Rights and Duties of Man (binding for all member states of the Organization of American States), arts. 11, 12 and 14; and European Convention on Human Rights, arts. 10 and 11.

[8] *Tae Hoon Park v Republic of Korea*, Communication 628/1995, Views of the Human Rights Committee, 20 October 1998, para. 10.3. See also, e.g., *Appleby and Others v United Kingdom*, Judgment of the European Court of Human Rights, 6 May 2003, para. 39.

In the first place, it is qualified by the various qualifications that apply to the rights to freedom of expression, assembly and association themselves. Thus, for example, under article 19(3) of the International Covenant on Civil and Political Rights, restrictions may be imposed on freedom of expression, 'but these shall only be such as are provided by law and are necessary: (a) for respect of the rights or reputations of others; (b) for the protection of national security or of public order (*ordre public*), or of public health or morals'. Similar stipulations apply under other treaties, both in relation to freedom of expression and in relation to freedom of assembly and association. We review these stipulations in more detail below. Secondly, the right to protest is qualified by the prohibition of abusive invocation of rights. This prohibition is expressed in article 5(1) of the Civil and Political Rights Covenant in the following terms: 'Nothing in the present Covenant may be interpreted as implying for any State, group or person any right to engage in any activity or perform any act aimed at the destruction of any of the rights and freedoms recognized herein or at their limitation to a greater extent than is provided for in the present Covenant.' Again, similar prohibitions apply under other treaties.

Finally, the right to protest is qualified by the permission which is given under some human rights treaties, among them the Civil and Political Rights Covenant, for states to derogate from their obligations with respect to certain human rights in time of 'public emergency'.[9] Rights to freedom of expression, assembly and association are, in theory, among the rights which can be the subject to derogating measures. However, we say 'in theory' because derogation is only permitted if it can be considered necessary and proportionate to the exigencies of the situation confronted, and in most situations the restrictions which can ordinarily be imposed for the protection of national security, public order, and so on, under article 19(3) of the Covenant (quoted above) and other similar provisions are likely to be sufficient, with the result that the necessity of derogation may be difficult to establish.[10]

[9] See esp. International Covenant on Civil and Political Rights, art. 4; American Convention on Human Rights, art. 27; European Convention on Human Rights, art. 15. The Human Rights Committee has expressed the view that a 'mass demonstration involving instances of violence' may itself be a public emergency, but that this would generally be one in which derogating measures could not be justified. See Human Rights Committee, General Comment 29 (States of emergency: art. 4), 24 July 2001, para. 5.

[10] Human Rights Committee, General Comment 29 (States of emergency: art. 4), 24 July 2001, para. 5.

Protest as an offence

What obligations are entailed for states by the right to protest? In this section and the succeeding two sections we outline three kinds of obligations. We begin here with the 'negative' obligation not to make protest an offence. What is the scope of this obligation? Or, to turn that question the other way around, in what circumstances can the right to protest justifiably be restricted? We noted in the previous paragraph that the right to protest is subject to the various qualifications that apply to the rights through which it is protected, under article 19(3) of the Covenant and other corresponding provisions. The effect of these qualifications is that restriction of the right to protest will be justifiable where it is framed with certain legitimate interests in view (such as national security, public safety, public order, and the protection of the rights of others), provided that the specific restriction imposed can be considered a necessary and proportionate measure with respect to those interests, and provided also that it is laid down in national laws which are precise and accessible to all.

In one case before the Human Rights Committee, the complainant had been fined for distributing leaflets and raising a banner outside a building in Finland where official talks were taking place with a visiting dignitary.[11] She argued that this violated her rights to freedom of expression and assembly under articles 19 and 21 of the Covenant. The Committee upheld her complaint on the grounds that restriction of the right to protest is *only* justifiable in the circumstances described above, and those circumstances did not obtain in this case. In another case, a Korean complainant had been penalised following conviction for offences arising out of his participation in protests against government policy.[12] He argued that this violated his right to freedom of expression under article 19 of the Covenant, and again, the Committee upheld the complaint. In doing so, it said that the paramount importance of the right to freedom of expression in this context means that 'any restrictions to the exercise of [the right to freedom of expression] must meet

---

[11] *Kivenmaa v Finland*, Communication 412/1990, Views of the Human Rights Committee, adopted 31 March 1994.

[12] *Tae Hoon Park v Republic of Korea*, Communication 628/1995, Views of the Human Rights Committee, adopted 20 October 1998.

a strict test of justification'.[13] That strict test had not been met here. While the Government had invoked national security as a justifying interest, it had not been able to specify the 'precise nature' of the threat to national security posed by the applicant's activities.

A large number of applications have been brought under the European Convention on Human Rights by people who have incurred criminal liability as a result of participation in protests. The determination of whether this has involved a violation of state obligations with respect to the right to protest has been shaped by the doctrine of the 'margin of appreciation', elaborated by the European Court of Human Rights. Some examples will illustrate the significance of this concept. In one case, the applicant was arrested and fined for distributing leaflets and carrying a placard at a military parade in Austria, as part of a campaign to challenge the purchase of certain military aircraft.[14] He complained that this violated his right to freedom of expression, protected by article 10 of the European Convention. The Court dismissed this complaint, accepting the Government's argument that what was in issue was instead a justifiable restriction of his right to freedom of expression under article 10(2). Under this latter provision, the right to freedom of expression:

may be subject to such formalities, conditions, restrictions or penalties as are prescribed by law and are necessary in a democratic society, in the interests of national security, territorial integrity or public safety, for the prevention of disorder or crime, for the protection of health or morals, for the protection of the reputation or rights of others, for preventing the disclosure of information received in confidence, or for maintaining the authority and impartiality of the judiciary.

For the Court, the applicant's arrest and conviction were directed to one of the legitimate interests contemplated in article 10(2), namely the 'prevention of disorder'. The course followed by the authorities had been based on provisions of national law. As to whether the arrest and conviction could be considered necessary and proportionate, it was within the Government's 'margin of appreciation' to decide what measures

---

[13]   *Tae Hoon Park v Republic of Korea*, Communication 628/1995, Views of the Human Rights Committee, adopted 20 October 1998, para. 10.3.

[14]   *Chorherr v Austria*, Judgment of the European Court of Human Rights, 25 August 1993.

were required to maintain public order, and the particular measures taken were not, in the Court's assessment, excessive.

Another case concerned complaints by five people who had been arrested in the United Kingdom while engaged in a series of different kinds of protests on different issues.[15] Among other allegations, they argued that their right to freedom of expression had been violated. Three of the applicants had been arrested while handing out leaflets protesting against the sale of fighter helicopters. The European Court of Human Rights accepted their argument that there was no basis for their arrest in English law. It followed that the restriction of their right to freedom of expression did not satisfy the proviso of being laid down in national law—or 'prescribed by law', in the language of article 10(2)—and, accordingly, could not be justified. Of the remaining two applicants, one had been arrested while obstructing a grouse shooting party, the other while obstructing the construction of a motorway extension. Following their arrest, both had refused to commit themselves to not repeating their activities by being 'bound over'. The European Court dismissed their complaint. In contrast to the arrest of the other three applicants, the arrest of these applicants was seen to have a basis in English law. At the same time, these arrests were also seen to be directed to legitimate interests—the 'prevention of disorder', along with two other interests mentioned in article 10(2), the 'protection of the rights of others' and (in view of their refusal to be 'bound over') the 'maintenance of the authority of the judiciary'. On the question of whether the action taken by the British authorities was necessary to protect those interests, the Court again referred to the Government's margin of appreciation, and stated its own assessment that the action taken had not been excessive.

Let us mention one final case brought under the European Convention, which arose out of a widely publicised protest that occurred in Paris in 1996, where a group of non-nationals without residence permits ('sans papiers') and their supporters occupied a church, to draw attention to the difficulties faced by non-nationals in France in having their immigration status reviewed.[16] The applicant was spokesperson for the group, and was among those arrested and eventually

---

[15] *Steel and Others v United Kingdom*, Judgment of the European Court of Human Rights, 23 September 1998.

[16] *Cissé v France*, Judgment of the European Court of Human Rights, 9 April 2002.

deported and excluded from French territory. She complained that this violated her right to freedom of peaceful assembly, protected in article 11 of the European Convention. Noting that the occupation of the church was illegal under French law, the French Government argued that she had not been engaged in 'peaceful assembly'. However, there was no evidence of any violence associated with the protest, nor of any obstruction to religious services, and the European Court of Human Rights dismissed this argument. As the applicant observed, the legality or otherwise of an assembly under national law cannot be relevant in this regard, for national law may impose an excessive restriction on freedom of peaceful assembly. Did French law do that in this case? The Court held that it did not. No violation of the applicant's right to freedom of peaceful assembly was held to have occurred, as the action taken by the French authorities was regarded as justifiable by reference to article 11(2) of the Convention. Under that provision, '[n]o restrictions shall be placed on the exercise of [the right to freedom of assembly] other than such as are prescribed by law and are necessary in a democratic society in the interests of national security or public safety, for the prevention of disorder or crime, for the protection of health or morals or for the protection of the rights and freedoms of others.' For the Court, the evacuation of the church had been directed to the legitimate aim of preventing disorder, by bringing an end to an illegal act. Thus, the illegality of the protest, while not relevant to the question of whether the protesters were exercising the right to peaceful protest, *was* seen as relevant to the legitimacy of restrictions imposed with respect to that right. Furthermore, the Court considered that the Government had acted within its margin of appreciation in deciding that evacuation was required in the circumstances. For the Court, the 'symbolic and testimonial value of the applicant's and other immigrants' presence had been tolerated sufficiently long' for the interference not to appear unreasonable.[17]

Violence against protesters

We have so far been examining the 'negative' obligation of states not to prevent demonstrations by making protest an offence. But being

[17] Para. 52.

arrested is by no means the only obstacle a protester may face. Protest may equally be prevented where protesters are not able to protest safely, and without threat of violence at the hands of the police or other private citizens. The danger of police brutality is, of course, a real one in many situations.[18] Where force is used which goes beyond the minimal force necessary to effect a lawful arrest, violence by the police or other state officials is likely to violate the rights to security of the person and protection from inhuman treatment. If protesters are killed, there may additionally be a violation of the right to life unless the use of lethal force can be shown to have been necessary and proportionate. But what of violence by other private citizens, such as those engaged in a 'counter-demonstration'? Does the right to protest impose on states an obligation to protect protesters from other private citizens who would harm them?

This question was considered by the European Court of Human Rights in a case against Austria, decided in 1988.[19] The applicants were a group of doctors campaigning against abortion. They held two demonstrations which were disrupted by counter-demonstrators, shouting and throwing eggs and clumps of grass. Police officers deployed along the route were unable to prevent this. In proceedings before the Austrian courts, the doctors claimed that the police had failed to provide sufficient protection for the events. These claims were not successful. The applicants then took their case to Strasbourg, complaining that their rights under the European Convention had been violated. They initially argued that their right to freedom of assembly, protected in article 11 of the Convention, had been violated. However, this argument failed before the European Commission of Human Rights, and before the European Court the focus was instead on the further claim that the doctors' rights under article 13 of the Convention had been breached. Under article 13, '[e]veryone whose rights and freedoms as set forth in this Convention are violated shall have an effective remedy before a national authority'.

The applicants contended that they had been denied an effective remedy for their complaint under article 11. It is sufficient for the

---

[18] See T. Mertes, 'Grassroots Globalism' 17 New Left Review (2002), 101, esp. 108.

[19] Plattform "Ärtze für das Leben" v Austria, Judgment of the European Court of Human Rights, 25 May 1988.

purposes of article 13 that an applicant have an 'arguable case' that his or her rights and freedoms under the Convention have been violated, even if the Court is not ultimately persuaded that a violation has occurred. Did the applicants have an arguable case that their right to freedom of assembly had been violated? They could not do so unless the Austrian authorities were seen to have a duty to provide protection against violence by counter-demonstrators.

Indeed, the Court held that the Austrian authorities had this duty. As it reasoned,

[a] demonstration may annoy or give offence to persons opposed to the ideas or claims that it is seeking to promote. The participants must, however, be able to hold the demonstration without having to fear that they will be subjected to physical violence by their opponents; such a fear would be liable to deter associations or other groups supporting common ideas or interests from openly expressing their opinions on highly controversial issues affecting the community. In a democracy the right to counter-demonstrate cannot extend to inhibiting the exercise of the right to demonstrate.[20]

It followed for the Court that '[g]enuine, effective freedom of peaceful assembly cannot...be reduced to a mere duty on the part of the State not to interfere: a purely negative conception would not be compatible with the object and purpose of Article 11'. Rather, article 11 'sometimes requires positive measures to be taken, even in the sphere of relations between individuals'.[21] In the event, the Court decided that the applicants did not have an arguable case, as the authorities had taken reasonable and appropriate measures to protect those demonstrating, and the demonstration had been able to conclude without damage or serious clashes. Nonetheless, the principle recognised by the Court that the right to protest imposes on states an obligation to protect protesters from other private citizens remains important.

Privatisation of protest space

We have reviewed the 'negative' obligation of states not to make protest an offence and the 'positive' obligation of states to provide protection from counter-demonstrators. Yet these obligations still by no means

---

[20] Para. 32.   [21] Ibid.

speak to all the obstacles which a protester may face. One further obstacle we highlight here takes on particular significance against the background of the developments we noted in introducing this discussion. This is the privatisation of protest space. For just as the right to protest may be prevented where protesters are exposed to criminal liability or risk injury at the hands of their opponents, so too it may be prevented where they lack access to places where meaningful protest can occur. To what extent, then, is the right to protest understood to entail an obligation to ensure access to such places?

Again, this question has been considered by the European Court of Human Rights. The issue arose in connection with a complaint against the United Kingdom, decided in 2003.[22] An educational institution based in the town of Washington (England) sought planning permission to build on an area then in use as playing fields. The applicants wished to persuade the planning authorities not to grant the permission, as these were the only playing fields in the vicinity of the Washington town centre which were available for community use. The town centre of Washington was itself privately owned. It had originally been built by a state-owned corporation, and had then been sold to a private company, which had developed it as a shopping mall. Wishing to stage their protest in the town centre, the applicants tried to set up stands and collect signatures for a petition at the entrance to the shopping mall. Security guards employed by the owner told them to leave. For a short time the manager of one hypermarket within the mall allowed them to set up stands and collect signatures inside that store. However, the applicants' subsequent efforts to obtain permission from the owner of the town centre to continue their protest were not successful. Their request was met with the reply that the 'owner's stance on all political and religious issues is one of strict neutrality', and permission was refused. Before the European Court of Human Rights, the applicants argued that their rights to freedom of expression and freedom of assembly had been violated.

The applicants' argument under the European Convention was twofold. On the one hand, they contended that the state was directly responsible for an interference with their freedoms of expression and

---

[22] *Appleby and Others v United Kingdom*, Judgment of the European Court of Human Rights, 6 May 2003.

assembly. This responsibility arose, they maintained, from the state's failure, at the time when the town centre was being sold to its current owner, to require the latter to enter into a 'walkways agreement', under which access by people wishing to exercise their right to protest would be assured. On the other hand, the applicants also contended that the state owed a 'positive obligation to secure the exercise of their rights' within the mall. According to them, access to the town centre was essential for the exercise of their rights of protest, as it was the most effective way of communicating information and ideas to their fellow citizens. The Court dismissed the first of these arguments, rejecting the notion that the Government bore direct responsibility for the restriction of the applicants' rights to freedom of expression and assembly. The only issue, for the Court, was 'whether the Government have failed in any positive obligation to protect the exercise of the applicants' Article 10 [and 11] rights from interference by others', and specifically, by the owner of the town centre/shopping mall.[23] The Court decided that the Government had not. For one thing, freedoms of expression and assembly were not the only Convention rights at stake. A balance needed to be struck, for '[r]egard must also be had to the property rights of the owner of the shopping centre under Article 1 of Protocol No. 1', which protects the right to peaceful enjoyment of one's possessions.[24] Moreover, with regard to freedoms of expression, article 10 of the Convention 'does not bestow any freedom of forum for the exercise' of that right.[25] Inasmuch as patterns of social interaction were admittedly changing, the Court was not persuaded that this required the 'automatic creation of rights of entry to private property'. That said, the Court did allow that:

where however the bar on access to property has the effect of preventing any effective exercise of freedom of expression or it can be said that the essence of the right has been destroyed, the Court would not exclude that a positive obligation could arise for the State to protect the enjoyment of Convention rights by regulating property rights.[26]

By way of example, the Court cited the phenomenon of the corporate town, where an entire municipality is controlled by a private body.[27] In the present case, however, the Court did not consider that refusal to

[23] Para. 41.   [24] Para. 43.   [25] Para. 47.   [26] Ibid.
[27] See, e.g., *Marsh v Alabama*, 326 U.S. 501 (1946) (US Supreme Court).

allow the applicants to conduct their protest in the town centre had prevented any effective exercise of their rights or destroyed the essence of those rights. The applicants had available to them, and had indeed employed, other means for conducting their campaign, such as calling door-to-door and seeking exposure in the local media.

Protest and economic liberalisation

The case just discussed illustrates the way advancing privatisation may affect the right to protest, and the way such a process may be ratified through human rights procedures. The European Court of Human Rights invoked the right to peaceful enjoyment of one's possessions to justify the exclusion of protest from a privately owned town centre, as if the latter were just another possession to be quietly enjoyed, like its manager's back garden or living room. Economic liberalisation has like-wise been addressed from the standpoint of its relation to protest activity in cases before the European Court of Justice. In one case, decided in 1997, the Commission of the European Communities sought a ruling with respect to complaints it had repeatedly received about the passivity of the French authorities in the face of protest activities by French farmers directed against agricultural products from other member states of the European Union.[28] These activities included the interception of lorries, violence against lorry drivers, and threats against supermarkets selling such products. The French Government did not seek to defend its inaction by reference to the farmers' right to protest, and the Court of Justice held that, in failing to intervene, the French Government had breached its obligations with respect to the free movement of goods under Community law.

By contrast, the right to protest was successfully invoked to justify restriction of economic freedoms in a later case before the Court of Justice involving Austria.[29] An environmental campaigning organisation was granted permission to organise a demonstration on a motorway to draw attention to the public health dangers associated with the

---

[28] *EC Commission v France*, Case C-265/95, Judgment of the European Court of Justice, 9 December 1997, [1997] ECR I-6959.

[29] *Eugen Schmidberger, Internationale Tranporte und Planzüge v Austria*, Case C-112/00, Judgment of the European Court of Justice, 12 June 2003, [2003] ECR I-5659.

ever-increasing transit traffic of heavy goods vehicles. In consequence of the demonstration, the motorway was closed to traffic for 30 hours. A road transport company whose lorries regularly used the motorway complained that the grant of permission for the demonstration was inconsistent with Community law norms providing for the free movement of goods. The Austrian Government argued that the restriction on free movement arising from the demonstration was limited and reasonable, and that assessment of the interests at stake should lean in favour of the freedoms of expression and assembly. The Court of Justice ruled that indeed there had been no breach of Community law. In its analysis, the case raised the question of the need to reconcile freedoms of expression and assembly—which it deemed 'the fundamental pillars of a democratic society'[30]—with free movement of goods. Against this background, the Court considered it significant that, whereas in the earlier French case the protesters' aim was to prevent the movement of goods, in this case obstruction of free movement was simply the temporary consequence of a protest inspired by environmental concerns. Overall, the Court was persuaded that the Austrian authorities had been justified in taking the view that the 'legitimate aim of [the] demonstration could not be achieved...by measures less restrictive of intra-Community trade'.[31]

'Michael Moore starves the poor'

Between 1999 and 2002 Mike Moore was Director-General of the World Trade Organization. After his tenure ended, he wrote a book entitled *A World Without Walls: Freedom, Development, Free Trade and Global Governance*, reflecting on his experiences in that role.[32] On the cover of the book is an intriguing picture. It is a photograph of what appears to be an 'anti-globalisation' rally, and in the foreground is an enormous figure with a *papier maché* head—perhaps someone on stilts—wearing a suit inscribed with the letters 'WTO' and clearly designed to resemble Mike Moore. Around the figure's neck hangs a placard, much like the self-denouncing placards which at various times and in various places criminal offenders have sometimes been made to wear. The placard reads: 'Michael Moore starves the poor'.

[30] Para. 79.   [31] Para. 93.
[32] M. Moore, *A World Without Walls* (Cambridge: Cambridge, University Press, 2003).

Funny, self-mocking and perhaps a little vain, Moore's cover is above all a celebration of protest. We have seen that human rights law joins in that celebration, supporting the entitlement to engage in peaceful protest as a right of 'paramount importance in any democratic society'. Under international human rights law, governments are required to justify restrictions on freedoms of expression, assembly and association, and show that those restrictions are necessary and proportionate with respect to specified legitimate interests and aims. Within the framework of the European Convention on Human Rights an obligation has also been recognised to take reasonable and appropriate measures to protect the safety of protesters, and ensure that they are able to express their views. The European Court of Human Rights has said furthermore that, where a bar on access to property has the 'effect of preventing any effective exercise' of rights to freedom of expression or assembly or of 'destroying the essence' of those rights, it 'would not exclude' that governments are required to enable protest by regulating property rights. In connection with the EU legal order, the idea that economic freedoms may legitimately be restricted for the sake of the right to protest has received clear endorsement by the European Court of Justice.

But, of course, Moore's cover is not only a celebration of protest. It is also a co-optation of protest. By putting that photograph on the cover of his book (or, we should more accurately say, by proposing or agreeing that his publisher should put it there), Moore is co-opting protest at two levels. One level is personal. With this arresting picture, Moore is aestheticising 'anti-globalisation' protest to help sell his book. He is draining political struggle of its oppositional force, and commodifying it as a marketing tool. The other level of co-optation, however, is political. Moore is telling us here that the WTO is accountable, transparent and responsive to its critics. As former Director-General, he is showing us that, when it comes to this institution, there is no stifling of dissent, no refusal to confront resistance; opinions naturally differ on questions of trade liberalisation policy, but the important thing, reflected in this book jacket, is that the governance is good. What could anyone have to complain about? In terms of our earlier discussion, Moore's cover belongs to a strategy of managing dissent, and deploying it to legitimate the WTO's project of economic liberalisation. Does human rights law share in this aspect of Moore's engagement with protest? Certainly, the repeated characterisation of protest rights as badges of democratic legitimacy can be understood as part of a management strategy that co-opts dissent to validate the status quo. Moreover, if under international human rights law governments are required to justify restrictions on freedoms of expression, assembly and association, we have seen that this can also *enable* governments to justify and hence legitimate those restrictions. In the end, our conclusion has to be that human rights law, like globalisation itself, both facilitates protest and sets limits to the challenges that may be raised against prevailing political and economic arrangements.

Racism

In the late 1980s Paul Gilroy wrote a book called *There Ain't No Black in the Union Jack*.[1] His subject was racism in the United Kingdom, and his central theme was the importance of race as a factor shaping social structures, processes and events. Both in academic studies and in policy debates, he argued, race was not being taken nearly as seriously as it needed to be. The book was reissued in 2002, with a new introduction by the author. Gilroy speculated that one of the reasons why people still wanted to read his book was that British racism had not gone away. At the same time, however, he observed that things had changed *around* that racism. By 2002, the arguments for taking race seriously had become uncontroversial. If anything, he wrote, '[race] is likely to be taken too seriously while racism is not taken seriously enough'.[2] What does Gilroy mean by this? Why here and in another book published in 2000 does he now contend that the fight against racism must renounce the category of race for the sake of the 'rehabilitation of politics'?[3] And, whether or not that is right, how might the changed circumstances which inform Gilroy's argument bear upon anti-racist initiatives within the framework of international human rights law?

Race, racism and anti-racism

In recent decades a number of important shifts have affected the ideas and practices associated with race, racism and anti-racism. While these shifts cannot be observed in all countries, and while they have nowhere entailed the complete supercession of earlier notions, each points to

---

[1] P. Gilroy, *There Ain't No Black in the Union Jack* (London and New York: Routledge, first pub'd 1987, reissued 2002).　　　　　　　　　　　　　　　　[2] Ibid., xvii.
[3] P. Gilroy, *Against Race* (Cambridge, Mass.: Harvard University Press, 2000), 41.

a notable reorientation of thought and activity. It will be valuable to begin by taking brief stock of some of the changes involved.[4]

Race

The most obvious changes relate to the concept of race. When it was first elaborated, primarily in the late 18th and 19th centuries, race was a theory about biology. People were classified as belonging to different races according to their physical morphology and especially their physiognomy, and different races were in turn classified as being more or less advanced in the progression from earlier forms. Thus, accounts of race were initially a matter of providing descriptions, measurements and, above all, pictures of skulls, noses, hair, skin tones, and so on, generally presented comparatively and glossed with indications of evolutionary significance. As we now understand, racial science developed in conjunction with the legitimation of indigenous dispossession and colonial rule. It lent support to the idea of a European 'civilising mission', and also helped in its day to justify slavery.

During the course of the 20th century, however, racial science came widely to be viewed as embarrassing and dangerous, in large part due to its implication in fresh devastation in the context of the Nazis' 'final solution' and the *apartheid* regime in South Africa. But race did not disappear. Rather, it was recast as a theory, not about biology, but about culture. From this 'culturalist' perspective, traditions, customs and more generally ways of life are what count, far more than physical attributes. Moreover, differences in ways of life do not make some people superior and others inferior. All cultures are equally worthy of respect. The point is simply that they are just that: *cultures*, in the sense of distinct entities with an essential character and authentic form all of their own. As such, cultures are understood to correspond to a variety of human collectivities, but perhaps most prominently the nation. Thus, race is often elided with nation, which is seen to derive its strength and solidarity as a political community from the shared traditions, values and ways of its members.

---

[4] See further International Council on Human Rights Policy, *The Persistence and Mutation of Racism* (Versoix: ICHRP, 2000) and S. Fredman (ed.), *Discrimination and Human Rights: the Case of Racism* (Oxford: Oxford University Press, 2001). See also J. Swarc, *Faces of Racism* (London: Amnesty International, 2001).

Racism

Linked to this shift in conceptions of race, changes are also evident in
the phenomenon of racism. These changes can be observed on at least
three levels. In the first place, they can be observed on the level of the
logics of racism. If race was initially a theory about biology, this enabled
a form of racism which was based on the idea that biology is destiny,
and that biologically determined difference should translate into social
hierarchy. As just noted, that idea has become widely discredited, and
differences between people are today conceived less as genetic facts than
as cultural products, and hence less as properties of nature than as outcomes of history. But just as the concept of race did not disappear but
instead mutated in the light of this new perspective, so too did the phenomenon of racism. The new culturalist conception of race enabled a
new culturalist form of racism. This emphatically rejects racial hierarchy,
and embraces—even celebrates—social diversity. At the same time, however, it warns that too much diversity endangers solidarity, for social life
works best when people cleave to their own kind. From the perspective
of culturalist racism, biology is not destiny, but cultural identity is. In
effect, as many have observed, this form of racism abandons biological
determinism, only to replace it with cultural determinism: while differences between people are recognised as historical and hence contingent
in their causes, they are treated as necessary in their effects.

A key feature of this shift in the logics of racism is the way culturalist
racism takes up and absorbs the critique of biology-based racism. In this
sense, as has been remarked, it 'attacks . . . anti-racism from the rear, and
actually co-opts and enlists its arguments'.[5] This process of co-optation
and enlistment seems to be an ongoing one, and Slavoj Žižek offers an
intriguing illustration of the further mutations of racism.[6] Discussing
racism towards the people of his own Balkan region, Žižek points to the
emergence of a new form of racism which he calls 'reflexive racism'. As
he explains, 'traditional' forms of racism have denigrated the 'Balkan
Other' as 'despotic, barbarian, orthodox, Muslim, corrupt, Oriental', on
behalf of authentic values figured as 'Western, civilized, democratic,
Christian'. Today, however, racism is also, and perhaps more commonly,
manifested through characterisations of the Balkans as 'the terrain of

[5] M. Hardt & A. Negri, *Empire* (Cambridge, Mass.: Harvard University Press, 2000), 191.
[6] S. Žižek, *The Fragile Absolute* (London: Verso, 2000).

ethnic horrors and intolerance, of primitive irrational warring passions, to be opposed to the post-nation-state liberal-democratic process of solving conflicts through rational negotiation, compromise and mutual respect'.[7] By 'reflexive racism' Žižek intends this move whereby racism is attributed to or fixed on others, and from a standpoint which claims for itself the high ground of multiculturalism, value-pluralism and anti-racism. When we portray others as unworthy of respect because they are, always have been, and always will be, a hopeless bunch of racist bigots, we create the basis for a new form of racism that again assaults anti-racism by co-opting it.

A second level on which changes can be observed concerns the *practices* of racism. Here we can trace a shift, like that which we have just seen in relation to the logics of racism, from relatively simple forms to more complex and subtle ones. What was initially involved was straight-forward and officially mandated segregation, domination and killing. In some cases—such as Nazi Germany and South Africa—the official mandate included an extremely detailed framework of laws and admin-istrative regulations affecting all aspects of life. While practices of this kind may still exist in some countries, there can be little doubt that they have declined in recent decades and that their legitimacy has been sub-stantially eroded. In this regard, decolonisation, the civil rights move-ment in the United States, and the struggle against *apartheid* in South Africa—crucial spurs to anti-racist initiative—have had a profound impact. Today, self-determination is a human and people's right; geno-cide is an international crime; and most countries have laws prohibiting racial discrimination. Once again, however, we must be cautious, for, of course, the decline of particular racist practices does not necessarily spell the decline of racism, just as the proscription of particular conduct does not necessarily signal the achievement of social change. In fact, the decline and proscription of certain racist practices have by no means put an end to racism. Rather, new racist practices have developed in response to the shift from official racism to official anti-racism.

At the centre of the new practices is the phenomenon known as 'institutional racism'. This phrase was coined in the 1960s in the context of American civil rights activism, to highlight that racism was not just a matter of individual acts, but also, and perhaps more consequentially,

---

[7] S. Žižek, *The Fragile Absolute* (London: Verso, 2000), 4–5.

of the functioning of public and private institutions. Thus, racism could not be understood and overcome without analysis of the ways in which social, economic, political, legal and administrative institutions systematically excluded, marginalised and disfavoured African-Americans. In the late 1990s an inquiry in United Kingdom, set up under legislation regulating the police force, considered a complaint from the perspective of institutional racism. Two black teenagers had been attacked and killed by a group of white youths, none of whom had been charged. The parents of one of the victims, Stephen Lawrence, complained that the police investigation had been flawed by racism. The report of the inquiry concluded that there had indeed been a combination of professional incompetence, failure of leadership and racism, and that the racism involved could not be grasped as a series of individual racially motivated acts, but had rather to be considered a case of institutional racism. This it characterised as '[t]he collective failure of an organisation to provide an appropriate and professional service to people because of their colour, culture or ethnic origin'.[8] A key element in institutional racism is racial profiling—or, as it is sometimes less abstractly called in the United States, 'driving while black'. This expression referred originally to the hugely disproportionate numbers of African-Americans stopped and searched in their cars under powers conferred on the police in narcotics and other legislation, and has since come synecdochically to evoke all forms of racial profiling. What is fascinating about 'driving while black' is that it precisely captures the unofficial, informal and generally covert nature of institutional racism. No legislature would ever pass a law to prohibit driving while black, yet experience suggests that in practice this is an offence.

Thirdly, we can observe changes affecting the *context* of racism. One aspect of these changes, already noted, is the shift from official racism to official anti-racism. Contemporary forms of racism are generally structured around the denial or repression of racism. Thus, the shift from relatively simple logics and practices to more complex ones has also brought such strategies as the encoding of racist discourse, the minimisation of racist phenomena as isolated and exceptional, the foregrounding of 'success stories' of anti-racist policy, and so on. Another, related aspect of the contemporary context of racism concerns the resignification of racism as a management

[8] *The Stephen Lawrence Inquiry—Report of an Inquiry by Sir William Macpherson of Cluny* (London: The Stationery Office, 1999) Cm 4262-I, para. 6.34.

issue. As official anti-racism has been embraced, racism has emerged as a technical or management problem, to be addressed using tools primarily developed within the domain of corporate activity. Thus, a familiar feature of the output of companies and government agencies in many countries is the mission statement proclaiming equality of opportunity for all. While no doubt valuable, such statements help to sustain the denial or repression just mentioned when they appear to exhaust the range of measures that are required. We expand on this point further below.

Beyond these developments, and reinforcing them, the context of racism has also been affected by wider historical shifts. If racism originally belonged with colonialism and its legitimating ideology of the 'civilising mission', today it is caught up in the processes of globalisation. Among the many ambiguous outcomes of these processes is the contemporary conjunction of borderlessness and nationalism. While goods, services and money move around the world ever more freely, restrictions on the movement of people remain, and in some contexts rise. Thus, racism is frequently encoded as hostility towards immigrants and asylum-seekers, portrayed as culturally ill-adapted to be decent, law-abiding and self-sufficient members of society. Likewise, while globalising processes are associated with cultural convergence and global orientation, they have also been consonant with identity politics and resurgent ethno-nationalism. Thus, racism is commonly manifested in xenophobia and social exclusion directed not only against immigrants and asylum-seekers, but also against citizens and permanent residents who are figured as culturally out of place. And again, while globalisation promotes forms of restructuring and liberalisation that have brought benefits to many people, these developments have also been linked to the widening of social inequalities and the creation or deepening of poverty, with particular consequences for those already disadvantaged and hence most vulnerable. Against this background, racism often works by 'blaming the victims'; that is to say, by treating the increasing deprivation of those subject to racial discrimination as proof that they are culturally incapable of being productive, and accordingly have only themselves to blame for their situation.

Anti-racism

Turning to the final dimension of this brief survey, anti-racism, it is obvious that the mutations involving racism just outlined alter in some quite significant ways the context and challenges of anti-racist struggle. For one thing, the culturalist turn makes clear that biology-based conceptions of race are not the only problem. Culturalist conceptions too can become the basis for exclusionary practices justified by reference to nationalist and other myths. It follows that *all* determinisms need to be challenged, whether they are linked to genetic inheritance or cultural tradition. At the same time, secondly, the emergence of new, more subtle forms of racism, in connection with the embrace of official anti-racism, has made charges of racism more difficult to prove than was previously the case. When racism co-opts anti-racism, the line between the two begins to blur, and separating them comes to depend on refocusing attention on the lived experience of racism and its social impacts for those affected. Thirdly, the embrace of official anti-racism has also made anti-racist struggle harder to organise and advance. A culture of denial has developed in which anti-racist concerns are routinely dismissed and delegitimated, as expressions of 'political correctness' and so on. Besides, if the problem of racism appears to have been overcome, or at any rate reduced to the kind of proportions that good management can rectify, why mobilise against it? Indeed, the relative demobilisation of anti-racism compared to earlier phases in the history of racism is frequently remarked upon. In this context, it becomes crucial to reawaken the earlier sense of urgency and scale. For, as just discussed, not only has racism not disappeared; in some respects it is actually being aggravated in contemporary conditions.

A fourth way in which anti-racism has been affected by the changes we have highlighted, and the last one we mention here, is for some commentators the most significant. This concerns the depoliticisation of racism. As is widely recognised, racism is inseparable from the wider social and economic systems through which wealth and power are distributed at local, national and global levels. Victims of racism frequently suffer economic deprivation and social marginalisation, and in some cases are denied access to all but the lowest-status jobs. These disadvantages in turn heighten the vulnerability of those affected to further deprivation and marginalisation when pressures arise. And just as some suffer in consequence of racism, some also benefit. In this sense racism is more specifically inseparable from the exploitative dimensions of social and economic systems—a point that was especially vivid in the context of colonialism and *apartheid*, but is also apparent and perhaps even intensifying in current realities. It follows that not only are corporate mission statements insufficient to overcome racism; anti-racist education, though important and necessary, is also insufficient. Rather, political change is required. Yet here again the impact of the culturalist turn can be observed. For whereas colonialism and *apartheid* were challenged as political problems, and whereas some forms of contemporary racism continue to be challenged on that same basis, many contemporary manifestations of racism are treated as cultural problems to be solved by better multicultural strategies.[9]

We are now in a position to consider Paul Gilroy's claim, mentioned at the beginning, that today race is taken too seriously, while racism is not taken seriously enough, and that in these circumstances the fight against racism must renounce the category of race for the sake of the rehabilitation of politics. Gilroy certainly recognises that race has in the past served an immensely important and indeed historically pivotal role in relation to the identities, solidarities and oppositional movements created by victims of racism in many places. The mobilisation of civil rights struggle in the United States around 'black power' is just one well-known instance of this. But, while Gilroy also recognises that race continues to fulfil this role in some contexts, he warns that race may not be equal to the task of renewing awareness of the political implications of racism. As an example, he highlights the way phrases like 'race riots' can become consoling myths, whereby racial difference or incompatible culture are held to explain outbreaks of violence that need rather to be understood and addressed in terms of economic disadvantage and social exclusion.[10] Gilroy concludes that, if the political stakes of racism are to be grasped, a more complex analysis is called for than one structured around race. This is an intriguing claim, and we will return to it again at the end. In the meantime, let us turn now to consider how international human rights law stands with respect to race, racism and anti-racism. What kind of anti-racist agenda has developed within the framework of human rights, and what resources does that agenda contain for helping to ensure that race does not, as Gilroy fears, get in the way of the fight against racism?

---

[9] See, e.g., Durban Declaration and Programme of Action, adopted by the World Conference against Racism, Racial Discrimination, Xenophobia and Related Intolerance, September 2001, UN Doc. A/CONF.189/12.

[10] For this example, see P. Gilroy, *There Ain't No Black in the Union Jack* (London and New York: Routledge, first pub'd 1987, reissued 2002), xxi.

Human rights and anti-racism

When the Covenant of the League of Nations was being drafted in 1919, a proposal to include a provision on racial equality did not succeed. As the debates on the proposal confirm, official racism was at that time the norm for many of those states involved.[11] This changed in the second half of the 20th century, and today anti-racism is an integral part of international human rights law, with three principal components outlined in this section. The first is concerned with the specification of international crimes. The second is concerned with racial discrimination as an obstacle to the enjoyment of human rights. The third is concerned with the charge that in particular circumstances anti-racist initiatives themselves breach human rights.

Genocide, crimes against humanity, war crimes

In the first place, then, racism may constitute the commission of an international crime. This is the case where genocide is involved, and also in the context of *apartheid* as a crime against humanity, and in certain other circumstances as well. As recognised in the 1948 Convention on the Prevention and Punishment of the Crime of Genocide, the crime of genocide entails killing or certain other acts when 'committed with intent to destroy, in whole or in part, a national, ethnical, racial or religious group, as such'.[12] The crime of *apartheid* was first elaborated in the 1973 Convention on the Suppression and Punishment of the Crime of *Apartheid*, and is there explicitly modelled on the 'policies and practices of racial segregation and discrimination [then] practised in southern Africa'.[13] As more recently generalised and redefined in the Rome Statute of the International Criminal Court as a crime against humanity, *apartheid* refers to killing, forced population transfer, torture, rape and other similar acts when 'committed in the context of an institutionalized regime of systematic oppression and domination by one racial group over any other racial group or groups and committed with the intention of maintaining that regime'.[14]

---

[11] Concerning this proposal (put forward by Japan) and the debates surrounding it, see P.G. Lauren, *The Evolution of Human Rights: Visions Seen* (Philadelphia: University of Pennsylvania Press, 1998), 99–101, 125–7.   [12] Genocide Convention, art. II
[13] Art. II.   [14] Statute of the International Criminal Court (1998), art. 7(2)(h).

Beyond these crimes, racism may also be the basis for other forms of international criminal responsibility. In particular, the Rome Statute recognises as a crime against humanity 'persecution against any identifiable group or collectivity' on (among others) racial grounds, in connection with an act of the kind with which crimes against humanity are concerned, or in connection with genocide or war crimes as defined by the Statute.[15] 'Persecution' is stated to refer to the 'intentional and severe deprivation of fundamental rights contrary to international law by reason of the identity of the group or collectivity'.[16] In the context of proceedings before the International Criminal Tribunal for the former Yugoslavia, persecution has been defined as 'the gross or blatant denial, on discriminatory grounds, of a fundamental right, laid down in international customary or treaty law, reaching the same level of gravity' as other acts that may constitute crimes against humanity under the Tribunal's Statute.[17] The Tribunal has stressed, furthermore, that acts of persecution 'must be evaluated not in isolation but in context, by looking at their cumulative effect'.[18] War crimes, for their part, are defined in the Rome Statute as including the commission of 'outrages upon personal dignity, in particular humiliating and degrading treatment',[19] and racism could clearly be relevant in determining whether this has occurred.

Racial discrimination

These situations in which racism constitutes an international crime are particularly conspicuous instances of a wider concern, reflected in international human rights law, with racism as an obstacle to the enjoyment of human rights. At the centre of this concern is the concept of racial discrimination. Thus, the Universal Declaration of Human Rights states that '[e]veryone is entitled to all the rights and freedoms set forth in this Declaration, without distinction of any kind'.[20] Among the (non-exhaustive) grounds of impermissible distinction mentioned are race, colour, national or social origin, and birth. The International Covenants on Civil and Political Rights and Economic, Social and Cultural Rights

---

[15] Art. 7(1)(h).   [16] Art. 7(2)(g).

[17] *Prosecutor v Kupreškić and Others* (Case IT-95-16-T), Judgment of the International Criminal Tribunal for the former Yugoslavia, 14 January 2000, para. 621.

[18] Ibid., para. 622.   [19] Art. 8(2)(b)(xxi) and (c)(ii).   [20] Art. 2.

contain similar provisions,[21] and the Civil and Political Rights Covenant also protects the right to the equal protection of the law.[22] The various regional human rights treaties likewise include non-discrimination guarantees (African Charter of Human and Peoples' Rights;[23] American Convention on Human Rights;[24] and European Convention on Human Rights[25] and Protocol 12 thereto),[26] as do many other treaties besides. Beyond these treaties, racial discrimination is correspondingly prohibited under generally applicable international law, and indeed has been categorised as a violation of a peremptory norm of international law (*jus cogens*).[27]

In some of these cases, the non-discrimination guarantee applies to all legal entitlements. Thus, for instance, the International Covenant on Civil and Political Rights asserts in article 26 the right 'without any discrimination to the equal protection of the law', and stipulates that 'the law shall prohibit any discrimination and guarantee to all persons equal and effective protection against discrimination on any ground'. In other cases, the non-discrimination guarantee applies only to the specific rights protected, and in that sense is not an 'autonomous' or 'standalone' guarantee. For example, the European Convention on Human Rights provides in article 14 that the 'enjoyment of the rights and freedoms set forth in this Convention shall be secured without discrimination on any ground'. As this indicates, article 14 is only concerned with non-discrimination in relation to the rights protected. Thus, as it is said, it only applies 'in conjunction with' a Convention right. The European Court of Human Rights has made clear that this does not mean that a Convention right must actually have been violated, nor even that in the particular circumstances the state concerned must have obligations in connection with one. But it does mean that the facts of the case must 'fall within the ambit' of a right protected by the Convention.[28] In 2000 a Protocol to the Convention was adopted with the aim of creating a fully autonomous right to be free from discrimination. Under

---

[21] Art. 2(1) and (2) respectively.   [22] Art. 26.   [23] Arts. 2 and 3.

[24] Arts. 1(1) and 24.   [25] Art. 14.   [26] Art. 1.

[27] See Report of the International Law Commission, adopted at its 53rd session, 2001, UN Doc. A/56/10, 207. See also J. Crawford, *The International Law Commission's Articles on State Responsibility: Introduction, Text and Commentaries* (Cambridge: Cambridge University Press, 2002), 188.

[28] *Karner v Austria*, Judgment of the European Court of Human Rights, 24 July 2003, para. 32.

Protocol 12, '[t]he enjoyment of any right set forth by law shall be secured without discrimination on any ground, such as [among others] race'.[29] The Protocol also provides that '[n]o one shall be discriminated against by any public authority on any ground such as those mentioned in paragraph 1'.[30]

These various treaties assert the right to non-discrimination on a range of grounds including race and related categories. In the specific context of racial discrimination, the acts that may constitute racial discrimination, and the obligations that are associated with the elimination of those acts, were first specified in detail in the International Convention on the Elimination of All Forms of Racial Discrimination, and this treaty remains a key focus of efforts to address racism as an obstacle to respect for human rights. The Convention defines racial discrimination as 'any distinction, exclusion, restriction or preference based on race, colour, descent, or national or ethnic origin which has the purpose or effect of nullifying or impairing the recognition, enjoyment or exercise, on an equal footing, of human rights and fundamental freedoms in the political, economic, social, cultural or any other field of public life.'[31] Definitions of injustice or oppression are always subject to challenge and reinterpretation, as excluded issues, overlooked problems and neglected groups come insistently into view. In this respect the definition of racial discrimination is no exception. Discussions have revolved primarily around four aspects: the distinctively 'racial' character of racial discrimination; the issue of what should count as 'discrimination' in this context; the domains of life affected, whether public or also private; and an exclusion, explained below, which relates to non-nationals. Let us look briefly at each of these aspects in turn.

With regard to the distinctively 'racial' character of racial discrimination, attention has recently focused on caste-based discrimination, of the kind faced by the *dalits* (untouchables) in India. The Committee on the Elimination of Racial Discrimination, established under the Racial Discrimination Convention, has affirmed that discrimination indexed to caste, as a form of descent-based discrimination, is to be regarded as falling within the Convention definition.[32] Turning to the second question of what should count as discrimination in this context, the Convention

---

[29] Art. 1(1).   [30] Art. 1(2).   [31] Art. 1(1).

[32] See Committee on the Elimination of Racial Discrimination, General Recommendation 29 (Descent: art. 1(1)), 1 November 2002, esp. para. 1.

makes clear that measures taken by way of 'affirmative action' or 'positive discrimination' to ensure equal enjoyment or exercise of human rights, 'shall not be deemed racial discrimination'.[33] More positively, it provides that such measures 'shall [be taken] when the circumstances so warrant' in order to guarantee the full and equal enjoyment of human rights by all.[34] This is subject to the proviso that the measures do not, as a consequence lead to the 'maintenance of unequal or separate rights for different racial groups after the objectives for which they were taken have been achieved'.[35] The Committee on the Elimination of Racial Discrimination has stated that, in considering whether a differentiation constitutes discrimination, what counts is whether the criteria of differentiation are legitimate when 'judged against the objectives and purposes of the Convention' or fall within article 1(4) just quoted. It has also stated that, in determining whether a measure has an effect contrary to the Convention, what counts is whether the action has an 'unjustifiable disparate impact' on a particular racial or other group.[36]

These things said, affirmative action is by no means all that is at stake in the question of what should count as discrimination. Would that it were, and that the only problems arising in this context were matters of over-zealous remedial action by governments! In fact, of course, problems also arise with respect to the characterisation of specific practices, and in particular institutional racism and the various subtle or 'indirect' forms of discrimination often associated with it. This issue was brought into focus in 2004 in an important case under the European Convention on Human Rights. Two men of Roma origin were fatally shot by an officer of the Bulgarian military police in the course of an attempt to arrest them.[37] Upon the application of family members of those killed, the European Court of Human Rights found the state responsible for 'intentional deprivation of life', failure to conduct an effective investigation into the use of lethal violence by the military police, and failure to protect life, contrary to article 2 of the Convention, which guarantees the right to life. However, the applicants also argued that the state was responsible for racial discrimination with respect to that right, contrary

---

[33] Art. 1(4).   [34] Art. 2(2).   [35] Art. 2(2). See also art. 1(4).

[36] Committee on the Elimination of Racial Discrimination, General Recommendation 14 (Definition of discrimination (art. 1, para.1)), 22 March 1993, para. 2.

[37] *Nachova and Others v Bulgaria*, Judgment of the European Court of Human Rights, 26 February 2004.

to article 14 of the Convention. Preceding this case had been a number of other complaints against Bulgaria arising out of the deaths of Roma in police custody.[38] In dealing with those complaints, the Court had declined to uphold the claim that article 14 had been breached. While acknowledging that 'serious arguments' had been adduced about racism against Roma on the part of law enforcement and criminal investigation authorities in Bulgaria, the Court had said that it could not 'conclude beyond reasonable doubt that the [acts and omissions complained of] were motivated by racial prejudice'.[39]

In this 2004 case, by contrast, that concern for compelling evidence of racist motivation in relation to particular acts and omissions gave way to a new attention to the institutional or systemic character of the racism at issue. In the first place, the state was held responsible for failing to investigate facts and collect evidence which could have clarified the allegations of racism. In the Court's words, the authorities had failed in their duty under article 14 of the Convention, taken together with article 2, to take 'all possible steps to establish whether or not discriminatory attitudes may have played a role in events'.[40] Additionally, the failure of the national authorities to fulfil that duty was seen as relevant to the substantive allegation of discrimination on their part. Noting the difficulties of proving racist motivation, especially at the stage of European Court proceedings, the Court decided that 'in cases where the authorities have not pursued lines of inquiry that were clearly warranted in their investigation into acts of violence by State agents and have disregarded evidence of possible discrimination, it [the Court] may, when examining complaints under Article 14 of the Convention, draw negative inferences or shift the burden of proof to the respondent Government'.[41] Given the circumstances of this case, and also the fact precisely that it was not the first complaint under the Convention about racist violence against Roma at the hands of Bulgarian state agents, the Court considered that indeed the burden of proof shifted to

---

[38] See *Velikova v Bulgaria*, Judgment of the European Court of Human Rights, 18 May 2000 and *Anguelova v Bulgaria*, Judgment of the European Court of Human Rights, 13 June 2002.

[39] See, e.g., *Velikova v Bulgaria*, Judgment of the European Court of Human Rights, 18 May 2000, para. 94.

[40] *Nachova and Others v Bulgaria*, Judgment of the European Court of Human Rights, 26 February 2004, para. 163.   [41] Para. 169.

the Government, 'which must satisfy the Court, on the basis of additional evidence or a convincing explanation of the facts, that the events complained of were not shaped by any prohibited discriminatory attitude on the part of State agents'.[42] Since the Bulgarian Government had failed to supply the necessary evidence or explanation, the Court held that the prohibition on racial discrimination had been violated. The state had not secured the right to life without discrimination on grounds of race, in violation of article 14 of the Convention, taken together with article 2.

The third issue we mentioned above concerns the domains of life affected. The definition of racial discrimination in the Racial Discrimination Convention refers to the nullification or impairment of rights and freedoms in the 'political, economic, social, cultural or any other field of public life'. This leaves somewhat ambiguous the extent to which racial discrimination in the private sphere—the domain of private employment, housing, services, and so on—is also encompassed. However, the Convention goes on to oblige states parties to prohibit and bring to an end 'racial discrimination by any persons, group or organization',[43] and the Committee on the Elimination of Racial Discrimination has expressed the view that indeed the obligation to eliminate racial discrimination applies to all domains of life. In its words, '[t]o the extent that private institutions influence the exercise of rights or the availability of opportunities, the State Party must ensure that the result has neither the purpose nor the effect of creating or perpetuating racial discrimination'.[44] Other treaties can be understood in similarly general terms. Protocol 12 to the European Convention referred to above may appear to be an exception, in that it asserts the right not to 'be discriminated against by any public authority'.[45] As observed in the Explanatory Report relating to the Protocol, the reference here to 'public authority' raises the question of the extent to which states parties to the Protocol are obliged to take measures to prevent or remedy discrimination where that discrimination occurs in relations between private persons. According to the Explanatory Report, positive obligations of this sort may apply to relations between private persons for which 'the state

[42] Para. 171.   [43] Art. 2(1)(d).

[44] Committee on the Elimination of Racial Discrimination, General Recommendation 20 (Non-discriminatory implementation of rights and freedoms (art. 5)), 15 March 1996, para. 5.   [45] Art. 1(2).

has a certain responsibility'; the examples given relate to employment, access to restaurants, and access to services such as medical care, water and electricity. With regard to 'purely private matters', by contrast, protection of the right to privacy is seen as likely to preclude state action with respect to racial discrimination.[46]

A final aspect, and one that takes on particular significance at a time when—as highlighted earlier—nationality serves increasingly as a cipher for race, and racism draws fuel from xenophobia, is the exclusion from the scope of racial discrimination of certain restrictions on the rights of non-nationals. Thus, after defining racial discrimination, the Racial Discrimination Convention goes on to state in article 1:

(2) This Convention shall not apply to distinctions, exclusions, restrictions or preferences made by a State Party to this Convention between citizens and non-citizens.

(3) Nothing in this Convention may be interpreted as affecting in any way the legal provisions of States Parties concerning nationality, citizenship or naturalization, provided that such provisions do not discriminate against any particular nationality.

That this does not rule out a concern with discrimination linked to nationality is made clear in one of the few complaints brought before the Committee on the Elimination of Racial Discrimination under the communications procedure in the Convention. A man of Tunisian nationality permanently resident in Denmark had an application for credit refused by a Danish bank, on the ground that it was the bank's policy not to lend to non-citizens. He complained that this policy was a covert form of racial discrimination. The Committee was of the opinion that the failure of the Danish authorities to initiate a proper investigation into this complaint violated the applicant's rights under the Convention, inasmuch as he was denied an effective remedy for invoking the state's obligation to prohibit racial discrimination 'by any persons, group or organization'.[47] This opinion also illustrates the point that state obligations may extend to discrimination in the private sphere.

---

[46] Explanatory Report on Protocol 12 to the European Convention on Human Rights, prepared by the Steering Committee for Human Rights, and adopted by the Committee of Ministers, 4 November 2000, para. 28.

[47] Art. 6, with Art. 2(1)(d). *Ziad Ben Ahmed Habassi v Denmark*, Communication 10/1997, Opinion of the Committee on the Elimination of Racial Discrimination, 17 March 1999.

The Committee on the Elimination of Racial Discrimination has reaffirmed that 'differential treatment based on citizenship or immigration status' may constitute discrimination under the Racial Discrimination Convention.[48] While recognising that distinctions between citizens and non-citizens may be legitimate for some purposes, such as voting rights, the Committee recalls that states parties to the Racial Discrimination Convention have non-discrimination obligations under general international human rights law, and must 'guarantee equality between citizens and non-citizens in the enjoyment of [human rights] to the extent recognized under international law'.[49] The 1990 Convention on the Protection of the Rights of All Migrant Workers and Members of their Families may also be relevant in this regard, although it has attracted few ratifications.[50] In the context of the International Covenant on Civil and Political Rights, it has been stated that 'the general rule is that each one of the rights of the Covenant must be guaranteed without discrimination between citizens and aliens', and that only exceptionally are some of the rights recognised in the Covenant applicable to citizens alone. These latter rights include electoral rights and rights of entry and residence, though even where rights of entry and residence are concerned, it has been noted that non-nationals 'may enjoy the protection of the Covenant, . . . for example, when considerations of non-discrimination, prohibition of inhuman treatment and respect for family life arise'.[51]

Within the European Union legal order, an enlarged conception of racial discrimination has been elaborated, which in some important respects points beyond the various limitations or ambiguities of the Racial Discrimination Convention just highlighted. An EU Directive, adopted on 29 June 2000, aims to 'lay down a framework for combating discrimination on the grounds of racial or ethnic origin, with a view to putting into effect in the Member States the principle of equal treatment.'[52] The principle of equal treatment is stated to mean that 'there

---

[48] See Committee on the Elimination of Racial Discrimination, General Recommendation 30 (Discrimination against non-citizens), 5 August 2004, para. 4.

[49] Ibid., para. 3.

[50] This Convention entered into force on 1 July 2003, though adherences remain largely confined to labour-exporting states.

[51] Human Rights Committee, General Comment 15 (The position of aliens under the Covenant), 11 April 1986, paras. 2 and 5.

[52] Directive 2000/43/EC, OJ L 180/22, 19 July 2000, art. 1.

shall be no direct or indirect discrimination based on racial or ethnic origin'.[53] 'Direct discrimination' is taken to occur 'where one person is treated less favourably than another is, has been or would be treated in a comparable situation on grounds of racial or ethnic origin'. 'Indirect discrimination' is taken to occur 'where an apparently neutral provision, criterion or practice would put persons of a racial or ethnic origin at a particular disadvantage compared with other persons, unless that provision, criterion or practice is objectively justified by a legitimate aim and the means of achieving that aim are appropriate and necessary'. At the same time, the Directive states that 'harassment' is deemed to be discrimination 'when an unwanted conduct related to racial or ethnic origin takes place with the purpose or effect of violating the dignity of a person and of creating an intimidating, hostile, degrading, humiliating or offensive environment'.[54] The Directive also makes clear that it is not concerned only with public authorities or activities, but rather extends to 'all persons, as regards both the public and private sectors'.[55] On the other hand, the Directive retains a limitation with respect to nationality. Thus, it is stated not to 'cover difference of treatment based on nationality' and to be 'without prejudice to provisions and conditions' relating to entry and residence, and to 'any treatment which arises from the legal status of' those who are not EU nationals.[56]

Anti-racism and free speech

We have so far been considering circumstances in which racism undermines human rights, whether through mass atrocities like genocide or *apartheid* or through discriminatory practices that do not involve international criminality. However, what of the contention that *anti-racism* may itself undermine human rights? The primary context in which this danger is said to arise is the proscription of incitement to racial hatred and related activities, and the concern is with the implications of that proscription for freedom of expression and sometimes for freedoms of assembly, association, information, thought or other rights and freedoms as well. National legal systems deal with this in a variety of ways. In some countries, such as the United States, overwhelming importance is attached to freedom of expression, and anti-racist measures are correspondingly

[53] Art. 2(1).   [54] Art. 2(3).   [55] Art. 3(1).   [56] Art. 3(2).

limited. In other countries, such as Germany and Austria, very strict prohibitions on (neo-)Nazi organisations and Holocaust denial have been put in place. At the international level, stipulations exist in a number of treaties requiring that certain racist activities be made offences. Thus, the Racial Discrimination Convention obliges states parties to 'declare an offence punishable by law all dissemination of ideas based on racial superiority or hatred, incitement to racial discrimination, as well as all acts of violence or incitement to such acts against any race or group of persons of another colour or ethnic origin, and also the provision of any assistance to racist activities, including the financing thereof.'[57] States parties are also obliged to proscribe organisations which promote or incite racial discrimination and to prohibit participation in such organisations or activities.[58] Similar provisions are included in other treaties.[59]

Within the framework of international human rights law, the question of whether anti-racist measures clash with rights to freedom of expression has surfaced in a series of cases involving prosecution for Holocaust denial or similar offences. In one such case, brought before the Human Rights Committee, the applicant had been prosecuted in France for the offence of contesting the crimes against humanity for which the Nazi leaders were tried and convicted by the Nuremberg Tribunal in 1945–6.[60] He argued that this violated his right to freedom of expression under the International Covenant on Civil and Political Rights (article 19(2)). While the Covenant recognises the right to freedom of expression, it also recognises the need to restrict that right in some circumstances. Thus, article 19(3) provides:

The exercise of the rights provided for in paragraph 2 of this article carries with it special duties and responsibilities. It may therefore be subject to certain restrictions, but these shall only be such as are provided by law and are necessary:
(a) For respect of the rights or reputations of others;
(b) For the protection of national security or of public order (*ordre public*), or of public health or morals.

---

[57] Art. 4(a).   [58] Art. 4(b).

[59] See, e.g., International Covenant on Civil and Political Rights, art. 20; American Convention on Human Rights, art. 13, para. 5.

[60] *Faurisson v France*, Communication 550/1993, Views of the Human Rights Committee, adopted 8 November 1996.

In the Committee's view, the prosecution of the applicant was justified by reference to this stipulation. The prosecution was pursuant to provisions of French law which were directed to ensuring respect for the rights and reputation of others, and were necessary to secure that aim. In particular, '[s]ince the statements made by the author, read in their full context, were of a nature as to raise or strengthen anti-semitic feelings, the restriction served the respect of the Jewish community to live free from fear of an atmosphere of anti-semitism'.[61] As to the issue of necessity, the Committee accepted the French Government's contention that the restriction was vital to the struggle against racism, since—at least in the applicant's case—Holocaust denial served as a coded form of anti-semitism.

What conclusions can be drawn from this survey of approaches to anti-racism within the framework of international human rights law? How adequate are the various norms and interpretations for addressing the problem of racism in an age of official anti-racism? While the phenomenon of institutional racism has not always been fully grasped, there are signs that its implications for the understanding of non-discrimination guarantees are beginning to be registered. The emerging recognition of indirect discrimination may also be a step in that direction. On the other hand, the overriding preoccupation with discrimination may be a limiting factor, inasmuch as the issue of comparators inevitably arises. From that perspective, the notion that racism is an attack on the dignity and rights of others may appear more promising. This notion may appear more promising too from the perspective of Paul Gilroy's claim that taking race seriously today requires renouncing (or at any rate, reducing in significance) the category of race and rehabilitating the dimension of politics. Racial discrimination depends on a consideration of distinctions based on the specific ground of race (or colour, national origin, etc.). So to speak, it insists on that ground. By contrast (and perhaps counter-intuitively, given the etymology of the word), racism may be less insistent on, or invested in, race, in that it can often be approached in terms of a more complex and multifaceted analysis.

But is Gilroy right? At the beginning of this discussion we mentioned some of the reasons motivating his argument. It will be worth noting one

---

[61] *Faurisson v France*, Communication 550/1993, Views of the Human Rights Committee, adopted 8 November 1996, para. 9.6.

further reason, which he illustrates through an example that interestingly mirrors the discussion of 'reflexive' racism in relation to the Balkans put forward by Slavoj Žižek. Gilroy recounts that at an anti-racist march in England, held in the area where Stephen Lawrence and another boy had been murdered not long before,

[c]onflict over the behaviour of the marchers erupted after the event [between the police and organisers of the march]. This was something more than the routine cycle of mutual denunciation. In particular, the police claimed that antiracist marchers had singled out black officers and made them special targets for hostility and attack. One of the policemen . . . was Constable Leslie Turner. Turner said he had been attacked because he was black. He told the newspapers, 'It was the white demonstrators. There were no black people there that I could see. They singled me out as being a traitor.'[62]

While Gilroy observes that Constable Turner may well have been mistaken, he wants us to reflect on the possibility that there was a measure of truth in Turner's perception of what went on. Reflecting on that possibility, we can see once again the blurring of racism and anti-racism. Just as Žižek points to the way racism absorbs anti-racism, so here Gilroy directs attention to the way anti-racism slips back into racism. If even 'dedicated antiracist and antifascist activists remain wedded to the most basic mythologies and morphologies of racial difference', then, as he observes, the world at large has little chance to escape its allure.[63] Does this mean that racism is simply unavoidable, like gravity and mortality? No, to note the residual racism within anti-racism is not to suggest that racism must or will always be with us. But it does tend to confirm that race may be getting in the way of the fight against racism. It does tend to indicate that anti-racism may now demand, in Gilroy's words, that we 'step away from the pious ritual in which we always agree that "race" is invented but are then required to defer to its embeddedness in the world'.[64]

---

[62] P. Gilroy, *Against Race* (Cambridge, Mass.: Harvard University Press, 2000), 50–1.
[63] Ibid., 51.   [64] Ibid., 52.

Religion

If for Karl Marx religion was the pacifying 'opium of the people',[1] today it is more commonly denounced for the opposite tendency. Religion, we hear, mobilises people to extravagant, intemperate and violent *action*; it stirs them to kill, maim, terrorise, tyrannise, self-harm. Insofar as religion is indeed linked to action of this sort, it seems hardly congenial to the promotion of human rights. Yet the promotion of human rights is precisely an enterprise in which religious conviction has always played an important part. Religious organisations helped to launch the human rights movement, and remain to this day some of the most engaged and effective actors within it. How then does religion stand with respect to human rights? In what follows we explore something of the complex and contested relationship between human rights and religion, beginning with this question of the character of religious traditions as obstacles to or forces for the enjoyment of human rights. In the second part of our discussion, we turn the enquiry around, and ask how human rights law stands with respect to religion. What are the scope and limits of the right to religious freedom in international human rights law? To what extent does the recognition of this right provide support for those wishing to challenge state-imposed restrictions on religious life? At the end, we address the often heard remark that the human rights movement constitutes itself a kind of religion. If true, we ask, is this something that should be celebrated, or should it rather be a source of dismay?

Religion and human rights

In assessing the bearing of religion for human rights, we are faced with a task that is complicated by at least three levels of diversity. In the first

[1] See 'Towards a Critique of Hegel's *Philosophy of Right*: Introduction' (1844) in D. McLellan, *Karl Marx: Selected Writings*, 2nd edn. (Oxford: Oxford University Press, 2000), 71, 72.

place, as is routinely recalled in discussions of this topic, there is not religion, but rather a plurality of *religions*. Different religious traditions obviously relate differently to human rights. Secondly, each of the major religious traditions itself relates to human rights in a variety of ways. The same religion can be invoked to support widely divergent practices, institutions and orientations. Finally, those religious practices, institutions and orientations are, for their part, experienced and explained in ways that are similarly diverse in their implications for human rights. To give an example to which we will return later, the wearing of the Muslim headscarf or *hijab* is for some a symbol of female subordination; for others, on the contrary, it is a mark of empowerment and an aid to the active involvement of women in public life. These points make very clear that detailed assessment depends on context-specific analysis. That said, we can gain some initial insight into the role of religion with respect to human rights through attention to a number of general or overarching issues.

Legitimacy

One general issue which has long preoccupied scholars of human rights, and continues to do so, is the question of religious justifications. To what extent can, or should, human rights be justified in terms of religion? In an essay on the relationship between religion and human rights, Louis Henkin argues that the aspiration of international human rights law to universality is inconsistent with religious grounding. As he explains, 'for the human rights movement insistence on the nontheistic foundations of the contemporary human rights idea reflects a quest for universal acceptance and universal commitment to a common moral intuition articulated in specific agreed-upon terms'.[2] Thus, human rights 'are not, and cannot be, grounded in religious conviction'. Rather, the 'human rights ideology is a fully secular and rational ideology whose very promise of success as a universal ideology depends on its secularity and rationality'.[3] According to Henkin, the secular ground—or, as he calls it, the '*ur* value or principle'—upon which human rights rest is 'the principle of human dignity'.[4] Michael Ignatieff likewise maintains that

---

[2] L. Henkin, 'Religion, Religions, and Human Rights' 26 *Journal of Religious Ethics* (1998), 229, 234.   [3] Ibid., 238.

[4] Ibid., 231 (emphasis omitted).

the prospects for universal human rights depend on eschewing religious authority—even if, for him, the relevant secular basis is expressed not in the concept of human dignity, but rather in the need to protect 'human agency'.[5] He praises the drafters of the Universal Declaration of Human Rights for avoiding all reference to God. One factor in that decision was the atheism of the Communist delegations, but Ignatieff contends that the secular framing of the Declaration also reflects a more general awareness that what was required was a 'pragmatic common denominator designed to make agreement possible across a range of divergent cultural and political viewpoints'.[6]

For these scholars, the fact that no set of religious beliefs commands universal assent means that human rights must rest on some secular value, whether that secular value is human dignity or human agency. The premise of this proposition is certainly correct. But does the conclusion necessarily follow? It only follows if we assume that human rights must rest on a single value—*ur* value, principle, common denominator—that is acceptable to all or most people. Yet it is by no means clear that this is required. As Amy Gutmann contends in a response to Ignatieff's analysis,

it is not necessary that any *single* grounding be acceptable to all supporters, whether the grounding be human agency or some other secular or religious conception of what makes human rights important. What a human rights regime relies on, instead, are plural foundations, no one of which needs to be authoritative to all human rights defenders. Plural foundations make a human rights regime more broadly acceptable to people.[7]

According to Gutmann, the pragmatic point taken by the drafters of the Universal Declaration was not that the Declaration needed a single secular common denominator, but rather this point that it needed plural foundations. In her reading, allusions can be found in the text of the Declaration to a variety of justificatory ideas and concepts, among them human dignity and human agency, but also equal creation and equal brotherhood.[8]

[5] M. Ignatieff, 'Human Rights as Idolatry' in M. Ignatieff, (A. Gutmann, ed.), *Human Rights as Politics and Idolatry* (Princeton: Princeton University Press, 2001), 53, 55–7.
[6] Ibid., 64.
[7] A. Gutmann, 'Introduction' in M. Ignatieff, (A. Gutmann, ed.), *Human Rights as Politics and Idolatry* (Princeton: Princeton University Press, 2001), vii, xxii.
[8] Ibid., xxiv–xxv.

And yet, the question still remains: *why* does the human rights regime need plural foundations? Why, for that matter, does it need any ethical, religious or other extra-legal foundations at all? Some scholars (among them Ignatieff) indeed argue that foundational argument is redundant where human rights are concerned. To them, the only issues that arise are prudential or pragmatic.[9] On the other hand, those scholars generally find it difficult to explain why human rights should be respected, protected and defended without referring to some underlying value or interest said to be of particular importance (such as, in Ignatieff's case, human agency), even if (as in his case) that value or interest does not correspond to the kind of metaphysical concept we commonly recognise as foundational. Returning, then, to the question of why this is so, what purpose is served by appeal to (plural) foundations, the answer appears to have something to do with *legitimacy*. By legitimacy, we mean the quality that makes law seem justified, appropriate and morally compelling. The significance of foundations is that they contribute to endowing human rights law with this quality. They help to make it legitimate. And if that is so, then plural foundations help to maximise the legitimacy of human rights law in a diverse world. From this perspective, foundations are themselves a prudential or pragmatic issue, inasmuch as they affect the practical prospects of international human rights law. Thus, Diane Orentlicher warns that those who reject all religious foundations for human rights fail to take 'adequate account of a crucial fact: universal acceptance of the human rights idea depends upon its legitimation *within* diverse religious traditions, and not just *alongside* them'.[10] More than that, according to Abdullahi An-Na'im, those who reject all religious foundations fail to take adequate account of the fact that 'human rights need to be "owned" by different peoples around the world, instead of being perceived as simply another facet of Western hegemony', and religious legitimation is often vital to that ownership.[11]

---

[9]   See also R. Rorty, 'Human Rights, Rationality and Sentimentality' in S. Shute and S. Hurley (eds.), *On Human Rights* (New York: Basic Books, 1993), 111.

[10]   D. Orentlicher, 'Relativism and Religion' in M. Ignatieff, (A. Gutmann, ed.), *Human Rights as Politics and Idolatry* (Princeton: Princeton University Press, 2001), 141, 155.

[11]   A. An-Na'im, 'The Synergy and Interdependence of Human Rights, Religion and Secularism' in J. Runzo, N.M. Martin and A. Sharma (eds.), *Human Rights and Responsibilities in the World Religions* (Oxford: Oneworld Publications, 2003), 27, 40.

Compatibility

We have considered the relevance of religion for the legitimacy or 'ownership' of human rights. But another important issue in debates about human rights and religion concerns the extent to which particular religious traditions are actually compatible with respect for human rights. The question of compatibility with the human rights of women has received perhaps the greatest attention. As Donna Sullivan observes, '[w]omen's rights activists in a number of national settings have stressed the need to transform religious law and practice, not only as a means of ending gender-based restrictions on specific human rights, but also as an essential step toward dismantling systemic gender inequality'.[12] Conversely, the 'most comprehensive challenges mounted by states to the international norms guaranteeing women's rights, and their application, have been couched as defenses of religious liberty'.[13] Among the phenomena involved are laws that deny or limit women's capacity to own and inherit property, marriage and divorce laws that are biased against women, and laws that impose discriminatory restrictions on the admissibility of women's evidence in legal proceedings, together with customs of dowry murder, 'honour' killing and widow suicide, and norms that affect reproductive choice, access of girls to education, and the forms and conditions of women's work.

At the same time, concerns have been raised about the compatibility of religious laws and practices with norms guaranteeing the rights of convicted prisoners not to be subjected to torture or to inhuman or degrading punishment, the rights of non-believers and those wishing to renounce their religion, and the rights of gay men and lesbians. All the major religious traditions are implicated. Thus, for example, attention has focused on Christian justifications for proscribing same-sex relations and restricting reproductive choice and Jewish laws that disadvantage women in relation to divorce and the admissibility of legal testimony. However, at the international level it has been in the context of Islam that some of the most contentious issues have arisen. These issues have mostly revolved around the imposition of cruel punishments such as amputation, stoning and flogging, along with the maintenance of

---

[12] D. Sullivan, 'Gender Equality and Religious Freedom: Toward a Framework for Conflict Resolution', 24 *New York University Journal of International Law and Politics* (1992), 795.   [13] Ibid.

gender-biased personal laws, exclusions of women from public life, proscriptions on apostasy, and restrictions on the rights of non-believers. Against this background, some argue that Islam is fundamentally incompatible with international human rights law—whether they intend this as a problem for Islam or for international human rights law. Others point out that, like all religious traditions, Islam is not a seamless monolith, but is rather a multiplicity of interpretations and practices which are themselves contested and revisable. Thus, it is neither fundamentally incompatible, nor fundamentally compatible, with human rights law. There is today a substantial literature exploring the relationship between Islamic traditions and human rights. In one useful study, Khaled Abou El Fadl outlines some of the obstacles and potentialities within Muslim thought which shape that relationship.[14]

According to Abou El Fadl, approaches to human rights within Muslim thought can be analysed in terms of two predominant orientations, which he labels 'apologetic' and 'exceptionalist'. The *apologetic* orientation asserts that Islamic tradition is entirely consistent with international human rights law, and indeed that it is superior to that law in its regard for human rights. Thus, in order to realise human rights, all that is necessary is to give full expression to Islamic doctrines. While this orientation can be understood as an attempt to reaffirm self-worth in societies weakened by colonial ideology, Abou El Fadl contends that it induced 'an artificial sense of confidence, and an intellectual lethargy that neither took the Islamic tradition nor the human rights tradition very seriously'.[15] In his assessment, apologists 'responded to the intellectual challenges of modernity and to universalist Western paradigms by adopting pietistic fictions about the presumed perfection of Islam, and eschewed any critical evaluation of Islamic doctrines'.[16] The *exceptionalist* orientation, although it goes back further, is linked, in Abou El Fadl's account, with the emergence of Islamic fundamentalism, or what he calls the 'puritan movement', calling for a return to 'authentic' Islam through the re-implementation of *sharia* law. This orientation reaches much the same conclusion as the apologetic orientation, but differs in insisting on the exclusive validity of Islamic codes. Thus, exceptionalism

---

[14] K. Abou El Fadl, 'The Human Rights Commitment in Modern Islam' in J. Runzo, N.M. Martin and A. Sharma (eds.), *Human Rights and Responsibilities in the World Religions* (Oxford: Oneworld Publications, 2003), 301.   [15] Ibid., 307.
[16] Ibid., 306.

rejects 'all universalisms, except the universals of Islam'.[17] As Abou El Fadl explains, 'the puritans did not deny, in principle, that human beings have rights'; they simply 'contended that rights could not exist unless granted by God'. For this reason, 'there is no effort to justify international rights on Islamic terms but simply an effort to set out the divine law, on the assumption that such a law, by definition, provides human beings with a just and moral order'.[18]

Between the apologetic and exceptionalist orientations, Abou El Fadl shows that much got obscured which can support Muslim reform movements today. If Islamic tradition is currently used to justify practices inconsistent with international human rights law, it also contains resources that can be used to challenge those practices, or at least some of them. Confirming this point, scholars have argued, for example, that provisions mandating cruel punishments should be read in the light of stipulations requiring strict adherence to procedural guarantees and admitting wide-ranging defences to criminal liability, the effect of which could be to reduce the scope for imposition of those punishments almost to vanishing point.[19] The concern here, then, is with the way the apologetic and exceptionalist orientations have dominated and constrained Muslim thinking about human rights. At the same time, as Abou El Fadl highlights, those orientations have also dominated and constrained non-Muslim thinking about the interrelation of human rights and Islam. He points to a number of generalisations about Islamic law commonly found in human rights scholarship which, 'to say the least, are not based on historical texts generated by Muslim jurists'.[20] These include the idea that Islamic law is concerned primarily with duties, rather than rights, and the idea that, insofar as Islamic law is concerned with rights, its conception of rights is collectivist, rather than individualist. Abou El Fadl shows how these ideas owe more to Western orientalism and (often convergent) Muslim apologetics and exceptionalism than

[17] Ibid., 309.   [18] Ibid., 310.

[19] See, e.g., A. An-Na'im, 'Towards a Cross-Cultural Approach to Defining International Standards of Human Rights: The Meaning of Cruel, Inhuman or Degrading Treatment or Punishment', in A. An-Na'im (ed.), Human Rights in Cross-Cultural Perspectives (Philadelphia: University of Pennsylvania Press, 1992), 19.

[20] K. Abou El Fadl, 'The Human Rights Commitment in Modern Islam' in J. Runzo, N.M. Martin and A. Sharma (eds.), Human Rights and Responsibilities in the World Religions (Oxford: Oneworld Publications, 2003), 301, 337.

to serious engagement with Islamic thought, which, according to him, largely sidesteps the dualities in question. Thus, he contends, Muslim thought asserts both duties and rights, and is neither collectivist nor individualist, revolving instead around other concepts and structures of argument.

The right to religious freedom

We have so far been speaking about the bearing of religion for human rights. Let us now shift perspectives, and begin to consider how, for its part, international human rights law bears upon religion. Specifically, our questions are: how does human rights law protect the right to freedom of religion? In what circumstances are restrictions on this right acceptable? And to what extent does this right justify restriction of other rights, such as the rights to freedom of expression, assembly, and association?

Religious freedom

We noted earlier the view of Louis Henkin and Michael Ignatieff that the universality of human rights is inconsistent with any religious grounding. Whether or not that is true, it is certainly the case, as Henkin observes, that the Universal Declaration of Human Rights 'is not anti-religious; it is not even nonreligious'. Rather, it provides 'an essential support for religion, for religions'.[21] The right to freedom of religion is recognised in article 18 of the Declaration: 'Everyone has the right to freedom of thought, conscience and religion; this right includes freedom to change his religion or belief, and freedom, either alone or in community with others and in public or private, to manifest his religion or belief in teaching, practice, worship and observance.' Freedom of religion is likewise guaranteed in the International Covenant of Civil and Political Rights,[22] and in the various regional human rights treaties (the African Charter of Human and Peoples' Rights;[23] the American Convention on Human Rights;[24] and the European Convention on

---

[21] L. Henkin, 'Religion, Religions, and Human Rights' 26 *Journal of Religious Ethics* (1998), 229, 234.   [22] Art. 18.

[23] Art. 8.

[24] Art. 12. See also American Declaration on the Rights and Duties of Man (1948), art. III.

Human Rights).[25] Article 18 of the Civil and Political Rights Covenant is the subject of a detailed General Comment of the Human Rights Committee (General Comment 22),[26] to which we return below.

Wherever human rights instruments prohibit discrimination and guarantee the right to equality before the law, religion is an explicit ground of impermissible discrimination. Within the framework of EU law, far-reaching provisions concerning religious discrimination are laid down in a Directive on equal treatment in employment and occupation, adopted in 2000.[27] Religious discrimination is also addressed in the UN Declaration on the Elimination of All Forms of Intolerance and of Discrimination Based on Religion or Belief, adopted by the General Assembly in 1981. While, unlike some similar documents, this Declaration has not been followed up by the adoption of a treaty in corresponding terms, it has had considerable influence on the interpretation of other instruments, including treaties such as the Convention on the Rights of the Child. Since 1987 the UN Commission on Human Rights has mandated a Special Rapporteur to investigate problems associated with the right to freedom of religion or belief, and the Declaration has also served as the basis for the work of that Special Rapporteur.[28]

Buttressing these stipulations on freedom of religion and religion-based discrimination is a range of further norms that protect the rights of religious communities and their members. Among these are norms establishing the crime of genocide, defined in the Convention on the Prevention and Punishment of the Crime of Genocide as killing and other very serious acts 'committed with intent to destroy, in whole or in part, a national, ethnical, racial or religious group, as such'.[29] The crime of persecution, included within the category of crimes against humanity in the Rome Statute of the International Criminal Court, is also relevant here. Persecution in this context is said to refer to the 'intentional and severe deprivation of fundamental rights contrary to international law by reason of the identity of the group or collectivity'.[30] Under the Rome Statute,

[25] Art. 9. See further C. Evans, *Freedom of Religion under the European Convention on Human Rights* (Oxford: Oxford University Press, 2001).

[26] Human Rights Committee, General Comment 22 (The right to freedom of thought, conscience and religion: art. 18), 30 July 1993.

[27] Directive 2000/78/EC, OJ L 303/16, 2 December 2000.

[28] See, e.g., Report of the Special Rapporteur on freedom of religion or belief, Abdelfattah Amor, UN Doc. E/CN.4/2004/63, 16 January 2004.

[29] Art. II.   [30] Art. 7(2)(g). See further Racism*.

persecution against 'any identifiable group or collectivity' on religious grounds is a crime against humanity where it is committed 'as part of a widespread or systematic attack directed against any civilian population, with knowledge of the attack' in connection with other crimes against humanity or in connection with genocide or war crimes. Finally, the rights of religious communities and their members are protected through guarantees of minority rights. Thus, the International Covenant on Civil and Political Rights, in article 27, protects the rights of members of religious minorities, 'in community with the other members of their group, to . . . profess and practice their own religion'. Expanding on this provision, the UN Declaration on the Rights of Persons Belonging to National or Ethnic, Religious and Linguistic Minorities sets forth a catalogue of rights designed to protect, among other things, religious freedom.[31]

Scope and limits

The right to religious freedom encompasses a number of distinct, if interrelated, elements. In the first place, there is the right to *have* a religion or belief of one's choice. This is closely linked to the right to freedom of thought and conscience. One issue that has been raised in this connection is refusal to perform military service on the ground of conscientious objection. In its General Comment 22, the Human Rights Committee proposes that the right to conscientious objection, while not explicitly guaranteed in the Covenant, 'can be derived from' the right to freedom of religion or belief, inasmuch as the obligation to use lethal force may seriously conflict with one's freedom of thought and conscience, and with the right to have a religion or belief of one's choice.[32]

Secondly, there is the right to *manifest* one's religion or belief, whether individually or in community with others, whether in public or in private, and whether through worship, observance, practice or teaching. On this aspect, the Human Rights Committee proposes that the concept of religious manifestation should be understood as referring to a broad range of acts.[33] Included in the Committee's illustrative list are ritual and ceremonial acts and the symbols, buildings and objects associated with

[31] GA Res. 47/13, adopted 18 December 1992.
[32] Human Rights Committee, General Comment 22 (The right to freedom of thought, conscience and religion: art. 18), 30 July 1993, para. 11.
[33] Ibid., para. 4.

them, the observance of holidays and days of rest, the observance of dietary regulations, the wearing of particular clothing or head coverings, participation in rituals associated with certain stages of life, and the use of a particular language. According to the Committee, religious manifestation should also be taken to encompass the choice of religious leaders and teachers, the establishment of seminaries and religious schools, and the preparation and distribution of religious texts and other publications.

Following on from this, a third element of the right to freedom of religion is the right to *ensure the education of one's children* in conformity with one's religion or belief. In some treaties this is guaranteed in connection with the right to freedom of conscience and religion;[34] in other treaties it is guaranteed in connection with the right to education.[35] Either way, as the Human Rights Committee explains, this right of parents and guardians implies the right to undertake private religious instruction. It also means that state school instruction in a particular religion must be accompanied by 'non-discriminatory exemptions or alternatives', and that more general religious education must be provided in a 'neutral and objective way'.[36]

Fourthly, in certain formulations the right to religious freedom encompasses the right to *adopt* a religion of one's choice, that is to say, the right to change one's religion. This is included in article 18 of the Civil and Political Rights Covenant, but was omitted from the UN Declaration on the Elimination of All Forms of Intolerance and of Discrimination Based on Religion or Belief, and also does not appear in article 8 of the African Charter.

The right to religious freedom is not unqualified. However, the ways in which it may be restricted are closely circumscribed, and are more limited than is the case for many human rights. For one thing, while under some human rights treaties states parties are entitled to derogate from certain of their obligations in time of war or other 'public emergency', under two key treaties this does not apply to the right to freedom of religion. That right must be fully respected at all times.[37] Moreover, whereas restrictions can be imposed on religious freedom,

[34] E.g., International Covenant on Civil and Political Rights, art. 18(4).

[35] E.g., First Protocol to the European Convention on Human Rights, art. 2.

[36] Human Rights Committee, General Comment 22 (The right to freedom of thought, conscience and religion: art. 18), 30 July 1993, para. 6.

[37] See International Covenant on Civil and Political Rights, art. 4(2), and American Convention on Human Rights, art. 27(2). The corresponding provision of the European

the treaties also provide that they can only be imposed on the *manifestation* of religion.[38] The right to *have* and (insofar as applicable) to *adopt* a religion of one's choice cannot be restricted, and nor can the right of parents or guardians to see to the religious education of their children. In a similar vein, article 19 of the Civil and Political Rights Covenant provides that the right to hold opinions without interference is not subject to limitation. A notable case before the African Commission of Human and Peoples' Rights concerned acts of harassment, persecution and discrimination against Christians in Sudan.[39] The African Commission held that the unanswered complaints pointed to a violation of the right to the right to have or 'profess' a religion of one's choice, protected in article 8 of the African Charter of Human and Peoples' Rights.

Finally, even with respect to the manifestation of religion, certain grounds of restriction that commonly apply to other human rights do not apply. For instance, restriction cannot be justified by reference to national security. That said, restriction of the right to manifest religion can be justified by reference to public health, public safety and the protection of the rights of others, among other grounds. In one case before the Human Rights Committee, the complainant was a Sikh who had been dismissed from his job with a Canadian state railway company after refusing to wear safety headgear.[40] He argued that the dismissal violated his right to manifest his religion by wearing a turban. Against this, the Canadian Government maintained that the restriction on his freedom to manifest his religion was a justifiable measure for public health and safety, and the Committee accepted that contention. Likewise, the European Commission on Human Rights accepted some years earlier that a Sikh could be prosecuted in the United Kingdom for

Convention on Human Rights (art. 15(2)) does not mention the right to freedom of religion. However, derogations under the European Convention must not be inconsistent with a state's other international obligations (European Convention, art. 15(1)), with the result that derogation with respect to the right to freedom of religion will not be possible where the state is also a party to the International Covenant on Civil and Political Rights.

[38] A possible exception may be the African Charter of Human and Peoples' Rights (art. 8).

[39] Communications 48/90, 50/91, 52/91 and 89/93 *Amnesty International and Others v Sudan*, Thirteenth Activity Report 1999–2000, Annex V.

[40] *Singh Binder v Canada*, Communication 208/1986, Views of the Human Rights Committee, adopted 9 November 1989.

failing to wear a crash-helmet while riding a motorcycle.[41] Despite these decisions, the right of Sikhs to be exempted from obligations to wear crash-helmets and other headgear has been recognised in many countries, including the United Kingdom.

More recently, the issue has arisen of whether restrictions on the wearing of the Muslim *hijab* are justifiable limitations of the right to manifest religion. In 2001 the European Court of Human Rights considered a complaint by a primary school teacher in Switzerland who had been prohibited from wearing the *hijab* while carrying out her professional duties.[42] Before being asked to stop wearing the *hijab* in class, the applicant had worn it for several years without comment from parents or school authorities. Nonetheless, the Court accepted the Government's argument that the prohibition was a justifiable restriction of the applicant's right to manifest her religion, with the legitimate aims of 'protection of the rights of others, public safety and public order'. At stake for the Court was the need to 'protect pupils', especially very young and impressionable pupils, 'by preserving religious harmony'. Dismissing the applicant's complaint as manifestly ill-founded, the Court also expressed the view that the wearing of the *hijab* 'is hard to square with the principle of gender equality', and hence 'difficult to reconcile ... with the message of tolerance, respect for others and, above all, equality and non-discrimination that all teachers in a democratic society must convey to their pupils'.[43]

In a later case against Turkey, the Court confronted a similar complaint, this time by a university student.[44] The applicant was a medical student who had been prevented from attending classes and taking examinations because she wished to wear the *hijab*. Again the claim that this violated the right to religious freedom failed. The Court said that it could not 'lose sight of the fact that there are extremist political movements in Turkey which seek to impose on society as a whole their religious symbols and conception of a society founded on religious precepts'.[45] For the Court, 'it is the principle of secularism ... which is the paramount consideration underlying the ban on the wearing of

[41] *X v UK*, Applic. 7992/77, (1978) 14 DR 234.
[42] *Dahlab v Switzerland*, Decision of the European Court of Human Rights, 15 February 2001. The complaint was ruled inadmissible.   [43] Ibid., para. 1.
[44] *Leyla Sahin v Turkey*, Judgment of the European Court of Human Rights, 29 June 2004.   [45] Ibid., para. 109.

religious insignia in universities'.[46] However, approaches to the meaning of secularism are variable, and the right of Muslim women and girls to wear the *hijab* in public educational institutions is recognised in many European countries. On the other hand, in February 2004 the French National Assembly approved a law banning the wearing of conspicuous religious symbols in state schools. Around that time demonstrations were held throughout France, as well as elsewhere, asserting the right to wear the *hijab* as an aspect of religious freedom.

Restriction of other rights

Beyond the right to freedom of religion and the various norms addressing religion-based discrimination and threats to religious communities, religious rights may also be protected through restriction of other rights. For example, the right to freedom of assembly may be restricted for the sake of preventing incitement to violence against a religious community. Likewise, the right to freedom of expression may be restricted for the sake of accommodating religious sensibilities, as in the offence of blasphemy. In a complaint against Austria under the European Convention on Human Rights, the applicant was a film society which was prevented from showing a film said to be offensive to Catholics, who formed the majority in the relevant area.[47] The applicant complained that this violated its right to freedom of expression, protected in article 10 of the Convention. Like the right to freedom of religious manifestation, the right to freedom of expression can justifiably be restricted where this is necessary to protect public order and the rights of others. The European Court of Human Rights accepted the Government's argument that the seizure of the film was indeed necessary to ensure 'religious peace' in the region and also to 'prevent that some people should feel the object of attacks on their religious beliefs in an unwarranted and offensive manner'.[48] Thus, there was no violation of article 10.

Alternatively, religious freedom may be upheld by limiting restriction of other rights, or by condemning such restriction as discrimination. An example can be found in another case before the European Court

---

[46] Para. 110.

[47] *Otto-Preminger-Institut v Austria*, Judgment of the European Court of Human Rights, 9 September 1994.   [48] Ibid., para. 56.

of Human Rights against Austria.[49] The applicant converted from Catholicism to become a Jehovah's Witness. In subsequent divorce proceedings, she and her husband were in dispute over custody of their children. The national court awarded custody to the husband, apparently on the sole basis of the applicant's religion. The applicant argued that this constituted discrimination with respect to her right to respect for family life, protected in article 8 of the Convention. Under article 14 of the Convention the rights guaranteed in the Convention must be secured without discrimination on any ground, including religion. The European Court of Human Rights upheld the applicant's argument, finding that, indeed, the applicant's right to respect to family life had been affected by religion-based discrimination. Thus, there had been a violation of article 8, taken in conjunction with article 14.

As in the context of the wearing of the *hijab*, however, religious pluralism may not only be the basis for asserting a complainant's rights; it may also be taken to justify restricting a complainant's rights. In a striking example of this, the European Court of Human Rights dismissed a complaint arising out the dissolution of the Turkish *Refah Partisi* (Welfare Party).[50] The Turkish Constitutional Court had ordered the dissolution on the ground that this political party was a 'centre of activities contrary to the principles of secularism', inasmuch as statements had been made by leading figures associated with it calling for the replacement of the current political order with a theocratic system based on *sharia* (Islamic law). The complainants—the party itself, along with its chairman and vice-chairman—argued that this violated a number of their rights under the European Convention, among them the right to freedom of association protected in article 11. Rejecting this claim, the European Court accepted the Turkish Government's argument that the Constitutional Court's decision had been a justifiable restriction on the applicants' freedom of association. Among the various aims for which freedom of association may legitimately be restricted under article 11, the European Court accepted that in this case the restriction pursued the legitimate aims of 'protection of national security and public safety, prevention of disorder or crime and protection of

---

[49] *Hoffmann v Austria*, Judgment of the European Court of Human Rights, 23 June 1993.

[50] *Refah Partisi (The Welfare Party) and Others v Turkey*, Judgment of the European Court of Human Rights (Grand Chamber), 13 February 2003.

the rights and freedoms of others'.[51] The Court considered that the dissolution of *Refah Partisi* was not disproportionate to these aims, for '[p]luralism and democracy are based on a compromise that requires various concessions by individuals or groups of individuals, who must sometimes agree to limit some of the freedoms they enjoy in order to guarantee greater stability of the country as a whole'.[52] The Court expressed particular concern that 'sharia...clearly diverges from Convention values, particularly with regard to its criminal law and criminal procedure, its rules on the legal status of women and the way it intervenes in all spheres of private and public life in accordance with religious precepts'.[53]

Human rights as religion

Our discussion to this point has revolved around systems of religious (or other) belief and their relationship to human rights. In this final section we give brief consideration to another dimension of the interrelation of religion and human rights, which concerns the idea that the human rights movement has emerged as itself a type of religion, albeit a non-theistic one. Elie Wiesel expresses what is now almost a commonplace of human rights commentary when he writes that the 'defense of human rights has, in the last fifty years, become a kind of worldwide secular religion'.[54] From one angle, this seems like a development strongly to be welcomed. As Wiesel explains, '[the defense of human rights] has attracted millions of members and sympathizers...Its mission is to defend victims of injustice and despair, and in the field of therapy to heal those whose mind and soul have been mutilated, wherever they exist and whoever they are'.Viewed from another angle, however, the religious, or religion-like, features of the human rights movement may appear more troubling.

---

[51] *Refah Partisi (The Welfare Party) and Others v Turkey*, Judgment of the European Court of Human Rights (Grand Chamber), 13 February 2003, para. 67.

[52] Ibid., para. 99.

[53] Ibid., para. 123 (concurring in this respect with the view earlier expressed by a Chamber of the European Court of Human Rights).

[54] E. Wiesel, 'A Tribute to Human Rights' in Y. Danieli, E. Stamatopoulou and C. Dias (eds.), *The Universal Declaration of Human Rights: Fifty Years and Beyond* (Amityville, NY: Baywood Publishing, 1999), 3.

In the view of Michael Ignatieff, treating human rights as a secular religion '[turns] it into a species of idolatry'.[55] By this he means that a worshipful or reverential attitude is adopted, which fails to subject the premises of human rights to critical scrutiny. Ignatieff wants to discourage us from approaching human rights as a belief system, with the sacredness or inviolate dignity of human beings as its central article of faith. Rather, he insists, humanism must subject its own premises to the same critical examination to which it subjects religious convictions. If it fails to do that, it falls into a 'cultlike credulity', and becomes 'simply inconsistent'.[56] Amy Gutmann agrees that human rights should not be idolised. But for her the issue is not so much inconsistency. It is the danger of 'worshipping human rights rather than valuing the lives of the people who are supposed to be protected by human rights'.[57] David Kennedy highlights this danger in an essay on the ambiguous character of human rights activism. As he sees it, what is problematic about treating human rights as a secular religion is that it leads us to overlook the need to identify and consider the actual impacts of articulating, institutionalising and enforcing human rights for the people whose interests are at stake.[58] In particular, we become apt to overlook the need to identify and consider the *negative* impacts. Rather than approaching human rights as an 'object of devotion', Kennedy urges us to adopt a more pragmatic or strategic approach, which appreciates both benefits and costs, and weighs each in specific contexts. In a striking phrase, borrowed from the presumptively antithetical language of utilitarianism, he proposes that human rights should become an object of 'calculation' in this sense.

We have reviewed three ways in which human rights relate to religion. In the first place, we have seen that religion may be used to justify the abuse of human rights; at the same time, it may be used to enhance the legitimacy of human rights. Secondly, we have seen that international

[55] M. Ignatieff, 'Human Rights as Idolatry' in M. Ignatieff, (A. Gutmann, ed.), *Human Rights as Politics and Idolatry* (Princeton: Princeton University Press, 2001), 53.

[56] Ibid., 83.

[57] A. Gutmann, 'Introduction' in M. Ignatieff, (A. Gutmann, ed.), *Human Rights as Politics and Idolatry* (Princeton: Princeton University Press, 2001), vii, xxv–xxvi.

[58] D. Kennedy, 'The International Human Rights Movement: Part of the Problem?' *European Human Rights Law Review* (2001) 245, 246. See further D. Kennedy, *The Dark Sides of Virtue* (Princeton: Princeton University Press, 2004).

human rights law may be invoked to defend religious life; at the same time, it may be used to restrict the activities of religious people and organisations. Finally, we have seen that the defence of human rights may be approached as a religion in itself, an object of devotion; at the same time, it may be approached as an object of calculation. In the light of the discussion as a whole, it is not difficult to grasp the dangers of devotion in this context. Human rights can serve a variety of ends, agendas and interests, including contradictory or competing ones. Moreover, behind the assertion of any given right, and shaping its meaning and prospects, is invariably also a variety of concerns. When schoolgirls demonstrate on the streets of Paris asserting the right to wear the *hijab* as an aspect of the right to religious freedom, they may be shouting about religious rights. But they are also shouting about racism, nationalism, the second class status of French Muslims, the containment of Islam, and the 'war on terror', with all its multifarious effects. Does the demand for religious rights express these concerns, or does it muffle them? In turn, would the recognition of those rights reduce Muslim marginalisation or reinforce it, promote women's equality or undermine it, curb racist violence or inflame it? Far from supplying determinate answers, the assertion of religious rights belongs with our debates about injustice and how best to challenge and redress it. And of course, at least in some traditions, so does religion itself.

Sexuality

Sexuality is, of course, about sex. But, as our discussion here will confirm, it is also about access to pensions, custody of children, tenancy rights, and security of employment, to mention just a few of the further topics that are raised. If these rather unsexy matters are also at stake, this is because, like many other categories of human identification and inter-action, sexuality names a domain of power relations. Social goods and opportunities are differentially distributed, according to a 'sex-gender system' in which some forms of relationship, activity, and identity are privileged, while others are disfavoured and disciplined. Sustaining this system is a wide range of practices and institutions that mark out dis-favoured relationships, activities and identities as abnormal, unnatural or deficient. While these practices and institutions encompass many domains of life, law is among those domains, and, especially in recent decades, the effort to secure legal change and put in place legal protection has been a key focus of moves to redress the injustices of prevailing sex-gender arrangements.

We have so far been speaking rather abstractly, but the concrete context of these moves has been primarily the movement for lesbian, gay and transsexual rights. In what follows we examine some of the ways in which international human rights law has been linked to the activities of this movement. We begin with challenges to laws that criminalise same-sex relations. We then look at challenges to laws and administra-tive practices that discipline same-sex relations by somewhat more subtle or indirect means, involving discrimination against gay men and lesbians with respect to matters beyond sexual life. The final part of our discussion is concerned with challenges to laws and administrative prac-tices that affect the legal status of transsexual people. At a few points we will refer to the path-breaking work of Michel Foucault on the history of sexuality. In one of the most frequently quoted passages from that study, Foucault writes: 'Where there is power, there is resistance'.[1] The questions for us here revolve around the role of human rights with regard to resistance in the field of sexuality. How have human rights supported that resistance? How has that resistance in turn reshaped human rights? What are the enduring limitations of a human rights strategy in this field?[2]

Homosexuality and criminal law

The starting point for challenges to laws and administrative practices affecting same-sex relations is the phenomenon of 'heteronormativity', whereby heterosexual relations are treated as the norm and all other kinds of sexuality as deviations from that norm. The simplest, or crudest, expressions in law of heteronormativity are laws criminalising same-sex relations. We begin with these, as they were the focus of some of the earliest moves to use human rights in connection with demands for change in the sphere of sexuality.

The first cases were brought within the framework of the European Convention on Human Rights. In 1981 the European Court of European Rights considered a complaint by Jeffrey Dudgeon against the United Kingdom arising out of the criminalisation of homosexuality in Northern Ireland.[3] Dudgeon argued that the existence of a law criminalising private consensual sex between men violated his right to respect for private life, protected in article 8 of the European Convention. Article 8 is not unqualified, and interference with the right to respect for private life can be justified where it is necessary and proportionate

---

[1] M. Foucault (R. Hurley, trans.), *The Will to Knowledge (The History of Sexuality Vol. 1)* (London: Penguin, 1978), 95.

[2] See further E. Heinze, *Sexual Orientation: A Human Right: An Essay on International Human Rights Law* (Dordrecht: Martinus Nijhoff, 1995); R. Wintemute, *Sexual Orientation and Human Rights—The United States Constitution, the European Convention, and the Canadian Charter* (Oxford: Oxford University Press, 1997); R. Wintemute, and M. Andenas (eds.), *Legal Recognition of Same-Sex Partnerships: A Study of National, European and International Law* (Oxford: Hart Publishing, 2001).

[3] *Dudgeon v United Kingdom*, Judgment of the European Court of Human Rights, 23 September 1981.

to the pursuit of a number of specified aims, one of which is the protection of morals. The United Kingdom Government maintained that the protection of morals justified interference in this case. In the Court's assessment, however, the moral context which might once have supported that contention no longer prevailed. Accordingly, the Court upheld Dudgeon's argument that this was an unjustified interference with his right to respect for private life, and hence a violation of the United Kingdom's obligations under article 8. Seven years later, it delivered a similar judgment upon a complaint against Ireland,[4] and again later still in a claim against Cyprus.[5]

Alongside his arguments about the violation of his right to respect for private life, Dudgeon actually also argued that the criminalisation of homosexuality constituted *discrimination* with respect to that right, contrary to article 14 of the European Convention. Under article 14, the rights protected in the Convention must be secured 'without discrimination on any ground such as sex . . . or other status'. For the Court, however, it could 'not be said that a clear inequality of treatment [was] a fundamental aspect of the case', and no decision was rendered on this aspect of Dudgeon's claim.[6] As we shall see, the question of discrimination has become central to the Court's analysis of many of the other issues affecting same-sex relations that have been raised in subsequent years. Among these is the issue of the age of consent to male homosexual relations. In 1997 the European Commission of Human Rights accepted an applicant's argument that a United Kingdom law fixing the age of consent to male homosexual relations at 18, while the age of consent to heterosexual relations was 16, constituted discriminatory treatment with respect to the right to private life.[7] Using the now standard language of 'sexual orientation discrimination', the Commission qualified the difference in ages of consent as an unjustified 'difference based on sexual orientation'.[8] In two cases against Austria, the European Court of Human Rights subsequently confirmed this point that

[4] *Norris v Ireland*, Judgment of the European Court of Human Rights, 26 October 1988.

[5] *Modinos v Cyprus*, Judgment of the European Court of Human Rights, 25 March 1993.

[6] *Dudgeon v United Kingdom*, Judgment of the European Court of Human Rights, 23 September 1981, para. 69.

[7] *Sutherland v United Kingdom*, Report of the European Commission of Human Rights, 1 July 1997.   [8] Ibid., para. 50.

differential ages of consent constitute discrimination on the grounds of
sexual orientation, in violation of article 14, taken in conjunction with
article 8.[9]

If the European Convention was the earliest context in which international human rights norms were invoked to challenge prohibitions or
restrictions on same-sex relations, and if it remains among the most significant contexts, it has not been the only framework for initiatives of
this sort. In 1994 the Human Rights Committee considered a complaint
about the consistency with the International Covenant on Civil and
Political Rights of legal provisions that criminalised homosexual behaviour in the state of Tasmania in Australia.[10] The Committee ruled that
the provisions constituted an arbitrary and unreasonable interference
with the applicant's right to privacy, in violation of article 17 of the
Covenant. The Committee also observed that, inasmuch as the rights
protected in the Covenant have to be secured 'without distinction of
any kind, such as [among others] sex',[11] the reference here to sex (and in
article 26, guaranteeing equal protection of the law) should be understood as including sexual orientation. Thus, it has been made clear that
the rights protected in the Covenant must be secured without discrimination on the grounds of sexual orientation—and not only the right to
privacy, but all the other rights, including the right to equal protection
of the law, as well. Similar statements have been made with respect to
the International Covenant on Economic, Social and Cultural Rights.
In a General Comment on the right to health, the Committee on
Economic, Social and Cultural Rights affirmed that sexual orientation
is among the prohibited grounds of discrimination, and among the
relevant grounds for considering equality of treatment, under that
Covenant.[12]

Liability to prosecution, actual prosecution, and/or homophobic
violence have also been the basis for arguments under the Convention
on the Status of Refugees. Under the Convention, refugee status
depends on having a well-founded fear of persecution on any of several

[9] See, e.g., *S.L. v Austria* and *L. and V. v Austria*, Judgments of the European Court of
Human Rights, 9 January 2003.
[10] *Toonen v Australia*, Communication 488/1992, Views of the Human Rights
Committee, adopted 31 March 1994.   [11] Art. 2(1).
[12] See Committee on Economic, Social and Cultural Rights, General Comment 14
(The right to the highest attainable standard of health: art. 12), 11 August 2000, para. 18.

stated grounds, including 'membership of a particular social group'.[13] In a number of cases national courts and administrative bodies have recognised the category of 'particular social group' to encompass gay men and lesbians, and that practice is reflected in interpretive guidelines on this aspect of the Refugee Convention issued by the United Nations High Commissioner for Refugees.[14] At the same time, United Nations human rights reports have considered the point at which (liability to) prosecution shades into persecution from the perspective of a range of human rights, among them (in situations of lethal homophobic violence) the right to life.[15]

Sexual orientation discrimination

Laws criminalising same-sex relations may be the simplest, or crudest, expressions in law of heteronormativity, but they are not the only expressions, nor necessarily the most potent ones. Michel Foucault highlights this point in his study of the history of sexuality mentioned earlier. Foucault describes there how modernity is associated with a shift in the way sexual life is governed. In place of the relatively simple processes of earlier times, centred principally on taboos and prohibitionary laws taking the form of taboos, came a more complex and multifaceted system of regulation. As he explains, this system operates less 'by punishment' than 'by control',[16] and, while it may still be 'locally dependent on procedures of prohibition',[17] it extends well beyond those procedures and is not reducible to them. Foucault was especially concerned to call attention to the role within this system of institutions and practices that do not form part of the apparatus of government; medicine, psychiatry, psychology, biology, demography and pedagogy are among the fields of knowledge and activity that he considered especially

[13] Art. 1A(2).

[14] UNHCR, Guidelines on International Protection: 'Membership of a particular social group' within the context of Article 1A(2) of the 1951 Convention and/or its 1967 Protocol relating to the Status of Refugees, Doc. HCR/GIP/02/02, 7 May 2002.

[15] See, e.g., Report of the Special Rapporteur on Extrajudicial, Summary or Arbitrary Executions, Asma Jahangir: UN Doc. E/CN.4/2003/3, 13 January 2003. See also, regarding the death penalty, e.g., Commission on Human Rights, Resolution 2003/67, para. 4(d).

[16] M. Foucault (R. Hurley, trans.), *The Will to Knowledge (The History of Sexuality Vol. 1)* (London: Penguin, 1978), 89.   [17] Ibid., 49.

significant. But his analysis also has important implications for our understanding of the role of institutions and practices that *do* form part of the apparatus of government. In particular, he reminds us that the contribution of law to the regulation of sexual life includes the specification of criminal offences, but by no means stops at that. For behind the heavy hand of the criminal law (and whether supporting it or, with decriminalisation, displacing it) is always an array of other (civil, administrative, labour, etc.) laws and official practices which enforce heteronormativity, not through punishment, but rather through control. Since the late 1990s these too have been contested on the terrain of international human rights law. Let us turn now to consider some of the decisions and developments that have resulted.

One case, brought against Portugal under the European Convention on Human Rights, concerned child custody.[18] A gay man was denied custody of his child, in circumstances which left no doubt that his homosexuality was the decisive criterion in the decision. The European Court of Human Rights accepted his argument that this constituted discrimination with regard to his right to respect for family life, contrary to article 8 of the Convention, taken in conjunction with article 14. Sidestepping the issue of whether discrimination on grounds of sexual orientation is a form of discrimination on grounds of 'sex' (as explicitly proscribed in article 14), the Court simply observed that the list of prohibited grounds of discrimination in article 14 is 'illustrative and not exhaustive', and that sexual orientation is 'undoubtedly covered'.[19] In a later case against France, the Court confronted an application by a gay man who was refused authorisation to adopt a child.[20] Again, the circumstances left no doubt that the decision not to authorise adoption was based decisively on the applicant's homosexuality. Under French law unmarried people could adopt, and the applicant claimed that he was the victim of discrimination on grounds of sexual orientation, contrary to article 14, taken in conjunction with article 8. On this occasion, however, the European Court of Human Rights declined to uphold the applicant's argument. While accepting that the applicant's homosexuality had been crucial to the decision of the French authorities, and while noting that article 14 therefore applied in principle, the Court considered

---

[18] *Salgueiro da Silva Mouta v Portugal*, Judgment of the European Court of Human Rights, 21 December 1999.   [19] Ibid., para. 28.
[20] *Fretté v France*, Judgment of the European Court of Human Rights, 30 January 2002.

that the different treatment of a gay would-be adopter like the applicant compared to a straight would-be adopter was justifiable. In this regard, the Court held that the diversity of national approaches to gay adoption within the Council of Europe member states made it appropriate to concede to the national authorities a significant measure of discretion, or (in the Court's terminology) a 'wide margin of appreciation', on this issue.

Another series of cases has raised the issue of discrimination with respect to the rights of partners of gay men and lesbians. In one case before the Human Rights Committee, a complaint was made against Australia in connection with an entitlement to a surviving dependant's pension.[21] The applicant, a gay man, was in a relationship for 38 years. His partner died, and, as the latter had been a war veteran, he claimed a pension under legislation which provided benefits for the surviving dependants of war veterans. His claim was refused. Under the legislation, pensions were payable only to surviving spouses or to unmarried partners in circumstances where a war veteran had been living with a person of the opposite sex. Before the Human Rights Committee the applicant argued that this was inconsistent with his right to equal treatment before the law. The Committee accepted this argument, ruling that the difference in treatment of same-sex couples and different-sex couples constituted discrimination on grounds of sexual orientation, contrary to article 26 of the International Covenant on Civil and Political Rights. In another case within the framework of the European Convention on Human Rights concerning succession to tenancy rights, the European Court of Human Rights was likewise persuaded that the failure to treat a gay partner in the same way as an unmarried heterosexual partner constituted discrimination with respect to the right to a home, contrary to article 14 of the Convention, taken in conjunction with article 8.[22]

In the context of European Community law, a challenge to discriminatory practices of this kind failed in 1998.[23] The applicant worked for a British train company which granted travel concessions to married

---

[21] *Young v Australia*, Communication 941/2000, Views of the Human Rights Committee, adopted 6 August 2003.

[22] *Karner v Austria*, Judgment of the European Court of Human Rights, 24 July 2003.

[23] *Grant v South-West Trains Limited*, European Court of Justice, Case C-249/96, 17 February 1998, [1998] ECR I-621.

employees' spouses, as well as to the 'common law opposite sex spouses' of unmarried employees. The applicant, a lesbian, was refused travel concessions for her partner, and she argued that this violated her rights under Community law. The European Court of Justice dismissed her claim. Rejecting the argument that norms of Community law which proscribed sex discrimination should be construed to include discrimination based on sexual orientation, the Court of Justice considered that there was no sex discrimination here because a (gay) male employee would have been treated in the same way as the applicant. His same-sex partner too would have been refused travel concessions. Clearly, as many commentators have remarked, the Court chose an inappropriate comparator; the discrimination which the applicant sought to highlight was not discrimination between lesbians and gay men, but discrimination between lesbians and heterosexual women (or, for that matter, heterosexual men). For the Court of Justice, however, this latter form of discrimination was not inconsistent with Community law. After 1998, important changes came into effect which modified that situation. The Treaty of Amsterdam was in fact the first international treaty explicitly to address discrimination on grounds of sexual orientation.[24] The Treaty amended the EC Treaty so as to confer on the Council of the European Communities competence to take action aimed at eliminating various forms of discrimination, among them discrimination based on sexual orientation.[25] Pursuant to this amendment, the Council issued in 2000 a Directive on equal treatment in employment and occupation, which imposes on EU states obligations with respect to the elimination of direct and indirect forms of sexual orientation discrimination.[26]

At the centre of these various challenges and initiatives is, as we have seen, the concept of discrimination. And at the centre of that concept, in turn, is the question of comparators. The 1989 European Court of Justice case just mentioned makes clear that everything hinges on the choice of comparator. Let us, then, look at one further context in which administrative practices have been impugned through human rights law. In 1999 the European Court of Human Rights ruled on a series of cases brought against the United Kingdom by members of the armed forces

[24]   See art. 2, inserting a new provision into the EC Treaty.
[25]   See, now, art. 13(1) EC Treaty (as renumbered following the entry into force of the Treaty of Nice).   [26]   Directive 2000/78/EC, OJ L 303/16, 2 December 2000.

who had been discharged because they were lesbian or gay.[27] The applicants argued that the dismissals and the investigations which led up to them interfered with their right to privacy. The British Government argued that any interference was justifiable. Under article 8(2) of the European Convention, interference can be justified where it is in the interests of national security, and is necessary, as well as proportionate to these interests. The British Government contended that the exclusion of homosexuals from the armed forces was a necessary and proportionate measure for maintaining morale and hence fighting power. The Court was not persuaded of this, and held in these cases that the applicants' right to private life had indeed been violated. Insofar as there was evidence to substantiate the Government's contention, the Court noted that it was 'founded solely upon the negative attitudes of heterosexual personnel towards those of homosexual orientation'.[28] To treat the negative attitudes of heterosexual personnel as sufficient justification for maintaining the ban on homosexuals in the armed forces was simply to capitulate to those attitudes. More than that, it was to disregard the extent to which the ban itself fostered and sustained them.

Gender identity and legal status

Our focus to this point has been on laws and administrative practices affecting same-sex relations. We have seen how heteronormativity has been enforced, not just through the interdiction of sexual activity, but also through the control of benefits, families, careers, and so on. To that extent, Foucault's account of the way sexuality is governed in modern societies proves enduringly instructive. But beyond that account, we can also take from Foucault's work another idea of a more general kind, which underpins his whole project of investigating the history of sexuality. This is the striking insight that our sexual identities, while experienced as personal—and indeed intimate—facts, are at another level historical artefacts. They are products of history—not simply properties of individuals, but outcomes of a social process. That social process,

[27] *Smith and Grady v United Kingdom* and *Lustig-Prean and Beckett v United Kingdom*, Judgments of the European Court of Human Rights, 27 September 1999.

[28] *Smith and Grady v United Kingdom*, Judgment of the European Court of Human Rights, 27 September 1999, para. 96.

moreover, is in significant part a 'discursive' process, in that it is shaped by the concepts and categories we use in talking about life and the world. Thus, the concepts and categories used by many of us today are such that, as Tamsin Spargo observes, 'I am likely to think of my sexuality in terms of a range of possible identities—straight, gay, lesbian, bisexual— which are themselves bound up with my gender classification. I may consider myself to be a gay man or a straight woman, but I'd have trouble thinking of myself as a lesbian man'.[29] As Spargo also observes, what makes identifying as a lesbian man seem preposterous is the existence of 'apparently stable genders attached to appropriate biological sexes'.[30] But what if those genders are not so stable? In this final section we consider a series of cases in which transsexual people have invoked human rights to challenge legal and administrative practices denying recognition of reassigned gender identity.

The earliest claims concerning gender identity were, again, brought under the European Convention on Human Rights. In 1986 the European Court of Human Rights ruled on an application by Mark Rees against the United Kingdom.[31] Rees was a post-operative transsexual, who sought to have his birth certificate amended to reflect his reassigned gender. The authorities refused to make the change. Given the exposure of his intimate history to which this decision subjected him in a variety of contexts, Rees argued that the British Government had failed to protect his right to respect to his private life, and was thus in violation of article 8 of the Convention. As the decision also prevented him from marrying, he additionally argued that the Government had failed to protect his right to marry, contrary to article 12 of the Convention. The Court dismissed both claims. With respect to the privacy claim, the Court considered that the British Government had acted within its 'margin of appreciation' in refusing to amend the register. Supporting this conclusion was the Court's assessment that (as in the later case concerning gay adoption) the diversity of approaches to the legal status of transsexuals within the member states of the Council of Europe meant that the British Government was entitled to a wide margin of appreciation in dealing with this issue. With respect to the

[29] T. Spargo, *Foucault and Queer Theory* (Cambridge: Icon, 1999), 51.
[30] Ibid., 54.
[31] *Rees v United Kingdom*, Judgment of the European Court of Human Rights, 25 September 1986.

marriage claim, the Court simply stated that in its opinion 'the right to marry guaranteed by article 12 refers to the traditional marriage between persons of the opposite biological sex'.[32]

The rights invoked by Rees were subsequently invoked again on a number of occasions. In one case against France, decided in 1992, the European Court upheld the applicant's complaint.[33] Under the French system of civil status, a variety of life events are recorded on birth certificates, and the Court was of the view that the failure of the French authorities to record gender reassignment violated the applicant's right to respect for her private life. Within the EU legal order as well, the dismissal of a male-to-female transsexual from an educational establishment in the United Kingdom on the ground of her transsexualism was successfully challenged in 1996 as sex discrimination, contrary to Community law.[34] The European Court of Justice rejected the UK Government's argument that the relevant comparator was a female-to-male transsexual. The fact that a woman who had become a man would have been dismissed too did not mean there had been no sex discrimination, because the point here was to protect people against unfavourable treatment 'by comparison with persons of the sex to which he or she was deemed to belong before undergoing gender reassignment'.[35]

As for the remainder of the cases invoking rights under the European Convention to legal recognition of reassigned gender identity, these were mostly attempts to persuade the European Court of Human Rights to reconsider its decision in Rees. The Court, however, adhered to that position throughout the 1990s, though, in doing so, it repeatedly restated an observation made already in Rees (and no doubt ringing increasingly hollow to the applicants with each iteration) that the need for appropriate legal measures to redress the difficulties faced by transsexuals should nonetheless be kept under review, 'having regard

---

[32] Para. 49.

[33] B. v France, Judgment of the European Court of Human Rights, 24 June 1992.

[34] P. v S. and Cornwall County Council, Case C-13/94, Judgment of the European Court of Justice, 30 April 1996, [1996] ECR I-02143. See also K.B. v National Health Service Pensions Agency, Case C/117/01, Judgment of the European Court of Justice, 7 January 2004, (not yet reported).

[35] P. v S. and Cornwall County Council, Case C-13/94, Judgment of the European Court of Justice, 30 April 1996, [1996] ECR I-02143, para. 21.

particularly to scientific and societal developments'.[36] As if to underscore the salience of such developments, the Court pondered at some length in these judgments on the relative significance of chromosomal and other biological factors, compared to psycho-social factors, in determining gender identity. The Court also generally described in some detail the physical modifications which the applicant's body had undergone, often adding some words as well about the applicant's character and behaviour as a member of his or her reassigned sex.

In 2002 the Court was finally convinced to reconsider its earlier decisions concerning the United Kingdom.[37] A key factor in this regard appears to have been the fact that changes regularising the legal status of transsexuals had by then occurred in a considerable number of countries, if not actually within the Council of Europe, then on a global scale; there was now 'clear and uncontested evidence of a continuing international trend in favour... of legal recognition of the new sexual identity of post-operative transsexuals'.[38] As to medical and scientific considerations, it was also significant for the Court that 'transsexualism has wide international recognition as a medical condition for which treatment is provided in order to afford relief'.[39] While the Court observed that that treatment still did not enable a transsexual to acquire all the characteristics of the assigned sex, the principal unchanging aspect of gender identity was the chromosomal element. Yet '[i]t is not apparent to the Court that the chromosomal element, amongst all the others, must inevitably take on decisive significance for the purposes of legal attribution of gender identity for transsexuals'.[40] Thus, the importance was implicitly affirmed of psycho-social factors and self-ascription in the determination of gender. The Court concluded that the Government was no longer acting within its margin of appreciation in refusing legal recognition of the reassigned gender of post-operative transsexuals, and had thus failed to respect their right to private life, protected in article 8. Furthermore, the Court found no justification for barring the rights of transsexuals to marry. Inasmuch as the United Kingdom Government argued that transsexuals had not been deprived

[36] *Rees v United Kingdom*, Judgment of the European Court of Human Rights, 25 September 1986, para. 47.

[37] *Goodwin v UK* and *I v UK*, Judgments of the European Court of Human Rights, 3 July 2002. The references in the discussion that follows are to *Goodwin*.

[38] Para. 85.   [39] Para. 81.   [40] Para. 82.

of the right to marry because they remained able to marry a person of their former opposite sex, the Court rejected this as 'artificial'. In the case of the applicant, the Court observed that she 'lives as a woman, is in a relationship with a man and would only wish to marry a man. She has no possibility of doing so'.[41] Thus, in refusing to grant legal recognition to the reassigned gender of a transsexual, the United Kingdom had also failed to respect her right to marry.

Sexuality and the limits of human rights

Let us now try to draw together some of the threads of this discussion. In introducing the subject of international human rights law as a vehicle for pursuing demands for lesbian, gay and transsexual rights, we raised a number of questions about the role of human rights in relation to those demands. How have human rights supported them? How have they in turn reshaped human rights? What are the enduring limitations of a human rights strategy in this field? As we have seen, human rights have supported the effort to redress injustice with respect to same-sex relations and gender crossing in some notable ways. These have been based primarily on the idea that sexuality and gender identity belong to the sphere of private life, and are protected accordingly by the right to respect for privacy. Prohibitions of discrimination and rights to equal treatment have also been interpreted to take account of discrimination on grounds of sexual orientation or gender identity. And, at least in the context of transsexuality (though not yet in the context of same-sex relationships), the right to marry has likewise been recognised as a right that should belong to everyone. Within the EU, initial reluctance to deal with sexual orientation discrimination has given way to some significant developments both with regard to employment and employment-related discrimination, and more generally with respect to conceptualisations of marriage and the family.[42]

It is, of course, the case that most of the initiatives we have reviewed are European, whether they have unfolded within the framework of the

---

[41] Para. 101.

[42] In addition to the employment-related issues already discussed, see Charter of Fundamental Rights of the EU, art. 9 (guaranteeing the 'right to marry', without reference to the notion, reflected in art. 12 of the European Convention and other instruments, that marriage must be between a man and a woman).

EU legal order or the European Convention on Human Rights. However, as Ralph Sandland comments in a study of the 2002 European Convention cases on transsexual rights, 'legal changes have rippled around the world', and the willingness of the European Court of Human Rights in those cases to take into account global trends, even though no common European approach had yet emerged, marks a shift from its earlier more limited compass. To that extent, these decisions seem to affirm the 'global nature of gender politics in the twenty-first century'.[43] On the other hand, this may itself be a European perspective, in that gender and sexuality politics may well appear less global when viewed from other vantage points. Or rather, we need to remember that globalisation is associated with contradictory trends, which include convergence and the destabilisation of established ways, but also renewed parochialism and the effort to restrain change by appeal to local traditions. This applies no less to the globalisation of gender and sexuality politics than to globalisation in any other field of activity and interaction.

What, then, of the further limitations of a human rights strategy in this field? In addressing this question it will be helpful to return a final time to the work of Michel Foucault, and in particular to three themes elaborated in his history of sexuality and other writings. One is expressed in his famous claim that homosexuality is a modern phenomenon. What Foucault meant by this was not, of course, that same-sex desire did not exist in pre-modern times. Rather, his point was that it was not identified with a particular form of life or category of people. As he explains, whereas sodomy was formerly a class of forbidden acts, there emerged in conjunction with the more complex processes for enforcing heteronormativity in modern societies the concept of 'homosexuality' and of the 'homosexual' as a particular individual. In Foucault's words, '[t]he sodomite had been a temporary aberration; the homosexual was now a species'.[44] Moreover, the homosexual was a species understood as entirely defined by his sexuality: 'Nothing that went into his

---

[43] R. Sandland, 'Crossing and Not Crossing: Gender, Sexuality and Melancholy in the European Court of Human Rights' 11 *Feminist Legal Studies* (2003) 191, 199. A further illustration of this might be the judgment of the United States Supreme Court in *Lawrence v Texas*, 16 July 2003, 539 U.S. 558 (2003), in which the Supreme Court took into account the jurisprudence of the European Court of Human Rights with regard to homosexuality.

[44] M. Foucault (R. Hurley, trans.), *The Will to Knowledge (The History of Sexuality Vol. 1)* (London: Penguin, 1978), 43.

total composition was unaffected by his sexuality. It was everywhere present in him ... It was consubstantial with him'.[45] Our review of challenges to laws and administrative practices that discriminate against gay men and lesbians certainly bears out this last claim. Through these laws and administrative practices, gay men and lesbians are indeed treated as defined by their sexuality, inasmuch as this is made relevant to matters such as parenting, employment and benefits entitlements that have nothing to do with sexual activity. At the same time, however, Foucault sensitises us to the ambiguities of identity politics. For, as many have observed, the challenges themselves have the effect of reinforcing the phenomenon whereby gay men and lesbians are taken to comprise a 'species', minority or (in the language of refugee law) 'particular social group' that remains marginal and subordinate with respect to the heterosexual genus, majority and generality of society.

A second theme concerns what Foucault refers to as the 'medicalization of the sexually peculiar'.[46] On his account, once sexuality was not simply the subject of proscriptions, but also of widely dispersed forms of regulation, detailed procedures were established of examination, observation and scrutiny, and, with them, elaborate conceptions of health and of pathology. As he explains, sexuality became something to be '[detected]—as a lesion, a dysfunction, or a symptom—in the depths of the organism, or on the surface of the skin, or among all the signs of behavior'. In the process, it also became a source of pleasure or prurient interest for those doing the detecting. In Foucault's words, the 'power which thus took charge of sexuality ... wrapped the sexual body in its embrace', occasioning a new 'sensualization of power'.[47] Here there is obvious resonance with our review of challenges to laws and administrative practices affecting transsexuals. Where reassigned gender is not recognised, the body of the transsexual is, in effect, put constantly before the eyes of the world. The violation of the right to respect for private life stands in this context for an imaginative exposure to all those to whom one must produce unamended official documents. Here too, however, the process of vindicating this right is not without its ambiguities, for, as we have seen, close and perhaps prurient attention is paid to the details of psychiatric examinations, counselling sessions, and surgical procedures, and to the various physical changes and psycho-social effects

[45] Ibid.   [46] Ibid., 44.   [47] Ibid.

that have resulted—all of that attention, moreover, strongly indicative of the belief that what is in issue is really less gender identity than sexual peculiarity, a sexual peculiarity called 'transsexualism'. Once again, this highlights the danger of entrenching marginality in the process of trying to attack it.

The final theme we mention here points to an important link between the two issues of sexual orientation and gender identity we have discussed. Foucault and, to a greater extent, later scholars working within the tradition of queer theory have shown how the same heteronormativity that structures the discursive processes associated with sexuality also structures the discursive processes associated with gender.[48] Among other things, control of sexuality depends upon, and invests in, a strict binarism of gender categories: you have to be either a man or a woman. In tandem with this academic work, the possibilities for disrupting that strict binarism have also been explored. The term 'transgender' is sometimes used to refer to those who cross gender boundaries in more ambiguous, provisional and often confusing ways than do transsexual people. The relevance of heteronormativity in relation to gender-crossing is, again, reflected in our review of human rights jurisprudence. When deciding finally to reverse the position adopted in the *Rees* case with respect to the legal recognition in the United Kingdom of reassigned gender identity, the European Court of Human Rights made clear its sense that the time had arrived for change. Why? Because 'the unsatisfactory situation in which post-operative transsexuals live in an intermediate zone as not quite one gender or the other is no longer sustainable'.[49] As Sandland observes, the Court expresses here a 'horror of ambiguous gender identity'.[50] The applicant had to belong to one sex or the other, and since she was no longer a man, she had to be recognised as a woman. More specifically, she had to be recognised as a straight woman. As noted earlier, the Court upheld her right to marry on the basis that she lived with a man and 'would only wish to marry a man'.[51] Within the context of the

[48] See esp. J. Butler, *Gender Trouble* (London: Routledge, 1990).

[49] *Goodwin v UK*, Judgment of the European Court of Human Rights, 3 July 2002, para. 90.

[50] R. Sandland, 'Crossing and Not Crossing: Gender, Sexuality and Melancholy in the European Court of Human Rights' 11 *Feminist Legal Studies* (2003) 191, 202.

[51] *Goodwin v UK*, Judgment of the European Court of Human Rights, 3 July 2002, para. 101.

Court's discussion of post-operative gender identity, it appears that this was a kind of proof of successful gender-crossing, and that heterosexuality thus goes hand in hand with the right to recognition in the new gender. As preposterous and uncanny as a lesbian man, the Court may be suggesting, is a transsexual who is homosexual. To be sure, the applicant in this case in fact identified as a straight woman, and the horror of ambiguous gender identity was (for very obvious and entirely understandable reasons) also hers. Nonetheless, as Sandland again remarks, the danger here is that 'gains for post-operative transsexuals are at the expense of further shoring up the construction of homosexuality as *the* fundamental deviation'.[52] In common with the other limitations we have highlighted, this is not an argument for eschewing the tools offered by human rights law, whether in the struggle for transsexual rights or other rights. But it is an argument for remaining alert to the unintended consequences and often double-edged outcomes which the use of those tools may produce.

---

[52] R. Sandland, 'Crossing and Not Crossing: Gender, Sexuality and Melancholy in the European Court of Human Rights' 11 *Feminist Legal Studies* (2003), 191, 204.

Terrorism

Since 11 September 2001 many people have come to believe, if they did not already, that terrorism is one of the most serious threats we face in the world today. Others have come to believe that counter-terrorism—the 'war on terror'—is one of the most serious threats we face in the world today. These two groups of course overlap: for some people there is grave danger associated with both terrorism and counter-terrorism. The concern about terrorism does not require much explanation. But why the concern about counter-terrorism? One aspect of the answer has to do with human rights, and relates to the action taken in many countries in the name of combating terrorism. In August 2003 UN Secretary-General Kofi Annan expressed disquiet that 'under the guise of terrorism, governments all around the world are using the T-word—and tagging people with it—to abuse their rights.'[1] Reflected in this statement is the widely voiced anxiety that terrorism has become a pretext for disregard for human rights. From one perspective, the problem is conceptual inflation. The label 'terrorism'—Annan's 'T-word'—is being overused, in connection with repressive measures that are out of proportion with the security threats claimed to justify them. From another perspective, however, the problem runs deeper than that, and belongs with the concept of terrorism itself. For Conor Gearty, terrorism is a 'confusing and distracting label,'[2] which 'has never been a useful or intelligent way of describing political violence', and is now all the more dangerous for its vacuity; as such, it should be '[expelled] from public affairs'.[3] In what follows we examine and evaluate these views, as responses to the complex interrelation of terrorism, counter-terrorism, security and human rights.

---

[1] K. Annan, quoted in *International Herald Tribune*, 1 August 2003.
[2] C. Gearty, *The Future of Terrorism* (London: Phoenix, 1997), 19.   [3] Ibid., 3.

Terrorism and human rights

The first thing to note about the concept of terrorism is that this is not a straightforward descriptive term, like tequila or tessellation. To call an act terrorism is to assert not just that it possesses certain characteristics, but that it is wrong. This obviously means that there is a lot at stake in the definition of terrorism. Indeed, the question of how terrorism should be defined is the subject of a longstanding debate within the United Nations, now focused on the drafting of a Comprehensive Convention on International Terrorism. Driving this debate is, on the one hand, a well-founded concern to pin the concept down, and so prevent vague and potentially very broad usages which threaten to shut down the avenues of non-violent dissent. On the other hand, there is the fact that terrorism remains an intensely, and perhaps essentially, contested concept, inasmuch as it is bound up with the legitimacy of violence in particular contexts. Clearly, not all subversive violence is illegitimate, for many national heroes were armed rebels, and (to refer only to relatively recent history) violent struggle was necessary to achieve most transitions from colonial rule. If there is concern about shutting down the avenues of non-violent dissent, so too, then, there is concern about how the boundary is drawn between legitimate and illegitimate instances of violent dissent. We will return later to consider whether the word terrorism may now be more trouble than it is worth. For the moment we simply use it, but without entering the fray with any definition of our own.

Let us now take up the question of how terrorism may affect human rights.[4] To begin with, there is obviously the subversive violence itself, together with its financing and organisation. Under more than a dozen

---

[4] On the interrelation of human rights and terrorism, see further F. Andreu-Guzman (ed.), *Terrorism and Human Rights No. 2: New Challenges and Old Dangers* (Geneva: International Commission of Jurists, 2003); Lawyers Committee for Human Rights, *Imbalance of Powers: How Changes to Law and Policy since 9/11 Erode Human Rights and Civil Liberties* (New York: Lawyers Committee for Human Rights, 2003); International Council of Human Rights Policy, *Human Rights After September 11* (Versoix: International Council of Human Rights Policy, 2002); and United Nations High Commissioner for Human Rights, 'Digest of Jurisprudence of the UN and Regional Organizations on the Protection of Human Rights While Countering Terrorism' (2003) www.unhchr.ch/html/menu6/2/digest.doc.

treaties, some of which date back many decades, acts such as placing bombs in public places, seizing control of aircraft, kidnapping people and holding them hostage, and collecting or providing funds for these or similar activities, are made offences, and states parties are placed under obligations designed to ensure that those responsible are brought to justice.[5] This may lead to prosecution in the territory of one of the states parties to these treaties. Depending on the circumstances, there may additionally be the possibility of prosecution before an *ad hoc* international tribunal[6] or the International Criminal Court.[7] (See further International Crimes★.) Beyond this question of the responsibility of those who carry out or assist in an attack, however, it is in the various initiatives framed as strategies of counter-terrorism that the ongoing impact of terrorism for human rights becomes evident. Arrests and deportations carried out in the United States and other countries after 11 September 2001 highlight some of the issues that may arise. These include discrimination and racial profiling, and denial of the right

---

[5] See, e.g., Convention on Offences and Certain other Acts Committed on Board Aircraft, 1963; Convention for the Suppression of Unlawful Seizure of Aircraft (1970); Convention for the Suppression of Unlawful Acts against the Safety of Civil Aviation (1971); Convention on the Prevention and Punishment of Crimes against Internationally Protected Persons, including Diplomatic Agents (1973); International Convention against the Taking of Hostages (1979); Convention on the Physical Protection of Nuclear Material (1980); Protocol for the Suppression of Unlawful Acts of Violence at Airports Serving International Civil Aviation, supplementary to the Convention for the Suppression of Unlawful Acts against the Safety of Civil Aviation (1988); Convention for the Suppression of Unlawful Acts against the Safety of Maritime Navigation (1988); Protocol for the Suppression of Unlawful Acts against the Safety of Fixed Platforms located on the Continental Shelf (1988); International Convention for the Suppression of Terrorist Bombings (1997); International Convention for the Suppression of the Financing Of Terrorism (1999). At the regional level, see, e.g., OAS Convention to Prevent and Punish Acts of Terrorism Taking the Form of Crimes against Persons and Related Extortion that are of International Significance (1971); European Convention on the Suppression of Terrorism (1977), and Protocol amending the European Convention on the Suppression of Terrorism (2003, not yet in force); States of the South Asian Association for Regional Cooperation Regional Convention on Suppression of Terrorism (1987); and Inter-American Convention Against Terrorism (2002).

[6] See, e.g., *Prosecutor v Galić*, Judgment of the International Criminal Tribunal for the former Yugoslavia (Case IT-98-29-T), 5 December 2003, paras. 63–138 (finding the defendant responsible for the crime of terror against the civilian population in Sarajevo).

[7] For example, the act may be subject to the jurisdiction of the Court as a crime against humanity, or as the war crime of intentionally directing attacks against the civilian population as such. See Rome Statute of the International Criminal Court, arts. 7, 8(2)(b)(i) and 8(2)(e)(i).

to freedom of speech and freedom of assembly. They also include incommunicado detention, prolonged detention without charge or on minor charges, denial of the right to challenge the lawfulness of detention, ill-treatment of detainees, inhuman or degrading conditions of detention, and denial of access to legal representation or monitoring of conversations with lawyers. And they include illegal deportation and constraints on the proper consideration of refugee claims.

The transfer of prisoners from Afghanistan and elsewhere to a United States military base at Guantánamo Bay in Cuba further illustrates the way detention of 'terrorist suspects' may affect human rights, as well as (in some cases) raising questions under international humanitarian law. Held in extremely harsh conditions, without charge and with only very limited access to lawyers and the outside world, the detainees were deprived for over two years of the chance to challenge the legality of their detention.[8] At the same time, the introduction of special procedures for the eventual trial of those detained before military commissions points to a series of additional concerns relating to due process and the right to life. Among these are concerns about the lack of independence of the commissions, their power to admit secret evidence, denial of the right of appeal, and the prospect that the death penalty may be imposed in circumstances that do not guarantee a fair trial.[9] Although Camp Delta at Guantánamo Bay has become emblematic of these concerns, the 'war on terror' has resulted in the detention without charge of large numbers of people by United States authorities in Afghanistan and Iraq as well, and in recourse to the practice of targeted assassination. In connection with the International Covenant on Civil and Political Rights, the Human Rights Committee has affirmed that state obligations under the Covenant continue to apply during armed conflict.[10] The Committee has also affirmed that state obligations continue to

---

[8] In June 2004 the US Supreme Court ruled that 'the federal courts have jurisdiction to determine the legality of the Executive's potentially indefinite detention of individuals who claim to be wholly innocent of wrongdoing.' See *Rasul et al. v George W. Bush, President of The United States et al.*, 28 June 2004, Part IV.

[9] See further International Commission of Jurists, *Military Jurisdiction and International Law: Military Courts and Gross Human Rights Violations*, vol. 1 (Geneva: International Commission of Jurists, 2004).

[10] See Human Rights Committee, General Comment 31 (The nature of the general legal obligation imposed on states parties to the Covenant), 29 March 2004, para. 11. The Committee explains that '[w]hile, in respect of certain Covenant rights, more specific rules of international humanitarian law may be specially relevant for the purposes

apply outside a state's territory, with respect to those 'within the power or effective control' of its forces.[11]

Finally, and more generally, human rights are affected by a range of legislative, administrative and policy measures adopted in many countries. Special arrangements for the investigation and prosecution of 'terrorist' crime, and for the expulsion or exclusion of those suspected of involvement in it have been a feature of the law of the United Kingdom, the United States and a number of other countries for many decades. After 11 September 2001 these arrangements were strengthened and also introduced elsewhere. In this regard encouragement was provided by a resolution adopted by the United Nations Security Council on 28 September 2001 (resolution 1373), under which the governments of states members of the UN are obliged to take steps to combat terrorism in a variety of ways, and to report to a committee—the Counter-Terrorism Committee—on the action they have taken. Among the changes that have been made since Security Council resolution 1373 have been moves to enlarge the legal and operational capacities of governments with respect to surveillance, detention, and immigration control. Thus, police and security services have been granted enhanced powers to search premises and people, and to monitor communications. Systems of internment or indefinite preventive detention have been introduced or expanded. And immigration laws and asylum procedures have been modified to extend the circumstances in which deportation can occur.

These developments raise concerns about arbitrary detention, and about the protection of privacy, the principle of non-refoulement, and the rights of refugees. They also raise concerns about discrimination, especially as in some contexts powers to detain apply exclusively to non-citizens. With these points in mind, and alongside its comments mentioned above about the scope of application of the International Covenant on Civil and Political Rights, the Human Rights Committee has emphasised that enjoyment of rights under the Covenant is not limited to citizens of states parties. Rather, it 'must also be available to all individuals, regardless of nationality or statelessness, such as asylum seekers, refugees, migrant workers and other persons, who may find themselves in [a state party's] territory or subject to [its] jurisdiction'.[12] More generally, and given that

of the interpretation of Covenant rights, both spheres of law are complementary, not mutually exclusive'.

[11] Ibid., para. 10.   [12] Ibid.

the various police, security and immigration powers created are typically linked to a very broad category of offences, itself based on an extremely loosely defined concept of terrorist activity, these and other measures adopted under the banner of counter-terrorism raise concerns about the criminalisation of protest and the chilling of public debate.

Counter-terrorism and human rights

In an article published in February 2002, Bruce Ackerman expressed the fear that further attacks in the United States like those of the previous year would lead to the further strengthening of measures of the kind we have just reviewed, giving rise to a 'destructive cycle [that] will prove devastating to civil liberties'.[13] He wrote: 'It is tempting to respond to this grim prospect with an absolutist defence of traditional freedom: no matter how large the event, . . . we must insist on the strict protection of all rights all the time.' But Ackerman made clear that he did not share this view.

If pedantic respect for civil liberties requires government paralysis, no serious politician will hesitate before sacrificing rights to the war against terrorism... To avoid a repeated cycle of repression, defenders of freedom must consider a more hard-headed doctrine, one that allows short-term emergency measures, but draws the line against permanent restrictions... And governments shouldn't be permitted to run wild even during the emergency—many extreme measures should remain off-limits.[14]

Although he does not mention international human rights law, Ackerman could be describing it here. For international human rights law precisely eschews the 'absolutist defence' he rejects, in favour of the 'hard-headed doctrine' for which he calls. At the same time, that 'hard-headed doctrine' contains stipulations designed to prevent 'permanent restrictions' and restrain governments from 'running wild', just as he recommends. The relevant regime can be found in treaty provisions permitting derogation from certain human rights commitments in times of national emergency. It is also reflected in customary international law, which proceeds from the assumption that emergency measures are at times

---

[13] B. Ackerman, 'Don't Panic', *London Review of Books*, 7 February 2002, 15.
[14] Ibid.

considered necessary and establishes a human rights-based framework for their regulation. Let us examine what is involved.[15]

By 'derogation' is meant in this context a modification that allows for the temporary curtailment of human rights. The effect of a valid derogation is to excuse what in other circumstances would be a violation of state obligations. But note that this is only the effect of a *valid* derogation. In permitting the temporary curtailment of human rights, the point is also to regulate and restrict it. Provisions for derogation are included in six human rights treaties: the International Covenant on Civil and Political Rights,[16] the European Convention on Human Rights,[17] the Revised European Social Charter,[18] the American Convention on Human Rights,[19] the Commonwealth of Independent States Convention on Human Rights and Fundamental Freedoms,[20] and the Arab Charter of Human Rights (not yet in force).[21] At the same time, as indicated, emergency measures are regulated under customary international law. In this regard, the obligations that follow from non-treaty obligations to protect human rights have been clarified in a series of influential instruments. These instruments mostly take the form of guidelines for the legitimate promulgation and implementation of emergency regimes, and can be found in reports of the UN Special Rapporteur on Human Rights and States of Emergency,[22] along with unofficial, 'expert' statements, such as the Paris Minimum Standards of Human Rights Norms in a State of Emergency,[23] and the Turku Declaration on Minimum Humanitarian Standards.[24]

Despite some divergences and differences of focus, these various derogation provisions and emergency guidelines establish a substantially common framework for the regulation of emergency measures. Article 4 of the Civil and Political Rights Covenant will serve as a guide to the key features of this. Under article 4(1):

In time of public emergency which threatens the life of the nation and the existence of which is officially proclaimed, the States Parties to the present

[15] See further J. Fitzpatrick, *Human Rights In Crisis* (Philadelphia: University of Pennsylvania Press, 1994); and A.-L. Svensson-McCarthy, *The International Law of Human Rights and States of Exception* (Dordrecht: Martinus Nijhoff, 1998).

[16] Art. 4.   [17] Art. 15.   [18] Part V., art. F.   [19] Art. 27.
[20] Art. 35.   [21] Arts. 4(b) and (c).
[22] See esp. the Special Rapporteur's Tenth Report, UN Doc. E/CN.4/Sub.2/1997/19.
[23] International Law Association, Report of the Sixty-First Conference, London, 1985, 56.   [24] See UN Doc. E/CN.4/1995/116.

Covenant may take measures derogating from their obligations under the present Covenant to the extent strictly required by the exigencies of the situation, provided that such measures are not inconsistent with their other obligations under international law and do not involve discrimination solely on the ground of race, colour, sex, language, religion or social origin.

From this paragraph and others like it, a number of principles are generally drawn. First, derogation will only be justified where there is a 'public emergency which threatens the life of the nation' (the principle of exceptionality). Secondly, that emergency must be 'officially proclaimed' (the principle of publicity). Thirdly, the emergency measures must be 'strictly required by the exigencies of the situation' (the principle of proportionality). This is understood to entail that the derogation must be necessary, as well as proportionate to the circumstances said to demand it. Fourthly, the emergency measures must be 'not inconsistent with [the state's] other obligations under international law' (the principle of consistency). Among these other obligations will be obligations under international humanitarian law, and also under other treaties from which derogation is not permitted, such as the International Covenant on Economic, Social and Cultural Rights and the International Convention on the Rights of the Child. Fifthly, the emergency measures must not involve discrimination on whatever grounds are specified in the article permitting derogation (the principle of non-discrimination). In the case of article 4(1), the grounds are 'race, colour, sex, language, religion or social origin'. An additional procedural principle laid down in article 4(3), which applies also under the other derogation provisions, is that the emergency measures must be notified to the depositary of the relevant treaty (the principle of notification). With regard to derogations under article 4, this means that they must be notified to the UN Secretary-General. The point of this is obviously to enable monitoring of derogation from human rights obligations.

These principles place significant limits on the extent to which, in Ackerman's phrase, governments can 'run wild during emergencies'. Perhaps the most important safeguards against this, however, are reflected in article 4(2):

No derogation from articles 6 [the right to life], 7 [the prohibition on torture and cruel, inhuman or degrading treatment and punishment], 8 (paragraphs 1 and 2) [the prohibition on slavery], 11 [the right not to be imprisoned for non-fulfilment of a contractual obligation], 15 [the prohibition on retrospective application of criminal law], 16 [the right to recognition as a legal person] and 18 [the right to freedom of thought, conscience and religion] may be made under this provision.

As this makes clear, certain rights are not subject to derogation in any circumstances. While the list of non-derogable rights is not identical in all the various treaties that allow derogation, nor in all the instruments that deal with emergency measures by reference to customary international law obligations in the field of human rights, the principle of consistency tends to ensure that a highest common denominator of non-derogability prevails. In an influential General Comment of the Human Rights Committee, issued in August 2001, the Committee emphasises and elaborates on this aspect of article 4.[25] Of particular importance is the non-derogability of the right to life, the prohibition on torture and cruel, inhuman or degrading treatment and punishment, and the right to freedom of thought, conscience and religion. In the corresponding provision of the American Convention on Human Rights, it is provided that, alongside these and other non-derogable rights, the status of non-derogability also attaches to 'the judicial guarantees essential for the protection of such rights'.[26] This has been held to encompass the idea that the right to seek a judicial determination of the lawfulness of detention (*habeas corpus*) may never be abrogated.[27] While no such stipulation is included in article 4 of the Civil and Political Rights Covenant, the Committee considers that it is implicit in article 4(2) and, indeed, in the Covenant as a whole, that procedural guarantees must always remain in place to protect non-derogable rights.[28] In consequence, access to a court, along with other fundamental safeguards against arbitrary detention and principles of due process must themselves be counted among the rights from which no derogation is permissible.

Applying the corresponding provision in the European Convention on Human Rights (article 15), the European Court of Human Rights

---

[25] Human Rights Committee, General Comment 29 (States of emergency: art. 4), 24 July 2001.   [26] Art. 27(2).

[27] See *Habeas Corpus in Emergency Situations*, Advisory Opinion of the Inter-American Court of Human Rights, OC-8/87, 30 January 1987.

[28] Human Rights Committee, General Comment 29 (States of emergency: art. 4), 24 July 2001, para. 15. See also paras. 11 and 16.

has accepted that terrorism justifies derogation in a number of cases. These have arisen out of measures implemented in the United Kingdom and Turkey. However, in a complaint brought by Ireland against the United Kingdom in the 1970s, the Court had occasion to observe that this leaves unaffected state obligations with respect to the prohibition on torture and inhuman or degrading treatment and punishment.[29] More recently, in a series of complaints against Turkey, the Court has also confirmed that derogation will not excuse prolonged incommunicado detention. In one case, some of the applicants were held incommunicado for at least 23 days.[30] While the Court accepted that Turkey had grounds for lodging a notice of derogation under article 15 of the Convention, it considered that in this respect the measures adopted contravened the principle of proportionality. Incommunicado detention for such a lengthy period could not be regarded as 'strictly required by the exigencies' of the crisis on which the respondent government relied. In another case, the applicant was held incommunicado for at least 14 days, and during this time was tortured.[31] Emphasising the importance of procedural safeguards, the Court observed that the denial of access to a lawyer, doctor, relative or friend, coupled with the absence of any realistic possibility of challenging the detention before a court, meant that the applicant had been 'left completely at the mercy of those holding him'.[32] For the Court, as for the Human Rights Committee, the non-derogability of the prohibition on torture and inhuman or degrading treatment and punishment implies that basic procedural guarantees must always remain in place. In the Court's words, 'prompt judicial intervention may lead to the detection and prevention of serious ill-treatment, which . . . is prohibited by the Convention in absolute and non-derogable terms'.[33]

To this point, we have been focusing on the ways in which international human rights law seeks to combine 'hard-headed doctrine' with

[29] *Ireland v United Kingdom*, Judgment of the European Court of Human Rights, 18 January 1978.

[30] *Demir & Ors. v Turkey*, Judgment of the European Court of Human Rights, 23 August 1998.

[31] *Aksoy v Turkey*, Judgment of the European Court of Human Rights, 18 December 1996.   [32] Ibid., para. 83.

[33] Ibid., para. 76.

stipulations that stop governments 'running wild'—or, to recall some of Ackerman's other phrases, the ways in which human rights law sets aside 'pedantic respect for civil liberties' so as to prevent 'government paralysis', while also 'putting many extreme measures off-limits'. To some observers, derogation provisions remain still too pedantic in their respect for civil liberties. To others, paralysis is a less realistic fear here than repression, and these provisions do too little to restrain governments. How, then, should we understand and evaluate these provisions? Is derogation more a matter of protecting human rights or legitimating government action? Notices of derogation under the European Convention and the Civil and Political Rights Covenant lodged by the Government of the United Kingdom in December 2001 prompt reflection on this question.[34] The derogations were made in connection with legislation providing for the indefinite detention of non-nationals 'suspected of involvement in international terrorism'. The legislation was subsequently used as a basis for the long-term detention of a number of individuals at Belmarsh prison and other high-security facilities. Under the European Convention, non-nationals may be held so long as 'action is being taken [against them] with a view to deportation'.[35] The rationale of the derogation was that the legislation concerned non-nationals against whom action could not be taken with a view to deportation, since, if deported, the individuals involved would face the risk of torture or other ill-treatment in the place to which they were sent, and under established principles of Convention law that in turn would entail a breach of United Kingdom obligations under the Convention.[36] In its notice of derogation the British Government referred to UN Security Council resolution 1373, and asserted that '[t]here exists a terrorist threat to the United Kingdom from persons suspected of involvement in international terrorism. In particular, there are foreign nationals present in the United Kingdom who are suspected [of involvement in international terrorism] and who are a threat to the national security of the United Kingdom'.

---

[34] Note Verbale registered at the Council of Europe, 18 December 2001; Notification of the United Kingdom's Derogation from Article 9 of the International Covenant on Civil and Political Rights, 18 December 2001.   [35] Art. 5(1)(f).

[36] See *Chahal v United Kingdom*, Judgment of the European Court of Human Rights, 15 November 1996.

Security and human rights

What is the relationship between human rights, counter-terrorism and national security? In August 2003 the UN High Commissioner for Human Rights published a large document entitled 'Digest of Jurisprudence of the UN and Regional Organizations on the Protection of Human Rights While Countering Terrorism'.[37] In the introductory section of this document, it is explained that derogation provisions and emergency guidelines are part of a process by which '[h]uman rights law has sought to strike a fair balance between legitimate national security concerns and the protection of fundamental freedoms'.[38] From this perspective, the problem with counter-terrorism is that the measures adopted sometimes tilt the balance too heavily in favour of national security; sometimes too much freedom is taken away. That is a very familiar analysis, and it has obvious appeal. Yet there are a number of grounds for wondering whether the idea that what is needed is a balance between human rights and national security is really the most accurate and helpful way of expressing the challenge we confront.

In the first place, the call for a balance between human rights and national security concentrates attention on the total quantity or *aggregate* of freedom that remains to be enjoyed once security measures are put in place. Yet what is in issue is also the *distribution* of that freedom among individuals and groups. In an article about the counter-terrorist measures introduced or proposed in the United States after September 11, Ronald Dworkin argues that 'the familiar metaphors of "trade-off" and "balance" are deeply misleading', insofar as they suggest that ' "we"— Americans in general—must decide what mixture of security and personal freedom we want for ourselves'.[39] In reality, however:

None of the administration's decisions and proposals will affect more than a tiny number of American citizens: almost none of us will be indefinitely detained for minor violations or offenses, or have our houses searched without our knowledge, or find ourselves brought before military tribunals on grave charges carrying the death penalty. Most of us pay almost nothing in personal freedom when such measures are used against those the President suspects of terrorism.[40]

---

[37] Available at www.unhchr.ch/html/menu6/2/digest.doc.   [38] Ibid., 3.
[39] R. Dworkin, 'The Threat to Patriotism', *New York Review of Books*, 28 February 2002, 44, 48.   [40] Ibid.

Further reinforcing this point is the fact that some of the measures to which Dworkin refers apply exclusively to non-citizens, in the manner of those aspects of the United Kingdom legislation mentioned above. Dworkin concludes that the question actually faced is not how much freedom should be traded for how much security, or 'where our interest lies on balance'. It is 'what justice requires', what fairness demands, and what is involved in this context in treating everyone with equal concern and respect.[41] If this is right, then the problem posed by counter-terrorism is not just equilibrium, but also equality, and not just freedom, but also justice.

That said, the problem is also freedom, and in another sense the kind of measures to which Dworkin refers do affect all citizens. This is because of the danger that emergency will transmute into normality. One circumstance in which that can happen is when emergency measures are extended indefinitely, so that they become effectively permanent. But another is when measures originally justified as necessary to deal with exceptional conditions become part of the ordinary law. An example is the limitation of the 'right to silence' in the United Kingdom. The principle that adverse inferences may not be drawn from silence under police questioning was originally qualified in connection with legislative responses to the 'Troubles' in Northern Ireland; however, this qualification was later expanded to cover anyone under police questioning in England or Wales. Secondly, then, the balancing approach is inadequate because it treats the issue of the relationship between human rights and national security in a synchronic manner, focusing on its character at a particular moment. Yet experience suggests that the significance of emergency measures for human rights also needs to be considered diachronically, with a view to the effects over time. What needs to be taken into account is that emergency measures have a tendency to escape their original context, and become engines of a general levelling down in the protection of human rights.

Our third point is linked to this. Thinking in terms of a balance between human rights and national security is problematic because it leads us to assume that counter-terrorist measures really do weigh on the side of—in the sense of improving the prospects for—security. As many have observed, however, this is not an assumption we can safely make. Rather, we have to consider the possibility that the enterprise of combating terrorism

[41] Ibid.

may itself contribute to insecurity. One way it may do that is by oversimplifying analysis, flattening out specificity, and reifying terrorist activity as a thing that exists in isolation from its context and determinants. As Conor Gearty explains, 'the language of terrorism is the enemy of context, forcing the analysis of any situation down a blind alley of anger at certain violence and blindness towards the rest. It blinkers the discussion of any particular political problem which has manifested itself in violence by compelling a concentration on that violence to the exclusion of the broader picture.'[42] Viewed through the optic of counter-terrorism, subversive violence appears as a prepolitical fact or force of nature, rather than a social phenomenon and product of historical conditions. It appears as something we must repress, but cannot hope to understand. Yet, as we know from Sigmund Freud, as well as from our own personal experience, repression only leads to displacement. Ultimately, ending subversive violence depends on examining it as the outcome of processes that may involve and implicate us.

Let us mention one final misgiving about the idea of a balance between human rights and national security, which has to do with the implicit message that, if only the right balance can be maintained, the dangers posed by counter-terrorism will disappear. To return to a point we raised at the beginning of this discussion, the challenge from this perspective is to keep the T-word in its proper place. That is to say, it is to prevent conceptual inflation, by holding the line on what really constitutes terrorism. Yet terrorism will always exceed the limits of our efforts to hold the line on what really constitutes it. In part that is because it is a contested concept, which is inseparable from disagreements about the legitimacy of violence in particular contexts. But in part it is also because terrorism is a *justificatory* concept, the distinctiveness of which lies in its capacity to exploit fears and mobilise support for the introduction of laws and procedures that would otherwise be unacceptable. To portray the problem in terms of imbalance, misuse, or conceptual inflation is to miss the character of terrorism as—in Gearty's phrase—a 'verbal Trojan horse'.[43] With it comes the 'self-justifying authoritarianism of the exigencies of "counter-terrorism"'. And with that, in turn, comes the danger of 'quietly, apparently morally, destroying all unacceptable dissent'.[44]

[42] C. Gearty, *The Future of Terrorism* (London: Phoenix, 1997), 24.
[43] Ibid., 55.   [44] Ibid., 56.

Torture

In 1874 Victor Hugo declared that torture had 'ceased to exist'.[1] Until about a century earlier, the practice of torture had been central to the administration of criminal justice in Europe. Suspects would be 'put to the question' on the basis that only confessions could establish truth, and only torture could produce valid confessions. From the early 18th century, however, European states began to enact legislation to abolish the use of torture. This reform had been urged by Voltaire, Montesquieu and perhaps most famously Cesare Beccaria, who wrote at length on the immorality and irrationality of treating torture as the 'crucible of truth'.[2] When abolition came, it was widely celebrated as a sign of newly enlightened consciousness. More recent historiography offers a somewhat different perspective, relating the abolition of torture to the changing structure of power in the late modern world and, in particular, to the emergence of a new system of social control which no longer depended on hurting people's bodies but set its sights instead on the more ambitious project of reprogramming their minds. Either way, the upshot was that by the end of the 19th century torture had been largely displaced from the ordinary criminal law.

Despite this, Victor Hugo spoke, of course, far too glibly, and too soon. He may have been partly right, in that the incidence of torture appears to have declined significantly in Europe in the last decades of the 19th century. But it continued to be used in European colonies and elsewhere. And it spectacularly recrudesced throughout the world in the 20th century. During this period, regimes of systematic torture were established that dwarfed in scale, scope and sophistication the much more limited uses of torture of earlier times. These regimes also differed

[1] Quoted in E. Peters, *Torture* (Philadelphia: University of Pennsylvania Press, 1996), 5.

[2] See C. Beccaria (R. Davies, trans.), *On Crimes and Punishments and Other Writings*, edited by R. Bellamy (Cambridge: Cambridge University Press, 1995), 39.

from earlier practices in another respect. They moved torture into the shadowy realm of 'intelligence operations' carried out by 'security police' at 'interrogation centres', generally on an undisclosed or at any rate unacknowledged basis. In the 21st century, one notable development so far is that this aspect has come under strain. With the advent of digital photography and the possibility for circulating images by electronic means, torture has taken on renewed, and indeed unprecedented, visibility. These things said, it has not generally been reintroduced as part of ordinary criminal procedure. The abolitionist laws first passed in Europe in the early 18th century now extend worldwide, and are reinforced by an international framework of norms and institutions aimed at the elimination of torture. In what follows we examine that international legal framework. At the same time, we take stock of the fact that, notwithstanding changes since Beccaria's day, the idea he denounced of torture as the crucible of truth has not disappeared.

Prohibition and criminalisation

The international legal prohibition of torture is a multifaceted norm, the basis at once of an internationally protected human right, a duty imposed on those engaged in armed conflict, and a form of international criminal liability. Let us consider each of these facets in turn.

The right not to be tortured is part of a broader right not to be subjected to torture or to inhuman or degrading treatment or punishment. This is sometimes expressed in terms of the right to personal integrity, and is also reflected in specific guarantees of the right to humane treatment whilst in detention. Thus, the Universal Declaration of Human Rights proclaims in article 5 that '[n]o one shall be subjected to torture or to cruel, inhuman or degrading treatment or punishment'. The International Covenant on Civil and Political Rights repeats this stipulation in article 7, and also states in article 10(1) that '[a]ll persons deprived of their liberty shall be treated with humanity and with respect for the inherent dignity of the human person'. The various regional human rights systems contain similar provisions. All guarantee the right not to be subjected to torture or to inhuman or degrading treatment or punishment (see the African Charter of Human and Peoples' Rights;[3] American Convention on

___

[3] Art. 5.

Human Rights;[4] and European Convention on Human Rights).[5] In addition, the American Convention and African Charter explicitly assert the right to personal integrity,[6] while the American Convention joins the Civil and Political Rights Covenant in making specific reference to the right to humane treatment of those who are deprived of their liberty.[7]

In all of these treaties the right not to be subjected to torture or to inhuman or degrading treatment or punishment is guaranteed in absolute terms. That is to say, it contains no qualifying conditions under which restrictions may legitimately be imposed. It is also exempted from the application of 'derogation' provisions, under which governments are permitted to take measures that do not meet normal standards of human rights protection in order to deal with the exigencies of a war or other 'public emergency'. Thus, wherever derogation is allowed, a proviso is attached to the effect that this does not apply to a series of rights which invariably include the right not to be ill-treated. Pointing to these features, human rights courts and supervisory bodies have repeatedly stressed the absolute, unqualified and non-derogable nature of the right not to be subjected to torture or to inhuman or degrading treatment or punishment. In the words of the Human Rights Committee, 'no justification or extenuating circumstances may be invoked to excuse a violation' of this right.[8] One implication of this, highlighted by the European Court of Human Rights, is that the 'requirements of [a criminal] investigation and the undeniable difficulties inherent in the fight against crime, particularly with regard to terrorism, cannot result in limits being placed on the protection to be afforded in respect of the physical integrity of individuals'.[9] We will return to this aspect later.

Alongside stipulations of the kind just mentioned within larger catalogues of human rights, there also exist a number of treaties and other instruments that have been specifically adopted to address torture and related issues. The Convention against Torture and Other Cruel, Inhuman or Degrading Treatment or Punishment obliges states parties

[4] Art. 5(2).   [5] Art. 3.   [6] See arts. 5(1) and 4 respectively.

[7] See art. 5(2). See also American Declaration of the Rights and Duties of Man, art. XXV.

[8] Human Rights Committee, General Comment 20 (replaces General Comment 7 concerning prohibition of torture and cruel treatment or punishment: art. 7), 10 March 1992, para. 3.

[9] *Tomasi v France*, Judgment of the European Court of Human Rights, 25 June 1992, para. 115.

to take a series of steps designed to protect and enforce the right not to be subjected to torture.[10] We outline some of these in the succeeding section. For the present, it is sufficient to note that a key aim of this treaty is to reverse the impunity which is commonly enjoyed by those responsible for acts of torture. Even if the latter are not prosecuted in their home country, the Torture Convention seeks to ensure that they can, and will, be prosecuted wherever else they may go in the world. To this end, states parties are obliged to make torture a criminal offence within their national law,[11] and to establish jurisdiction with respect to that offence. Jurisdiction must be established in cases where the act was committed on their territory or by one of their nationals;[12] at the same time, it must also be established in cases where those connections are lacking but a person alleged to be responsible for acts of torture is present within their territory and they do not extradite him or her.[13] Faced with an allegation of torture in relation to someone within its territory, a state party's obligation is then to undertake an investigation and, if the circumstances so warrant, arrest that person,[14] and either extradite him or her for trial in another state or, failing extradition, submit the case to its own prosecutorial authorities.[15] This is the so-called 'extradite or prosecute' rule. In the Americas, a similar approach structures the Inter-American Convention to Prevent and Punish Torture.

A different approach is followed in the European Convention for the Prevention of Torture and Inhuman or Degrading Treatment or Punishment, and in the 2002 Protocol to the Convention against Torture and Other Cruel, Inhuman or Degrading Treatment or Punishment. Whereas the focus of the Torture Convention and the Inter-American Convention is on combating impunity and ensuring prosecution, the focus of these two more recent treaties is on the prevention of torture through on-site monitoring.[16] Both treaties set up bodies which are

[10] Regarding this Convention, see further A. Boulesbaa, *The UN Convention on Torture and the Prospects for Enforcement* (The Hague: Nijhoff, 1999).

[11] Art. 4. This obligation extends to attempt, complicity and participation. See art. 4(1).

[12] Art. 5(1). Jurisdiction may also be established in cases where the act was committed against one of their nationals.   [13] Art. 5(2).

[14] Art. 6.   [15] Art. 7.

[16] Regarding the European Convention for the Prevention of Torture, see M.D. Evans & R. Morgan, *Preventing Torture: A Study of the European Convention for the Prevention of Torture and Inhuman or Degrading Treatment or Punishment* (Oxford: Oxford University Press 1998).

mandated to visit places where detainees are held, and to make recommendations for strengthening the protection of detainees from torture or other ill-treatment. The 2002 Protocol also requires states parties to set up national bodies with a corresponding mandate. Outside the framework of these treaties, visits to places where torture is alleged to be widespread and systematic can also be proposed by the UN Special Rapporteur on Torture. Established by the UN Commission on Human Rights in 1985, the role of the Special Rapporteur includes raising specific allegations with governments, and preparing reports on issues relevant to the eradication of torture. Reports frequently contain detailed findings, based on visits to the countries concerned.

As the work of the Special Rapporteur confirms, the right not to be tortured entails obligations for all states, whether or not they are parties to any relevant treaty. Indeed, the prohibition of torture is widely considered to have the status of a principle of *jus cogens* or 'peremptory' norm of general international law.[17] By this is meant that it is not only binding on all states; it is also a norm from which no derogation is permitted, so that any treaty purporting to derogate from it would be void. In connection with this norm and with the various treaty provisions mentioned earlier, a series of resolutions of international and regional organisations have been adopted that lend specificity to the right not to be tortured and its implications for governments and others. These include resolutions of the UN General Assembly and other UN bodies setting out detailed standards for the treatment of detainees,[18] codes of conduct for law enforcement officials,[19] and relevant principles of medical ethics to be taken into account by doctors and other health workers.[20] Key elements

---

[17] See *Prosecutor v Furundžija*, Case IT-95-17/1-T, Judgment of the International Criminal Tribunal for the former Yugoslavia, 10 December 1998, para. 153.

[18] Body of Principles for the Protection of All Persons under Any Form of Detention or Imprisonment, adopted by UN GA Res. 43/173, 9 December 1988; Basic Principles for the Treatment of Prisoners, adopted and proclaimed by UN GA Res. 45/111, 14 December 1990. See also Standard Minimum Rules for the Treatment of Prisoners, approved by ECOSOC Res. 663C (XXIV), 31 July 1957, and amended by ECOSOC Res. 2076 (LXII), 13 May 1977.

[19] Code of Conduct for Law Enforcement Officials, adopted by UN GA Res. 34/169, 17 December 1979.

[20] Principles of Medical Ethics relevant to the Role of Health Personnel, particularly Physicians, in the Protection of Prisoners and Detainees against Torture and Other Cruel, Inhuman or Degrading Treatment or Punishment, adopted by UN GA Res. 37/194, 18 December 1982.

have recently been distilled in two texts: the Guidelines and Measures for the Prohibition and Prevention of Torture, Cruel, Inhuman or Degrading Treatment or Punishment in Africa, elaborated at a meeting held on Robben Island, South Africa;[21] and the Principles on the Effective Investigation and Documentation of Torture and Other Cruel, Inhuman or Degrading Treatment or Punishment, annexed to a resolution of the UN General Assembly in 2000.[22]

We have so far been considering torture as a violation of internationally protected human rights. However, as indicated earlier, the prohibition on torture is also the basis for a duty imposed on all those involved in armed conflict. In the context of international armed conflict, people who engage in acts of torture or inhuman treatment against prisoners of war and other detainees commit grave breaches of the Geneva Conventions.[23] The Conventions impose a duty on states parties to search for individuals alleged to have committed or ordered grave breaches, and to prosecute those individuals.[24] Grave breaches may also be punished as war crimes under national law,[25] as well as before the International Criminal Court.[26] The Rome Statute additionally provides that torture can be prosecuted as a war crime before the International Criminal Court where it is committed in the context of civil war or other non-international armed conflict.[27] This is the case, whether the accused was fighting on the government side or with the insurgents. At the same time, jurisdiction is also conferred on the International Criminal Court with respect to acts of torture committed outside the context of armed conflict, where the acts constitute a crime against humanity. This depends upon whether they were committed 'as part of a widespread or systematic attack directed against any civilian population, with knowledge of the attack'.[28] The Rome Statute provides a definition of torture for this purpose, according to which torture refers to the 'intentional infliction of severe pain or suffering, whether physical or mental,

---

[21] Adopted by the African Commission on Human and Peoples' Rights, 23 October 2002.   [22] Annexed to UN GA Res. 55/89, 4 December 2000.

[23] See arts. 130 and 147 of the Third and Fourth Geneva Conventions of 1949 respectively. Further grave breaches are established in arts. 11 and 85 of Protocol I of 1977.

[24] See arts. 49, 50, 129 and 146 of the four Geneva Conventions of 1949 respectively.

[25] See, e.g., US War Crimes Act, as amended in 1997, introducing Section 2441 in Title 18 of the US Code.   [26] Art. 8(2)(a)(ii). See also art. 8(2)(b)(xxi) and (xxii).

[27] Art. 8(2)(c)(i). See also art. 8(2)(e)(vi) and (xi).   [28] Art. 7(1)(f).

upon a person in the custody or under the control of the accused'.[29] War crimes and crimes against humanity involving torture have been the subject of numerous prosecutions before the International Criminal Tribunal for the former Yugoslavia and the International Criminal Tribunal for Rwanda.

At the same time, international criminal liability with respect to torture can also be invoked in national courts. Many states have legislation which provides for extraterritorial jurisdiction to try those suspected of torture. Under this legislation, jurisdiction is exercised notwithstanding that the acts in issue took place abroad, and were committed by non-nationals. We noted above that jurisdiction of this kind is demanded by the Torture Convention. It is also required to be introduced under the Inter-American Convention to Prevent and Punish Torture. More recently, the International Criminal Tribunal for the former Yugoslavia has stated that this type of national jurisdiction is likewise permissible outside the framework of those treaties: 'it would seem that one of the consequences of the *jus cogens* character bestowed by the international community upon the prohibition of torture is that every State is entitled to investigate, prosecute and punish or extradite individuals accused of torture, who are present in a territory under its jurisdiction'.[30] These things said, attempts in a number of western European countries to secure the extradition or prosecution of heads of state and other high-level Ministers for involvement in torture or other international crimes have mostly failed. In the case of an incumbent Foreign Minister, the International Court of Justice has determined that the principle of sovereign immunity bars criminal proceedings before the courts of another state.[31] In the case of a former head of state, the proceedings in England against General Pinochet did not result in the General's extradition for trial in Spain. But they did point to the important possibility that, once a head of state ceases to hold office, sovereign immunity may not apply to prevent extradition or prosecution on charges of torture.[32]

---

[29] Art. 7(2)(e).

[30] *Prosecutor v Furundžija* (Case IT-95-17/1-T), Judgment of the International Criminal Tribunal for the Former Yugoslavia, 10 December 1998, para. 156.

[31] *Democratic Republic of the Congo v Belgium*, Judgment of the International Court of Justice, 14 February 2002.

[32] *R v Bow Street Metropolitan Stipendiary Magistrate and Others, ex parte Pinochet Ugarte (No. 3)* [1999] 2 Weekly Law Reports 827.

The right not to be tortured

Let us now examine in more detail the scope of the right not to be tortured in international human rights law. What kind of conduct is covered? What obligations are entailed for governments and others? With respect to this second question, particular attention is today focused on the issue of safeguards and other precautionary measures which must be put in place to ensure that torture does not occur.

Conduct

As indicated earlier, the right not to be tortured is part of a broader right not to be subjected to torture or to inhuman or degrading treatment or punishment. In dealing with complaints against states parties to the International Covenant on Civil and Political Rights, the Human Rights Committee has not generally found it necessary to distinguish between these various forms of ill-treatment. Thus, where an applicant has been treated or punished in a manner inconsistent with article 7 of the Covenant, the Human Rights Committee has simply said so, without specifying that the conduct constituted torture or one of the other categories of prohibited ill-treatment.[33] By contrast, the European Court of Human Rights has been anxious to stress the existence of a 'special stigma' where torture is concerned. An early statement of this appeared in 1977. Following a complaint by Ireland, the Court considered interrogation methods used by United Kingdom officials at detention centres in Northern Ireland.[34] The European Commission on Human Rights had earlier concluded that these methods involved torture. For the Court, it was necessary to 'have regard to the distinction, embodied in Article 3 [of the Convention], between this notion [torture] and that of inhuman or degrading treatment'.[35] In its assessment, the distinction 'derives principally from a difference in the intensity of the suffering inflicted',

---

[33] See, e.g., *El-Megreisi v Libyan Arab Jamahiriya*, Communication 440/1990, Views of the Human Rights Committee, adopted 23 March 2004, in which the Committee concluded that Mr El-Megreisi, 'by being subjected to prolonged incommunicado detention in an unknown location, is the victim of torture and cruel and inhuman treatment, in violation of articles 7 and 10, paragraph 1, of the Covenant'. See para. 5.4.

[34] *Ireland v United Kingdom*, Judgment of the European Court of Human Rights, 13 December 1977.   [35] Ibid., para. 167.

for 'it appears ... that it was the intention that the Convention, with its distinction between "torture" and "inhuman or degrading treatment", should by the first of these terms attach a special stigma to deliberate inhuman treatment causing very serious and cruel suffering.'[36] With respect to the interrogation methods in issue in this case, the Court accepted that they constituted inhuman and degrading treatment, but considered that they 'did not occasion suffering of the particular intensity and cruelty implied by the word torture as so understood'.[37] Accordingly, the United Kingdom Government was adjudged responsible for inhuman and degrading treatment, but not torture. Inasmuch as this judgment was celebrated by some as a 'triumph' for the Government,[38] it appears that attaching a special stigma to torture may carry the risk of sanctifying the idea that other forms of violence are broadly acceptable.

The European Court of Human Rights has, however, observed that the boundary between inhuman and degrading treatment, on the one hand, and torture, on the other, is not fixed. In a complaint against France, decided in 1999, the Court noted that 'certain acts which were classified in the past as "inhuman and degrading treatment" as opposed to "torture" could be classified differently in future'.[39] In its view, the 'increasingly high standard being required in the area of the protection of human rights and fundamental liberties correspondingly and inevitably requires greater firmness' in the qualification of violations.[40] The applicant in this case had been severely assaulted while in police custody. There were medical certificates recording his injuries. However, in subsequent proceedings against the police officers concerned, the latter claimed that he had sustained the injuries resisting arrest, and the French Government pointed out that the national courts had not yet ruled finally on this claim. For the European Court, the outcome of national proceedings against officials involved could not affect the responsibility of the state. What counted was that no satisfactory explanation had been provided for the injuries sustained. Reiterating a point made on a number of previous occasions, the Court declared that, 'where an individual is taken into police custody in good health but is found to be injured at the time of release, it is incumbent on

---

[36] Ibid.   [37] Ibid.

[38] See reference to an article in *The Daily Telegraph* in J. Conroy, 'The Internment', *Granta*, Spring 1992, 223.

[39] *Selmouni v France*, Judgment of the European Court of Human Rights, 28 July 1999, para. 101.   [40] Ibid.

the State to provide a plausible explanation of how those injuries were caused, failing which a clear issue arises under Article 3 of the Convention'.[41] Here the seriousness of the injuries was considered to justify the conclusion that acts of torture had indeed occurred.[42]

Beyond the right not to be ill-treated, the specificity of torture is unavoidably confronted where one is dealing with the international crime of torture. Under the Torture Convention, torture is defined as:

any act by which severe pain or suffering, whether physical or mental, is intentionally inflicted on a person for such purposes as obtaining from him or a third person information or a confession, punishing him for an act he or a third person has committed or is suspected of having committed, or intimidating or coercing him or a third person, or for any reason based on discrimination of any kind, when such pain or suffering is inflicted by or at the instigation of or with the consent or acquiescence of a public official or other person acting in an official capacity . . .[43]

Leaving aside for the moment the issue of the agents involved, this definition points to three elements which feature in most accounts of torture by courts and supervisory bodies concerned with human rights and international criminality. In a judgment rendered in 2002 the International Criminal Tribunal for the former Yugoslavia characterised these constituent elements as follows.

  (i) The infliction, by act or omission, of severe pain or suffering, whether physical or mental.
 (ii) The act or omission must be intentional.
(iii) The act or omission must aim at obtaining information or a confession, or at punishing, intimidating or coercing the victim or a third person, or at discriminating, on any ground, against the victim or a third person.[44]

In this case, three Bosnian Serb soldiers were being tried in connection with the 'sexual enslavement' and repeated rape of a group of Muslim women. The Tribunal observed that the first element was established once rape had been proved, since the act of rape necessarily implies severe pain

---

[41] *Selmouni v France*, Judgment of the European Court of Human Rights, 28 July 1999, para. 87. [42] Ibid., para. 105.
[43] Art. 1(1).
[44] *Prosecutor v Kunarac, Kovac and Vukovic* (Case IT-96-23 & IT-96-23/1-A), Judgment of the International Criminal Tribunal for the former Yugoslavia (Appeals Chamber), 12 June 2002, para. 142.

or suffering.[45] As to the second element, the Tribunal said that, even if the perpetrators' motivations were mixed, it was sufficient that they 'intended to act in a way which, in the normal course of events, would cause severe pain or suffering, whether physical or mental, to [their] victims'.[46] Considering the third element, the Tribunal was clear that the acts had been committed for the purpose of intimidating or coercing the victims, and with intent to discriminate against and subordinate them as Muslims. In the case of one of the soldiers, it considered that the acts had also been committed with the purpose of obtaining information.

Returning now to the issue of the agents involved, it may be noted that article 1(1) of the Torture Convention defines torture in terms that depend on the involvement of public officials, or at least of persons acting in an official capacity. What of torture that does not involve persons who are public officials or others acting in an official capacity? An example of this might be torture by non-state militias. The Committee Against Torture, established to supervise compliance with the Torture Convention, has said that where, in the absence of a central government, armed factions are exercising *de facto* some of the functions normally exercised by a legitimate government, 'the members of those factions can fall, for the purposes of the application of the [Torture] Convention, within the phrase "public officials or other persons acting in an official capacity" contained in article 1'.[47] However, what of the situation where there remains a central government, and those responsible for acts of torture cannot plausibly be characterised as public officials or others acting in an official capacity? According to the International Criminal Tribunal for the former Yugoslavia, the definition in article 1(1) of the Torture Convention should not be read as an exhaustive statement of what counts as torture for all international legal purposes.[48] In the

---

[45] With regard to the character of rape as torture, see also *Aydin v Turkey*, Judgment of the European Court of Human Rights, 25 September 1997.

[46] *Prosecutor v Kunarac, Kovac and Vukovic* (Case IT-96-23 & IT-96-23/1-A), Judgment of the International Criminal Tribunal for the former Yugoslavia (Appeals Chamber), 12 June 2002, para. 153.

[47] *Elmi v Australia*, Communication 120/1998, Views of the Committee Against Torture, adopted 14 May 1999, para. 6.5. The complaint here concerned the threat of torture in Somalia.

[48] *Prosecutor v Kunarac, Kovac and Vukovic* (Case IT-96-23 & IT-96-23/1-A), Judgment of the International Criminal Tribunal for the former Yugoslavia (Appeals Chamber), 12 June 2002, para. 147.

Tribunal's assessment, the definition in article 1(1) does not 'wholly [reflect] customary international law regarding the meaning of the crime of torture generally'.[49] In particular, 'the public official requirement is not a requirement under customary international law in relation to the criminal responsibility of an individual for torture outside the framework of the Torture Convention'.[50] Viewed in this light, the Torture Convention is to be understood as imposing an 'extradite or prosecute' obligation in a limited set of situations, which represent only a subset of those covered by the crime of torture under general or customary international law. Beyond the Torture Convention, conduct by non-state actors may also constitute the crime of torture.

Obligations

Let us turn now to the obligations entailed for states and others by the right not to be tortured. An initial obligation is to prohibit the use of torture. One issue, upon which we have not yet touched, is the imposition of corporal punishment. We have mentioned article 1(1) of the Torture Convention, in which torture is defined for the purpose of the Convention. After setting out the definition, article 1(1) stipulates that for this purpose torture 'does not include pain or suffering arising only from, inherent in or incidental to lawful sanctions'. On one interpretation, the effect of this stipulation is to exclude corporal punishment from the definition of torture, at least where it is prescribed under, and carried out in accordance with, national law, as in this case it is a 'lawful sanction'.[51] In a report of the UN Special Rapporteur on Torture, a different interpretation is put forward. According to the Special Rapporteur, the reference in article 1(1) to 'lawful sanctions' is not a reference to sanctions that are duly authorised under national law; it is a reference to sanctions that have *international* legitimacy. In his words, 'the "lawful sanctions" exclusion must necessarily refer to those sanctions that constitute practices widely accepted as legitimate by the international community, such as

---

[49] *Prosecutor v Kunarac, Kovac and Vukovic* (Case IT-96-23 & IT-96-23/1-A), Judgment of the International Criminal Tribunal for the former Yugoslavia (Appeals Chamber), 12 June 2002, para. 147.   [50] Ibid., para. 148.

[51] On some versions of this interpretation, corporal punishment may nonetheless constitute 'cruel, inhuman or degrading' punishment.

deprivation of liberty through imprisonment, which is common to almost all penal systems'.[52] From this perspective, the point of the 'lawful sanctions' exclusion is to bar the argument that the inherently painful character of such penalties as imprisonment brings them within the definition of torture.[53] The Special Rapporteur makes clear his view that 'corporal punishment is inconsistent with the prohibition of torture and other cruel, inhuman or degrading treatment or punishment'.[54] In a number of countries the legal basis for corporal punishment is Islamic law. According to some scholars, it is not possible, as a matter of Islamic law, to ban the imposition of certain kinds of corporal punishment for certain offences, though the imposition of these punishments can be considerably reduced through more expansive interpretation of norms relating to defences to criminal liability, rules of procedural fairness, and so on.[55]

Beyond the practice of imposing sentences of corporal punishment, there is, of course, the issue of the use of torture against people in detention, especially pre-trial or extra-judicial detention. This is what was at stake in the various cases to which we have referred, and it is central also to the policy debates on which we will later comment. In 1987 a Commission of Inquiry in Israel led by retired judge Moshe Landau reported on interrogation practices then being used by the Israeli security service in connection with counter-terrorism.[56] The Commission approved official directives which in certain circumstances authorised investigators to apply what was referred to a

[52] Nigel Rodley, Report of the Special Rapporteur on Torture, UN Doc. E/CN.4/1997, 10 January 1997, section I.A. See further N.S. Rodley, *The Treatment of Prisoners under International Law* (2nd edn.) (Oxford: Oxford University Press, 1999).

[53] For the argument that a 'trace of "torture"' remains in modern systems of incarceration, see M. Foucault (A. Sheridan, trans.), *Discipline and Punish* (London: Penguin, 1977), 16.

[54] UN Doc. E/CN.4/1997, 10 January 1997, section I.A.

[55] See, e.g., A. An-Na'im, 'Towards a Cross-Cultural Approach to Defining International Standards of Human Rights: The Meaning of Cruel, Inhuman or Degrading Treatment or Punishment' in A. An-Na'im (ed.), *Human Rights in Cross-Cultural Perspectives* (Philadelphia, University of Pennsylvania Press, 1992), 19. On this issue, see further Culture★, Religion★, and Universality★.

[56] *Report of the Commission of Inquiry Regarding the General Security Service's Interrogation Practices With Respect to Hostile Terrorist Activities* (the 'Landau Report'), excerpted in 23 *Israel Law Review* (1989) 146.

'moderate degree of physical pressure'. Among the practices encompassed within this phrase were some that involved serious physical injury and the risk of death. The directives were later challenged before the Supreme Court of Israel. In a judgment rendered in 1999 the Supreme Court ruled that security service investigators were not lawfully authorised to use what for its part it called 'physical means'.[57] Since there was 'no statutory instruction endowing a [security service] investigator with special interrogating powers that are either different or more serious than those given the police investigator',[58] counter-terrorist investigators had to follow normal procedures, and these excluded the practices in question. However, the Court did not rule out that such statutory instruction might be provided in the future, adding that '[i]f it will nonetheless be decided that it is appropriate for Israel, in light of its security difficulties to sanction physical means in interrogations . . ., this is an issue that must be decided by the legislative branch which represents the people. We do not take any stand on this matter at this time.'[59] The Court also drew a distinction between 'the granting of permission to use physical means for interrogation purposes *ab initio*' and 'the ability to potentially escape criminal liability *post factum*', by invoking the defence of 'necessity'.[60] With respect to the latter, the Court made clear that, in the event of criminal charges being brought against a security service officer in connection with counter-terrorist investigations, its decision was not to be read as precluding reliance on the necessity defence. Thus, the judgment left open both the possibility of future legislative enactment authorising torture, and the possibility that security service officers involved in torture might be exonerated from criminal liability.

This brings us to a further aspect of the obligations entailed for states and others by the right not to be tortured. We have already noted the application of the 'extradite or prosecute' rule in this context. The obligation or right to extradite persons suspected of torture has an important obverse, expressed in the Torture Convention in article 3(1): 'No State Party shall expel, return ("refouler") or extradite a person to

---

[57] *Public Committee Against Torture in Israel and Others v State of Israel and Others*, Judgment of the Supreme Court of Israel, 6 September 1999.   [58] Ibid., para. 32.

[59] Ibid., para. 39.

[60] Ibid., para. 14. The Court stated that this distinction had been accepted by all the applicants in the case.

another State where there are substantial grounds for believing that he would be in danger of being subjected to torture.' Explaining this provision in a General Comment on article 3, the Committee Against Torture has said that the obligation not to expel, return or extradite people to states in which there is a substantial risk of their facing torture applies not only to the state to which a person is immediately expelled etc., but also to any other state to the authorities of which he or she may subsequently be turned over.[61] With respect to the risk which engages the obligation, the Committee has said that this should be 'personal and present',[62] to an extent that goes 'beyond mere theory or suspicion', but need not 'meet the test of being highly probable'.[63] In a case to which we have already referred above, the Committee considered a complaint by a person whom the Australian authorities were proposing to return to Somalia.[64] The applicant alleged that, if returned there, he would be in danger of torture at the hands of armed factions. The Committee accepted this claim, and also accepted the applicant's argument that, in the absence of a central government in Somalia, members of armed factions should be regarded as public officials or other persons acting in an official capacity for the purpose of article 1(1) of the Convention. On this basis, the Australian authorities were said to be under an obligation not to return the applicant to Somalia. While other treaties do not contain an explicit stipulation along the lines of article 3 of the Torture Convention, the idea that people must not be deported or extradited to countries in which they face a serious risk of torture has been seen as implicit in the prohibition of torture. To give one example, the European Court of Human Rights rendered judgment in 1996 on an application by a person whom the United Kingdom authorities were proposing to deport to India, in circumstances where there was a real risk that he would face torture there.[65] The Court held that the applicant's deportation would violate the obligation of the United Kingdom with regard to torture and other ill-treatment under article 3 of the European Convention.

---

[61] Committee Against Torture, General Comment 1 (Implementation of art. 3 of the Convention in the context of art. 22: art. 3), 21 November 1997, para. 2.

[62] Para. 7.   [63] Para. 6.

[64] *Elmi v Australia*, Communication 120/1998, Views of the Committee Against Torture, adopted 14 May 1999, para. 6.5.

[65] *Chahal v United Kingdom*, Judgment of the European Court of Human Rights, 26 October 1996.

To this point we have noted the obligation of states to prohibit and criminalise torture and to refrain from deporting, expelling or extraditing people to countries where they will be at risk of torture. In tandem with these obligations, considerable prominence is given in all discussions of torture to a range of further issues relevant to the prevention of torture. The obligation to take steps to prevent torture is made explicit in the Torture Convention (article 2(1)): 'Each State Party shall take effective legislative, administrative, judicial or other measures to prevent acts of torture in any territory under its jurisdiction.' Again, however, this simply expresses what is regarded as implicit in other treaties and general international human rights law. Certainly, it is widely recognised that effective protection of the right not to be tortured calls for more than prohibition, criminalisation, and *non-refoulement*. In the first place, attention is required to procedural safeguards regarding arrest and detention. As Amnesty International has long argued, incommunicado detention sets the scene for torture. To protect detainees from acts of torture, procedures must be put in place to ensure that people who are arrested are brought promptly before a court. They must also have the right of access to a lawyer, the right to independent medical examination, and the right to seek *habeas corpus* while in detention. The requirement that a family member or friend be informed of the arrest is also considered crucial. In one case before the European Court of Human Rights, the applicant had been detained incommunicado in Turkey for at least 14 days, during which time he had been tortured.[66] The Court highlighted the link between disregard for the right to personal liberty and security and vulnerability to torture. In its words, 'the denial of access to a lawyer, doctor, relative or friend and the absence of any realistic possibility of being brought before a court to test the legality of the detention meant that [the applicant] was left completely at the mercy of those holding him'.[67]

Secondly, effective protection of the right not to be tortured also entails that state authorities have a duty to investigate complaints about abuses. This is stipulated in article 12 of the Torture Convention, and has been expressed by the Human Rights Committee in the following terms: 'The right to lodge complaints against maltreatment prohibited by article 7 [of the Civil and Political Rights Covenant] must be recognized

---

[66] *Aksoy v Turkey*, Judgment of the European Court of Human Rights, 26 November 1996.   [67] Ibid., para 83.

in the domestic law. Complaints must be investigated promptly and impartially by competent authorities so as to make the remedy effective'.[68] This aspect assumes particular significance in the context of disappearances. Thirdly, there is a duty to ensure that evidence obtained through torture cannot be relied upon in an eventual trial (except as evidence that acts of torture have occurred). Again, this is highlighted by the Human Rights Committee: 'It is important for the discouragement of violations under article 7 [of the Civil and Political Rights Covenant] that the law must prohibit the use of [sic] admissibility in judicial proceedings of statements or confessions obtained through torture or other prohibited treatment'.[69] The admissibility of evidence obtained as a result of torture is also precluded by article 15 of the Torture Convention. A fourth dimension of the obligation to take steps to prevent torture concerns the implementation of procedures for ongoing review of criminal justice arrangements and practices. Article 11 of the Torture Convention refers to the obligation to 'keep under systematic review interrogation rules, instructions, methods and practices as well as arrangements for the custody and treatment of [detainees and others] . . . with a view to preventing any cases of torture'.

Fifthly, there is the important issue of training. The prohibition of torture entails that all those who might have a role in the custody, questioning or treatment of detainees and prisoners must be informed that torture is prohibited and receive appropriate training and instructions with a view to preventing it. Those involved are likely to include, among others, police officers, criminal investigators, prison guards and doctors, whether they have the status of public officials or private contractors, and whether they are civilians or military personnel.[70] Following on from this, it is clear that, as affirmed by the Human Rights Committee, those who refuse to carry out orders to perpetrate, encourage or tolerate acts of torture must not be punished or penalised in any way.[71] A final dimension of the obligation to take steps to prevent torture relates to equipment used to inflict torture. On the one hand, the need has been highlighted for governments to monitor the use of law enforcement and

---

[68] Human Rights Committee, General Comment 20 (replaces General Comment 7 concerning prohibition of torture and cruel treatment or punishment: art. 7), 10 March 1992, para. 14.   [69] Ibid., para. 12.
[70] Again, this is stressed by the Human Rights Committee, ibid., para. 10. It appears also in the Torture Convention in art. 10.   [71] Ibid., para. 13.

restraint equipment, to ensure that it is not being used inconsistently with the prohibition on torture and other ill-treatment. On the other hand, attention has more recently turned to the need to prevent the production of, and trade in, objects specifically designed to inflict torture.[72] The UN Special Rapporteur on Torture has expressed the view that the enactment of legal and other measures to stop the production of, and trade in, equipment specifically designed to inflict torture or other cruel, inhuman or degrading treatment is part of the general obligation, reflected in the Torture Convention, to take effective measures to prevent ill-treatment of this sort.[73]

Torture and the 'melancholic healer'

In January 2003 *The Economist* ran a cover-story on torture.[74] To illustrate the story, the front of the magazine carried a sketch of a man hooded and bound to a chair, his head bowed in abjection. Above the picture, the title read: 'Is torture ever justified?'[75] From the perspective of international human rights law, the answer is clear. As we have seen, treaties and other instruments ban the use of torture in absolute and unqualified terms. No restrictions are permitted to be imposed on the right not to be tortured, nor is this right subject to modified application or 'derogation' during times of national emergency. Beyond this, acts of torture constitute international crimes, including war crimes when committed during armed conflict, and crimes against humanity when committed as part of a widespread or systematic attack on a civilian population. Plainly, international human rights law rejects the notion that torture is ever justified. Is it right to do this? Taking up *The Economist*'s question, *should* torture be prohibited at all times and for all purposes?

[72] See, e.g., Amnesty International, 'The Pain Merchants: Security equipment and its use in torture and other ill-treatment', AI Index: ACT 40/008/2003.

[73] Theo van Boven, Study of the situation of trade in and production of equipment which is specifically designed to inflict torture or other cruel, inhuman or degrading treatment, its origin, destination and forms, 13 January 2003, UN Doc. E/CN.4/2003/69, para. 35.   [74] *The Economist*, 11–17 January 2003.

[75] *The Economist* ran another cover-story on torture in its 8–14 May 2004 issue. This time the picture on the cover was a photograph, not a sketch, and the title read 'Resign Rumsfeld'. For discussion of some aspects of the scandal surrounding this and related photographs, see Victims★.

In 1971 General Jacques Massu, a soldier in the French Army who had been in charge of Algiers at the time of the Algerian War, published memoirs in which he acknowledged that torture had been used under his command. Unrepentant, he claimed that this was 'the only way he could get advance knowledge of terrorist plans and avert the deaths of innocent people'.[76] Sixteen years later, the Israeli Commission of Inquiry approved the use of 'moderate physical pressure' in counter-terrorist investigations. Explaining this decision, the Commission referred to statements by security service investigators who had characterised the situation they faced in the following terms: '[W]e are talking about the "cleaning of sewers" the existence of which endangers State security, and this unpleasant mission has been imposed upon us. One cannot clean sewers without dirtying oneself.'[77] As noted in the previous section, the Commission's decision was later challenged before the Supreme Court of Israel. In setting out the issues it had had to consider, the Court reported that the State's attorneys, like the Commission before them, had invoked the 'ticking time bomb' argument. The Court's account of the well-known scenario which underpins this argument went like this.

A given suspect is arrested by the [security services]. He holds information respecting the location of a bomb that was set and will imminently explode. There is no way to defuse the bomb without this information. If the information is obtained, however, the bomb may be defused. If the bomb is not defused, scores will be killed and maimed. Is a [security service] investigator authorized to employ physical means in order to elicit information regarding the location of the bomb in such instances?[78]

The Court decided, as we saw, that the answer was no. However, its concern to leave open the possibility for security service investigators to be excused from eventual criminal liability suggests that it did not find the ticking time bomb argument wholly unpersuasive. Indeed, the judges made plain their unease about the consequences of barring the security services from employing a tool which the latter had said was

[76] D. Johnson, 'General Jacques Massu' (Obituary), *The Guardian*, 28 October 2002. According to Johnson, Massu later expressed regret at his use of torture, following the publication of the memoirs of one of his victims in 2000.

[77] Report of the Commission of Inquiry Regarding the General Security Service's Interrogation Practices With Respect to Hostile Terrorist Activities, excerpted in 23 *Israel Law Review* (1989) 146, 162 (para 2.40 of the Report).

[78] *Public Committee Against Torture and Others v State of Israel and Others*, Judgment of the Supreme Court of Israel, 6 September 1999, para. 33.

'indispensable to fighting and winning the war on terrorism'.[79] 'We are', they wrote, 'aware of the harsh reality of terrorism in which we are, at times, immersed. Our apprehension... that this decision will hamper the ability to properly deal with terrorists and terrorism disturbs us.'[80]

Since 11 September 2001 many influential officials and commentators have proposed that the ticking time bomb argument likewise needs to be considered in the United States. According to Judge Richard Posner of the Seventh Circuit Court of Appeals, 'only the most doctrinaire civil libertarians... deny [that] if the stakes are high enough, torture is permissible. No one who doubts that this is the case should be in a position of responsibility'.[81] The view that torture may be used in some circumstances has similarly been expressed by lawyers advising the United States Administration on the treatment of detainees at Guantánamo Bay and elsewhere.[82] For Harvard law professor Alan Dershowitz the absolute prohibition of torture is not only naive, but also hypocritical and ultimately illiberal. As he explains, 'I have no doubt that if an actual ticking bomb situation were to arise, our law enforcement authorities would torture. The real debate is whether such torture should take place outside of our legal system or within it. The answer to this question seems clear: if we are to have torture, it should be authorized by the law'.[83] Dershowitz has proposed that legislation should be introduced, under which judges would have to issue a 'torture warrant' before torture was used. This would be more honest, he suggests, than quietly condoning torture in counter-terrorist investigations while publicly condemning it. More importantly, it would protect those affected from unregulated and arbitrary action. In his words, '[d]emocracy requires accountability and

---

[79] Report of the Commission of Inquiry Regarding the General Security Service's Interrogation Practices With Respect to Hostile Terrorist Activities, cited in *Public Committee Against Torture and Others v State of Israel and Others*, Judgment of the Supreme Court of Israel, 6 September 1999, para. 9.   [80] Ibid., para. 40.

[81] Quoted in S. Levinson, 'The Debate on Torture: War Against Virtual States' 50 *Dissent* (Summer, 2003).

[82] See, e.g., 'Working Group Report on Detainee Interrogations in the Global War on Terrorism: Assessment of Legal, Historical, Policy, and Operational Considerations' (Draft Report to US Defence Secretary Donald Rumsfeld), 6 March 2003, available at news.findlaw.com/wp/docs/torture/30603wgrpt.html. The analysis in this report revolves mainly around United States law and United States reservations to relevant human rights treaties.

[83] A. Dershowitz, Commentary, *Los Angeles Times*, 8 November 2001. See also A. Dershowitz, *Why Terrorism Works* (New Haven: Yale University Press, 2002), chap. 4.

transparency, especially when extraordinary steps are taken. Most important, it requires compliance with the rule of law. And such compliance
is impossible when an extraordinary technique, such as torture, operates
outside of the law'.[84] From this perspective, the absolute prohibition of
torture may make sense as a response to the practice of torture in tyrannical regimes. But—so the argument runs—torture is not only used to
prop up tyrannical power; in today's world it is also used in democratic
states to save innocent people from being killed or maimed, and it
behoves such states to ensure that this is not left to the discretion of
secret policemen in underground cells, but instead operates within a
framework of law.

The idea that torture is sometimes, exceptionally, justified has not
gone unchallenged.[85] Before turning to the challenges, we should note
one further way in which justification for acts of torture may be provided, albeit implicitly. This is by simply avoiding the word torture.
Dershowitz, Posner and the advisers to the United States Administration
are in fact relatively unusual in their willingness to use the language of
torture. More commonly, as in the case of the Israeli Commission of
Inquiry and Supreme Court, the talk is of 'moderate physical pressure',
'physical means', and the like. But, of course, avoiding the word torture
is not the same as avoiding torture. The practice may simply be shielded
behind euphemism. Alternatively, torture may be 'defined away', by
reducing its field of reference to the point where very little remains to
be 'caught' by the prohibition. An example of this can be found in a
memorandum prepared for the United States Justice Department in
August 2002.[86] According to the memorandum, '[p]hysical pain amounting to torture must be equivalent in intensity to the pain accompanying
serious physical injury, such as organ failure, impairment of bodily function, or even death'.[87] While at one level this kind of argumentation
may seem to affirm the prohibition, insofar as it acknowledges the illegitimacy of acts called 'torture', the shrinkage of that category indicates

[84] Ibid.
[85] For a hilarious satire of the proposals, see J. Gray, 'A Modest Proposal For Preventing
Torturers in Liberal Democracies From Being Abused, and For Recognising Their
Benefit to The Public', *New Statesman*, 17 February 2003, 22.
[86] J.S. Bybee, 'Memorandum for Alberto R. Gonzales, Counsel to the President, Re:
Standards of Conduct for Interrogation under 18 U.S.C. §§ 2340–2340A', 1 August 2002.
[87] Ibid., 1.

otherwise. In essence, an implicit claim is made for the legitimacy of conduct that would be regarded as torture under international human rights law. How, then, has this claim been challenged? What can be said in defence of the international legal prohibition on torture and its unqualified ban, valid even in a ticking time bomb situation? Among the various arguments that have been or might be put forward, let us mention here four.

The first and simplest to state is the claim that torture is just wrong, and should never be regarded as legitimate, whatever the consequences. The playwright Ariel Dorfman makes this argument, and, in doing so, evokes the famous passage in Dostoevsky's *The Brothers Karamazov* in which Ivan invites his brother Alyosha to imagine that he is 'charged with building the edifice of human destiny, whose ultimate aim is to bring people happiness, to give them peace and contentment at last, but that in order to achieve this it is essential and unavoidable to torture just one little speck of creation', just one little child. Imagining this, Ivan asks, '[w]ould you agree to be the architect under those conditions?'. 'No', replies Alyosha quietly, 'I wouldn't agree'.[88] For Dorfman, Alyosha's 'No' expresses the sense that acts of torture will 'eternally corrode and corrupt us'. 'What Aloysha is telling Ivan', Dorfman writes, 'in the name of humanity, is that he will not accept responsibility for someone else torturing in his name'.[89] He will not accept to have paradise for all bought at the cost of hell for even one—one, moreover, Dorfman reminds us, who on at least some occasions, we must assume, will be as innocent and harmless as the child in Ivan's hypothetical.

A second argument revolves around the practical significance of what was referred to in *The Economist* cover-story mentioned earlier as the 'taboo against torture'.[90] If we must expect that torture will occur, the claim here is that it is nonetheless important that it should remain contrary to the law. Those committing acts of torture should know those acts are wrong. And those who are victims of acts of torture should not be delivered by the law to their tormentors. Israeli legal scholar Mordechai Kremnitzer has developed this argument in a response to the report of

[88] F.M. Dostoevsky (I. Avsey, trans.), *The Brothers Karamazov* (Oxford: Oxford University Press, 1994), 308.

[89] A. Dorfman, 'Are there times when we have to accept torture?', *The Guardian*, 8 May 2004.   [90] 'Is torture ever justified?', *The Economist*, 11–17 January 2003, 23.

the Commission of Inquiry on the authorisation of torture in Israel. Where the use of torture is authorised, he writes, '[t]he law, which generally grants protection, permits the suspect's injury, obligates him to suffer it (as he may not resist) and thus renders him legally helpless. More significant than the actual physical blow and suffering themselves— which should not be taken lightly—is the knowledge that... "one has given one's back to the smiters" [Isaiah, 50:6], that the legal barrier which protects one's most valuable assets—one's body and one's liberty—has been lifted. The law itself, intended for one's protection, has turned its back and dealt one a blow'.[91] From this perspective, the idea of legalised torture is a travesty of the rule of law, inasmuch as the law is supposed to protect citizens from violence and treat them as innocent until proven guilty, yet in Alan Dershowitz's proposal it is made to vindicate their serious injury at the hands of state agents.

A third objection to the legalisation of torture concedes that torture *is* perhaps justified in a ticking time bomb situation, but observes that in practice it is all too often used in other, less extreme situations. On this analysis, torture should not be legalised because no law could prevent the inevitable slide from exceptional use into a routinised system of torture. Thus, for example, Amnesty International called attention to the emergence in Israel of a 'pattern of torture or ill-treatment', and reported that, even after the Supreme Court's decision in 1999, this development proved difficult to reverse.[92] American legal scholar Richard Weisberg highlights that 'the dividing of an abhorrent practice into "good torture" and "bad torture" sets the stage for a full-blown acceptance of the practice'.[93] He writes: 'No one...wants to seem wide-eyed when facing the "ticking bomb" hypothetical... [but] it may be the instrumentalists who are being naive'. After all, you can't know whether you have the right person. And even if you do have the one who knows where the bomb is, you can't be sure he or she will tell you

[91] M. Kremnitzer, 'The Landau Commission Report—Was the security service subordinated to the law, or the law to the "needs" of the security service?' 23 *Israel Law Review* (1989) 216, 251, quoted in N. Belton, *The Good Listener* (London: Phoenix, 1998), 415.

[92] See *Amnesty International Report 1992* (London: Amnesty International, 1992), 153 and Amnesty International, '2002 UN Commission on Human Rights: Rights at Risk', AI Index IOR/41/025/2001, 1 December 2001, 15.

[93] R. Weisberg, 'Response to Sanford Levinson' 50 *Dissent* (Summer, 2003), 92.

the truth. Information gained through torture is notoriously unreliable. 'Because of this, you end up sanctioning torture in general.'[94]

A final argument is of a different order to the three we have just mentioned. Rather than arguing that torture is or is not justified in a ticking time bomb situation, the contention here is that the question of whether or not torture is justified in this situation is the wrong question. It misses the point that torture is not about getting information, but about asserting power. As we have seen, that is a point often missed as well in international human rights law. Yet, on this analysis, to treat the question 'Where is the bomb?' as the *motive* for torture is to take the torturer's self-justification too seriously. It is to credit his cruelty with a rationale that could ultimately be found in the 'answer'. Historian Edward Peters recalls that in George Orwell's *Nineteen Eighty-Four* the information extracted from Winston Smith is already known to his interrogators. Their aim in torturing him is simply to establish his co-operation.[95] Peters contends that this is indeed the way torture works. 'It is not primarily the victim's information', he writes, 'but the victim, that torture needs to win—or reduce to powerlessness.'[96] In her celebrated study of the 'body in pain', Elaine Scarry concurs. On her account, the torturer's 'question' and the victim's 'answer' form part of an elaborate ritual for converting 'absolute pain into the fiction of absolute power'.[97] With torture, she writes, the 'interrogator' stages a performance of overwhelming power in which the victim's '[w]orld, self and voice are lost, or nearly lost'. The 'answer' becomes 'a way of saying, yes, all is almost gone now, there is almost nothing left now, even this voice, the sounds I am making, no longer form my words but the words of another'.[98]

In a book about the life and work of a British activist who set up an organisation to help victims of torture, Neil Belton warns of the danger of taking torturers' self-exculpations too seriously. The ticking time bomb scenario is a fantasy, he writes, 'exhumed and revived whenever torture needs a justification'.[99] Belton calls it 'one of the most insidious

---

[94] R. Weisberg, 'Response to Sanford Levinson' 50 *Dissent* (Summer, 2003) 92–3, quoting David Cole.

[95] E. Peters, *Torture*, 2nd edn. (Philadelphia: University of Pennsylvania Press, 1996), 161.

[96] Ibid., 164.

[97] E. Scarry, *The Body In Pain* (Oxford: Oxford University Press, 1985), 27.

[98] Ibid., 35.   [98] N. Belton, *The Good Listener* (London: Phoenix, 1998), 216.

and durable of post-war fantasies'.[100] Rather than going along with the claim that torture is the unfortunate duty of those charged with the task of getting the information to avert the catastrophe, rather than accepting the representation of torture as the thankless work of those who descend into the political sewers so that the rest of us can move safely about the streets, he contends that we should resist these ideas, and hold on instead to the *philosophes'* vision of a world without torture. In his words, '[t]he vision of a world that does not include torture is essential, and possible; the fantasy of the melancholic healer who imagines that he is saving the world, finding the bomb, curing the plague, is what we have to fear'.[101]

[100] Ibid., 411.   [101] Ibid., 399.

Universality

Central to international human rights law is the idea that human rights are rights with universal significance. These are rights you have because you are a human being, rather than because you belong to a particular political community. In this sense, and despite the existence of import-ant region-specific arrangements, human rights norms and institutions presuppose universality, as well as having its greater practical realisation as their stated goal. What, then, of the diversity of values and forms of life that so manifestly characterises our world? How is this presupposition to be squared with that diversity? How does that diversity affect efforts to realise this goal? These questions have been the subject of long–standing, and sporadically very intense, debate, both within the human rights movement and between it and its critics. In what follows we review some of the arguments that have emerged.

Relativism

One response to the evident fact of global cultural heterogeneity often goes by the name 'relativism'. Before examining what this entails in the context of human rights, let us take brief stock of the tradition of ethical relativism which is evoked.

Ethical relativism

In general terms, relativism in ethics is concerned with the limits of our capacity, and entitlement, to evaluate moral systems. Two key claims are involved.[1] On the one hand, there is a claim that no single moral

[1] See D. Wong, 'Relativism' in P. Singer (ed.), *A Companion to Ethics* (Cambridge, Mass.: Blackwell Publishers, 1993). 442.

code can be said to have universal validity. This is sometimes called 'meta-ethical relativism'. In some extreme forms, it leads to the contention that no basis exists for evaluating, and hence criticising, beliefs about right and wrong. That is to say, it leads to the contention that all moral codes have equal merit. More commonly, however, meta-ethical relativism is not seen as negating the possibility of criticism, for even if there is no single moral code with universal validity, it does not follow that every code is as good as every other. Some beliefs about how we should live can still be shown to be more adequate and compelling than their alternatives.

A second claim associated with ethical relativism is the claim that it is wrong in principle for people in one society to criticise and try to change the values of another. This is sometimes called 'normative relativism'. Inasmuch as it enjoins toleration in intersocietal relations, it is exposed to the obvious objection that toleration is itself a value. How can the universal validity of *this* value be upheld, while the universal validity of values in general is denied? The diversity which exists over moral beliefs patently extends also to the attitudes adopted towards that diversity, and it is not logically open to the relativist to reject an attitude of intolerance. But then, as noted above, more moderate forms of ethical relativism recognise that not all cultural norms command equal respect. Some norms deserve to be condemned, and any account of the right way to behave in intersocietal relations must take that into account. Approached from this angle, normative relativism simply asserts the value of toleration, accepting that that value might be outweighed by other values in particular circumstances.

The two claims we have highlighted in connection with ethical relativism are clearly linked. But, while meta-ethical relativism belongs to a very long-standing debate about the relationship between morality and custom stretching back in European thought to the ancient Greek philosophers, normative relativism is a much more recent extension of the relativist logic. In particular, normative relativism is often associated with developments in the field of anthropology, whereby studies documenting the 'primitive' practices of people in far-off lands came to be seen as colonialist rationalisations. Twentieth century anthropologists began to repudiate the assumptions of superiority that had informed such studies. Some within the discipline appear to have concluded that absolute toleration is the only legitimate spirit in which to confront a foreign culture. For most, however, what was required was not to become wholly disengaged and uncritical, but rather to eschew arrogance and imperiousness, and root anthropological enquiry in new, more respectful forms of intercultural encounter.

Relativism and human rights

Let us now return to relativism in relation to human rights. In some versions, this tracks extreme ethical relativism with a two-fold claim about the limits of international human rights norms and processes. In the first place, there is the idea that human rights are Western constructs, with no universal validity. Since the foundational instruments—the Universal Declaration of Human Rights and the two International Covenants on Human Rights—were drafted at a time when most African and Asian societies still remained under colonial rule, or were only just emerging from it, the claim here is that the system remains marked by the exclusionary process that gave birth to it. Human rights, it is argued, can have no purchase in societies which were not adequately represented in the meetings that defined them—societies which, moreover, do not share the liberal and socialist worldviews that decisively shaped the norms laid down. To hold otherwise is simply to perpetuate imperialism in new form.

This takes us to the second contention, that it is wrong to use human rights as a basis for criticising and seeking to change institutions and practices in non-Western societies. From this perspective, those in powerful countries must begin to recognise the right of other societies to organise their collective lives in their own ways and for their ends. Intersocietal relations should be governed by the principle that these ways and ends are multiple and incommensurable, and defy evaluation by reference to a Western-defined, or indeed any single, standard. Human rights, instead, recycle the colonialist project of remaking the world in the image, or at any rate at the service, of the West. In doing so, they supply the latest fig leaf by which cultural subordination and economic exploitation are masked and legitimated as a 'civilising mission'.

These points are certainly understandable, especially as there can be little doubt that human rights norms can—and often do—operate ideologically, to rationalise interventionist policies aimed at ensuring that change in developing states remains consistent with the economic interests of industrialised countries. However, as in the case of ethical relativism, this most extreme variant—with its total denial of the validity of human rights in some parts of the world—is not widely espoused. Relativism retains enduring appeal, and in recent years has received renewed impetus in connection with arguments about the significance for human rights of 'Asian values', 'Islamic fundamentalism', and the 'clash of civilisations'. (For discussion of some of these arguments, see Culture★ and Religion★.) But the claim is not generally so much about the validity of human rights as it is about their protection in diverse contexts.

Just as meta-ethical relativism is best understood not as negating the possibility of evaluation but simply as denying the existence of any single objective or Archimedean standpoint from which valid evaluation can occur, and just as normative relativism is best understood not as banning criticism outright but simply as enjoining toleration as one important value among others, so too relativism in relation to human rights is best seen as a reminder that context counts. Human rights are not just abstract. They must be made meaningful in specific social conditions, each of them unique in its political institutions, cultural traditions and economic circumstances, and each of them entailing as well a unique set of opportunities and threats from the standpoint of ensuring respect for human rights.

Of course, even (and perhaps especially) the most ardent colonialist recognised that societies differ. But for such a person differences were to be explained as the result of backwardness, ignorance or inhumanity on the part of those outside the metropole. From this evolutionary perspective, there was one truly human way to live, one enlightened pattern of social organisation and, while some societies had mastered it, others, sadly, had not. The most important message of relativism is that that mindset cannot inform international human rights law. Whatever the universality of human rights is to mean, it cannot refer to an evolutionary process according to which some societies instantiate the norms that others are enjoined to embrace. The specificity of life in different places—all places—must be taken seriously.

Universality

Understood in this way, relativism supplies a valuable counterweight to an attitude that has had devastating impact historically, and is by no means without influence today. It helps us to see why we must ask the questions with which we began. But it does little to answer those questions, little to show us what a more adequate approach to universality might involve. Proceeding, then, from a recognition that no one has a monopoly of insight into 'truly human ways to live', how should the universality of human rights be conceived and pursued?

Thick and thin morality

Once again it will be instructive to begin with some points drawn from the field of ethics. What does it mean to say that a moral concept has universal significance, and how does that significance come about? This is a vast topic, the focus of many different perspectives and debates. We confine ourselves to one account which will be particularly useful for our purpose, that of Michael Walzer in his book *Thick and Thin*.[2]

Walzer seeks in this book to clarify the character and basis of universality in the moral domain by means of a contrast between two types of morality. One arises in the context of 'particularist' moral discourse, the discourse—as he puts it—which we have 'among ourselves, here at home'.[3] When we argue over taxation or discuss welfare policy, we talk in a way that few who have not lived in our society for a long time could fully understand. We appeal to shared values, draw on local traditions, invoke home truths. Walzer calls this 'thick' morality—thick in the sense that it is embedded in a society's history, politics and culture, and thus thick too in the anthropologists' sense that, if it is to be grasped by outsiders, quite detailed ethnographic description will be needed. The other kind of morality is that which arises in the context of universalist moral discourse, the discourse which we have with 'people abroad, across different cultures'.[4] This does not depend on having lived in any particular place or on being familiar with any particular traditions, values or truths. No detailed social descriptions are required to convey this morality. It is intelligible to everyone, accessible everywhere, resonant in settings that seem otherwise far apart. Walzer calls this 'thin' morality, and explains it as a disembedding of, or abstraction from, recurrent features of diverse thick moralities.

[2] M. Walzer, *Thick and Thin* (Notre Dame, Ind.: University of Notre Dame Press, 1994), esp. Introduction and Chapter 1. [3] Ibid., xi.
[4] Ibid.

What happens, in his account, is that morality 'reveals itself thinly . . . on specific occasions', when the need arises to create a moral language for talking across cultural boundaries and invoking shared humanity.[5] Out of the diversity of thickly conceived values and practices in different societies, certain recurrent features come into relief. These could be common principles, or they could simply be convergent outcomes. Either way, the similar or overlapping aspects provide a basis from which it becomes possible to abstract. In Walzer's words, thin morality consists of normative patterns that are 'reiterated in different times and places, and that are seen to be similar even though they are expressed in different idioms and reflect different histories and different versions of the world'.[6] Note here the reference to features being 'seen' as similar. It is a distinctive feature of thin morality, for him, that it is *seen*, or reveals itself, or is recognised. If thick morality is (or should be) a function of argument, of persuading others that the beliefs you espouse are just and the interpretations you urge are right, thin morality has a different dynamic. It is 'less the product of persuasion than of mutual recognition among the protagonists of different fully developed moral cultures'.[7]

In associating universalist moral discourse with 'thin' morality, Walzer is, of course, using the word 'thin' in a very special sense. In particular, he is concerned to stress that it should not be taken to imply either that the values in question are insignificant or trivial, or that the convictions involved are shallow or weakly held. On the contrary, he suggests that the reverse is likely to be true. At issue here is morality 'close to the bone', morality at its most urgent and its most obvious. He gives the example of watching on television scenes of people marching in the streets of Prague in 1989. In some cases their banners read simply 'Truth' and 'Justice'. Walzer observes that the marchers could be confident in demanding those things that everyone in the world would support their cause. More refined claims might misfire or be lost on others but, however little is known about the marchers and their circumstances, there is something in their appeals to truth and justice that everyone can recognise. Thus, in this field 'thinness and intensity go together, whereas with thickness comes qualification, compromise, complexity, and disagreement'.[8]

---

[5] M. Walzer, *Thick and Thin* (Notre Dame, Ind.: University of Notre Dame Press, 1994), 4.

[6] Ibid., 17. [7] Ibid. [8] Ibid., 6.

Were a catalogue to be made of moments like that of watching the
marchers in Prague in 1989, Walzer proposes that the end product might
be 'a set of standards to which all societies can be held—negative
injunctions, most likely, rules against murder, deceit, torture, oppression
and tyranny'. Together these standards—articulations of thin morality—
would express a kind of 'moral minimum', the unproblematic core of all
the more maximalist and contentious meanings given to moral concepts
in specific contexts.[9] In summary, then, the claim is that moral discourse
is conducted in two distinct, if interrelated, registers. Thick morality,
rooted in the particularities of history, politics and culture, is for use within
societies. Thin morality—or 'minimalist' morality—is abstracted from
those particularities for the sake of engagement across societies.

Universality and human rights

Returning now to human rights, to what extent are we confronted with
something like Walzer's thin or 'minimalist' morality? Is it the case that
here too the basis for universality is the articulation of shared features
within otherwise diverse normative systems?

Writing in 1947, Jacques Maritain expressed the view that this is
indeed how the universality of human rights should be understood.
Maritain's comments appear in a survey of perspectives on the philosophical foundations of human rights commissioned by UNESCO as
a contribution to the elaboration (then underway) of the Universal
Declaration of Human Rights.[10] For him, what made it possible even to
contemplate such a Declaration was the fact that people in different
societies can often be shown to agree on principles of action, however
much they may disagree over the reasons for adopting those principles.
In his words, a 'common denominator' exists at the 'point where in
practice the most widely separated theoretical ideologies and mental
traditions converge'. Our 'speculative ideas' may be irreconcilable, but
for the purpose of a charter of human rights it is enough that our 'practical ideas' very frequently coincide.[11] The question is: how far do they
coincide? What are the 'extent and limits of the practical agreement on
human rights'?[12]

---

[9] Ibid., 10.
[10] UNESCO, *Human Rights: Comments and Interpretations* (New York: Greenwood, 1949).
[11] Ibid., 10.   [12] Ibid., 16.

Maritain's point was reaffirmed later in the same volume, in a statement of the study's conclusions.[13] UNESCO had sought the views of scholars on the philosophical foundations of human rights from the perspective of many different traditions, including the Marxist, Chinese, Islamic and Hindu traditions. Reviewing the various analyses presented, the authors of the concluding statement found it striking and significant that 'common convictions' had often been expressed in terms of disparate moral-philosophical worldviews. On the other hand, differences among the contributors had led to 'varied and even opposed interpretations of fundamental rights'. It followed for the concluding statement's authors that the challenge was to search for 'common principles' which might help in overcoming obstacles to agreement over rights. At the same time, efforts had to be made to identify divergences which might help in anticipating conflict over the interpretation of rights.[14]

This way of conceiving the challenge of constructing a universally applicable body of human rights norms is echoed in much subsequent work. In countless studies, oriented to countless specific preoccupations, the question is raised of the extent to which practical agreement obtains with respect to human rights. To take just one example from another UNESCO study published in 1986, it has been observed that Islamic traditions depart significantly from the rights proclaimed in the Universal Declaration in some respects, but in other respects reflect a very long-standing recognition of the right to life, freedom of religion, the right to asylum, the right to a basic income, etc.[15] As in the earlier UNESCO survey, universality is viewed in this work as a function of cross-cultural consensus. The aim is to show how, even where the language of human rights has not traditionally been used or has even been repudiated, equivalent concepts have developed. Values have been promoted and objectives advanced which likewise assert the fundamentality of human dignity and the legitimacy of demands for freedom and security.

An approach to the universality of human rights along these lines—let us label it 'cross-cultural consensus'—has obvious appeal. As Raimundo Pannikar has argued, there is considerable scope for demonstrating the

[13] UNESCO, *Human Rights: Comments and Interpretations* (New York: Greenwood, 1949), 258. The statement was prepared by a committee chaired by E.H. Carr.

[14] Ibid., 261–2.

[15] See M.A. Sinaceur, 'Islamic Tradition and Human Rights' in A. Diemer *et al.*, *Philosophical Foundations of Human Rights* (Paris: UNESCO, 1986), 193.

existence throughout the world of functional analogues, or in his phrase 'homeomorphic equivalents', of human rights concepts.[16] From the perspective of this approach, differences of language, culture and history need not mislead us into overlooking commonalities of policy and practice. The more diligent we are in showing where those commonalities hold, the firmer our basis for treating human rights as rights with universal, rather than merely particular, significance. The more careful we are in noting where those commonalities end, the stronger our capacity to anticipate and hence defuse conflicts over interpretation. These things are certainly true, but we should not allow them to obscure another consideration of vital importance. This is that, where human rights are concerned, universality is not simply a presupposition. It is also, and more centrally, a *project*. Whether in relation to liberal societies or other societies, the point is always to enhance and expand the protection of human rights. In part this is because safeguards against human rights abuse can always be improved. But in part it is also because interpretations of human rights must always remain revisable, so that what counts as compliance today may be made to count as abuse tomorrow.

A major limitation of the cross-cultural consensus approach, then, is that it is too static. It does not speak to the need for change that is, or should be, the rationale and enduring message of international human rights law. Nor (to compound the problem) does it speak to the potentials for change that arise within the various cultural contexts considered. Instead, it tends to encourage the view that cultures are fixed essences, ever and always the same. And if cultures are fixed essences, then relations among them are established truths. Cross-cultural agreement with respect to human rights either exists or it does not. Where such a reifying perspective is fostered, awareness is apt to be occluded of the changing, and hence changeable, articulations of human rights with culture. This has at least two serious consequences. In the first place, it raises the risk that human rights will simply reflect a least common denominator of the norms and procedures now (or at some point in the past) in place across the world. Recall Walzer's thin morality, explained in a manner that closely parallels the cross-cultural consensus approach to human rights. In his account, thin or universalist morality corresponds

[16] R. Pannikar, 'Is the Notion of Human Rights a Western Concept?' 120 *Diogenes* (1982), 75, 77.

to a 'moral minimum', which he envisages as most likely made up of a series of negative injunctions, such as 'rules against murder, deceit, torture, oppression and tyranny'. If this likewise suggests the scope of universal human rights, then international human rights law might have something to say about some of the most egregious forms of violence and unfreedom, but will have little capacity to address more everyday, if often at least equally debilitating, crises and problems, such as illiteracy, homelessness, disease, and hunger.

A second, related, consequence of the reifying tendency just highlighted is that it masks the extent to which human rights can play a part in shaping cultural norms and practices, even as those norms and practices shape what is possible by way of universal human rights. Recall, again, Walzer's thin morality. While in his account thick or particularist morality is a function of argument and persuasion, thin morality simply 'reveals itself'. Walzer's moral minimum is 'less the product of persuasion than of mutual recognition among the protagonists of various fully developed moral cultures'. Where the universality of human rights is approached in similar fashion, we are led to assume that the time for debate and decision is over; the only available mode of engagement now is recognition—the recognition of given facts. Yet, for the most part, the facts of global cultural diversity are not given, but rather made and remade in ongoing processes of interpretation, contestation and negotiation. And for the most part too, these are processes which international human rights law can potentially—and does actually—enter and inform.

With these points in mind, another way of approaching the universality of human rights is to start from a conception of human rights as instruments for change, and from a conception of cultures as contexts of change. Rather than viewing traditions solely in terms of their practical agreement or overlap with one another, we are then encouraged to view them additionally in terms of the capacity of each to be reconsidered, reinterpreted and reconfigured. The focus, accordingly, is not just on identifying commonalities among norms and institutions. It is also on identifying vacillations, instabilities, contradictions, and disagreements within them, and the transformative potentials thereby entailed. Thus, we proceed from the idea that the most significant commonality among traditions may be difference within them.

A version of this approach—let us call it 'cross-cultural critique'—can be found in the work of Abdullahi An-Na'im.[17] An-Na'im's central concern is with the 'cultural legitimacy' of international human rights standards, especially in Africa and Asia. By cultural legitimacy he means the extent to which the standards are regarded as justified, proper and appropriate by those whom they affect. In An-Na'im's assessment, a major cause of disregard for human rights is their lack of cultural legitimacy in societies that have different traditions from those with reference to which the foundational instruments were largely framed. He considers, however, that this gap can still be filled. In his words, 'I believe not only that universal cultural legitimacy is necessary, but also that it is possible to develop it retrospectively in relation to fundamental human rights through enlightened interpretations of cultural norms'.[18] In making this argument, An-Na'im rejects what we have called the cross-cultural consensus approach in favour of what we have termed cross-cultural critique. He dismisses the notion that 'human rights should be founded on the existing least common denominator among [the world's] cultural traditions'. As he writes, 'restricting international human rights to those accepted by prevailing perceptions of values and norms . . . would not only limit these rights and reduce their scope, but also exclude extremely vital rights.' Instead, it is necessary to expand the 'area and quality of agreement among the cultural traditions of the world', so as to provide cultural legitimacy for a wider range of human rights claims.[19]

The crucial point for An-Na'im is that such an expansion can be accomplished. He observes that 'most of the published works tend to treat cultural traditions from a static and ahistorical point of view, with little regard for the constant evolution and change of cultural norms and

[17] Among An-Na'im's many writings on this theme, see, e.g., 'Problems of Universal Cultural Legitimacy for Human Rights' in A. An-Na'im and F. Deng (eds.), *Human Rights in Africa* (Washington, DC: The Brookings Institution, 1990), 331 and 'Toward a Cross-Cultural Approach to Defining International Standards of Human Rights: The Meaning of Cruel, Inhuman or Degrading Treatment or Punishment' in A. An-Na'im (ed.), *Human Rights in Cross-Cultural Perspective* (Philadelphia: University of Pennsylvania Press, 1992), 19.
[18] A. An-Na'im, 'Toward a Cross-Cultural Approach to Defining International Standards of Human Rights: The Meaning of Cruel, Inhuman or Degrading Treatment or Punishment' in A. An-Na'im (ed.), *Human Rights in Cross-Cultural Perspective* (Philadelphia: University of Pennsylvania Press, 1992), 20–1.   [19] Ibid., 21.

institutions'.[20] Once the historicity of traditions is taken into account, it becomes clear that much can be achieved through a combination of 'internal dialogue' and cross-cultural exchange. In his various writings An-Na'im has provided many examples to illustrate the role and prospects of internal dialogue. One relates to the concept of cruel, inhuman and degrading punishment and its bearing for Islamic punishments, such as flogging and amputation of the hand.[21] Even if under Islamic law the use of such punishments cannot formally be excluded, he contends that it can be severely restricted, perhaps even to vanishing point. For instance, established interpretations of Qur'anic principles concerning standards of proof can be revised. So too can understandings of the elements of offences, defences, and so on. In this regard, An-Na'im recalls that '[i]n the normal course of events, powerful individuals and groups tend to monopolize the interpretation of cultural norms and manipulate them to their own advantage'. He continues: 'it is vital for disadvantaged groups to challenge this monopoly and manipulation [by using] internal cultural discourse to offer alternative interpretations' that reflect their own interests.[22] The place of cross-cultural exchange is, as he sees it, to help in initiating and carrying forward such struggles. In his account, cross-cultural dialogue should be aimed at enlarging the foundations for human rights, and a key aspect of this is 'support for the proponents of enlightened perceptions and interpretations within a culture'.[23]

In the work of Maritain and An-Na'im can be found, then, two approaches to the universality of human rights. One invites enquiry into the extent and limits of the cross-cultural consensus that exists regarding human rights. The other invites consideration of the prospects for expanding and deepening that consensus by means of a critical engagement between cultural traditions and human rights. In most writings, of course, these two approaches co-occur (along with other approaches); the difference is largely one of emphasis, rather than of

[20] A. An-Na'im, 'Problems of Universal Cultural Legitimacy for Human Rights' in A. An-Na'im and F. Deng (eds.), *Human Rights in Africa* (Washington, DC: The Brookings Institution, 1990), 353–4.

[21] See A. An-Na'im, 'Toward a Cross-Cultural Approach to Defining International Standards of Human Rights: The Meaning of Cruel, Inhuman or Degrading Treatment or Punishment' in A. An-Na'im (ed.), *Human Rights in Cross-Cultural Perspective* (Philadelphia: University of Pennsylvania Press, 1992), 19.   [22] Ibid., 27–8.

[23] Ibid., 27.

kind. But the contrast is helpful in bringing out the limits of a very influential account of universality. In particular, what 'thin' universality tends to obscure is that, as Walzer himself observes, the 'crucial commonality of the human race is particularism: we participate, all of us, in thick cultures that are our own'.[24] The argument and persuasion that characterise our 'thick' life at home should not be uncoupled from the discourse we have with others abroad. Likewise, the 'qualification, compromise, complexity and disagreement' that are the hallmarks of 'thick' morality should not be isolated from the 'intensity' of our shared concerns. For the cross-cultural consensus available now need not—and cannot—suffice. If the protection of human rights is to be enhanced and extended, attention must be turned to our ongoing experiences of uncertainty, disagreement and renegotiation. Perhaps paradoxically, it seems that the key to universality in human rights is not so much consensus, but dissensus.

Universality/universalism

Animating international human rights law, as we noted at the beginning, is the idea that human rights are rights of universal significance. With this idea comes both the presupposition that these rights are universal in principle and the goal of making them more universal in practice. What emerges from our discussion? As to the presupposition, we have noted that universality must not simply be elided with the norms and practices of any single society or set of societies. As relativist arguments remind us, contexts count. At the same time, however, we have also observed that contexts are neither monolithic nor fixed, and that the goal of realising universality may not be best served by an approach that treats them as such. Rather than scrutinising diverse traditions for their points of commonality and difference, each tradition should also be considered with a view to its contradictory and contested character, and to its capacity for change. This suggests that the work of establishing a universal basis for human rights should become less a matter of recording consensus among cultures than of harnessing dissensus within them, and less a matter of recognising facts than of intervening in, and providing orientation for, historical processes.

[24] M. Walzer, *Thick and Thin* (Notre Dame, Ind.: University of Notre Dame Press, 1994), 83.

One way of summarising this approach to the reconciliation of universality and diversity is to refer to a distinction that has been drawn between universalism and universality.[25] For this purpose, 'universalism' is the attempt to eliminate particularity and achieve uniformity at global level; 'universality' is the attempt to bring out and develop the global resonance of particular ideas. Universality thus departs from universalism in accepting limitations. Disavowing uniformity as an imperious and in any event self-defeating aim, universality contents itself instead with generality. But there is a reward. For whereas universalism tends to choke off possibilities with doctrine, universality helps to open up traditions, and draw out transformative resources that remain latent or suppressed within them. Our point, then, is that the universal significance of human rights is a case of universality, not universalism. We speak not of uniformity but of generality, not of doctrine but of critique, and not of the demise of particularity but of its future in relation to the global circulation of human rights ideas.

[25] See R. Wisse, *The Modern Jewish Canon* (New York: The Free Press, 2000), 19.

Victims

Victims, victimhood, victimisation, victimology, the victim movement. Our discussion here revolves around these words, which direct attention to the experiences, needs and claims of those who have suffered harms of various kinds, and to the approaches, controversies and outcomes that have materialised in this regard.

Both the academic discipline of victimology and the victim movement have mostly been concerned with criminal harms, that is to say, with victims of *crime*.[1] Victimology developed as a corrective to the dominant focus within criminology on perpetrators, and raises questions about the relationship between victims and offenders, the factors that affect vulnerability to criminal victimisation, the needs of victims and the services that should be available to them, and the place of victims within the criminal justice system. For its part, the victim movement developed in response to a variety of agendas. In the United States, where it is most evolved, victim activism appears to have been mobilised primarily by dissatisfaction with the 'excessive' character of defendants' rights, and the most vocal elements remain those campaigning for the limitation of defendants' rights and the adoption of punitive approaches to criminal justice, including in some cases expanded use of the death penalty. In other countries the victim movement's origins and orientation are very different. In the United Kingdom, for example, it grew out of voluntary initiatives to provide support at local level to victims of crime, and its ambitions continue to centre on the provision of victim services.

Despite this emphasis on criminal victimisation, it is obvious that criminal conduct is by no means the only kind of harm of which a person may

---

[1] See further L. Zedner, 'Victims' in M. Maguire, R. Morgan & R. Reiner (eds.), *Oxford Handbook of Criminology* (Oxford: Oxford University Press, 2002), chap. 13.

be a victim. Among the many other, overlapping forms of possible victimisation is the violation of human rights. Some scholars of victimology have promoted an approach that takes in issues of human rights, and connects them to crime-related concerns.[2] This is sometimes referred to as a human rights-based approach to victimology. One aspect of it is interest in victims' rights. Advocacy for victims' rights spans many segments of the contemporary victim movement, including those oriented to the provision of victim support. While the demands are not uniform, rights are commonly asserted with regard to victims' treatment in criminal investigations and trial procedures, the availability of compensation or restitution, and the provision of state-funded support services. In the United States and in some other countries, rights are also asserted to a say in sentencing and related aspects of the administration of penal policy.

Insofar as some of these rights now receive protection under international law (as described further below), it is evident that moves to connect issues of criminal victimisation with human rights have not only affected victimology. They have also affected human rights. The recognition of victims' rights is part of this. More generally, however, and in parallel with the promotion of human rights-based approaches to victimology, calls have emerged for a more victim-centred orientation within the field of human rights. By that is usually meant an approach which takes as its starting point the experience of victims. Rather than organising enquiry around the obligations of states, a victim-centred approach invites us to proceed from analysis of the abuses suffered, and to examine who is affected, by whom, how, and in what circumstances. Such an approach has also been understood to prompt reappraisal of the rights to remedies and reparations of those who are victims of human rights violations, and reconsideration too of the place of victims within systems of human rights monitoring and enforcement.

Evaluations of approaches that give a central place to victimhood vary quite considerably. Some observers are sharply critical of them, stressing their dangers and ill-effects. Others see a more positive role for victim-oriented study, activism and policy. Our interest here is in the initiatives and debates through which these various assessments have been

[2] See, e.g., R. Elias, *The Politics of Victimization: Victims, Victimology and Human Rights* (New York/Oxford: Oxford University Press, 1986). See also R.I. Mawby & S. Walkate, *Critical Victimology* (London: Sage Publications, 1994), 13 *et seq.*

reflected onto the field of human rights. We begin with a review of developments with regard to the recognition of victims' rights. If these developments have been impelled by a concern that human rights law and institutions need to become more victim-centred, we then outline a range of arguments which are animated by the contrary belief, that victim-centricity is a major limitation of the human rights system. As we shall see, these latter arguments cannot be easily dismissed. But, for their part, are they too quick to dismiss victimology from the study of human rights? Illustrating our remarks with reference to the Abu Ghraib torture scandal that broke in May 2004, we highlight at the end some of the ways in which the 'victim' question may yet remain instructive, and indeed urgent.

Victims' rights

Let us begin, then, with victims' rights. Where victims of crime are concerned, rights are left to be inferred from international instruments which for the most part sidestep the language of entitlements, and speak instead of the duties of relevant authorities, or of the arrangements that should be in place. An early initiative was the European Convention on the Compensation of Victims of Violent Crimes, adopted within the framework of the Council of Europe in 1983. States parties to this treaty are obliged to establish compensation schemes for the benefit of victims of serious crimes of violence or their surviving families. An important non-treaty instrument of this period is the UN Declaration of Basic Principles of Justice for Victims of Crime and Abuse of Power.[3] Adopted by the UN General Assembly in 1985, this deals again with criminal compensation, but also with a wide range of other victim-related issues, among them 'material, medical, psychological and social assistance', restitution by offenders, and participation in criminal proceedings. With regard to the latter, it is declared that the 'responsiveness of judicial and administrative processes to the needs of victims should be facilitated' by informing victims of their role and of the progress and outcome of the proceedings, and by allowing the views and concerns of victims to be presented and considered at appropriate stages.[4] In 2001 the European

---

[3] UN GA Res. A/RES/40/34, 29 November 1985.   [4] Para. 6(a) and (b).

Union adopted a Framework Decision on the 'standing of victims in criminal proceedings' which includes many of these same elements.[5] In conjunction with the various specific obligations laid down, the Framework Decision makes explicit reference to the obligation of EU member states to 'recognise the rights and legitimate interests of victims with particular reference to criminal proceedings'.[6]

The three instruments we have just mentioned are addressed to national criminal procedure. In the context of international criminal procedure, the Rome Statute of the International Criminal Court is widely considered to exemplify a 'victim–centred' approach. Under the Statute victims are entitled to make submissions on the issue of whether or not the Prosecutor should continue with the investigation, and also on the issues of jurisdiction and admissibility.[7] Where their 'personal interests... are affected', they are also entitled to have their views and concerns heard and considered at appropriate stages of the proceedings.[8] Of vital importance in this field is the protection of victims and others who give testimony from those who would harm them. The Statute obliges both the Prosecutor and the Court to take appropriate measures to protect victims and witnesses.[9] More generally, it obliges the Prosecutor to ensure that the investigation and prosecution are conducted in a manner that respects 'the interests and personal circumstances of victims' and takes 'into account the nature of the crime', especially where sexual or gender-based violence or violence against children is involved.[10] Protection arrangements and other assistance to victims are co-ordinated through a Victims and Witnesses Unit, established within the court registry.[11] Finally, the Rome Statute provides that the court 'shall establish principles relating to reparations to, or in respect of, victims, including restitution, compensation and rehabilitation'.[12] Perpetrators may be ordered to make reparations. Alternatively, reparations may come from a Trust Fund, set up for the benefit of victims of crimes within the jurisdiction of the International Criminal Court.[13]

Beyond these developments concerning the rights of victims in national and international criminal proceedings, there is the issue of the rights of those who are victims of a violation of human rights. Whether

---

[5] Council of the EU, Framework Decision of 15 March 2001.   [6] Art. 2(1).
[7] Art. 19(3).   [8] Art. 68(3)   [9] Art. 68(1).   [10] Art. 54(1)(b).
[11] Art. 43(6).   [12] Art. 75(1).   [13] Art. 75(2).

or not criminal proceedings have been or could be initiated against the offender, the question obviously arises of the victim's rights with respect to the violation itself. In a study prepared for the UN Commission on Human Rights, it is observed that remedies for violations of international human rights encompass the victim's right to information, access to justice, and reparation for the harm suffered.[14] In connection with the International Covenant on Civil and Political Rights, the Human Rights Committee has likewise reaffirmed that the recognition of rights goes hand-in-hand with an obligation on the part of states parties to ensure that people have accessible and effective remedies to vindicate those rights.[15] The Committee has also highlighted the obligation of states parties to make reparation to those whose Covenant rights have been violated. According to the Committee, this generally entails compensation, and, where appropriate, may involve restitution, rehabilitation, public apologies, changes to relevant laws and other measures, as well as bringing to justice those responsible for the violation.[16]

Victimhood and its limits

Our focus to this point has been on initiatives premised on the idea that it would be good if legal procedures could become more victim-centred. In this section we review a number of arguments in which victim-centricity is much less enthusiastically embraced. Here the focus is on victimhood considered not as a basis for rights and reforms, but rather in terms of its downsides and dangers.

It is a common feature of human rights treaties that procedures for complaining to supervisory organs are reserved to individuals who can claim to be the victim of a violation; complaints by other concerned individuals or organisations are generally inadmissible. Thus, for

[14] Final Report of Cherif Bassiouni, special rapporteur on the right to restitution, compensation and rehabilitation for victims of gross violations of human rights and fundamental freedoms, UN Doc. E/CN.4/2000/62, 18 January 2000, Annex (Draft Basic Principles and Guidelines on the Right to a Remedy and Reparation for Victims of Violations of Human Rights and Humanitarian Law), para. 11.

[15] Human Rights Committee, General Comment 31 (The nature of the general legal obligation imposed on states parties to the Covenant), 21 April 2004, para. 15.

[16] Ibid., para. 16.

instance, under the First Protocol to the International Covenant on Civil and Political Rights, complaints about violations of the Covenant may only be lodged with the Human Rights Committee by those who claim to be the victim of those violations.[17] The same applies under other treaties, such as the Convention on the Elimination of All Forms of Racial Discrimination[18] and the European Convention on Human Rights.[19] A long-standing theme of critical commentary on human rights enforcement is that this is too limited, and that the criteria for admissibility of complaints before human rights courts and supervisory bodies should be expanded to include those whose enjoyment of human rights is not itself in question.[20] However, while not insignificant, this kind of criticism still remains within the realm of procedural reform, and captures only a small part of what some observers see as the much wider and deeper problem of the human rights regime's investment in victimhood.

One concern has to do with the character of victims as objects of pity and compassion. As Makau Mutua observes, the image of the human rights victim is a 'powerless, helpless innocent' upon whom catastrophic events are visited.[21] Or rather, according to him, it is a collection of 'hordes of nameless, despairing, and dispirited masses'.[22] This way of presenting things defines victims in terms of misery, tragedy and damage. That is to say, it treats their experience of suffering as wholly definitive of their being, and obscures the extent to which they retain the capacity for action and initiative. It also obscures the extent to which that capacity for action and initiative may be a source of residual and ongoing pleasure: the pleasure of solidarity, the pleasure of expression, the pleasure of re-imagining the world.[23] As Mutua highlights, a key consequence of the idea of the victim as passive wretch is that, instead of thinking about what people are, or could be, doing to change their circumstances, we are encouraged to view them as objects of intervention by others. At the same time, those others—lawyers, activists, officials, and

---

[17] See art. I.   [18] See art. 14(2).   [19] See art. 34.

[20] See, e.g., American Convention on Human Rights, art. 44, reflecting a broader approach to admissibility.

[21] M. Mutua, *Human Rights: A Political and Cultural Critique* (Philadelphia: University of Pennsylvania Press, 2002), 11.   [22] Ibid., 28–9.

[23] On this aspect, see the critique of 'suffer-mongerers' by Wendy Brown and Janet Halley in the Introduction to W. Brown & J. Halley (eds.), *Left Legalism, Left Critique* (Durham, NC: Duke University Press, 2002), 1, 28–33.

the like—are encouraged to adopt modes of representation that give a central place to pathos. All too often, that means melodrama.[24] Melodrama is so routinised in human rights practice that we hardly notice it, but it has serious effects, especially for those depicted as victims. In effect, it steals their experience, and puts in its place a cheap and ghastly imitation.

A further misgiving about the human rights regime's investment in victimhood is of a different kind. Whereas Mutua highlights the image of victims as hordes of nameless, helpless masses, others emphasise the way human rights individuate injustice and focus on those singled out (often because they are politically active), at the expense of those affected in their everyday lives. Mahmood Mamdani calls attention to this aspect in commentary on the work of the South African Truth and Reconciliation Commission, which delivered its final report in 1998.[25] The Commission was mandated to address gross violations of human rights committed during the *apartheid* era. It took this category to refer to killing, torture, severe ill-treatment, and abduction or forced disappearance. As Mamdani observes, abuses of this sort represent a tiny fraction, and not necessarily the most troubling, of *apartheid*'s injustices, which also included subjection to pass laws, forced removals, sub-standard education, and so on. Yet the Commission's attachment to human rights victimhood meant that it could not grasp these things. It could address the suffering of militants, but not the suffering of ordinary people. Mamdani wants us to see the consequences of this for those excluded from the category of victims, both with regard to the distribution of reparations and with regard to the risk of signalling that their suffering was somehow less important, or at any rate less important to document. He also wants us to see the consequences for those permitted to remain comfortably outside the category of perpetrators. For if systemic subordination was not covered, then nor was responsibility as a beneficiary of systemic privilege.

[24] On this, see R. Meister, 'The Liberalism of Fear and the Counterrevolutionary Project' 16 *Ethics and Public Affairs* (2002) 118, 123.

[25] M. Mamdani, 'Reconciliation Without Justice', *Southern African Review of Books*, Issue 46, Nov./Dec. 1996 and 'When Does Reconciliation Turn Into a Denial of Justice?', *The Sam Nolutshungu Memorial Lecture Series* 15 (1988), cited in T. Borer, 'A Taxonomy of Victims and Perpetrators: Human Rights and Reconciliation in South Africa' 25 *Human Rights Quarterly* (2003) 1088, 1111–13.

Another danger of victim-centricity has also been the subject of discussion in the context of transitional justice. This has to do with the way victim-centred approaches tend to promote strategies that are framed in terms of reconciliation or healing. That obviously supports the establishment of processes such as the South African Truth and Reconciliation Commission. More generally, however, it prioritises counselling and other practices geared to alleviating psychological distress. As Brandon Hamber writes, 'the needs of victims are often relegated (or compartmentalized off) to the therapy room'.[26] Without minimising the importance of trauma counselling for victims of violence, the danger here is that problems may come to be seen as primarily psychological (or perhaps socio-psychological) which must also be understood as inescapably political. Like the de-emphasis of systemic forms of injustice mentioned above, the focus on trauma associated with abusive events or episodes may divert attention from more constant and structural forms of violence. In the process, it may obscure the need to transform social arrangements. It may also obscure the possibility that transforming social arrangements precisely depends on the existence of *unreconciled* victims, and on the mobilising energy that is produced when there is not just grief, but also grievance.[27]

The points we have touched upon so far have mostly been elaborated with specific reference to human rights, whether in the context of discussions of international human rights law or of national transitional justice. Let us now mention one final point of a more general nature, which concerns the way victimhood may become bound up with identity, and in turn with competition among victimised groups. This is a familiar phenomenon, highlighted by many observers. Thus, Ian Buruma refers to the 'Olympics of suffering',[28] while Marina Warner remarks that an 'economy of virtue...flourishes around claims to injustice'—an economy that risks turning into a 'black market in competitive injury, an inflationary spiral of self-pitying self-justification'.[29]

[26] B. Hamber, 'Dealing with the Past: Rights and Reasons for Truth Recovery in South Africa and Northern Ireland', 26 *Fordham International Law Journal* (2002–3) 1074, 1091.

[27] On this point, see further R. Meister, 'Human Rights and the Politics of Victimhood' 16 *Ethics and Public Affairs* (2002), 91.

[28] I. Buruma, 'The Joys and Perils of Victimhood', *New York Review of Books*, 8 April 1999, 4.

[29] M. Warner, 'Sorry: the present state of apology—Scene One: Io', published on www.openDemocracy.net.

The key peril here is self-justification, the claim to occupy a moral high ground where culpability for wrongdoing cannot arise. In an article about the complicity of the Rwandan Patriotic Front in abuses in the Democratic Republic of Congo, George Monbiot calls this 'victim's licence'. As he explains, 'we license the victim to keep committing the crime'.[30] Under victim's licence, the victim remains forever a victim, endowed with a moral authority which entails permanent blamelessness. Here, then, is a further facet of the relation between victimhood and human rights: in Monbiot's words, '[i]t is arguable that nothing so endangers world peace and human rights as official victimhood'.[31]

Asking the victim question[32]

We have looked at how recognition of victims' rights may improve the position of crime victims with respect to criminal investigations and proceedings, compensation or restitution, and access to support services. On the other hand, we have also seen something of the way victimhood, especially 'official' victimhood, may enable crime and help to perpetuate the conditions in which human rights abuse occurs. Let us now re-examine the possibility that, notwithstanding the downsides and dangers which have been highlighted, asking the victim question may yet promote justice. By the victim question, we actually mean a plurality of questions, of the kind suggested by the academic discipline of victimology. Included are not just issues of victims' rights, but the whole range of issues that come into view when the focus is on victims and victimisation. To faciliate our discussion, it will be helpful at this stage to introduce an illustrative case. As indicated earlier, we propose to refer to reports in May 2004 of the torture of Iraqi prisoners at the Abu Ghraib detention centre outside Baghdad. Central to these reports was a series of photographs released to the media, and featured in a number of those photographs was Private Lynndie England, a person said at one point to have achieved the dubious distinction of becoming 'the most loathed woman in the world'.[33] Was Lynndie England really so uniquely

---

[30] G. Monbiot, 'The Victim's Licence', *The Guardian*, 13 April 2004.   [31] Ibid.

[32] With apologies to Margaret Davies, from whose *Asking the Law Question* (Sydney: Lawbook Co., 2002, 2nd edn.) we borrow this formulation.

[33] M. Riddell, 'A New Monster-in-Chief', *The Guardian*, 9 May 2004.

loathesome, or were some relevant facts being ignored here? By refocusing attention on victims and victimisation, what can we eludicate?

In the first place, and most obviously, we can challenge the almost exclusive focus on the perpetrators of the acts of torture, and raise questions about the victims. Who were they? How did they come to be detained? Insofar as the acts of torture were said to have been designed to 'soften them up' for interrogation, what kind of information were they expected to furnish? By what right was that information demanded? To initiate enquiry into those issues is, in turn, to prompt a host of further and larger questions about the occupation of Iraq itself, and about the resistance to that occupation. We will return to some of those in a moment. Secondly, we can challenge the simple binary 'perpetrator/victim', and ask whether the perpetrators may also have been themselves in some sense victims. The point here is not to exonerate them, but to query their demonisation, and try to understand the context in which they acted as they did. More generally, the point is to investigate the relation between individual culpability and larger social forces and patterns.[34] From this perspective, a range of questions arises about Lynndie England and her colleagues. What were the personal circumstances that brought them to Iraq in the first place? How did they come to join the US military? Who taught them to smile and give the thumbs up in the midst of all that misery? And how did it become possible for them to believe that these acts were acceptable, and even part of their duties? Where did they get the idea that there was no need to treat Iraqis humanely?[35]

Thirdly, we can challenge the assumption that the victims were only those involved in the torture episode. If, as we saw earlier, victimhood can serve to individuate injustice and concentrate attention on those singled out, at the expense of those affected more systemically, it can also be used to widen the focus. Thus, we may ask about the many other victims of the hostilities and of the occupation, who were not at Abu Ghraib. How many people were killed, and are still being killed, as a direct or indirect result of the conflict? What are its long-term health

---

[34] For discussion of this issue in another context, see T. Borer, 'A Taxonomy of Victims and Perpetrators: Human Rights and Reconciliation in South Africa' 25 *Human Rights Quarterly* (2003) 1088, 1113.

[35] For some answers, see N. Klein, 'Children of Bush's America', *The Guardian*, 18 May 2004 and A. Lewis, 'Making Torture Legal', *New York Review of Books*, 15 July 2004, 4.

and environmental impacts? How has it affected people's livelihoods and family life? How is it linked to patterns of victimisation elsewhere in the world? Finally, we can challenge sensationalised, larcenous representations of the events by journalists, officials and activists. Certainly, as noted above, victimhood may, and very frequently does, invite melodrama. But asking the victim question also means asking the victim, letting the victim speak. And one of the most striking insights of victimology is that, when crime victims speak, they do not always say what we have been conditioned to expect. For example, it is reported that in the United Kingdom '[v]ictim surveys have consistently revealed that victims are no more punitive than the general public'.[36] In the context of efforts to develop methods of 'restorative justice', many victims have apparently shown a willingness to engage in direct mediation with offenders. With this in mind, let us listen to a victim of the Abu Ghraib torture, albeit an indirect one.

Michael Berg is the father of Nicholas Berg, an American who was murdered in Iraq by men claiming to act in retaliation for the torture of Iraqi detainees at Abu Ghraib. In an article published in a British newspaper, Berg writes that he is often asked why he attaches blame for his son's atrocious end to the Bush administration.[37] People ask: 'Don't you blame the five men who killed him?' Berg says that he blames them too, but that he takes comfort from the thought that 'when they did the awful thing they did, they weren't quite as in to it as they might have been'. He continues: 'I am sure that the one who wielded the knife felt Nick's breath on his hand and knew that he had a real human being there. I am sure that the others looked into my son's eyes and got at least a glimmer of what the rest of the world sees. And I am sure that these murderers, for just a brief moment, did not like what they were doing.' By contrast, he suggests, George Bush and Donald Rumsfeld are never in the position of not liking what they are doing. They are always fully in to it, and spin adverse outcomes in a way that deflects criticism and removes fault. He explains: 'George Bush, though a father himself, cannot feel my pain, or that of my family, or of the world that grieves for Nick, because he is a policymaker, and he doesn't have to bear

[36] L. Zedner, 'Victims' in M. Maguire, R. Morgan & R. Reiner (eds.), *Oxford Handbook of Criminology* (Oxford: Oxford University Press, 2002), 419, 443.

[37] M. Berg, 'George Bush never looked into Nick's eyes', *The Guardian*, 21 May 2004. (All the succeeding quotations are from this article.)

the consequences of his acts...Donald Rumsfeld said that he took responsibility for the sexual abuse of Iraqi prisoners. How could he take that responsibility when there was no consequence? Nick took the consequences.' Berg concludes: 'Even more than those murderers who took my son's life, I can't stand those who sit and make policies to end lives and break the lives of the still living.'

Women

Among the many facets of that complex phenomenon we call globalisation, one is rarely noticed, yet absolutely integral. This is the migration of millions of women from poor countries to rich ones, to serve as maids, nannies, elder-carers, and sometimes sex workers. In the book *Global Woman*, Barbara Ehrenreich and Arlie Hochschild call this the 'globalization of women's traditional role'[1] or, more generally and in a way that highlights its relative invisibility, the 'female underside of globalization'.[2] As they explain, '[i]n the absence of help from male partners, many women have succeeded in tough "male world" careers only by turning over the care of their children, elderly parents, and homes to women from the Third World.'[3] In turn, those Third World women have improved their material circumstances, or in some cases simply made it possible for their families to survive, only by going abroad and leaving their own children in the care of sisters, elderly parents, daughters taken out of school to look after younger siblings, or other women they have themselves employed who have made similar arrangements for their children.

Ehrenreich and Hochschild observe that some female migrants are brutally forced into domestic labour or sex work. Some too end up in the control of criminal employers who steal their passports, abuse them, and make them work for no pay. But these situations, while extremely serious, are relatively rare. Mostly, passports are retained, conditions are decent, and those employed are paid wages that enable them to send home significant remittances. Even in these more typical cases, however, Ehrenreich and Hochschild note that 'Third World migrant women achieve their success only by assuming the cast-off domestic roles of middle- and high-income women in the First World... And their [the

---

[1] B. Ehrenreich & A. Hochschild, 'Introduction' in B. Ehrenreich & A. Hochschild (eds.), *Global Woman* (London: Granta Books, 2003), 1, 13.   [2] Ibid., 3.
[3] Ibid., 2–3.

former's] "commute" entails a cost we have yet to fully comprehend'.[4] Whatever that cost is, it is presumably paid not just by the migrant women themselves, but also their families, and often especially the female members of those families.

Of course, the migration of women to undertake work of this sort is by no means a new phenomenon. What does appear to be new, however, is the scale of the current enterprise, in the sense of the numbers of people involved and the distances they are travelling. Ehrenreich and Hochschild highlight a series of migration routes that have become established in recent years.[5] Viewed as an ensemble, these routes suggest an alternative geography of globalisation.[6] Inasmuch as that alternative geography reflects a certain synergy between the needs of women from richer and poorer parts of the globe, Ehrenreich and Hochschild remark that that synergy itself reflects the unwillingness of men to share responsibility for household work and their determination to 'continue avoiding the second shift'.[7] More than that, it reflects the 'failure of First World governments to meet the needs created by [their] women's entry into the workforce'—needs for child care, paid parental leave, better working conditions, and so on.[8] And, of course, it reflects the limited options available within the countries of emigration, and the difficulties experienced by those countries' women in the face of poverty, economic restructuring, and national debt.

Against the background of this new configuration, we consider in what follows some key features of the normative framework through which international human rights law seeks to address women's inequality, inse- curity, and exploitation.[9] We begin with the problem of gender-based discrimination. We then consider efforts in recent years to develop norms

---

[4] B. Ehrenreich & A. Hochschild, 'Introduction' in B. Ehrenreich & A. Hochschild (eds.), *Global Woman* (London: Granta Books, 2003), 3.

[5] For maps, see B. Ehrenreich & A. Hochschild (eds.), *Global Woman* (London: Granta Books, 2003), 276 *et seq.*

[6] On this aspect, see further S. Sassen, 'Global Cities and Survival Circuits' in B. Ehrenreich & A. Hochschild (eds.), *Global Woman* (London: Granta Books, 2003), 254.

[7] B. Ehrenreich & A. Hochschild, 'Introduction' in B. Ehrenreich & A. Hochschild (eds.), *Global Woman* (London: Granta Books, 2003), 1, 9.   [8] Ibid., 8–9.

[9] For further reference, see R. Cook (ed.), *Human Rights of Women* (Philadelphia: University of Pennsylvania Press, 1994); J. Peters & A. Wolper (eds.), *Women's Rights, Human Rights* (London: Routledge, 1995); W. Benedek, E. Kisaakye & G. Oberleitner (eds.), *The Human Rights of Women: International Instruments and African Experiences* (London: Zed Books, 2002); and K. Knop (ed.), *Gender and Human Rights* (Oxford: Oxford University Press, 2004).

concerning violence against women and, more recently still, trafficking of women. Finally, we return at the end to the more benign context of voluntary migration from poor countries to rich ones. If a global redivision of 'women's work' is indeed underway, then the question arises of the implications of this for the project of overcoming the subordination of women. Put starkly, what does the struggle for gender justice mean at a time when, as Ehrenreich and Hochschild remark, resourceful and ambitious women from different parts of the world are coming together, not in the way feminists once liked to imagine, 'as sisters and allies struggling to achieve common goals', but rather as 'mistress and maid, employer and employee, across a great divide of privilege and opportunity'?[10]

Discrimination

The idea that gender-based discrimination contradicts the universality of human rights is reflected in some form in all the foundational instruments of international human rights law and in many subsequent treaties. In the Universal Declaration of Human Rights, it is affirmed that everyone is entitled to all the rights and freedoms proclaimed 'without distinction of any kind', and sex is among the illustrative grounds of prohibited distinction then mentioned.[11] Similar statements are included in the International Covenant on Civil and Political Rights and the International Covenant on Economic, Social and Cultural Rights.[12] In addition, both Covenants contain a specific provision recording the undertaking of states parties 'to ensure the equal right of men and women to the enjoyment of all [the rights] set forth in the present Covenant'.[13] The Civil and Political Rights Covenant also contains a guarantee of equality before the law and equal protection of the law, and in this respect requires that national law 'prohibit any discrimination and guarantee to all persons equal and effective protection against discrimination on any ground'.[14] Again, sex is among the illustrative grounds of discrimination that are mentioned.

---

[10] B. Ehrenreich & A. Hochschild, 'Introduction' in B. Ehrenreich & A. Hochschild (eds.), *Global Woman* (London: Granta Books, 2003), 1, 11.

[11] Art. 2.

[12] See International Covenant on Civil and Political Rights, art. 2(1), and International Covenant on Economic, Social and Cultural Rights, art. 2(2).

[13] See art. 3 of both Covenants.   [14] Art. 26.

414 INTERNATIONAL HUMAN RIGHTS LEXICON

Beyond these general instruments, there also exist a number of treaties and other international instruments that are specifically addressed to discrimination against women. These include treaties concerned with gender-based discrimination in a particular sphere, such as the Convention on the Political Rights of Women and the ILO Convention on Equal Remuneration for Men and Women Workers for Work of Equal Value (ILO Convention 100). Most notably, however, they include the Convention on the Elimination of All Forms of Discrimination against Women, which seeks to confront the phenomenon of gender-based discrimination as a whole. Regional human rights systems contain a similar range of non-discrimination guarantees. In the African Charter of Human and Peoples' Rights, American Convention on Human Rights, European Convention on Human Rights, and other similar instruments, it is again stated that everyone is entitled to the rights recognised without discrimination on grounds of sex.[15] In some cases provision is also included for equality before the law and equal legal protection.[16] At the same time, a number of women-specific treaties and other instruments have been adopted at the regional level. The most wide-ranging of these is the Protocol to the African Charter on Human and Peoples' Rights on the Rights of Women in Africa (not yet in force), adopted in 2003.

The practical significance of these various guarantees of non-discrimination depends crucially, of course, on how the central concept of discrimination is understood. What kinds of situation are encompassed? Whose conduct is implicated, and which spheres of life are in question? And what is entailed with respect to state obligations? What are the implications of non-discrimination guarantees for policy, procedure and law? Taking up these and related questions, feminist

[15] See African Charter on Human and Peoples' Rights, art. 2; American Declaration of the Rights and Duties of Man, art. II; American Convention on Human Rights, art. 1; European Convention on Human Rights, art. 14; Commonwealth of Independent States Convention on Human Rights and Fundamental Freedoms, art. 20(2); and Revised Arab Charter on Human Rights (2004) (not yet in force), art. 3.
[16] See African Charter on Human and Peoples' Rights, art. 3; American Declaration of the Rights and Duties of Man, art. II; American Convention on Human Rights, art. 24; Protocol 12 to the European Convention on Human Rights, art. 1; Commonwealth of Independent States Convention on Human Rights and Fundamental Freedoms, art. 20(1); and Revised Arab Charter on Human Rights (2004) (not yet in force), art. 11.

scholars and activists have challenged received ideas, and developed new conceptualisations that have transformed the way we understand and approach gender-based discrimination—and, for that matter, most other forms of discrimination as well.[17] An initial point is that non-discrimination cannot simply mean refraining from treating women less favourably than men. It must also entail the adoption of positive measures to redress discrimination. A further insight is that anti-discrimination measures cannot concern themselves only with the conduct of public officials, that is to say, with relations between individuals and government. Discrimination in the 'private' sphere of the workplace, school and home must also be addressed. Finally, we have learned that state obligations under non-discrimination guarantees cannot be limited to legislative reform and changes within the domain of public administration. Action must also be taken to support social movements engaged in contesting the ideologies that help to perpetuate discrimination by making it seem part of the natural, rational, or divinely ordained order of things.

These points are reflected in a General Comment by the Human Rights Committee in which the implications are elaborated of article 3 of the International Covenant on Civil and Political Rights.[18] This is the provision we referred to above which records the undertaking of states parties 'to ensure the equal right of men and women to the enjoyment of all civil and political rights set forth' in the Covenant. In the first place, the Committee states that, in implementing this provision, states parties must 'not only adopt measures of protection, but also positive measures in all areas so as to achieve the effective and equal empower-ment of women'.[19] Thus, for instance, 'positive measures [should be taken] to promote and ensure women's participation in the conduct of public affairs and in public office, including appropriate affirmative action'.[20] Secondly, the Committee emphasises that the obligation of

---

[17] We speak compendiously here, but in fact, of course, feminism is no monolith. For discussion of varieties of feminism and their distinctive perspectives on norms of gender-based discrimination in international human rights law, see C. Charlesworth & C. Chinkin, *The Boundaries of International Law* (Manchester: Manchester University Press, 2000), chap. 7, and N. Lacey, 'Feminist Legal Theory and the Rights of Women' in K. Knop (ed.), *Gender and Human Rights* (Oxford: Oxford University Press, 2004), 13.

[18] Human Rights Committee, General Comment 28 (Equality of rights between men and women: art. 3), 29 March 2000.   [19] Ibid., para. 3.

[20] Ibid., para. 29 (regarding the right to participate in public affairs, protected in art. 25 of the Covenant).

states parties to put an end to discriminatory actions applies to actions 'both in the public and the private sector'.[21] With regard to the private sector, one aspect highlighted by the Committee is that 'a large proportion of women are employed in areas which are not protected by labour laws and that prevailing customs and traditions . . . [constrain] access to better paid employment and to equal pay for work of equal value'.[22] Thirdly, and connectedly, the Committee asserts the responsibility of states parties to 'ensure that traditional, historical, religious or cultural attitudes are not used to justify violations of women's right to equality before the law and to equal enjoyment of all Covenant rights'.[23] Linked to this is a call to promote and develop strategies for challenging and transforming such attitudes.

Early complaints mostly involved straightforward or 'direct' forms of discrimination involving asymmetries of formal legal status. In one case before the Human Rights Committee, for example, a complaint was brought against Mauritius in connection with immigration legislation under which foreign men who married Mauritian women lost their right to reside in Mauritius and had to apply for a residence permit which could be refused or revoked at any time. The same did not apply to foreign women who married Mauritian men.[24] The complainants were a group of Mauritian women married to foreign men, and the Committee upheld the allegation that this arrangement violated their right to equality before the law, protected in article 26 of the Covenant. In another series of cases, against the Netherlands, the complaints concerned legislation which denied women social security and unemployment benefits in circumstances where men in the same position would have been entitled to those benefits.[25] Again, the Committee endorsed the claim that this violated the female applicants' rights under article 26. Direct discrimination of these kinds remains a serious concern, and not only in relation to immigration and benefits entitlements, but also in relation to the administration of justice, inheritance and property-ownership,

[21] Human Rights Committee, General Comment 28 (Equality of rights between men and women: art. 3), 29 March 2000, para. 4.   [22] Ibid., para. 31.

[23] Ibid., para. 5.

[24] *Aumeeruddy-Cziffra & Others v Mauritius*, Communication 35/1978, Views of the Human Rights Committee, adopted 9 April 1981.

[25] *Broeks v Netherlands*, Communication 172/1984, Views of the Human Rights Committee, adopted 9 April 1987; *Zwaan-de Vries v Netherlands*, Communication 182/1984, Views of the Human Rights Committee, adopted 9 April 1987.

and marriage, divorce and personal status—areas in which stark legal disparities exist in many countries. At the same time, however, attention has also turned to more subtle forms of discrimination against women. In particular, attention has turned to the way norms and arrangements that are on their face neutral become discriminatory in the real-world contexts of their application. Among these more subtle forms of discrimination are some that implicate international human rights law itself.

One aspect of this, to which we have already referred, concerns the traditional focus on public life and the conduct of public officials. If feminists have insisted that discrimination must also be addressed in the 'private' sphere of the workplace, school and home, they have noted in doing so that women are disproportionately affected by inequality, insecurity and exploitation in those arenas. Another, related aspect concerns the relative paucity of avenues for invoking economic and social rights within the international human rights system, and the justifying rhetoric of 'non-justiciability' which underpins that situation. While this may appear neutral in its impact, things again begin to look different when the point is registered that violations of labour, education and health rights are themselves gendered. As noted by the Human Rights Committee, a large proportion of women are employed in areas which are not protected by labour laws. The maids, nannies, elder-carers and sex workers of whom we wrote at the beginning will often be in this category. Likewise, as discussed elsewhere in this book, the overwhelming majority of children deprived of basic education, and adults unable to read, are female.[26] Let us highlight one final aspect, which has to do with the concept of discrimination itself, and in particular with the way that concept involves assessing female disadvantage by reference to male comparators. The trouble with this mode of assessment is that it captures only part of the reality. It fails to register forms of disadvantage that do not appear when the position of women is measured against, and hence mediated by, that of men. How, then, can human rights law be made to speak more fully and directly to the distinctive experiences of women? One answer has been found in the theme of violence against women.

[26] See further Education*. See also K. Watkins, *The Oxfam Education Report* (Oxford: Oxfam, 2000), 3 (referring to the existence 'at the very heart of education [of] a system of "gender apartheid" ').

Violence

Since the 1980s and especially 1990s violence against women has been a significant focus of organised activism and institutional engagement.[27] By violence against women is meant here a wide range of practices, including some that occur in all countries, such as domestic violence and custodial rape, and others that mostly occur in particular places or regions, such as dowry-related violence and 'honour killings'. Whereas violence of this sort may earlier have been of interest only to criminologists, sociologists, and anthropologists, or to social workers, welfare officers, and religious leaders, a key aim of the movement that emerged in the last decades of the 20th century was to increase its public visibility and reframe it as an issue of human rights.[28] Animating this aim was concern about inadequacies in the scope and enforcement of legal protections, and about factors that discouraged reporting and led to victims being blamed. The movement's influence is reflected in the documents adopted at successive World Conferences on Women, and especially the Beijing Declaration and Programme of Action, adopted in 1995. It is also reflected in the Vienna Declaration and Programme of Action, adopted at the World Conference on Human Rights in 1993. And it is reflected too in the appointment in 1994 of a UN Special Rapporteur on Violence against Women, whose reports describe and analyse violence of many different kinds and the actions that might be, and are being, taken to challenge it.[29]

Beyond these initiatives, a series of instruments has been elaborated on the theme of violence against women. The first was a General Recommendation adopted in 1992 in connection with the Convention on the Elimination of All Forms of Discrimination against Women.[30] In the General Recommendation, the Committee on the Elimination of

[27] See further P. Sen, 'Successes and Challenges: Understanding the Global Movement to End Violence against Women', in M. Kaldor, H. Anheier & M. Glasius (eds.), *Global Civil Society 2003* (Oxford: Oxford University Press, 2003), 119.

[28] See, more recently, Amnesty International, *It's In Our Hands: Stop Violence Against Women* (London: Amnesty International, 2004) (AI Index: ACT 77/001/2004).

[29] See, e.g., final report of Special Rapporteur Radhika Coomaraswamy, UN Doc. E/CN.4/2003/75, 6 January 2003.

[30] Committee on the Elimination of Discrimination Against Women, General Recommendation 19 (Violence against women), 29 January 1992.

Discrimination against Women highlights the obligation of states parties to the Convention to 'take positive measures to eliminate all forms of violence against women'.[31] In this regard the Committee affirms that states parties are not only responsible for eliminating violence by public authorities. They 'may also be responsible for private acts if they fail to act with due diligence to prevent violations of rights or to investigate and punish acts of violence'.[32] While in this document the Committee was constrained by the terms of the Convention to address violence against women through the lens of discrimination, in the following year the UN General Assembly adopted a Declaration on the Elimination of Violence against Women which put aside the concept of discrimination and cast the issue in more autonomous terms.[33] The Declaration asserts that violence against women constitutes a violation of the human rights of those victimised, and highlights a number of rights that may be affected, among them the right to life, the right not to be subjected to torture or other ill-treatment, the right to equality and equal legal protection, the right to be free from discrimination, the right to health, and the right to just and favourable conditions of work. The Declaration also reaffirms the obligations of states to '[e]xercise due diligence to prevent, investigate and, in accordance with national legislation, punish acts of violence against women, whether those acts are perpetrated by the State or by private persons'.[34]

In 1994 a treaty along similar lines to the UN Declaration was adopted within the framework of the Inter-American system—the Inter-American Convention on the Prevention, Punishment and Eradication of Violence against Women. Within the framework of the African system, the 2003 Protocol on the Rights of Women in Africa, mentioned earlier, distils the key elements of earlier documents.[35] The Protocol also addresses the related issue of 'harmful practices', a term used to refer to such practices as scarification and female genital cutting.[36] Discussion of these practices has provoked considerable controversy, encompassing questions not only of policy, but also of terminology and categorisation. Reflected in the Protocol is a human rights approach, in which states parties undertake to 'prohibit and condemn all forms of harmful practices which negatively affect the human

---

[31] Ibid., para. 4.   [32] Ibid., para. 9.
[33] UN GA Res. 48/104, adopted 23 February 1994.   [34] Ibid., art. 4(c).
[35] See esp. art. 4.   [36] Art. 5.

rights of women and which are contrary to recognised international standards'.[37] Among the rights which have been highlighted in this context are the right to health and the right to life. Whereas harmful practices are not undertaken with intent to injure, even if that is the outcome, the term 'traditional practices' is sometimes used in a way that brings these practices together with dowry murders, 'honour killings', widow burning (*sati*), and the like. Some of these latter forms of violence have been analysed from a human rights perspective in reports of the UN Special Rapporteur on Extrajudicial Executions.[38] Insofar as these practices are justified through arguments based on tradition, religion, or culture, questions have been raised about the participation of those affected in the interpretations that are put forward. Thus, Arati Rao writes of the need to investigate the status of the cultural interpreter, and to ask 'whose culture this is and who its primary beneficiaries are'.[39] In any event, as noted earlier, the Human Rights Committee has asserted the responsibility of states parties to the Civil and Political Rights Covenant to 'ensure that traditional, historical, religious or cultural attitudes are not used to justify violations of women's right to equality before the law and to equal enjoyment of all Covenant rights', including, of course, the right to life.[40]

An important dimension of the move to reframe violence against women in human rights terms concerns rape and other forms of sexual violence. In the context of the European Convention on Human Rights victims of rape have on a number of occasions asserted the responsibility of states for violations of their human rights. In one case against Turkey the applicant was raped and subjected to other forms of ill-treatment while in police custody.[41] The European Court of Human Rights upheld her complaint that this violated the prohibition of torture in article 3 of the Convention. For the Court, 'the accumulation of acts of physical and mental violence inflicted on the applicant and the especially cruel act of

---

[37] Art. 5.

[38] See Report of the Special Rapporteur on Extrajudicial, Summary or Arbitrary Executions, Asma Jahangir, 25 January 2000, UN Doc. E/CN.4/2000/3, 27 (para. 78 *et seq.*).

[39] A. Rao, 'The Politics of Gender and Culture in International Human Rights Discourse' in J. Peters & A. Wolper (eds.), *Women's Rights, Human Rights* (London: Routledge, 1995), 167, 174.

[40] Human Rights Committee, General Comment 28 (Equality of rights between men and women: art. 3), adopted 29 March 2000, para. 5.

[41] *Aydin v Turkey*, Judgment of the European Court of Human Rights, 25 September 1997.

rape to which she was subjected amounted to torture in breach of Article 3 of the Convention'. The Court added that it 'would have reached this conclusion on either of these grounds taken separately'.[42] In a later case against Bulgaria, the court was faced with a complaint arising out of the failure of the national authorities to initiate prosecutions in respect of the applicant's alleged rape by two men when she was 14.[43] Prosecutions had not been initiated because under Bulgarian law and practice cases were only prosecuted where there was evidence that the victim physically resisted the assault, and in this case that evidence was lacking. The applicant pointed out that consent could not be inferred from lack of physical resistance; the actual presence or absence of consent needed to be investigated on the basis of all relevant factors. In her contention, the failure of the Bulgarian authorities to undertake such an investigation, together with the prosecutorial practice of requiring evidence of physical resistance in all cases, had left her inadequately protected against rape and other sexual violence. The Court upheld this claim, and ruled the state in breach of its obligations under the prohibition on torture and other ill-treatment (article 3) and the right to private life (article 8). As it explained, 'States have a positive obligation inherent in Articles 3 and 8 of the Convention to enact criminal-law provisions effectively punishing rape and to apply them in practice through effective investigation and prosecution'.[44] This 'must be seen as requiring the penalisation and effective prosecution of any non-consensual sexual act, including in the absence of physical resistance by the victim'.[45]

Beyond these contexts in which states have been held responsible in connection with sexual violence, rape may also entail international criminal liability for the individual perpetrators. Under the Rome Statute of the International Criminal Court rape and other forms of sexual violence 'of comparable gravity' constitute crimes against humanity when committed 'as part of a widespread or systematic attack directed against any civilian population, with knowledge of the attack'.[46] These acts may also be subject to prosecution as war crimes[47] or, where the

[42] Ibid., para. 86.

[43] *M.C. v Bulgaria*, Judgment of the European Court of Human Rights, 4 December 2003. [44] Ibid., para. 153.

[45] Ibid., para. 166.

[46] Rome Statute of the International Criminal Court, art. 7(1)(g).

[47] Ibid., art. 8(2)(b)(xxii). See also art. 8(2)(b)(xxi).

requisites of the offence apply, acts of genocide.[48] Rape was likewise included among those acts which could be prosecuted as crimes against humanity and war crimes under the earlier Statutes of the International Criminal Tribunal for the former Yugoslavia and the International Criminal Tribunal for Rwanda.[49] In the first judgment delivered by the International Criminal Tribunal for Rwanda in 1998, the Tribunal found the accused criminally responsible in relation to multiple incidents of rape and other sexual violence.[50] In doing so, it defined rape for the purpose of the Tribunal's Statute as a 'physical invasion of a sexual nature, committed on a person under circumstances which are coercive'.[51] It used the broader term 'sexual violence' to refer to 'any act of a sexual nature which is committed on a person under circumstances which are coercive', whether physical contact is involved or not.[52] Though sexual violence not involving rape is not explicitly mentioned in the Tribunal's Statute, as it is in the later Statute of the International Criminal Court, the Tribunal considered it to come within the category of 'other inhumane acts' which may constitute crimes against humanity under the Statute.[53] The Tribunal emphasised that coercive circumstances do not need to be evidenced by a show of actual physical force. In its words, '[t]hreats, intimidation, extortion and other forms of duress which prey on fear or desperation may constitute coercion, and coercion may be inherent in certain circumstances, such as armed conflict'.[54] Sexual assault and enforced prostitution were defining features of the conflict that led to the establishment of the International Criminal Tribunal for the former Yugoslavia, and calls to deny impunity to those responsible are reflected in numerous indictments issued in that Tribunal with respect to rape and related crimes. One case concerned the detention of

---

[48] See Rome Statute of the International Criminal Court, art. 6.

[49] Statute of the International Criminal Tribunal for the former Yugoslavia, art. 5(g); Statute of the International Criminal Tribunal for Rwanda, arts. 3(g) and 4(e).

[50] *Prosecutor v Akayesu* (Case ICTR-96-4-T), Judgment of the International Criminal Tribunal for Rwanda, 2 September 1998.   [51] Ibid., para. 688.

[52] Ibid.

[53] See Statute of the International Criminal Tribunal for Rwanda, art. 3(i). The Tribunal also affirmed that sexual violence may also be a war crime ('outrage upon personal dignity') and an element that may evidence genocide ('serious bodily or mental harm'); see ibid., para. 688.

[54] *Prosecutor v Akayesu* (Case ICTR-96-4-T), Judgment of the International Criminal Tribunal for Rwanda, 2 September 1998, para. 688.

Muslim women in soldiers' residences and other places being used as military facilities, where they were mistreated in many ways, including being repeatedly raped.[55] The three accused were found guilty of rape, enslavement, and other crimes.[56] The Appeals Chamber reaffirmed that proof of the non-consensual character of sexual relations did not depend on specific evidence of force on the part of the perpetrators or resistance on the part of the victims. The victims' detentions amounted to 'circumstances that were so coercive as to negate any possibility of consent'.[57]

Trafficking

One form of violence against women which sets the phenomenon within a transnational context is the trafficking of women for forced prostitution. Trafficking invariably involves the violation of many fundamental rights, and also exposes those trafficked to further abuses in the country of destination, including violations of the right not to be subjected to forced labour and the right to humane treatment. Trafficking may additionally constitute a crime against humanity and hence engage the international criminal responsibility of individual traffickers. Under the Rome Statute of the International Criminal Court, trafficking may be subject to prosecution as the crime of enslavement, if it is committed 'as part of a widespread or systematic attack directed against any civilian population, with knowledge of the attack'.[58] Trafficking of women and girls is addressed in the Convention on the Elimination of All Forms of Discrimination against Women. Under article 6 of that Convention, states parties assume an obligation 'take all appropriate measures, including legislation, to suppress all forms of traffic in women and exploitation of prostitution of women'. Trafficking is also addressed

[55] *Prosecutor v Kunarac and Others* (Case IT-96-23 & IT-96-23/1-A), Judgment of the International Criminal Tribunal for the former Yugoslavia (Appeals Chamber), 12 June 2002.

[56] Regarding the crime of enslavement, see Statute of the International Criminal Tribunal for the former Yugoslavia, art. 5(c).

[57] *Prosecutor v Kunarac and Others* (Case IT-96-23 & IT-96-23/1-A), Judgment of the International Criminal Tribunal for the former Yugoslavia (Appeals Chamber), 12 June 2002, para. 132.

[58] Rome Statute of the International Criminal Court, art. 7(1)(c). See also art. 7(2)(c).

as an aspect of violence against women in the various treaties and other pronouncements on that theme mentioned above. Thus, the Committee on the Elimination of Discrimination against Women, in its General Recommendation on violence against women of 1992, highlights the practice of trafficking, and points to aspects of its contemporary context and effects.[59] Likewise, the UN Declaration on Violence against Women includes trafficking and forced prostitution within its illustrative enumeration of forms of violence against women.[60] And the Inter-American Convention on the Prevention, Punishment and Eradication of Violence against Women and Protocol to the African Charter on Human and Peoples' Rights on the Rights of Women in Africa record guarantees of protection against trafficking.[61]

As well as being recognised as a violation of human rights, an act of violence against women, and (where it is part of a wider assault on a civilian population) a crime against humanity, cross-border trafficking has also been approached as a form of transnational organised crime. In 2000 a Protocol was adopted supplementing the UN Convention against Transnational Organized Crime in this respect—the Protocol to Prevent, Suppress and Punish Trafficking in Persons, Especially Women and Children. The key obligation imposed on states parties to this Protocol is to make trafficking and related acts (such as complicity in trafficking and the organization of trafficking) criminal offences under national law.[62] There is also an obligation to take measures to prevent trafficking,[63] and to co-operate with law enforcement agencies in other countries to that end.[64] For the purpose of the Protocol, trafficking is defined in terms of a particular act, means, and purpose.[65] The act is 'recruitment, transportation, transfer, harboring or receipt of persons'. The means are the 'threat or use of force or other forms of coercion, of abduction, of fraud, of deception, of the abuse of power or of a position of vulnerability or of the giving or receiving of payments or benefits to achieve the consent of a person having control over another person'.

[59] Committee on the Elimination of Discrimination Against Women, General Recommendation 19 (Violence against women), 29 January 1992, para. 14.
[60] UN GA Res. 48/104, adopted 23 February 1994, art. 2(b).
[61] See Inter-American Convention on the Prevention, Punishment and Eradication of Violence against Women, art 2(b) (defining violence against women to include trafficking and related practices); Protocol to the African Charter on Human and Peoples' Rights on the Rights of Women in Africa, art. 4(c).   [62] Art. 5.
[63] Art. 9.   [64] Art. 10.   [65] Art. 3(a).

And the purpose is 'exploitation', stated to include 'at a minimum, the exploitation of the prostitution of others or other forms of sexual exploitation, forced labour or services, slavery or practices similar to slavery, servitude or the removal of organs'. The Protocol stipulates that the consent of the victim is irrelevant where any of the means just mentioned have been used.[66] Thus, it is recognised that involuntary transfer may occur in a wide range of contexts. In practice, victims of trafficking are not generally treated in their countries of destination as victims of human rights abuse, except in occasional cases where extreme cruelty is revealed. Rather, being generally undocumented, they are treated simply as illegal immigrants. The Protocol does not challenge this approach, though it does recognise the rights of trafficked people as victims of crime.[67] With regard to their repatriation, it provides that their return 'shall preferably be voluntary', and must in any event be effected 'with due regard for [their] safety'.[68] The Protocol also invites states parties to consider adopting legislative and administrative measures to allow victims of trafficking to remain, 'temporarily or permanently, in appropriate cases'.[69]

Global woman

Gender-based discrimination, violence against women and trafficking of women speak to important facets of the inequality, insecurity and exploitation of women in the world today. But they do not speak to the entirety of that inequality, insecurity and exploitation. To consider something of what may be missed, let us now return to the phenomenon with which we began, the phenomenon which Barbara Ehrenreich and Arlie Hochschild call the 'globalization of women's traditional role'.

In 1988 Carole Pateman wrote that the social contract was to be understood as a 'sexual contract'.[70] Today there is evidence that that sexual contract may be becoming globalised. Growth in the business of trafficking forms part of this process. At the same time, the migrations of women highlighted by Ehrenreich and Hochschild suggest that the global sexual contract is not limited to sexual services, but includes the various domestic functions which have traditionally been allocated to

---

[66] Art. 3(b).   [67] Art. 6.   [68] Art. 8   [69] Art. 7.
[70] C. Pateman, *The Sexual Contract* (Cambridge: Polity Press, 1988).

women as well, such as housekeeping, childcare and home nursing. These migrations further suggest that the global sexual contract is not confined to forced transfer and slave labour, but encompasses also voluntary moves by women who have chosen to go abroad and who get paid when they arrive there. Of course, the voluntariness of these women's emigration should not be overstated. If they choose to leave, this is generally because, as Arlie Hochschild observes, 'economic pressures all but coerce them to'. It is only because of 'the prevailing free market ideology [that] migration is viewed as a "personal choice", [and that its] consequences are seen as "personal problems"'.[71] It is also the case that some women start out as voluntary migrants and then later fall into the hands of traffickers. Trafficking is a complex, multi-episodal phenomenon, and there is no question that the line between it and voluntary migration is often fine. Nonetheless, it cannot capture the full range of ways in which women on the periphery of the global economic system are today being drawn, and drawing themselves, into what Saskia Sassen vividly calls 'survival circuits'.[72]

As Sassen explains, the mobilisation of women into survival circuits casts a new light on globalisation, challenging the dominant focus on the 'upper circuits' of global capital, and prompting us to consider also the 'lower circuits' and 'material infrastructure' that make possible the free flow of money and the moneyed.[73] At the same time, however, this mobilisation also casts a new light on feminism. Like other emancipatory discourses, feminism is, at least in part, an enterprise of 'silence breaking'.[74] In more visual terms, analyses are concerned with exposing to scrutiny aspects of reality that are more commonly hidden, unnoticed, or glossed over. Ehrenreich and Hochschild indeed exemplify this with their account of the 'female underside of globalization'.[75] What is fascinating about the globalisation of women's traditional role is that it turns the mirror back onto feminism itself. For (feminist) journalist

[71] A. Hochschild, 'Love and Gold' in B. Ehrenreich & A. Hochschild (eds.), *Global Woman* (London: Granta Books, 2003), 15, 27.

[72] S. Sassen, 'Global Cities and Survival Circuits' in B. Ehrenreich & A. Hochschild (eds.), *Global Woman* (London: Granta Books, 2003), 254.   [73] Ibid.

[74] See, e.g., 'Silence Breaking: The Women's Dimension of the Human Rights Box', *Human Rights Dialogue* (a publication of the Carnegie Council for Ethics and International Affairs), Summer 2000.

[75] B. Ehrenreich & A. Hochschild, 'Introduction' in B. Ehrenreich & A. Hochschild (eds.), *Global Woman* (London: Granta Books, 2003), 1, 2.

Polly Toynbee, the global redivision of domestic work is 'western feminism's dirty little secret'.[76] In her words, '[b]ehind the glorious image of the have-it-all-woman . . . too often lies a tale of the oppression of another woman . . . Liberation for high-fliers breaking through glass ceilings is only possible because of a flotilla of unseen, unheard women who care for their children, clean their homes and cook their meals while they live liberated like men'. Toynbee emphasises, as Ehrenreich and Hochschild do, that responsibility for this situation must be shared by 'men who still refuse to take an equal share in everything domestic'. Explanations are also to be found, she proposes, in 'the state's failure to provide universal childcare' and, more generally, in the 'long-hours culture' of contemporary capitalism.[77] In the end, however, the fact remains that the expanded options of some women are linked to the very limited options of others, and that the increasingly global character of this relation looks disturbingly like a new chapter in the long history of imperialist exploitation—a new chapter in which, as Hochschild puts it, what is extracted from the global South is no longer just rubber, ivory and gold, but also love.[78]

In a recent book about gender and human rights, Janet Halley calls into question the idea that 'feminism remains an utterly underdog movement needing complete and unbroken solicitude'.[79] Discussing conditions in North America, she remarks that there are 'plenty of places where feminism—far from slinking about underground—is running things. Sex harassment, child sexual abuse, pornography, sexual violence: these feminist justice projects have moved off the street and into state and corporate bureaucracies . . . In some important senses, *feminism rules*'.[80] And yet, she writes, feminism is 'without a theory and practice of its own role in governance, of itself as responsible wielder of power'.[81] Halley's point is not the 'post-feminist' or anti-feminist claim that traditional feminist preoccupations should be set aside. It is rather that feminism needs to develop a more self-critical form of investigation, of a kind which will enable us to see better the costs associated

---

[76] P. Toynbee, 'Mothers for sale', *The Guardian*, 19 July 2003. [77] Ibid.
[78] A. Hochschild, 'Love and Gold' in B. Ehrenreich & A. Hochschild (eds.), *Global Woman* (London: Granta Books, 2003), 15, esp. 26.
[79] J. Halley, 'Take a Break from Feminism?' in K. Knop (ed.), *Gender and Human Rights* (Oxford: Oxford University Press, 2004), 57, 65. [80] Ibid.
[81] Ibid.

with feminist gains, and who pays them. To be clear, the problem from this perspective is not the gains, but the costs and their distribution. Insofar as those costs are borne in distinctive ways and to a disproportionate extent by women, as in the context of the global redivision of domestic work, the problem thus belongs with the unfinished and ongoing business of feminist critique.[82] While much of what Halley describes may correspond to the experience of few countries other than the United States and Canada, this general point carries an important message for international efforts to promote women's human rights. In Toynbee's terms, western feminism needs to confront its dirty secrets, and formulate strategies for redressing the inequities they involve.

What, then, of 'global woman', with whom Ehrenreich and Hochschild seek to acquaint us? At one level, of course, there is no such person. There are only global *women*, billions of them, and, far from constituting a unity, the issue is precisely to what extent they are divided in wealth and opportunity, both within countries and across the world. At another level, however, global woman perhaps stands for the possibility of closing those divisions, and of developing a kind of solidarity, or at any rate a form of democratic global governance, that could improve the life chances of all women in relation to men and other women.

[82] On this point, see B. Ehrenreich, 'Maid to Order' in B. Ehrenreich & A. Hochschild (eds.), *Global Woman* (London: Granta Books, 2003), 85, 103.

Work

It is widely recognised that great changes have affected the world of work in recent decades. One of the clearest accounts of what is involved is provided by Naomi Klein in her book *No Logo*.[1] Klein's title alludes to the massive scaling down of manufacturing that has occurred in many countries of the global North, in favour of a focus on marketing. Instead of making their products themselves, companies are increasingly preferring to concentrate their energies—and enlarged proportions of their revenues—on developing their customer bases, promoting their brands. Clothes, shoes, computers, and other manufactured goods are today 'sourced', just like natural resources. And just like natural resources, they are mostly sourced from countries of the global South. But Klein points out that the change is not just about where goods are produced. It is also about how they are produced. Manufacturing has become an affair of individual 'orders', placed with contractors, and through them often a long chain of subcontractors, who must continually compete to fulfil specifications while offering the cheapest possible prices.

Linked to that private competition is the form of public competition that has been called the 'race to the bottom', in which governments are seen to vie to attract foreign investment by reducing social protections. Perhaps the most striking manifestation of this is the phenomenon of the 'export processing zone', or EPZ. Klein uses a vivid image to describe these zones: 'industrialization in brackets'. EPZs are placed, she writes, 'within a kind of legal and economic set of brackets' that entails wide-ranging exemption from normal requirements.[2] Extending the principle of the free trade zone, exemption is typically provided not just from export and import duties, but also from income and property taxes, and, now notoriously, from the enforcement of labour laws, health

[1] N. Klein, *No Logo* (London: Flamingo, 2001).   [2] Ibid., 207.

and safety regulations, and civil rights guarantees. Since the 1980s EPZs have proliferated throughout the developing world, as well as in some of the 'transition' states.[3] Their proliferation has caused considerable concern because of the sweatshop conditions in which the (mostly female) employees often work. In this connection, there is anxiety that order-driven manufacturing is fostering employment that is exploitative, unstable and insecure.

The rise of EPZs is associated with the globalisation of production. But the same logics are also affecting employment in rich countries, including service sector employment. Just as factories are being replaced by orders, so too service work once performed by employees is frequently today outsourced. To the extent that sales staff and others continue to be employed, the trend in many countries towards part-time work, home work and temporary work has been widely discussed. 'Flexible' scheduling is a term sometimes used to refer to the new pattern, though, as Klein observes, the flexibility involved is often not what workers have in mind when they aspire to more flexible working arrangements.[4] It is often a matter of organising things so as to ensure the inapplicability, or reduced applicability, of legal requirements regarding pay scales, employee benefits and job security. Thus, the challenge of making ends meet, rather than getting easier, can become more difficult, as companies slough off their responsibilities as employers, and turn away from the inconvenient reality that those who work for them need to earn a living.

What does this mean for the prospects of raising living standards? In a book entitled *The Corrosion of Character*, Richard Sennett writes of observing successive meetings of the World Economic Forum at Davos in Switzerland.[5] He reports that, after attending many sessions, he began to notice something about the business and political leaders present. This was that these extremely influential and generally confident individuals 'become acutely and personally uncomfortable, fidgeting or breaking eye contact or retreating into taking notes, if forced to discuss the people who, in their jargon, are "left behind".[6] He explains: 'They

---

[3] By far the largest concentration is today in China. According to ILO estimates, there are currently more than 5,000 EPZs throughout the world. Of the 40 million people who work in them, 30 million are in China. See www.ilo.org/public/english/dialogue/sector/themes/epz/stats.htm.

[4] See N. Klein, *No Logo* (London: Flamingo, 2001), 242.

[5] R. Sennett, *The Corrosion of Character* (New York: Norton, 1998).   [6] Ibid., 147.

know that the great majority of those who toil in the flexible regime are left behind, and of course they regret it'.[7] But, so the thought goes, such is the state of the world today. Implicit here is the intriguing suggestion that 'leaving behind' has, so to speak, overtaken 'catching up'. That is to say, 'catching up' has lost its power, even as myth. If that is correct, it raises many large and urgent questions. In what follows, we discuss some that implicate the international protection of labour rights. The key issue for us will be whether international human rights law can contribute to ongoing efforts to re-assert workers' rights and re-emphasise employers' responsibilities, and if so, how.

Human rights and work

The most obvious starting point for any enquiry into internationally protected workers' rights is the International Labour Organization. Established in 1919, the ILO was mandated to develop standards with regard to labour conditions. By the Declaration of Philadelphia of 1944, this mandate was expanded to include related aspects of social and economic policy. Since 1919, the Organization has adopted more than 180 treaties or 'conventions', some dealing with issues relevant to all workers, others concerned with particular sectors, social groups or types of work. We will have occasion to notice several in this discussion. Alongside these conventions, and elaborating on their provisions, a similar number of (non-binding) recommendations has also been adopted. Together, the various conventions and recommendations constitute what are referred to as 'international labour standards'. Supplementing them in turn is a range of declarations, codes of conduct and other documents issued by the International Labour Conference and other ILO organs. What is the relationship between international labour standards and human rights?

One way of answering that question is to refer to the fact that, in an attempt to make manageable the very substantial catalogue of standards that has been adopted over the years, the ILO has divided international labour standards into categories, and some of the categories are defined in terms of human rights. Specifically, eight ILO conventions have been designated as 'fundamental ILO conventions', on the ground that they

---

[7] Ibid.

are 'fundamental to the rights of human beings at work'.[8] These deal with freedom of association and the right to collective bargaining, forced or compulsory labour, child labour, and discrimination in respect of employment and occupation. We will return to highlight some further points relating to these conventions below. A further eight conventions and related recommendations have been designated 'basic human rights' standards.[9] These deal with rural workers' associations, the right of public employees to organise, the protection of workers' representatives, and the equal rights of workers with family responsibilities.

But reference to these ILO categorisations is only a very partial answer to the question of how international labour standards and human rights interrelate. Apart from other considerations, it says nothing about international human rights law, and about the wide range of work-related rights recognised in human rights treaties and other instruments. Here the initial reference-point is the Universal Declaration of Human Rights of 1948, which affirms in article 23 that:

(1) Everyone has the right to work, to free choice of employment, to just and favourable conditions of work and to protection against unemployment.

(2) Everyone, without any discrimination, has the right to equal pay for equal work.

(3) Everyone who works has the right to just and favourable remuneration ensuring for himself and his family an existence worthy of human dignity, and supplemented, if necessary, by other means of social protection.

(4) Everyone has the right to form and to join trade unions for the protection of his interests.

---

[8] Freedom of Association and Protection of the Right to Organise Convention 1948 (ILO Convention No. 87); Right to Organise and Collective Bargaining Convention 1949 (ILO Convention No. 98); Forced Labour Convention 1930 (ILO Convention No. 29); Abolition of Forced Labour Convention 1957 (ILO Convention No. 105); Discrimination (Employment and Occupation) Convention 1958 (ILO Convention No. 111); Equal Remuneration Convention 1951 (ILO Convention No. 100); Minimum Age Convention 1973 (ILO Convention No. 138); and Worst Forms of Child Labour Convention 1999 (ILO Convention No. 182).

[9] Rural Workers Organizations Convention 1975 (ILO Convention No. 141) supplemented by Recommendation No. 149; Labour Relations (Public Service) Convention 1978 (ILO Convention No. 151) supplemented by Recommendation No. 159; Workers Representatives Convention 1971 (ILO Convention No. 135) supplemented by Recommendation No. 143; and Workers with Family Responsibilities Convention 1981 (ILO Convention No. 156) supplemented by Recommendation No. 165.

In article 24 it is further affirmed that:

Everyone has the right to rest and leisure, including reasonable limitation of working hours and periodic holidays with pay.

Beyond these rights, the Universal Declaration recognises many other rights that are directly relevant to employment: the right to freedom of association,[10] the prohibition of slavery and servitude,[11] the right to social security in the event of unemployment,[12] the right to equal protection of the law,[13] and the right to enjoy these rights without discrimination.[14]

These and allied rights are protected in the two International Covenants of 1966. While the International Covenant on Economic, Social and Cultural Rights contains wide-ranging provisions on the right to work,[15] the right to just and favourable conditions of work,[16] trade union rights,[17] and the right to social security,[18] the International Covenant on Civil and Political Rights addresses the right to freedom of association (including the right to form and join trade unions),[19] the prohibition of slavery, servitude and forced or compulsory labour,[20] and the right to equal protection of the law.[21] Both Covenants guarantee the right to enjoy these rights without discrimination.[22] We will review some of these provisions in greater detail below. Particular aspects of workers' rights, and the work-related rights of particular social groups, are also protected in other treaties, such as the Convention on the Elimination of All Forms of Racial Discrimination, the Convention on the Elimination of All Forms of Discrimination against Women, the Convention on the Rights of the Child, and the Convention on the Protection of the Rights of All Migrant Workers and Members of their Families. At the same time, these rights are variously protected at regional level, within the framework of the African Charter of Human and Peoples' Rights, the European Convention on Human Rights and Revised European Social Charter, the European Union legal order, the Inter-American human rights system, and other regional human rights treaties.

---

[10] Art. 20(1).   [11] Art. 4(1).   [12] Arts. 25 and 22.   [13] Art. 7.
[14] Art. 2.   [15] Art. 6.   [16] Art. 7.   [17] Art. 8.   [18] Art. 9.
[19] Art. 22.   [20] Art. 8.   [21] Art. 26.
[22] International Covenant on Economic, Social and Cultural Rights, arts. 2(2) and 3; International Covenant on Civil and Political Rights, arts. 2(1), 3 and 26.

If we now re-visit the question 'what is the relationship between international labour standards and human rights?', it is evident that an important part of the answer concerns the relationship between international labour standards and international human rights law. In the 1960s and early 1970s Wilfred Jenks (legal adviser and eventually Director-General of the ILO) wrote extensively on this subject,[23] and a number of studies were also prepared by the ILO, among them a detailed comparative analysis of labour and human rights treaties.[24] In these works the establishment and early endeavours of the ILO are viewed as having foundational significance for the whole enterprise of international human rights protection. For their part, human rights treaties and other instruments are seen to constitute a regime of rights protection that complements and is supplemented by moves to protect the rights of human beings as workers in the context of international labour standards. A similar approach has been followed by later writers. Thus, Nicholas Valticos writes that 'it should be clearly understood that international labour standards, as a body, constitute a special category of human rights'.[25] In his assessment, 'the international labour Conventions provide, in a more specific and detailed manner, for the practical implementation, at the national level, of the series of principles embodied in more general terms in the UN Covenant on Economic, Social and Cultural Rights' and other international human rights treaties.[26]

Virginia Leary concurs that '[w]orkers' rights are human rights',[27] but observes that, despite this, and despite the studies just mentioned, there is yet another story to be told about interrelation of international labour standards and human rights, which has to do with levels of practical interaction. Historically, human rights activists have paid only limited attention to international labour standards. Likewise, labour leaders and

[23] See, e.g., C.W. Jenks, *Human Rights and International Labour Standards* (London: Stevens, 1960) and *Social Justice in the Law of Nations* (Oxford: Oxford University Press, 1970).

[24] 'Comparative Analysis of the International Covenants on Human Rights and International Labour Conventions and Recommendations' in *Official Bulletin* (Geneva: ILO, 1969), Vol. LII, No. 2, 181. For more recent analysis, see *International Labour Review* (1998), Vol. 137, No. 2: Special Issue 'Labour Rights, Human Rights'.

[25] N. Valticos, 'International Labour Standards and Human Rights: Approaching the Year 2000' 137 *International Labour Review* (1998) 135, 136–7.   [26] Ibid., 140.

[27] V. Leary, 'The Paradox of Workers' Rights as Human Rights' in L. Compa and S. Diamond (eds.), *Human Rights, Labor Rights, and International Trade* (Philadelphia: University of Pennsylvania Press, 1996), 22.

trade unions have seldom invoked human rights norms. In Leary's words, 'the human rights movement and the labor movement run on tracks that are sometimes parallel and rarely meet'.[28] The disjuncture is regrettable, she writes, for the 'status of workers' rights in a country is a bellwether for the status of human rights in general. The first sign of a deterioriating situation is often the violation of freedom of association'.[29] Certainly, labour leaders are among the most frequent victims of repression, and attempts by farm labourers, native peoples and industrial workers to organise in defence of their rights continue to meet with violence in many places.

Leary mentions a number of factors which may explain the existence of these parallel tracks. Perhaps the most significant is that the labour movement has tended to be more local in its focus than the human rights movement. Or rather, since national and international workers' associations quite obviously reach beyond local concerns, the point is more specifically that interest in labour rights has often been linked to protectionist or at any rate trade-oriented agendas which human rights organisations have not shared. During the Cold War interest in labour rights was also linked to foreign policy goals and West-East rivalries from which the major international human rights advocacy groups were anxious to distance themselves. To some extent, as Leary highlights, the pattern continues today. Concern about international labour relations appears, at least in part, to be driven by a perception that low wages, sweatshop conditions and child labour constitute a kind of subsidy, and lead to a form of 'social dumping', which gives the South an unfair advantage over the North in international trade. But if from this perspective disregard for labour rights is a trade problem, it is also a human rights problem—and a human rights problem of rather larger proportions than trade-focused analyses may allow.

Labour rights

In her book *Nickel and Dimed* Barbara Ehrenreich remarks that we have become accustomed to associating poverty with unemployment.[30] Of course, unemployment remains a major correlate, and indeed dimension,

---

[28] Ibid.   [29] Ibid.
[30] B. Ehrenreich, *Nickel and Dimed* (London: Granta Books, 2002), 219–20.

of social deprivation. But in today's contract-out, race-down economies and flexible, fragmented workplaces, it is important to recognise that poverty is also—and perhaps increasingly—a condition of working people. As Ehrenreich expresses it,

I grew up hearing over and over, to the point of tedium, that 'hard work' was the secret of success: 'Work hard and you'll get ahead' or 'It's hard work that got us where we are.' No one ever said that you could work hard—harder even than you ever thought possible—and still find yourself sinking ever deeper into poverty and debt.[31]

Against this background, let us now turn to consider in more detail the international protection of labour rights. Though the various aspects are interconnected, it will be convenient to look successively at rights that relate to employment, rights regarding pay and conditions, and rights to take collective action.

Employment

To highlight that poverty is not only associated with unemployment is not to suggest, quite obviously, that poverty is no longer associated with unemployment, or that levels of unemployment are no longer a concern. In the Declaration of Philadelphia the ILO Conference recognised as one of the Organization's obligations the promotion of policies and programmes that will achieve full employment.[32] As for international human rights law, we have already quoted article 23 of the Universal Declaration of Human Rights, in which mention is made of the right to work. This is guaranteed in a number of treaties, among them the International Covenant on Economic, Social and Cultural Rights,[33] the San Salvador Protocol to the American Convention on Human Rights,[34] and the Revised European Social Charter.[35] The right to work is not generally understood as an entitlement to be provided with work. But it is understood as a right of access to employment opportunities. In the language of the Economic, Social and Cultural Rights Covenant, it does include the 'right of everyone to the opportunity to gain his living by work which he freely chooses or accepts'.[36]

[31] B. Ehrenreich, *Nickel and Dimed* (London: Granta Books, 2002), 220.
[32] Art. III, Declaration of Philadelphia, Annex to the ILO Constitution.
[33] Art. 6.   [34] Art. 6.   [35] Part I (1) and Part II, art. 1.   [36] Art. 6(1).

This entails, in the first place, the provision of vocational guidance and training, the maintenance of free employment services, and the implementation of policies aimed at reducing unemployment. Read in conjunction with the obligation in the Covenant and other relevant treaties to secure the non-discriminatory enjoyment of the rights recognised, the right to work also imposes on states an obligation to ensure non-discrimination in hiring, promotion and dismissal. Secondly, then, measures are required to combat discrimination in the sphere of employment. This is reinforced by stipulations in treaties and other international instruments that are specifically addressed to the elimination of racial discrimination, sex discrimination, sexual orientation discrimination, and disability discrimination. A third entailment of the right to work concerns security of employment and protection against unfair dismissal more generally. Recognised in some human rights treaties and in international labour standards is the right not to have employment terminated without valid reasons and, in the event that it is terminated without valid reasons, the right to compensation or other appropriate relief.[37]

As just noted, the right to work is expressed as a right to gain one's living by work freely chosen or accepted. Of course, as we have known at least since Karl Marx, choice is a complicated concept in this context. It is fair to say that, when it comes to the voluntariness of work, labour rights set the bar quite low, in that the focus is on the prohibition of slavery, servitude and forced or compulsory labour. In the contemporary world, slavery mostly takes the form of debt bondage or 'bonded labour' (whereby work is extracted as security for a debt, without limitation as to the nature or duration of the obligation), trafficking (in which people are abducted or recruited through the use of coercion, fraud or deception) or forced labour (often associated with government or paramilitary action, in which people are forced to work under threat of violence or other punishment). Traditional slavery, involving the straightforward sale of human beings, also continues to exist in a few places.[38] In connection with efforts to abolish slavery in these and related forms, a large number

[37] See, e.g., Revised European Social Charter, Part II, art. 24; San Salvador Protocol to the American Convention on Human Rights, art. 7(d); and Termination of Employment Convention 1982 (ILO Convention No. 158).

[38] See 'The Burden of Slavery', New Internationalist, Issue 337, August 2001, 9. See further D. Weissbrodt and Anti-Slavery International, Abolishing Slavery and its Contemporary Forms (New York and Geneva: United Nations, 2002) (HR/PUB/02/4).

of treaties has been adopted, including two ILO Conventions on Forced Labour.[39] Provisions prohibiting slavery, servitude and forced or compulsory labour are also included in the Universal Declaration of Human Rights, the International Covenant on Civil and Political Rights and many regional human rights treaties.[40] Since 1974 the UN has mandated a Working Group (the 'Working Group on Contemporary Forms of Slavery') to lead the Organization's anti-slavery endeavours.[41]

Allegations of violations of the ILO Forced Labour Conventions have been examined on a number of occasions under ILO monitoring mechanisms. In 1998, for example, a Commission of Inquiry reported on violations of Convention No. 29 by Myanmar.[42] Likewise, complaints of forced or compulsory labour have been brought before human rights supervisory bodies. In one recent case the European Committee of Social Rights (which hears collective complaints under the Revised European Social Charter) considered a complaint against Greece about legislation governing the employment of military officers and merchant seamen.[43] The Committee expressed the view that arrangements whereby military officers could not resign their commissions for 25 years, and merchant seamen faced penal sanctions if they refused to carry out their duties even when there was no danger to the safety of the vessel or those on board, violated the right recognised in the Revised European Social Charter to earn one's living 'in an occupation freely entered upon'. The first case heard under the Revised European Social Charter's collective complaints procedure concerned child labour in

---

[39] Forced Labour Convention 1930 (ILO Convention No. 29) and Abolition of Forced Labour Convention 1957 (ILO Convention No. 105). See also Slavery, Servitude, Forced Labour and Similar Institutions and Practices Convention 1926; Supplementary Convention on the Abolition of Slavery, the Slave Trade and Institutions and Practices Similar to Slavery 1953; and Protocol to Prevent, Suppress and Punish Trafficking in Persons, Especially Women and Children 2000.

[40] Universal Declaration of Human Rights, art. 4 and International Covenant on Civil and Political Rights, art. 8. See also, e.g., European Convention on Human Rights, art. 4; American Convention on Human Rights, art. 6; African Charter on Human and Peoples' Rights art. 5; and Commonwealth of Independent States Convention on Human Rights and Fundamental Freedoms, art. 4.

[41] See, e.g., Report of the Working Group on Contemporary Forms of Slavery on its twenty-ninth session UN Doc. E/CN.4/Sub.2/2004/36, 20 July 2004.

[42] Report of the Commission on Inquiry appointed under article 26 to examine the observance of Myanmar of the Forced Labour Convention 1930 (No. 29), 1998.

[43] *International Federation of Human Rights v Greece*, Report of the European Committee of Social Rights, 5 December 2000.

Portugal and the failure of the Portuguese authorities to put in place an adequate regulatory and enforcement scheme for dealing with it.[44] The issue of minimum ages for work has strong historical and analytical links with the topic of slavery, and the right of children to be protected from work that is hazardous, exploitative or likely to interfere with their education is addressed in many of the anti-slavery treaties and provisions we have mentioned, as well as in the Convention on the Rights of the Child and the Worst Forms of Child Labour Convention (ILO Convention No. 182), adopted in 1999. (See further Children.*)

Pay and Conditions

Beyond the right to gain one's living, and to do so only by work freely chosen or accepted, Ehrenreich is certainly right that for a great many of the world's inhabitants the struggle to re-assert workers' rights and re-emphasise employers' reponsibilities is a struggle about pay and conditions. In the language of the Universal Declaration of Human Rights, what is in question is the right to 'just and favourable conditions of work'.[45]

Beginning with the issue of remuneration, we saw above that the Universal Declaration affirms that '[e]veryone who works has the right to just and favourable remuneration ensuring for himself and his family an existence worthy of human dignity, and supplemented, if necessary, by other means of social protection'.[46] The Universal Declaration also affirms that '[e]veryone, without any discrimination, has the right to equal pay for equal work'.[47] Both these rights are reflected in the International Covenant on Economic, Social and Cultural Rights,[48] and in other human rights treaties, such as the San Salvador Protocol to the American Convention on Human Rights[49] and Revised European Social Charter.[50]

---

[44] *International Commission of Jurists v Portugal*, Report of the European Committee of Social Rights, 9 September 1999. The Committee expressed the view that Portugal had violated its obligations under art. 7(1) of the Revised European Social Charter to 'provide that the minimum age of admission to employment shall be 15 years, subject to exceptions for children employed in prescribed light work without harm to their health, morals or education'.   [45] Art. 23(1).

[46] Art. 23(3).   [47] Art. 23(2).   [48] Art. 7(a).   [49] Art. 7(a).

[50] Part I (4) and Part II, art. 4(1) and (3). Regarding the right to equal pay for equal work, see also Treaty Establishing the European Community, art. 141 and EC Directive 2002/73/EC, 23 September 2002. And see African Charter on Human and Peoples' Rights, art. 15.

In the International Covenant on Economic, Social and Cultural Rights the right to a living wage is characterised as the right to 'remuneration which provides all workers, as a minimum, with: (i) fair wages...[and] (ii) a decent living for themselves and their families in accordance with the provisions of the present Covenant'.[51] This right and the right to equal pay for equal work are also reflected in international labour standards.[52] Already in 1919 the ILO Constitution counted the 'provision of an adequate living wage' and 'recognition of the principle of equal remuneration for work of equal value' among the improvements in working conditions 'urgently required'.[53]

Another aspect of the right to just and favourable conditions of employment concerns occupational health and safety. The right to 'safe and healthy working conditions' is recognised in the International Covenant on Economic, Social and Cultural Rights and the other treaties we have mentioned.[54] The Revised European Social Charter spells out the implications of this right for state obligations with respect to policy, regulation, enforcement and promotion.[55] These are spelled out in further detail in a large number of international labour standards, some of which remain quite broadly focused, while others are addressed to particular sectors or particular hazards. Examples of the broadly focused standards include the Occupational Health and Safety Convention and later Protocol[56] and the Prevention of Major Industrial Accidents Convention.[57] Examples of the more context-specific standards include the Protection against Accidents (Dockers) Convention,[58] the Safety and Health in Mines Convention,[59] the Safety and Health in Agriculture Convention,[60] and the Radiation Protection Convention.[61]

Linked to this, yet another aspect of the right to just and favourable working conditions concerns the limitation of working hours, the

[51] Art. 7(a).
[52] See, e.g., Equal Remuneration Convention 1951 (ILO Convention No. 100) and Minimum Wage Fixing Convention 1970 (ILO Convention No. 131).
[53] See Preamble to ILO Constitution.
[54] International Covenant on Economic, Social and Cultural Rights, art. 7(b); San Salvador Protocol to the American Convention on Human Rights, art. 7(e) and (f); Revised European Social Charter, Part I(3) and Part II, art. 3.   [55] See art. 3.
[56] ILO Convention No. 155 (1981) and Protocol thereto (2002).
[57] ILO Convention No. 174 (1993).
[58] ILO Convention No. 32 (1932) (revising an earlier ILO convention on this subject).
[59] ILO Convention No. 176 (1995).   [60] ILO Convention No. 184 (2001).
[61] ILO Convention No. 115 (1960).

entitlement to paid holidays, and related rights to rest and leave. The very first treaty adopted by the ILO in 1919 was the Hours of Work (Industry) Convention, which applied to industrial undertakings the principle of the eight-hour day and 48-hour week.[62] Since then, many more ILO conventions have been adopted regulating working hours in particular sectors. A number of conventions have also been adopted dealing with rest periods, educational leave and paid holidays. Within the framework of human rights law, article 24 of the Universal Declaration of Human Rights affirms the 'right to rest and leisure, including reasonable limitation of working hours and periodic holidays with pay'.[63] The International Covenant on Economic, Social and Cultural Rights guarantees these rights in similar terms,[64] and provisions on the subject can likewise be found in regional treaties and other instruments.[65]

In some countries a significant proportion of those who work harder than they ever thought possible and still find themselves sinking deeper into poverty and debt are migrants, whether legally in residence or undocumented. In 1990, a treaty was adopted within the framework of the United Nations with the aim of protecting the labour and related rights of non-nationals. Among the provisions of the Convention on the Protection of the Rights of All Migrant Workers and Members of their Families is the stipulation that '[m]igrant workers shall enjoy treatment not less favourable than that which applies to nationals of the State of employment in respect of remuneration and ... other conditions of work'.[66] The Convention further provides that states parties must 'take all appropriate measures to ensure that migrant workers are not deprived of any rights derived from this principle by reason of any irregularity in their stay or employment'.[67] To date, however, relatively few labour-importing states have become parties to this Convention. However heavily economies may depend on migrant labour, including undocumented migrant labour, governments have not generally been willing to recognise the special vulnerability of migrant workers to violations of their human rights.

---

[62] ILO Convention No. 1 (1919).   [63] Art. 24.   [64] Art. 7(d).
[65] San Salvador Protocol to the American Convention on Human Rights, art. 7(g) and (h); Revised European Social Charter, Part II, art. 2; EU Directive 93/104/EC, 23 November 1993 concerning 'certain aspects of the organization of working time'.
[66] Art. 25(1)(a).   [67] Art. 25(3).

In a recent Advisory Opinion, the Inter-American Court of Human Rights examined the position of undocumented migrant workers by reference to general human rights treaties and other instruments.[68] The Opinion was rendered at the request of the Government of Mexico, following a decision of the United States Supreme Court involving an undocumented Mexican worker in the United States.[69] Though the worker had been found to have been unlawfully dismissed (for trying to establish a union, an issue to which we will turn in a moment), he had been denied the right to back pay for work performed. The Mexican Government did not dispute that states may control entry and residence, and that migrants may be treated differently from nationals for some purposes (such as voting), but argued that, if undocumented migrant workers are employed, their labour rights must be respected and protected. In the Government's contention, this follows from the basic obligation of states to ensure human rights to everyone within their jurisdiction, and from related norms of non-discrimination, equality before the law, and equal protection of the law, both in Inter-American human rights law and in the Universal Declaration of Human Rights and International Covenant on Civil and Political Rights. The Inter-American Court of Human Rights endorsed this argument. In its words, '[w]hen assuming an employment relationship, the migrant acquires rights that must be recognized and ensured because he is an employee, irrespective of his regular or irregular status in the State where he is employed. These rights are a result of the employment relationship'.[70] Correspondingly, international human rights law imposes on the state an obligation 'to respect and guarantee the labor human rights of all workers, irrespective of their status as nationals or aliens, and not to tolerate situations of discrimination that are harmful to the latter in employment relationships established between private individuals'.[71]

Collective Action

We referred earlier to Richard Sennett's descriptions of the World Economic Forum at Davos, and his realisation that the participants

[68] *Legal Status and Rights of Undocumented Migrants*, Advisory Opinion of the Inter-American Court of Human Rights, 17 September 2003.
[69] *Hoffman Plastic Compounds v National Labor Relations Board*, 535 U.S. 137 (2002).
[70] *Legal Status and Rights of Undocumented Migrants*, Advisory Opinion of the Inter-American Court of Human Rights, 17 September 2003, para. 173(8).
[71] Ibid., para. 173(9).

become intensely uncomfortable when forced to discuss those 'left behind' in the current economic order. In conjunction with this, Sennett also reports on another realisation. For 'the rulers of the flexible realm', he writes, ' "[w]e" is . . . a dangerous pronoun'. If the chief executive officers 'dwell comfortably in entrepreneurial disorder', they 'fear organized confrontation'. And one—though perhaps only one—aspect of that is that they 'fear the resurgence of unions'.[72] This prompts consideration of the instrumental rights of workers, their rights to associate, organise, form and join trade unions, bargain collectively, and take collective action, such as strikes.

The right to freedom of association is recognised in the Universal Declaration of Human Rights,[73] the International Covenant on Civil and Political Rights,[74] and all the regional human rights systems.[75] Though this is understood to include the right to form and join trade unions, that right is explicitly reaffirmed in the Universal Declaration,[76] and is further elaborated in the International Covenant on Economic, Social and Cultural Rights[77] and in regional treaties, such as the San Salvador Protocol to the American Convention on Human Rights and the Revised European Social Charter.[78] Under these treaties, the right to form and join trade unions is variously linked to recognition of the right of those trade unions to form and join national and international federations, the right to bargain collectively, and (subject to obligations under collective agreements) the right to strike. In each relevant instrument, it is stipulated that associative and trade union rights may be subject to qualification (for example, to ensure essential services), but that any restrictions must be justified by reference to strict criteria.

The right of workers to form, join and run organisations to promote and defend their interests has similarly deep roots in international labour law. The importance of the general principle of freedom of association was proclaimed in 1919 in the preamble to the ILO Constitution, and

[72] R. Sennett, *The Corrosion of Character* (New York: Norton, 1998), 147.

[73] Art. 20(1).   [74] Art. 22.

[75] See, e.g., European Convention of Human Rights, art. 11; American Convention on Human Rights, art. 16; African Charter on Human and Peoples' Rights, art. 10; and Commonwealth of Independent States Convention on Human Rights and Fundamental Freedoms, art. 12.   [76] Art. 23(4).

[77] Art. 8.

[78] San Salvador Protocol to the American Convention on Human Rights, art. 8; Revised European Social Charter, Part I(5), Part II, arts. 5 and 6.

restated in 1944 in the Declaration of Philadelphia. In 1948 the ILO adopted a convention—the Freedom of Association and Protection of the Right to Organise Convention—affirming the 'right of workers and employers . . . to establish and, subject only to the rules of the organisation concerned, to join organisations of their own choosing without previous authorisation'.[79] The following year a further convention was adopted—the Right to Organise and Collective Bargaining Convention—under which the right of workers is recognised to 'adequate protection against acts of anti-union discrimination in respect of their employment' (for example, dismissal for attempting to establish a trade union).[80] The Convention is also the basis for state obligations to protect workers' associations against interference by employers, and to encourage the development and utilisation of machinery for regulating the terms and conditions of employment by means of collective agreements, that is to say, collective bargaining.[81]

Since 1951 adherence with these labour and related standards has been monitored by an ILO supervisory body, the Committee on Freedom of Association. Complaints about violation of the right to freedom of association have also come before human rights courts and monitoring bodies on numerous occasions. It needs to be signalled that by no means all of these complaints have been driven by concern about the instrumental value of freedom of association for collective bargaining and the defence of workers' rights regarding pay and conditions. In one well known case before the European Court of Human Rights, decided in 1981, the applicants complained about union security or 'closed shop' arrangements in place in the United Kingdom, under which membership of a trade union could be made a condition of employment.[82] The applicants did not wish to join the union, and argued that these arrangements violated their right to freedom of association, protected in article 11 of the Convention. The European Court of Human Rights upheld this argument, finding the United Kingdom in

[79] ILO Convention No. 87 (1948), art. 2.
[80] ILO Convention No. 98 (1949), art. 1.
[81] Ibid., arts. 2(2) and 4. See also the Collective Bargaining Convention 1981 (ILO Convention No. 154), under which states parties undertake to promote collective bargaining with a view to extending progressively the range of issues, branches of economic activity, and employees and employers covered.
[82] *Young, James and Webster v United Kingdom*, Judgment of the European Court of Human Rights, 26 June 1981.

violation of the Convention. In doing so, it lent support to a move already gaining momentum in that country to curtail the power of trade unions. Just over 20 years later, the European Court considered another complaint against the United Kingdom.[83] This time, however, the complaint was about the state's failure to protect workers and unions against anti-union discrimination. Employers were permitted to offer financial incentives to employees who would agree to limiting or eliminating union representation and collective bargaining. The applicants—one a trade union, the others disadvantaged employees who had not been willing to agree to this—claimed that this situation constituted a violation of their right to freedom of association. The Court upheld their claim, declaring that '[i]t is the role of the State to ensure that trade union members are not prevented or restrained from using their union to represent them in attempts to regulate their relations with their employers'.[84]

Core labour standards

Towards the beginning of this discussion we noted that the ILO has classified international labour standards into a number of categories, and that one category has been labelled 'fundamental ILO conventions'. Let us now return to that point, in order to introduce a final factor into the equation of internationally protected labour rights.

The designation of certain ILO conventions as fundamental was effected in 1998, through a resolution of the International Labour Conference entitled 'Declaration on Fundamental Principles and Rights at Work'.[85] But the aim of this Declaration was not just to advance a classificatory scheme for ILO conventions; the idea was also to affirm that the principles reflected in the fundamental conventions express core principles of international labour law, which are binding on all ILO member states, whether or not they have become parties to the relevant conventions. Thus, the ILO proclaims in the Declaration that all member states have an 'obligation . . . to respect, to promote and to realize, in good faith and in accordance with the [ILO] Constitution, the principles

---

[83] *Wilson & Others v United Kingdom*, Judgment of the European Court of Human Rights, 2 July 2002.   [84] Ibid., para. 46.
[85] Adopted June 1998.

concerning the fundamental rights which are the subject of those Conventions'. And this obligation is said to arise irrespective of whether a particular member state has ratified the 'fundamental' conventions, by virtue of the 'very fact of membership in the Organization'.[86] As noted above, the conventions in question are concerned with four issues: freedom of association and the right to collective bargaining; forced or compulsory labour; child labour; and discrimination in respect of employment and occupation.[87] In the Declaration, the ILO also commits itself to making full use of its resources to promote adherence to the principles reflected in these conventions.[88] Finally, the Declaration establishes a follow-up procedure of a promotional nature, involving the preparation of reports on the implementation of the fundamental principles.[89]

The term 'core labour standards' has gained currency as a name for the subset of international labour standards designated fundamental in this Declaration. We mentioned earlier that contemporary interest in international labour rights is linked, at least in part, to trade-related arguments about 'social dumping'. In the late 1990s these arguments, in turn, became linked to debate about the inclusion in international trade agreements of a 'social clause' that would permit trade sanctions for violation of workers' rights. The ILO Declaration on Fundamental Principles and Rights at Work is widely understood as an attempt to defuse that debate, by stepping up efforts to ensure compliance with core labour standards, but keeping those efforts within the framework of international labour law. In place, then, of modifications to international trade law, the ILO would sharpen its focus, and respond to the trade negotiators' anxieties. In this way, WTO-centred quarrels about the social clause could be put aside. At the same time, the ILO could retain its relevance in conditions of economic globalisation.

Since 1998 the ILO has devoted considerable energy to promoting core labour standards, and the Declaration is widely rated—to quote one typical statement—an important 'reaffirmation, by governments and both social partners [employers and workers], of the universality of fundamental principles and rights at a time of widespread uncertainty and questioning of those rights'.[90] For some analysts, however, a more

---

[86] Adopted June 1998, para. 2.   [87] See note 10 above.
[88] Adopted June 1998, para. 3.   [89] Ibid., para. 4.
[90] H. Kellerson, 'The ILO Declaration of 1998 on fundamental principles and rights: a challenge for the future', 137 *International Labour Review* (1998), 223, 227.

cautious assessment is warranted. Philip Alston highlights a number of grounds for concern about the implications of the Declaration for the protection of workers' rights.[91] While the Declaration is presented as complementing rather than altering the pre-existing ILO regime, and while its adoption has been accompanied by a campaign to promote the ratification of the fundamental ILO conventions, Alston argues that there is a danger that it will encourage the view that ratification of ILO and related human rights treaties is not necessary. More generally, there is a danger that it will foster an approach in which the focus is less on rights anchored in specific standards than on principles left to float free from those standards, and less on legal accountability for violations of labour rights than on 'soft' promotionalism. Alston is also worried that the concept of core labour standards risks eclipsing the larger panoply of labour rights, and encouraging a concentration within the ILO on what he considers an 'overly narrow' core.[92] Given that institutional time and resources are not unlimited, and since hierarchical ordering is, after all, part of the purpose of the Declaration, attention to non-core rights is almost inevitably downgraded.

From this perspective, the ILO Declaration has effectively—if unintentionally—co-opted criticism of the impact of economic liberalisation on labour rights. No one disputes that freedom of association, forced or compulsory labour, child labour, and discrimination in respect of employment and occupation are immensely important issues. But Alston's point is that soft promotionalism does justice neither to their importance, nor to the urgency of other issues. For in current conditions it is not only the rights covered by the Declaration that are coming under strain. It is also rights to safe and healthy working conditions, limited working hours, paid holidays, and vocational training. Above all, as highlighted above, it is the right to a living wage. At a time when products are giving way to brands, and jobs to contracts, the nature of employment is also changing. As Naomi Klein observes, 'the steady kind, with benefits, holiday pay, a measure of security and maybe even union representation'[93] is giving way to a new kind that makes workers seem like nothing so much as teenagers lending a hand in an affluent family business. In place of old-fashioned employment, there is now getting

---

[91] P. Alston, '"Core Labour Standards" and the Transformation of the International Labour Rights Regime' 15 *European Journal of International Law* (2004), 457.

[92] Ibid., 514.   [93] N. Klein, *No Logo* (London: Flamingo, 2001), 231.

some experience, earning a bit of money, or helping out when the orders come in. The idea that employees are trying to make a living, and that companies are responsible for those who work for them, appears to have lost something of its force.

Of course, this is not the case for everyone, and nor is it the case everywhere. But if the trend exists, it suggests that the need arises to refocus attention on the totality of ways in which the rights of workers are today compromised. In this context, international human rights law may assume renewed importance within the field of labour rights as a corrective to the ILO Declaration's narrowing thrust. To be sure, the Declaration does reassert the principle of freedom of association, and that principle has precious instrumental significance in relation to all workplace rights. However, with strong downward pressure on wages, benefits and job security, the promotion of freedom of association seems a poor substitute for the idea that governments have legal obligations to ensure the right to safe and healthy working conditions, the right to limited working hours and paid holidays, the right to vocational training, and the right to a living wage. Indeed, it seems a poor substitute for the idea that governments may be held legally accountable with respect to freedom of association itself.

*   *   *

Epilogue: On Human Rights

In a report by Oxfam, we meet Lucy (not her real name), a Kenyan factory worker who is employed in an export processing zone outside Nairobi.[94] Lucy's work involves sewing pockets onto children's jeans destined for Wal-Mart in the United States. Once, when her manager demanded that she work non-stop for two days and nights to meet a shipping deadline, her partner walked out, leaving her to raise their two children alone. 'He said he will come back when the condition of my work is good', she told her interviewer. 'Till today the condition is becoming worse.' One month she worked 20 hours of overtime and was

---

[94] The information in this paragraph comes from Oxfam, *Trading Away Our Rights: Women Working in Global Supply Chains* (Oxford: Oxfam International, 2004), 16.

paid only for six. There was no question of insisting. Trade unions are banned, and complaints are met with intimidation or dismissal. 'Supervisors abuse us', she explained. 'If we talk, they say "Shut your beak. Even a child can do your job."' At one point the factory's orders stopped for six weeks, and so did Lucy's pay. Her parents, who live in a village 150 kilometres away, agreed to take her children, and at the time she was interviewed for Oxfam's report she had not seen them for six months. '*If this EPZ could be better*', she said, '*and consider us as people, and give us leave and holidays, then I would be able to go and see the children.*'[95]

We recount Lucy's story at the end of this book because she captures here in one sentence the central claim of international human rights law: that denial of the means for a decent life and exclusion from a fair share in social goods and opportunities are to be grasped as forms of inhumanity. Of course, what counts in a particular context as a decent life and what passes for a fair share in social goods and opportunities are themselves the issues. As we have tried to show throughout our discussions, international human rights law can be used to orient those issues in a variety of different and often mutually incompatible directions. For example, it can be used to contest the denial of paid leave and holidays. But it can also be used to contest measures—such as union security or 'closed shop' stipulations—that help to secure entitlements of that sort in specific circumstances. Certainly, human rights law comes with no fixed agenda, and no progressive guarantee. Like other instruments of social action, it is routinely deployed in ways that lend (intended or unintended) support to relations of domination, and requires constant reappropriation for emancipatory purposes. What Lucy expresses with peerless clarity and concision is the distinctive *demand* that stands at the centre of all this, the demand that reverberates around the world as it connects with the diverse idioms of political struggle the universalising language of humanism: *consider us as people*.

[95] Emphasis added.

Index

Asterisks in the text and footnotes refer to other entries in this book.